Language Rights of the Citizen of the European Union

Ius, Lex et Res Publica
Studies in Law, Philosophy and Political Cultures

Edited by Barbara Janusz-Pohl and Anna Jaroń

Volume 21

PETER LANG

Aneta Skorupa-Wulczyńska

Language Rights of the Citizen of the European Union

PETER LANG

Bibliographic Information published by the Deutsche Nationalbibliothek
The Deutsche Nationalbibliothek lists this publication
in the Deutsche Nationalbibliografie; detailed bibliographic
data is available online at http://dnb.d-nb.de.

Library of Congress Cataloging-in-Publication Data
A CIP catalog record for this book has been applied for at the
Library of Congress.

Cover illustration: Courtesy of Benjamin Ben Chaim

ISSN 2191-3250
ISBN 978-3-631-88158-3 (Print)
E-ISBN 978-3-631-88289-4 (E-Book)
E-ISBN 978-3-631-87488-2 (EPUB)
DOI 10.3726/b19887

Peter Lang – Berlin · Bern · Bruxelles · New York ·
Oxford · Warszawa · Wien

www.peterlang.com

Table of contents

Acronyms and abbreviations

Cedefop	European Centre for the Development of Vocational Training
CEFR	Common European Framework of Reference
Charter	The Charter of Fundamental Rights of the European Union
CLIL	Content and Language Integrated Learning
CoE	Council of Europe
Commission	European Commission
COREPER	Committee of the Permanent Representatives of the Governments of the Member States to the European Union
Court of Justice	Court of Justice of the European Union
CRC	Convention on the Rights of the Child
EC	European Communities, European Commission
ECB	European Central Bank
ECC	European Consumer Centre
ECC-Net	European Consumer Centres' Network
ECHR	European Convention of Human Rights and Fundamental Freedoms
ECI	European Citizens' Initiative
ECML	European Centre for Modern Languages
ECRML	European Charter for Regional or Minority Languages
ECtHR	European Court of Human Rights
EDPS	European Data Protection Supervisor
EEC	European Economic Community
EESC	European Economic and Social Committee
EILC	European Indicator of Language Competence
EP	European Parliament
EPC	European Professional Card
EPSO	European Personnel Selection Office
ESLC	European Survey on Language Competences
EUIPO	European Union Intellectual Property Office, formerly: the Office for Harmonisation in the Internal Market (OHIM)
EU	European Union
EURATOM	European Atomic Energy Community
Eurojust	European Union Agency for Criminal Justice Cooperation
FCNM	Framework Convention for the Protection of National Minorities
GA	General Assembly (of the UN)
ICCPR	International Covenant on Civil and Political Rights
ICESCR	International Covenant on Economic, Social, and Cultural Rights
ICJ	International Court of Justice

LPP	Language Policy Programme
LT	Lisbon Treaty, Treaty of Lisbon
OJEU	Official Journal of the European Union
PCP	Product Contact Point
PSC	Point of Single Contact
TEC, EC Treaty	Treaty establishing the European Community
TEEC, EEC Treaty	Treaty establishing the European Economic Community
TEU	Treaty on European Union
TFEU	Treaty on the Functioning of the European Union
UDHR	Universal Declaration of Human Rights
UN	United Nations
UNESCO	United Nations Educational, Scientific and Cultural Organization
UNHRC	United Nations Human Rights Committee
VET	Vocational Education and Training

Introduction

1. Subject of the dissertation

Statistically Europe is the poorest continent in terms of languages. Out of more than 7100 living languages in the world only around 280 are European.[1] Still, linguistic diversity is considered to be an appropriate description of the sociolinguistic situation in the European Union. The organization is home to nearly 450 million people[2] of diverse linguistic, ethnic, and cultural backgrounds. The European Union[3] recognises 24 official and working languages[4] and over 60 autochthonous languages spoken over its geographical area. The languages are of different status. Most of them are spoken by few people and several are remarkably widespread.[5] The languages used within the EU are also enriched by those of the migrant population (allochthonous languages), not recognised by the Union. As their number is constantly growing, they are hard to keep track of. Despite the fact that the Union institutions find it difficult to include them in a coherent policy, they certainly colour the linguistic landscape of the EU.[6] The co-existence of a variety of languages in the EU resembles a linguistic mosaic, differing from Member State[7] to Member State and from region to region.

European linguistic patterns have been shaped by history, geographical factors and the mobility of people. Already in the seventeenth century, German philosophers, including Leibniz, called for a linguistic nationalism having observed that a nation and a language flourished together. They promoted the use of a national language in public discourse to promote unity across social strata and to educate the general population in a standard national language.[8] Later, language

1 The data available on https://www.ethnologue.com/guides/how-many-languages and is constantly updated [retrieved on 6 October 2020].

2 https://europa.eu/european-union/about-eu/eu-languages_en [retrieved on 20 August 2020].

3 The EU, the Union.

4 The status as of 6 October 2020. Following Brexit, the EU has not reduced the number of official languages.

5 Iñigo Urrutia and Iñaki Lasagabaster, "Language rights as a general principle of Community law", *German Law Journal*, Vol. 8, No. 5, 479.

6 László Marácz and Mireille Rosello (eds.), *Multilingual Europe, Multilingual Europeans*, Brill, 2012, 14.

7 The upper case is used with reference to the European Communities' Member States and later the European Union Member States.

8 William D. Davis and Stanley Dubinsky, *Language Conflict and Language Rights: Ethnolinguistic Perspectives on Human Conflict,* Cambridge University Press, 2018, 100.

matters gained importance in Europe in the post-Cold War years as they became one of the dimensions of the quest for a new society based on human rights. Since then, the issue of languages has triggered relevant international treaties, national legislation, and political initiatives. A new dimension assigned to the protection of languages in Europe originated from two sources: firstly, a doctrine of nationalism in terms of language matters, and secondly, the need to introduce legal and formal regulations on language use. The former was shaped through the complicated history of the continent and the relations between the states. The USSR's dominance over Europe, including obligatory courses of Russian aimed to shape the Russian identity, proves to have contributed to the strengthening of the native languages of the states affected by Russia. As a result, language was perceived as a carrier of tradition and an element of uniform national identity (one nation, one state, one language). Such an approach gained popularity at the outset of the twentieth century and directly affected the shape of the Old Continent. The latter was a consequence of nationalistic ideologies prevailing in the World Wars. The post-war situation required regulations assuring the national and linguistic identity of all the states, which would make Europeans avoid confrontation policies in favour of cooperation between nations.[9]

Such a state of affairs laid the foundations for the European idea of multilingualism. The European Communities'[10] (EC) approach to multilingualism was based on the principle of the equality of all the Member States' languages entrenched in democracy and modern concepts of human rights.[11] The EC embraced the principle of linguistic equality in order to express respect for the principal aims of most language policies of the Community Member States. Those, first and foremost, served to achieve and preserve unity and identity, where the need of a state common language of communication contributed to social cohesion and democracy in society.[12] Both the historical background of the continent and a strong impact of the Member State language policies shaped the European Union as the

9 Adam Pawłowski, "Zadania polskiej polityki językowej w Unii Europejskiej", *Polska polityka językowa w Unii Europejskiej*, 2008, 113–4.

10 The 'European Communities' comprised the European Economic Community, the European Coal and Steel Community and the European Atomic Energy Community. Upon the entry into force of the Treaty on European Union (Maastricht Treaty) in 1993, the European Economic Community was renamed the European Community and as such constituted the first of EU three pillars.

11 Miklós Kontra, Robert Phillipson, Tove Skutnabb-Kangas and Tibor Várady (eds.), *Language: A right and a resource: Approaching linguistic human rights*, Budapest: Central European University Press, 1999, 4–6.

12 Stefaan Van der Jeught, *EU Language Law*, Groninger: Europa Law Publishing, 2015, 48.

most multilingual international organization respecting the linguistic diversity of all mostly monolingual Member States.[13]

Multilingualism has been a cornerstone and a symbol of European integration since the beginning of the Community's existence. For its founders, the Member States' languages constituted part of Europe's rich and diverse cultural heritage and their linguistic equality aimed to contribute to social cohesion, and to be the source of tolerance and acceptance of differences between people.[14] European diversity in languages became a founding principle of the Community and in 2000, it became reflected in the Union's motto of 'unity in diversity'.[15] The equality of all Union official languages became a pragmatic assumption of the functioning of the EU institutions and bodies, which have consistently declared that they will maintain multilingual linguistic regimes in order to preserve the diversity of cultures and languages. The laws protecting the languages of Member States have been not only strategic directions, but also among the primary conditions for cooperation between the EU institutions and Union citizens.

The Union became the addressee of the Treaty requirements of respecting linguistic diversity of its Member States. The obligations imposed on the EU include both passive Union's respect for linguistic diversity while pursuing the Union policies and active actions aiming to achieve a particular state of affairs in respect of linguistic diversity and multilingualism.[16] As "a community of communication",[17] the EU developed democratic structures providing legitimacy for its actions and guaranteeing the democratic rights of Member States' citizens to have equal access to the EU institutions without language barriers.[18] Moreover, being aware of the fact that "diversity of languages means richness, but may also mean difference, divergence, and even mutual isolation,"[19] the Union has implemented its multilingualism strategy, the major aim of which is to promote foreign language learning

13 Sandra Mollin, *Euro-English: Assessing Variety Status*, Vol. 33, Gunter Narr Verlag, 2006, 57.

14 Anastazja Gajda, "Wielojęzyczność Unii Europejskiej", *Socjolingwistyka*, No. 27, 2013, 27.

15 Richard L. Creech, *Law and Language in the European Union: the Paradox of a Babel "United in Diversity"*, Groningen: Europa Law Publishing, 2005.

16 Artur Nowak-Far, *Prawo Unii Europejskiej. Języki, struktury, działanie w praktyce*, C.H. Beck, 2020, 300.

17 Sue Wright, *Community and Communication: the Role of Language in Nation State Building and European Integration*, Clevedon: Multilingual Matters Ltd, 2000.

18 Cornelis J.W. Baaij, *Legal Integration and Linguistic Diversity. Rethinking Translation in EU Lawmaking*, Oxford Studies in Language and Law, 2018.

19 Anne Lise Kjær and Silvia Adamo, "Linguistic Diversity and European Democracy: Introduction and Overview", in: Kjær Anne Lise and Silvia Adamo (eds.), *Linguistic Diversity and European Democracy*, Ashgate Publishing, 2013.

among Member States' citizens. The European Commission stresses that the ability to communicate in a number of languages brings not only enormous social benefits but also increases creativity, triggers mobility, and significantly enhances the employability of citizens.[20]

The growing linguistic diversity of the EU has evolved into an important social, legal, cultural, economic, and political fact of life.[21] With each successive enlargement, the languages of the new Member States were added to the list of Union official languages, which on the one hand highlighted the role of multilingualism, and on the other, increased complexity and created new challenges for the Union institutions, the Member States, and their citizens.[22] The problems concerned a variety of issues, including the interpretation of increasingly multilingual law equally valid in all the EU official languages. In this respect, the major challenge concerned the expression of the same content in different national languages, thus guaranteeing equal rights to all Union citizens. If, therefore, expression of the same rights in two languages may be a problem, it is obvious that the difficulty grows proportionately when there are over 20 languages.[23] Other major challenges have included the functioning of the EU institutions in an increasing number of languages as well as day-to-day linguistic difficulties resulting from the enhanced mobility and closer integration of the Union citizens. Whereas the former required from the EU institutions administrative capabilities to efficiently function in many languages, the latter experienced mostly by the movement of citizens operating in the public sphere. As a result of growing mobility for a variety of purposes, Member States' citizens found themselves in various formal, official, and public situations in which they became obliged to use an official language of the host State or were forced to pay the costs of a translator/interpreter. Individuals began to claim their language rights of varied nature, including the right to education in their language while staying in a host State, the right to use the language understandable by them before the Member State courts, the right not to be discriminated against based on language as a worker or self-employed person, or the right

20 Communication from the Commission to the Council, the European Parliament, the European Economic and Social Committee and the Committee of the Regions – A New Framework Strategy for Multilingualism COM (2005) 596. 22 November 2005. Not published in the Official Journal.

21 Patxi Juaristi, Timothy Reagan and Humphrey Tonkin, "Linguistic diversity in the European Union: An Overview", in: Xabier Arzoz (ed.), *Respecting Linguistic Diversity in the European Union*, Amsterdam, 2008, 47–9.

22 Arianna Kitzinger, *The Theory and Practice of Multilingualism in the European Union*, Saarbrücken: VDM Verlag Dr. Müller, 2009.

23 Adam Zienkiewicz and Michał Lasota, "Wielojęzyczność a interpretacja europejskiego prawa wspólnotowego", *Studia Prawnoustrojowe*, Vol. 9, 2009, 407.

to understand the labels of the product available on the market of their state, to name but a few.

The European Union's respect for linguistic diversity constitutes an important element of its respect for "the equality of the Member States before the Treaties as well as their national identities," as protected under Article 4(2) TEU.[24] Although the concept of 'national identity' does not have a clear definition in the EU,[25] it may undoubtedly be contended that national languages – often protected by the state constitutional legal orders[26] – constitute an essential element of a state's national identity.[27] As a result, respect for cultural and linguistic diversity, shaped as the Union's aim[28] and one of its fundamental rights[29] and values, may be read as an expression of the Union's respect for the national identities of its Member States. The Court of Justice[30] expressly ruled in its judgments that the Union's respect for the national identities of the Member States includes protection of their state official languages.[31] At the same time, it should be noted that 'national identity' stands for the identity of the state-building nations, i.e. nations constituting the majority in a given state.[32] Such understanding may justify the exclusion of national minorities'

24 OJ C202, 7 June 2016.

25 It is not known whether this is a cultural phenomenon which should be defined within the cultural, historical and linguistic context or this is a legal term which could be defined within a Member State constitutional order. Moreover, it is not apparent if 'national identity' is a Union term which requires autonomous interpretation by the Court of Justice or a term which owing to its nature should be defined in the same way by the Court of Justice and Member State constitutional courts, Source: *Andrzej Wróbel (ed.), Karta Praw Podstawowych Unii Europejskiej: Komentarz,* Wydawnictwo C.H. Beck, 2019, 727.

26 Armind Von Bogdandy and Stephan Schill, "Overcoming Absolute Primacy: Respect for National Identity under the Lisbon Treaty", *Common Market Law Review*, Vol. 48, 2011, 1249.

27 Kazimierz Lankosz (ed.), *Traktat o Unii Europejskiej. Komentarze Becka*, Warszawa: C.H. Beck, 2003, 137.

28 OJ C202, 7 June 2016, Article 3(3).

29 OJ C202/1, 7 June 2016, Article 22.

30 The Court of Justice of the European Union, formerly the Court of Justice of the EC.

31 Judgment of the Court of 28 November 1989 in the case C-379/87 *Anita Groener v Minister for Education and the City of Dublin Vocational Educational Committee*, ECLI:EU:C:1989:599; judgment of the Court of 12 May 2011 in the case C-391/09 *Malgožata Runevič-Vardyn and Łukasz Paweł Wardyn. Vilniaus miesto savivaldybės administracija and Others*, ECLI:EU:C:2011:291, para. 86; judgment of the Court of 16 April 2013 in the case C-202/11 *Anton Las v PSA Antwerp N*, ECLI:EU:C:2013:23, para. 25.

32 Wróbel (ed.), *Karta Praw Podstawowych Unii Europejskiej: Komentarz*, 2019, 724–5.

issues from the scope of analysis concerning Member States' national identities. From the EU's perspective, respect for diversity indicates that the limits for European integration are based on the statehood of the Member States, including the fundamental principles of the state system, protection of democracy, rule of law, and fundamental rights, as well as cultural and constitutional identity.[33] From the perspective of the Member States, the Union's respect for diversity guarantees that the essential elements of a state's national identity are observed.[34] As a consequence, the Union is prevented from disproportionate interference in the internal spheres concerning the national identity of a Member State.[35] This implies that the Union should identify and define such elements of national identity as are relevant for the EU actions and apply those which will in a least acute manner limit the national identities of its Member States.[36]

The language rights of the Union citizen constitute an important element of the EU's respect for linguistic diversity. Furthermore, observing the citizen's right to use a Member State national language, being also the EU official language, can be perceived as a manifestation of the EU's respect for the national identity of a Member State. Although the issue of language rights in the EU is important, as it may concern every Union citizen acting within the scope of the EU law, it remains largely unresolved. The scholarly contributions in the subject are rather sparse. Neither has the nature of the rights been established nor their legal status specified. I have identified two major reasons for that status quo. Firstly, the issue of language rights in the EU is not an easy one. The specificity of the EU as an international organization embodied by its autonomous legal order and high concentration of powers conferred by the Member States, on the one hand, and an unprecedented diversity of 24 official languages and lack of exclusive competences on the part of the Union in language matters, on the other, make the issue of language rights in the Union complex, multidimensional, sometimes vague and dependent on correlated factors. Secondly, the issue of languages, including language rights, has always been highly sensitive as it is tightly identified with the defence of Member State's national identity and sovereignty within the structures of the European Union as well as the underprivileged status of EU non-official languages.

As a result of the above, the Union's approach to language rights has taken a specific shape resulting from two of its objectives: respect for cultural and linguistic diversity, on the one hand, and striving for tightening and standardising cooperation between Member States, on the other. The effect is that to date language rights have often been the outcome of the EU's balancing between contradictory

33 Von Bogdandy and Schill, 1439–40.

34 Wróbel (ed.), *Karta Praw Podstawowych Unii Europejskiej: Komentarz,* 2019, 733.

35 Von Bogdandy and Schill, 1440.

36 Wróbel (ed.), *Karta Praw Podstawowych Unii Europejskiej: Komentarz,* 2019, 729–30.

cultural and economic objectives and acting in the light of the principle of subsidiarity and the principle of proportionality.

2. Thesis, research hypotheses and research problems

Thesis: the dissertation aims to verify the main thesis according to which the language rights of the Union citizen are an important element of the EU's respect for the national identities of its Member States guaranteed in the Treaties. The protection of these rights has been consistently strengthened in EU law, with citizenship of the Union playing an important role in this process.

Research hypotheses: in order to verify the main thesis of the dissertation, the following research hypotheses have been formulated:

1. Language rights are an integral part of the European Union language policy.
2. The European Union maintains a linguistic regime which constitutes the grounds for language rights.
3. Citizenship of the Union strengthens the protection of language rights of Member States' citizens.
4. The European Union respects selected language rights as fundamental rights.

Research problems: the analysis and justification of the above hypotheses require examination of the following research problems:

1. analysis of the European Union's language policy and its impact on language rights of Member States' citizens,
2. examination of the language rights of Member States' citizens resulting from the EU multilingual law,
3. investigation into the rights of Member States' citizens related to language use in communication with the EU institutions,
4. exploration of language rights resulting from the rights expressly granted to the Union citizen in the Lisbon Treaty,
5. investigation into the language rights arising from the universal human rights constituting general principles of EU law,
6. scrutiny of language rights resulting from the protection of fundamental rights laid down in the Charter of Fundamental Rights of the European Union.

3. Structure of the dissertation

The structure of the dissertation reflects to the above hypotheses and research problems. The dissertation consists of **four** chapters.

Chapter 1 deals with the analysis of the linguistic framework of the European Union. Firstly, the primary concepts of the EU language policy, such as respect for linguistic diversity and multilingualism, are introduced and discussed. Secondly, the analysis includes defining the concept of the EU language policy, specifying its components and legal grounds. The chapter examines the relevant Treaty provisions and the division of powers between the EU institutions and the Member States in the area of languages. Next, it analyses the implementation of the policy, including the EU multilingualism strategy as one of its components. Further, three major sources of the language rights of Member States nationals are distinguished. These are the rights arising from the EU language system (regime), rights related to Union citizenship and rights arising from the protection of fundamental rights in the EU. In order to demonstrate the unique character of the EU language policy, the last part of the chapter is dedicated to the analysis of the language policies of two important international organizations, i.e. the United Nations and the Council of Europe, with particular emphasis placed on the language rights of citizens of their members.

Chapter 2 discusses the language rights of the citizens of the Member States embedded in the EU linguistic regime. The first part of the chapter explores the status of languages distinguished in the EU: treaty/authentic languages, official languages and working languages. The second part of the chapter investigates the major principles governing the EU multilingual law, such as the principle of legal certainty, the principle of legal multilingualism, the principle of equal authenticity and the principle of the uniform interpretation and application of the law. The principles are analysed with the aim of verifying whether Member State citizens have the right to be unilingual, i.e. to base their knowledge about EU legal acts on one language version and at the same time to act in accordance with EU law. Next, language rights resulting from EU institutional multilingualism are analysed in the context of the external and internal linguistic regimes of the EU institutions. The rights subjected to examination include the right to send documents to the EU institutions and to receive replies in one of the EU official languages and the right to access court proceedings before the Court of Justice in one of the official languages of the Union. Finally, the impact of the internal restricted regimes of the EU institutions on the language rights of Member State citizens is scrutinised. The examined rights include the linguistic aspects of the citizen's right of access to information, including the information available on the EU institutions' websites, the right to participate in public consultations, and to take part in recruitment procedures for the EU institutions staff, and invitations to tenders.

Chapter 3 focuses on the examination of language rights related to citizenship of the Union. Firstly, the concept of citizenship of the Union is presented and its close relationship with the principle of non-discrimination on the grounds of nationality is demonstrated. Next, a catalogue of rights granted to the Union citizen under the Treaty of Lisbon is presented. The rights constitute a starting point for studying the language rights embedded in Union citizenship. Particular attention is paid to the language rights arising from the right to freely move and reside, read in conjunction with the principle of non-discrimination on the grounds of nationality. The following rights are examined in detail: the right of access to education in one's own language, the right to use one's own language before Member State courts, the right to choose one's name and surname, as well as the language rights of workers and self-employed persons. Subsequently, the rights of the Union citizen to petition the European Parliament, to apply to the European Ombudsman, and to address the EU institutions in one of the Treaty languages are analysed. Next, the linguistic aspects of other rights vested in the Union citizen are examined, including the right to receive diplomatic and consular protection, the right of access to the Union documents, and to submit the European Citizens' Initiative. The final part of the chapter studies the language rights of consumers stemming from their protection as parties to a contract or in disputes and when their health and safety are at stake.

Chapter 4 examines the scope of language rights protected as fundamental rights in the EU. Firstly, the international law background to the concept of language rights understood as (fundamental) human rights is presented. It includes the aims and scope of language rights protection, the individual and collective nature of the rights, language rights in the public and private sphere, as well as positive and negative aspects of the rights. Moreover, the first part of the chapter studies language rights as linguistic aspects of universal human rights protected under international law instruments, including freedom of expression, the right of non-discrimination on the grounds of language, the right to education, and procedural linguistic human rights. Secondly, language rights are set up in the context of the EU fundamental rights protection system. Two major sources of such rights are identified: firstly, the general principles of EU law, including international human rights instruments, in particular the European Convention for the Protection of Human Rights and Fundamental Freedoms (ECHR)[37] and the case-law of the Court of Justice, and secondly, the Charter of Fundamental Rights of the European Union (the Charter).[38] As the general principles of EU law are grounded in the relevant international human rights instruments discussed in the first part of the chapter, the further analysis focuses on the language rights embedded in the Charter. They entail linguistic aspects of the right to non-discrimination on the grounds of language and nationality, respect for linguistic diversity, the right to education, the citizen's rights as well as the right to a fair trial and the right of defence, with particular regard to the right to a translator/an interpreter in criminal proceedings. The last part of the chapter outlines the impact of the EU accession to the ECHR on the language rights of the Union citizen.

4. Research methods employed

The formulated thesis and research hypotheses are verified based on the analysis of the Treaties and relevant legislation, international law instruments, and political

37 European Convention for the Protection of Human Rights and Fundamental Freedom signed on 4 November 1950, entered into force on 3 September 1953. By 2020 ratified by 47 states.

38 OJ C 202/2, 7 June 2016.

documents, as well as academic studies on the subject matter (**dogmatic and legal method**). The **comparative legal method** is also used in order to examine the language policies of the EU, the United Nations, the Council of Europe, and the rights of individuals arising therefrom.

In addition, the **historical method** is employed to present the sources and evolution of language rights. The analysis includes legislative acts and other documents adopted by the Community/Union institutions.

The specific nature of the discussed subject matter and the objective of this dissertation need an interdisciplinary approach. For this reason, the research methods employed go beyond pure legal assessment. The methods used in the field of linguistics (**discourse analysis, including critical discourse analysis**) are applied mainly with reference to the conceptual apparatus adopted within the EU legal order. It constitutes the basis for the analysis of the EU primary and secondary law and the EU judicature.

5. Literature Review

Many questions asked in this study have been the subject of recent academic publications. Against the backdrop of the lack of the Union's clear position on language matters, and the growing mobility of Union citizens and Brexit, the issue of EU multilingualism and its future language policy have been scrutinised across a number of disciplines, in particular by linguists, translators, lawyer-linguists, and political analysts. The major research carried out in the field might be grouped as follows:

- interdisciplinary studies into EU multilingualism: Bruno De Witte (1990), Labrie Normand (1993), Roman Szul (2000), Lorna Carson (2003), Ammon Urlich (2006), Barbara Pozzo (2007), Xabier Arzoz (2008), Peter A. Kraus (2008), Charlotte Kemp (2009), Sue Wright (2009), László Marácz and Mireille Rosello (2012), Anne Lise Kjær and Silvia Adamo (2013), Anastazja Gajda (2013), Susan Šarčević (2017), Peter A. Kraus and François Grin (2018), Simona Montanari and Suzanne Quay (2019);
- studies dedicated to the analysis of EU language policy and the concept of the EU's respect for linguistic diversity: Bruno De Witte (1993, 2008), Jonathan Pool (1996), Thomas Ricento (2000), Peter A. Kraus (2008), Robert Philipson (2003), Richard L. Creech (2005), Xabier Arzoz (2008), Jacek Łuczak (2010), Robert Philipson (2011), Anne Lise Kjær and Silvia Adamo (2011), Sue Wright (2013), Florian Coulmas (2013), Peter A. Kraus and Rūta Kazlauskaitė-Gürbüz (2014), Petra Lea Láncos (2015), Glyn Williams and Gruffudd Williams (2016), Sue Wright (2016), Dave Sayers and Petra Lea Láncos (2017), Helder De Schutter (2018), Izabela Marcinkowska (2020); Artur Nowak-Far (2020);
- analysis of possible future scenarios for the EU language policy, including linguistic consequences of Brexit: Jacek Łuczak (2010), Goran Bandov (2013),

Michele Gazzola (2016), David Crystal (2017), Edgar W. Schneider (2017), Marko Modiano (2017);
- examination of institutional aspects of EU language policy (institutional multilingualism): Krystyna Michałowska-Gorywoda (2001), Richard L. Creech (2005), Phoebus Athanassiou (2006), Michele Gazzola (2006, 2016), Julian Currall (2010), Cornelis J.W. Baaij (2012), Domenico Cosmai (2014), Karolina Paluszek (2015), Nikos Vogiatzis (2016);
- research on EU legal multilingualism: Juha Raitio (2003), Agnieszka Doczekalska (2006, 2009, 2010, 2011, 2014, 2019), Barbara Pozzo and Valentina Jacometti (2006), Mattias Derlén (2009, 2011), Theodor Schilling (2010, 2011), Anne Lise Kjaer and Silvia Adamo (2011), Artur Nowak-Far (2012, 2016), Elina Paunio (2013), Karolina Paluszek (2014), Colin D. Robertson (2016), Susan Šarčević (2015, 2017), Cornelis J.W. Baaij (2012, 2018), Dagmara Kornobis-Romanowska (2018), Artur Nowak-Far (2020);
- analysis of educational and cultural aspects of multilingualism: Hanna Komorowska (2007), Magdalena Szpotowicz (2013), Aneta Skorupa-Wulczyńska (2016), Susan Šarčević (2017);
- study of the concept of European identity and its impact on national identities: Franciszek Grucza (2002), Jürgen Habermas (2005), Roman Szul (2007), Peter A. Kraus (2008), Aleks Szczerbiak and Paul Taggart (2008), Jeffrey T. Checkel and Peter J. Katzenstein (2009), Dario Castiglione (2009), Johnathan White (2012), Markus Prutch (2017), Anita Schnettger (2019);
- analysis of language rights in the EU context: Bruno de Witte (1992), Xabier Arzoz (2007), Iñigo Urrutia and Iñaki Lasagebaster (2007, 2008), Susanna Mancini and Bruno De Witte (2008), Theodor Schilling (2008), Stephen May (2011);
- exploration of language rights as human rights, including rights of national minorities: Mala Tabory (1980), Tove Skutnabb-Kangas and Robert Phillipson (1989, 1995, 2017), Patrick Thornberry (1992), Lauri Mälksoo (1998), Robert Dunbar (2001), Fernand de Varennes (1996, 1999, 2001), Sue Wright (2001), Xabier Arzoz (2007), Kristin Henrard (2010), Manuel Toscano Méndez (2012), Łukasz Wardyn (2012), Moria Paz (2013, 2014), Elżbieta Kuzborska and Łukasz Wardyn (2014), Elżbieta Kuzborska (2015, 2017), Fernand de Varennes and Elżbieta Kuzborska (2016); Bruno De Witte (2019);
- research on the concept of Union citizenship: Adam Łazowski (2003), Amanda Root (2007), Aleksander Gubrynowicz (2008), Adam Bodnar (2008), Peter Hilpold (2008), Thomas Marshall (2009), Izabela Skomerska-Muchowska and Anna Wyrozumska (2010), Alina Tryfonidou (2011, 2018), Dorota Pudzianowska (2013), Robert Grzeszczak (2013), Sandra Seubert and Oliver Eberl (2018).

As regards language matters in the EU, Polish academic research studies have focused on the analysis including: EU multilingualism and language policy (Gajda, Łuczak, Marcinkowska), institutional multilingualism (Michałowska-Gorywoda, Paluszek) and educational aspects of EU multilingualism (Komorowska, Szpotowicz), EU multilingual law (Doczekalska, Kornobis-Romanowska,

Nowak-Far, Paluszek), European identity (Szul, Grucza), and the language rights of national minorities (Wardyn and Kuzborska). Particular attention should be drawn to the latest monograph by Nowak-Far who analyses in detail the mechanisms of applying EU multilingual law at the level of terminology, syntax and from the perspective of law effectiveness. Moreover, the monograph recapitulates the academic achievements in respect of EU legal multilingualism. As the analysis made within this dissertation will also be affected by the research studies evaluating Union citizenship, it should be noted that the impact of Polish academics in this field is significant (Bodnar, Grzeszczak, Gubrynowicz, Łazowski, Pudziankowska, Skomerka-Muchowska and Wyrozumska).

Despite the intensified research in the field of broadly defined EU multilingualism, the matter of the language rights of the Union citizen has been only fragmentarily analysed. Although some of the above studies examine the issue of language rights within the EU, a gap in the analysis exists and it manifests a need to examine the language rights in a comprehensive way. The existing knowledge on the subject shows that there is no uniform legal framework for the protection of language rights in the EU, and the status of these rights has not been clarified. This dissertation aspires to fill the existing gap in this research field by specifying the legal grounds for such rights, including the EU law primary and secondary law, the case-law of the Court of Justice, and relevant international human rights instruments. It aims to organise and clarify the language-related entitlements vested in the Union citizen according to their origin and status.

The novelty of the dissertation consists in the fact that language rights are not analysed in the context of minority protection, although this aspect is also to be explored to the required extent, but in the context of the rights of individuals – citizens of the Union, who are not necessarily categorised as members of national or linguistic minorities. Moreover, within this study the Union citizen's language rights primarily refer to Member State national languages, not just any language. This is justified by the fact that the protection of Member State national languages constitutes the core of the EU's respect for the national identities of its Member States.

The analysis carried out within the framework of this dissertation includes the legal status and scholarly debates as of October 2020.

The British English standard is used throughout the dissertation.

1. Linguistic framework of the European Union

1.1 Opening remarks

The concepts of linguistic diversity and multilingualism have been an intrinsic element of European integration since its beginnings. They have been growing in importance together with the increasing number of EU Member States, which has triggered the rising number of EU official languages. As the European Union has become more and more diverse, its multilingualism has turned into an important social, cultural, economic, and political fact of life.[1] The expanding complexity of EU multilingualism has been creating new challenges for the European Union institutions, EU Member States, and their citizens. The EU institutions were forced to adapt their administrative capabilities to efficiently function in many languages, and the citizens enjoying the right to freely move and reside had to get used to operating in the public sphere in other than their native languages. As a result of the latter, citizens began to claim their language rights of varied nature, including the right to be educated in their mother tongue in a host Member State, the right to use language understandable to them before the court of the host State, the right not to be discriminated against based on language as a worker or self-employed person, or the right to understand the labels of a product available on the markets of their State, to name the key ones. So far, neither has the nature of such rights has been established nor their legal status specified. Moreover, there seem to be a variety of sources for such rights.

This chapter outlines the linguistic background to the functioning of the European Union. Its major purpose is to highlight the sources of the language rights of the citizen of the Union.[2] Moreover, the analysis aims to show that that the EU language policy is one of the three major sources of such rights, and to demonstrate that the policy embodying respect for national languages plays an important role in assuring the Union's respect for the national identities of its Member States. In this context, the chapter intends to display that the EU is the only international organization whose language policy is a source of enforceable language rights of the citizens of its Member States. At its various stages, the chapter introduces and discusses the major elements of the terminology used throughout the dissertation.

---

1 Patxi Juaristi, Timothy Reagan and Humphrey Tonkin, "Language diversity in the European Union", in: Xabier Arzoz (ed.) *Respecting Linguistic Diversity in the European Union*, 2008, 47–9.

2 Also referred to as the citizen of the European Union, the Union citizen, and the EU citizen.

The pivotal concepts of 'linguistic diversity', 'multilingualism', 'language policy', 'language planning', 'language rights', and 'linguistic regime' are introduced and explained. The notions of 'state language', 'national language' and 'official language' appear in the text. Their meanings are compliant with the definitions provided by Davis and Dubinsky (2018), according to which a state language is the one which fulfils the function of the state administration, government and official commerce; a national language is associated with a nation, and an official language is a state language that is mandated by law and is written into the constitution of a state.[3] In EU parlance, the concept of an official language prevails.

The chapter begins with an analysis of the primary concepts of the European Union language policy: linguistic diversity, and multilingualism. Next, the Union language policy is defined and its legal basis examined. Special attention is paid to two major components of the policy – status planning and acquisition planning. The former, which constitutes a primary legal dimension of the policy is only outlined, as it is analysed in-depth in chapter 2 of the dissertation. Following that, the component of acquisition planning implemented by way of the EU multilingualism strategy is investigated. The conclusions are drawn that, owing to the legal nature of the EU, the scope of language rights goes beyond the rights based on the norms embedded in the EU language policy. Language rights are also entrenched in the concept of Union citizenship and the EU fundamental rights protection system. Finally, with a view to demonstrating the distinct nature of the EU language policy, the chapter juxtaposes the EU language policy with the language policies of two important international organizations: the United Nations and the Council of Europe.

1.2 The concept of linguistic diversity in the European Union

In no way is the EU more diverse than in terms of languages.[4] The European Union respects linguistic diversity through the recognition of 24 official languages of its Member States[5] and approximately 60 autochthonous regional or minority languages spoken by around 40 million people over its geographical area.[6] Certainly,

---

3 William D. Davis and Stanley Dubinsky, *Language Conflict and Language Rights: Ethnolinguistic Perspectives on Human Conflict,* Cambridge University Press, 2018, 102.

4 Richard L. Creech, *Law and language in the European Union: the paradox of a Babel "United in Diversity"*, Groningen: Europa Law Publishing, 2005, 3–4.

5 Regulation No. 1 determining the languages to be used by the European Economic Community. Consolidated version of 1 July 2013. The number of official languages is lower than the number of the EU Member States, as some languages have the status of an official language in more than one Member State.

6 EU languages, https://europa.eu/european-union/about-eu/eu-languages_en [retrieved on 7 May 2019].

this is not the entire linguistic picture of the European Union. The Euromosaic study on the comparative analysis of minority language groups identified approximately a hundred minority linguistic groups in various EU Member States.[7] What is more, the number of languages is constantly growing owing to the mobility of Europeans and a notable influx of non-European migrants to the EU. Drawing on the Nettle's (1999) definition of linguistic diversity which amounts to "the total number of languages,"[8] it may be contended that all the languages, including national, regional, and minority languages as well as the languages of migrants, contribute to the linguistic landscape of the European Union.

The European appreciation of linguistic diversity stems from a particular concept of language embraced by the European Communities. Accordingly, language is a cultural phenomenon and a denominator of the identity of a community or society.[9] 'Diversity' in the EU has always been considered to mean 'respect' for differences rather than the mere existence of differences.[10] For this reason, respect for diversity of cultures, customs, religions, convictions, and languages has been the cornerstone of European integration since the very outset. Owing to such a unique approach to diversity, the European Union has never been considered a 'melting pot' in which differences are rendered down, but a 'salad bowl' in which diversity is celebrated and protected, and where a variety of native languages is a source of wealth, tolerance, and acceptance of differences between people as well as a bridge to greater solidarity, mutual understanding, and social cohesion.[11] Each of the many European languages is said to add its own unique facet to a shared European cultural heritage, where no language is superfluous and no European citizen feels that his or her language is marginalised or disrespected.[12]

The co-existence of many languages in Europe has become the European Union's aspiration to be united in diversity.[13] The motto of 'united in diversity' became the

---

7 Directorate-General for Education, Youth, Sport and Culture, *Euromosaic III. Presence of Regional and Minority Language Groups in the New Member States.* The study was initiated by the European Commission and published in 2006, 2009 and 2012.

8 Daniel Nettle, *Linguistic Diversity*, Oxford University Press, 1999.

9 Peter A. Kraus, "A one-dimensional diversity? European integration and the challenge of language policy", in: Xabier Arzoz (ed.), *Respecting linguistic diversity in the European Union* 2, 2008, 39–43.

10 Creech, 4.

11 Anastazja Gajda, "Wielojęzyczność Unii Europejskiej", *Socjolingwistyka*, No. 27, 2013, 27.

12 Communication from the Commission to the European Parliament, the Council, the European Economic and Social Committee and the Committee of the Regions – Multilingualism: an asset for Europe and a shared commitment COM(2008) 566.

13 Communication from the Commission to the Council, the European Parliament, the European Economic and Social Committee and the Committee of the Regions – A New Framework Strategy for Multilingualism COM(2005) 596.

official symbol of the Union, alongside the European flag and the anthem. Through its motto, the European Union formally confirmed that diverse cultures, traditions, and languages constituted a positive asset and one of the key values of Europe. The concept of respect for linguistic diversity was gradually strengthened and under the Lisbon Treaty it became one of the Union's objectives. As noted by Creech, in EU parlance, respect for linguistic diversity in practice translates into respect for the national languages of the Member States.[14] The principle of respect for national languages serves as a primary tool to demonstrate respect for the national identities of the Member States. The EU expresses this respect by refraining from interference in the national identities of its Member States and by undertaking measures to promote their linguistic and cultural wealth.[15]

The EU perceived the diversity of its Member States as "the waterway uniting what it separates in the archipelago of European identities".[16] Such an approach gave rise to the concept of European identity which had already been coined in 1973.[17] That was when the Declaration on European Identity was adopted in Copenhagen.[18] At that time, nine Member States declared an intention to build a European identity based on the attachment to common values and the principles of preserving national identity within the EU. The Declaration read as follows *"(...) The Nine [Member States of the European Communities] wish to ensure that the cherished values of their legal, political, and moral order are respected, and to preserve the rich variety of their national cultures. (...) 3. The diversity of cultures within the framework of a common European civilisation, the attachment to common values and principles, the increasing convergence of attitudes to life, the awareness of having specific interests in common, and the determination to take part in the construction of a United Europe, all give the European Identity its originality and its own dynamism."*[19]

Building a European identity based on respect for linguistic diversity was seen by the EU as an antidote to various types of fanaticism towards which the assertion of identity had slipped.[20] More than thirty years after the Declaration, the

14 Creech, 49.

15 Gajda, "Wielojęzyczność Unii Europejskiej", 7.

16 Kraus, "A one-dimensional diversity? European integration and the challenge of language policy", 85.

17 Roman Szul, "Tożsamość europejska a kwestia językowa w Unii Europejskiej", *Studia Regionalne i Lokalne, No.* 4, 2007, 66.

18 *Declaration on European Identity, Copenhagen,* 14 *December* 1973, Bulletin of the European Communities. December 1973, No. 12.

19 *Declaration on European Identity, para. 1(2).*

20 Proposals from the Group of Intellectuals for Intercultural Dialogue set up at the initiative of the European Commission, *A Rewarding Challenge: how the multiplicity of languages could strengthen Europe,* https://ec.europa.eu/education/sites/education/files/rewarding-challenge-report_en.pdf [retrieved on 23 July 2018].

European Commission reaffirmed that linguistic diversity was an instrument of building a European identity policy.[21] Moreover, the Council in the Resolution of 21 November 2008 on a European strategy for multilingualism, expressly confirmed that "linguistic and cultural diversity is part and parcel of the European identity; it is at once a shared heritage, a wealth, a challenge, and an asset for Europe."[22]

To clarify, European identity was categorised both as a cultural identity of shared values, and a political identity of shared democratic practices.[23] The concept of European cultural identity encountered considerable scepticism and reserve from philosophers, political scientists, and sociologists, including Harmsen and Wilson (2000)[24] and Checkel and Katzenstein (2009).[25] The broad criticism of European cultural identity triggered an alternative concept of a generic political identity of the Union. The term suggests that democratic structures and institutions have a crucial role in promoting political identity. The notion of political identity has also provoked notable criticism. Its critics such as Habermas (2005),[26] Szczerbiak and Taggart (2008),[27] and Castiglione (2009)[28] argued that the concept was too abstract and failed to raise any emotional bond among citizens of the EU Member States. White (2012) went further and claimed that 'European identity' was an empty phrase, an illusion, which was invented to respond to the genuine problem of governing Europe as one.[29] Nevertheless, there are academics including Kraus

21 Communication from the Commission to the Council, the European Parliament, the European Economic and Social Committee and the Committee of the Regions – A New Framework Strategy for Multilingualism COM(2005) 596.

22 Communication from the Commission to the European Parliament, the Council, the European Economic and Social Committee and the Committee of the Regions Multilingualism: an asset for Europe and a shared commitment COM(2008) 566.

23 Markus Prutsch, *Research for CULT Committee: European Identity*, European Parliament's Committee on Culture and Education, 2017, 5.

24 Robert Harmsen and Thomas M. Wilson (eds.), *Europeanization: Institution, Identities and Citizenship*, Amsterdam: Atlanta, GA: Rodopi (Yearbook of European Studies, 14), 2000.

25 Jeffrey T. Checkel and Peter J. Katzenstein (eds.), *European Identity*, Cambridge: Cambridge University Press, 2009.

26 Jürgen Habermas, *The Inclusion of the Other: Studies in Political Theory*, Cambridge: Polity Press, 2005.

27 Aleks Szczerbiak and Paul Taggart (eds.), *Opposing Europe? The Comparative Party Politics of Euroscepticism*, Oxford; New York, NY: Oxford University Press, 2008.

28 Dario Castiglione, "Political identity in a community of strangers", in: Jeffrey T. Checkel and Peter J. Katzenstein (eds.), *European Identity*, Cambridge: Cambridge University Press, 2009, 29–51.

29 Jonathan White, "A common European identity is an illusion", in: Hubert Zimmermann and Andreas Dür (eds.), *Key Controversies in European Integration*, Palgrave Macmillan, 2012.

(2008) who maintain that it is hardly doubted that a European identity based on linguistic diversity currently exists. However, it is highly doubted that it exists to the required extent. In his view, a politically resilient European identity is urgently needed for strengthening the legitimation basis of the EU.[30]

The debate on 'European identity' and Member State national identities revived in the face of Brexit. The UK's withdrawal from the European Union was regarded as the effect of the British weak sense of European identity.[31] Certainly, the British have been the most EU-sceptic nation in the EU since the 1990s with the peak reached in the Eurozone debt crisis in 2010.[32] The growing isolationist tendencies of the British may justify their decision of exit from the EU, but the question on the status quo of European identity remains open. Attachment to the EU is a complex phenomenon and building a sense of European identity is a long-lasting process. Its purpose is to demonstrate that identification with the Union does not exclude national identity. On the contrary, European identity coexists with Member State national identities. What is important is how strongly Europeans define themselves by their national identity and how much they identify themselves with the EU. According to the 2016 Eurobarometer, 39% of respondents defined themselves solely by their nationality, 51% defined themselves by their nationality and as Europeans, and only 2% of respondents saw themselves first of all as Europeans.[33] The 2019 Eurobarometer showed an increase in citizens' positive perception of the EU and optimism about its future.[34] Although this does not mean yet that Member State citizens identify more with the Union, such results may be a symptom of a reviving sense of European identity and diminishing Euroscepticism.

1.3 The concept of multilingualism in the European Union

The European Union's respect for linguistic diversity is closely connected with its concept of multilingualism. The interdependence between the two makes it necessary to determine first what is meant by EU multilingualism. To start with, it must be noted that the plain dictionary definition of multilingualism explains the term as an individual's ability to communicate in several languages (individual

30 Peter A. Kraus, *A Union of Diversity: Language, Identity and Polity-building in Europe*, Cambridge University Press, 2008.

31 Noah Carl, James Dennison and Geoffrey Evans, "European but not European enough: An explanation for Brexit", *European Union Politics, Vol.* 20, No. 2, 2019, 282–304.

32 Eurobarometer 85. European citizenship, May 2016.

33 Eurobarometer 85. European citizenship, May 2016.

34 Standard Eurobarometer 91. Spring 2019. Public opinion in the European Union. June 2019.

multilingualism, plurilingualism) as well as the co-existence of different languages within a community in one geographical/political area (social multilingualism). Such a definition is recognised by academics in the field, including Carson (2003),[35] Malinowska (2004),[36] Zygierewicz (2010)[37] and is commonly accepted by international organizations, such as the United Nations (UN)[38] and the Council of Europe (CoE).[39] Such an understanding of multilingualism has also been embraced by the European Union. Moreover, the European Commission assigns an additional meaning to the term by describing it as multilingualism strategy or language learning policy, i.e. the Union's policy aiming to promote conditions "conducive to the full expression of all languages, in which the teaching and learning of foreign languages can flourish".[40]

It must also be noted that multilingualism is a concept the meaning of which has expanded over time. Initially, multilingualism in the EU acquired a symbolic dimension and was regarded as the most prominent symbol of the Union's commitment to cultural and linguistic diversity.[41] Progressively, the term began to be used with regard to a multitude of matters related to language use in the EU, both in the public and private sphere. For this reason, a traditional understanding of multilingualism ceased to suffice to capture the full scope of the manifestations of linguistic diversity in modern societies in the EU, where the steady increase in European mobility entailed many new forms of social multilingualism.

With time, EU multilingualism has turned into an interdisciplinary phenomenon. The study of the EU regulations and directives[42] as well as of the publications

---

35 Lorna Carson (ed.), *Multilingualism in Europe. A Case Study*, PIE-P. Lang, Brussels, 2003.

36 Ewa Nikadem-Malinowska, *Język prawo–społeczeństwo*, University of Opole, 2004.

37 Anna Zygierewicz, "Wielojęzyczność Unii Europejskiej", *Analizy BAS*, No. 3 (28), 2010.

38 The dual meaning can be deduced from the publication placed on the UN website on multilingualism, https://www.un.org/Depts/DGACM/multilingualism.shtml [retrieved on 7 May 2019].

39 The CoE clearly differentiates between two concepts: 'multilingualism' and 'plurilingualism'. The former stands for the presence in a geographical area of more than one variety of language and the latter refers to the repertoire of languages spoken by individuals. Thus, in multilingual areas there may be monolingual or plurilingual individuals, https://rm.coe.int/16806a892c#_ Toc172301743, para. 3 [retrieved on 7 May 2019].

40 A New Framework Strategy for Multilingualism COM(2005) 596, 3.

41 Annarita Felici, "Translating EU law: Legal issues and multiple dynamics", *Perspectives: Studies in Translatology*, Vol. 18, No. 2, 2010, 95.

42 The examples being: Regulation No. 492/2011 on freedom of movement of workers, Directive 1999/44/EC on certain aspects of the sale of consumer goods and associated guarantees, Directive 2004/38 on the right of citizens of the Union and their

on the Union institutions' websites[43] confirm that the dictionary definition does not entail the full meaning of the term multilingualism used in the context of the European Union. What is more, the additional meaning assigned to multilingualism by the EU, understood as language learning policy, entails only some matters falling under the heading of EU multilingualism. Owing to its evolving nature, EU multilingualism has received much academic attention in recent years and has been studied from various perspectives, in particular by linguists, educators, sociologists, psychologists, and lawyers.[44] One of the major goals of academics was to establish the meaning and the scope of the term. Such an attempt was made *inter alia* by Carson (2003) who introduced a transparent and logical systematisation of EU multilingualism. She distinguished its three major facets in the EU, i.e. firstly, multilingualism within the EU official institutions and agencies, secondly, the interface between the EU bodies and the European public, and thirdly, multilingualism in the everyday life of EU citizens.[45]

The extensive research done so far reaffirms that the concept of multilingualism in the EU is still not finally defined. The LINEE Network of Excellence consisting of a group of 80 researchers investigating linguistic diversity and multilingualism in the EU proved in the Final Report on Challenges of Multilingualism in Europe (2011) that the picture was blurred. Academics claim that even the European policy-makers understand the term differently depending on the context. Some associate it with human rights and minority language protection, others with education policies or with its economic value.[46] The Report also presents the results of research projects[47] carried out by the LINEE Network which show that for the

---

family members to move and reside freely within the territory of the Member States, Directive 2005/29/EC on unfair commercial practices, Directive 2009/48/EC on the safety of toys, Directive 98/79/EC on in vitro diagnostic medical devices

43 European Parliament, Briefing of January 2017. Legal aspects of EU multilingualism, http://www.europarl.europa.eu/thinktank/en/document.html?reference=EPRS_BRI(2017)595914 [retrieved on 10 May 2019].

44 including: Carson, Philipson (2003), Creech (2005), Ammon, Pozzo and Jacometti (2006), Komorowska, Pozzo (2007), Arzoz, Kraus, Mancini and De Witte (2008), Derlén, Doczekalska, Kemp, Wright (2009), Łuczak (2010), Philipson, Schilling, Wright (2011), Marácz and Rosello (2012), Coulmas, Gajda, Kjær and Adamo, Paunio, Szpotowicz (2013), Doczekalska, Paluszek (2014), Láncos, Šarčević, Van der Jeught (2015), Gazzola, Nowak-Far, Robertson, Skorupa-Wulczyńska, Williams (2016), Šarčević, Sayers and Láncos (2017), Baaij (2018), Doczekalska, Montanari and Quay (2019), Nowak-Far (2020).

45 Carson, 19.

46 Final Report Summary of the research project – Languages in a network of European excellence (LINEE), 3 November 2011, https://cordis.europa.eu/project/id/28388/reporting [retrieved on 8 October 2020], 24.

47 Extensive analysis of particular LINEE's Work Packages can be found in the Report.

The aforementioned definitions imply that language policy serves two primary objectives – the maintenance of identity and ensuring effective communication. Firstly, identity is maintained by means of language, which is a fundamental, permanent, and intrinsic part of human identity. For this reason, the language policy is incorporated into an identity policy, which may be embodied in a dual nature of 'demos' and 'ethnos'. If 'demos' is an objective of a language policy, the policy aims at language uniformity. The ideal 'demos' assumes a homogenous community, single identity, and one language implying full unrestrained communication. If a language policy supports 'ethnos', it aims at the strengthening of a particular community. The ideal 'ethnos' means heterogeneous community, complex identity, and a multitude of languages, implying limited communication.[59] Secondly, language is also an external creation of a human being and a tool of communication. Therefore, language policy is also an inherent part of a communication policy.[60] The efficiency of any communication policy is characterised by three factors: 'symposia' (communication), 'glossa' (the existence of a language *per se*), and 'nomisma' (money). All the factors co-exist, intermingle and affect one another. Demos, ethnos, symposia, glossa, and nomisma are interdependent and interrelated values, the hierarchy of which determines the shape and direction of a given language policy.[61]

Language policy is a multi-faceted discipline and the achievement of its objectives entails three main aspects – legal, cultural and linguistic, as well as educational.[62] For this purpose, the competent authorities are obliged to adopt relevant statutes to carry out appropriate information, educational, and cultural policies, and to undertake appropriate measures and actions. The legal aspects of language policy relate to all the relevant regulations imposed by the state or by the organization in the scope of the language (languages) and its (their) use. Cultural and linguistic aspects include the totality of ideas, values, beliefs, attitudes, prejudices, myths, religious structures, and all the other cultural 'baggage' that speakers contribute to the language from their culture. Educational aspects of language policy aim at language acquisition and teaching. These three aspects are interrelated and affect one another. Pisarek noticed that the legal aspects of language policy should be brought to the forefront in all decisions concerning privileging a language or a group of languages and limiting other languages or their variants, which is often the case in international organizations.[63] In fact, the legal and regulatory aspects

59 Franciszek Grucza, "Język (narodowy) – tożsamość (narodowa) – integracja europejska", in: Elżbieta Jeleń [et al.](ed.), *Zmiany i rozwój języka oraz tożsamości narodowej–trendy w procesie integracji europejskiej (Language Dynamics and Linguistic Identity in the Context of European Integration)*, 2002, 38.

60 Grucza, 25.

61 Jacek Łuczak, *Polityka językowa Unii Europejskiej*, Oficyna Wydawnicza ASPRA-JR, 2010, 39.

62 Pisarek, 42.

63 Pisarek.

of a language determine the shape of the policy and form the grounds for any implementation activities. As noted by Wright (2016), language policy making also reflects on political events, economic and social processes, and also plays a crucial role in the distribution of power and resources in all societies.[64]

All the three major aspects of a language policy are reflected in language planning, which constitutes the actual phase of language policy implementation. Language planning is carried out by competent authorities in order to sort out language issues within a community and to influence the behaviour of the community members with respect to the acquisition, structure, or functional allocation of their language codes. Language planning is broken up into three components: status planning, acquisition planning, and corpus planning (the terms coined and defined by Haugen).[65] In principle, status planning within the language policy constitutes the major level of language planning which affects the social and legal position to which a language will be assigned. As status planning remains within the competence of the state or organization statutory institutions, the result of this process is publication of all relevant regulations imposed by a state or by an organization in respect of the language (languages) and its (their) use. In the course of the status planning, the variety of a language or varieties of languages that become official in a state or an organization and serve as a medium of its institutions, are established, and by way of that the means for interaction between the state and citizens are determined. Acquisition planning is a derivative of status planning, as relevant regulations adopted in the area of language acquisition must be compliant with the superior legislation specifying the status of languages. Although language acquisition is strictly related to education, it does not remain without impact on status and corpus planning, as it is a powerful tool affecting a shape of any language policy.[66] Corpus planning primarily deals with language standardisation processes including orthographic, lexical, and spelling correctness, harmonisation within the language, pronunciation, changes in language structure, vocabulary expansion, or style.[67]

1.4.2 EU language policy and its components

Based on the analysis of the notion of language policy, the EU language policy may be described as a policy embodied in deliberate activities of the EU institutions aimed at shaping the language situation within the organization. As the Union's language policy is a multilingualism policy, the European Union institutions undertake a series of activities to operate in many languages and make its Member

---

64 Sue Wright, *Language Policy and Language Planning. From Nationalism to Globalisation*, Palgrave Macmillan, 2016, 1.

65 Cooper, 45.

66 Łuczak, 30.

67 Kaplan and Baldauf, 20.

States and their citizens co-exist in multilingualism. The EU language policy includes the required components, with status planning and acquisition planning taking the lead. As noticed by Darquennes and Nelde (2006), corpus planning in the context of the EU language policy plays a minor role. It is of greater importance at a regional rather than supranational level.[68] This component does not constitute the focus of analysis made within this dissertation.

The immersion of the EU language policy in the principle of respect for linguistic diversity affects the status planning. The promotion of individual multilingualism and language learning exerts a significant impact on the acquisition planning. The component of status planning constitutes the key legal dimension of the EU language policy. It classifies the languages of the EU Member States into the treaty (authentic), official, and working languages of the European Union. As a result of this classification, the EU linguistic regime is established. The regime may be described as a multilingual language system which regulates the status of languages within the organization and specifies the languages which can be used in contacts between the European Union institutions, its Member States and their citizens, the rules of language use in the communication inside and between the institutions, as well as the language guarantees resulting from the principle of equal authenticity of Union multilingual law and international agreements entered into by the Union as an international organization. The component of acquisition planning is reflected in the EU multilingualism strategy. Within the framework of the strategy, the Union institutions, in particular the European Commission, take up relevant initiatives to encourage individuals to improve their language skills and master foreign languages and help the Member States develop educational tools and gather data to monitor progress in language teaching and learning.[69]

1.4.3 Legal framework for the EU language policy

1.4.3.1 Treaty provisions on language matters

In terms of time, the legal framework for the EU language policy may be divided into two phases: the period preceding the Lisbon Treaty (LT) and that following the Lisbon Treaty. An element linking the two periods is the institutional regime constantly based on Regulation No. 1 determining the languages to be used by the European Economic Community (Regulation No. 1/58).[70] It has remained virtually unchanged except for the relevant amendments extending the number of official languages upon every accession. Moreover, the link is also maintained by one treaty guarantee which justifies the European Union's principle of linguistic

68 Jeroen Darquennes and Peter Nelde, "German as a lingua franca", *Annual Review of Applied Linguistics, Vol.* 26, 2006, 61–77.

69 A New Framework Strategy for Multilingualism COM(2005) 596.

70 OJ 017, 1 July 2013.

equality – non-discrimination on the grounds of nationality. The guarantee has been enshrined in the law since the Treaty establishing the European Economic Community (TEEC) of 1958.[71]

The period of the language policy preceding the LT was earmarked by three main factors: prohibition of discrimination based on nationality, Community competence in the field of education and culture, and an ambivalent minority policy. Firstly, in the cases of *Cowan*[72] and *Martinez Sala*, the Court of Justice managed to specify the standards regarding linguistic requirements which amounted to discrimination and linked the discrimination based on language with discrimination based on citizenship. Secondly, the competence to pursue cultural cooperation and education policy was conferred by the Maastricht Treaty[73] and allowed the EU to adopt several programmes on language learning and the promotion of multilingualism among citizens. Thirdly, the EU seemed to apply double-standards in the field of minority protection. Out of all the EU institutions, only the European Parliament attempted to develop a common community standard of minority protection.[74]

The Lisbon Treaty is considered to be a breakthrough in respect of languages and their protection. In political terms, the LT reinforced multilingualism by making it a political necessity which determines the proper development of the European Union and the achievement of European goals.[75] In legal terms, the Treaty introduced new legal bases obliging the Union to respect and promote cultural and linguistic diversity. First of all, the principle of respect for linguistic diversity was incorporated into the Charter of Fundamental Rights of the European Union (Article 22 of the Charter) and thus its status changed into a fundamental right in the EU.[76] Respect for linguistic diversity was also enshrined in the Treaty on European Union (TEU), which includes a number of references to linguistic diversity. Firstly, the Preamble to the TEU refers to linguistic diversity as an intrinsic element of cultural inheritance by stating that the Union "draws inspiration from

---

71 Non-discrimination on the grounds of nationality – Article 7 TEEC, https://www.cvce.eu/obj/treaty_establishing_the_european_economic_community_rome_25_march_1957-en-cca6ba28-0bf3-4ce6-8a76-6b0b3252696e.html [retrieved on 20 January 2020].

72 Judgment of the Court of 2 February 1989 in the case 86/87 *Ian William Cowan v Trésor public. Reference for a preliminary ruling: Tribunal de grande instance de Paris – France*, ECLI:EU:C:1989:47.

73 OJ C 191, 29 July 1992.

74 Petra Lea Láncos, "Linguistic Diversity Meets the Free Movement of Workers: The Las Case", *Hungarian Yearbook of International Law & European Law*, 2015, 523.

75 Phoebus Athanassiou, *The Application of Multilingualism in the European Union Context, Legal Working Papers, No.* 2, March 2006, 7.

76 OJ C 202/2, 7 June 2016.

the cultural, religious, and humanistic inheritance of Europe". Secondly, respect for linguistic diversity is entrenched in the values on which the Union is founded (Article 2 TEU), such values encompass respect for human rights, including the rights of persons belonging to minorities, equality, tolerance, pluralism, and non-discrimination. Respect for linguistic diversity is also shaped as an aim of the Union. Article 3(3) TEU expressly provides that the European Union "shall respect its rich cultural and linguistic diversity, and shall ensure that Europe's cultural heritage is safeguarded and enhanced".[77]

The Treaty on the Functioning of the European Union (TFEU) also includes direct references to the principle of respect for linguistic diversity. Article 207(4)(a) TFEU[78] which constitutes the basis of the common commercial policy, falling under the exclusive competence of the Union, expresses respect for linguistic diversity in the context of commercial transactions. It obliges the Council to act unanimously in the field of cultural services if they bear a risk of exerting an adverse effect on cultural or linguistic diversity. Respect for linguistic diversity imposes on the Union a passive obligation not to conduct any policy which would prejudice the existing language diversity.[79] The TFEU also includes specific provisions on the promotion of linguistic and cultural diversity. Article 165 TFEU stresses that the Union should strive for "developing the European dimension in education, particularly through the teaching and dissemination of learning of the languages of the Member States, whilst fully respecting cultural and linguistic diversity".[80]

From a formal regulatory perspective, the recognition of linguistic matters and language rights in the primary sources of law, including the Charter, implies their importance in view of the principle of equality of the EU Member States. It must also be remembered that apart from the direct references to the protection of linguistic diversity, the Treaty provides other language-related guarantees which contribute to the implementation of the principle of respect for linguistic diversity, such as respect for national identity (Article 4(2) TEU), non-discrimination on the grounds of nationality (Article 18 TFEU, Article 21 of the Charter), or fundamental rights having linguistic aspects, in particular the right to a fair trial and right of defence (Articles 47 and 48 of the Charter) or the right to good administration (Article 41 of the Charter).

The Lisbon Treaty clearly attempts to strengthen language-related guarantees either by making them fundamental rights or by raising their status to such rights. As regards respect for national identity, the LT is more specific and elaborate when compared to the previous Treaties. The first reference to national identity appeared

77 OJ C 202/1, 7 June 2016.

78 OJ C 202/1, 7 June 2016.

79 Stefaan Van der Jeught, *EU Language Law*, Groninger: Europa Law Publishing, 2015, 90.

80 OJ 2016 C 202/1, 7 June 2016.

in the Maastricht Treaty[81] which stipulated that "the Union shall respect the national identities of its Member States". The LT describes this respect as intrinsically connected with "fundamental, political, constitutional, and regional structures, and self-government".[82] This wording indicates that national identity comprises, not only respect for culture, language or customs, but also respect for the identity of the state (fr. *état-nation*). The principle reinforces constitutional protection of the state structures. Although the extension of the principle does not expressly strengthen respect for national languages, it may be read as strengthening respect for Member State constitutional orders where national languages are protected as an essential element expressing the state's national identity.[83] Last but not least, Article 4(2) TEU does not constitute a norm of competence, nor does it provide sanctions for the infringement of an obligation to respect national identity. For this reason, the European Union is not allowed to provide general regulations protecting national identity. Hence, in the case of any violation of respect for national identity, a Member State could seek its rights only on the grounds of general rules of international liability.[84]

The changes introduced by the Lisbon Treaty outlined the direction the EU wants to pursue in terms of its language policy. The inclusion of the principle of respect for linguistic diversity into the TEU, the TFEU, and the Charter implies growing awareness in respect of language rights and illustrates the European Union's concern for linguistic diversity. A change in the status of respect for linguistic diversity may be seen as a step towards the intensification of language policy and strengthening of citizens' rights through the protection of languages, the identity of language users, as well as the promotion of building a European identity.

1.4.3.2 Division of powers in language matters

As regards the division of powers between the EU and the Member States in language matters, the Lisbon Treaty did not change anything in this respect. EU language policy still has two major limbs which fall under two categories of the European Union's competences. The first limb entails the classification of languages (status planning) which is explicitly regulated in hard law and exercised within the exclusive competence of the EU. Article 55 TEU recognises 24 treaty authentic languages: Bulgarian, Croatian, Czech, Danish, Dutch, English, Estonian,

81 Article F(1)TEU, OJ C 191, 29 July 1992.

82 Article 4(2) TEU, OJ C 202/1, 7 June 2016.

83 Lankosz (ed.), 137.

84 Anita Schnettger, "Article 4(2) TEU as a Vehicle for National Constitutional Identity in a Shared European Legal System", in: Christian Calliess and Gerhard van der Schyff (eds.), *Constitutional Identity in a Europe of Multilievel Constitutionalism*, Cambridge University Press, 2019, 9–38.

Finnish, French, German, Greek, Hungarian, Irish, Italian, Latvian, Lithuanian, Maltese, Polish, Portuguese, Romanian, Slovak, Slovenian, Spanish, and Swedish. The languages have equal status and the texts of the EU legal instruments are authentic in all treaty languages.

The second limb includes the so-called general division of competences in language matters, which covers the component of acquisition planning. The competences in the areas of education, vocational training, and culture are specified in Article 6 TFEU.[85] Accordingly, the Member States maintain their language policies and freely determine rules concerning the use of languages in their constitutions or otherwise, and indicate their official language(s) and language policy, including the recognition of regional and minority languages.[86] The Member States are also responsible for making progress in promoting linguistic diversity and foreign language learning (both at a regional and local level). The European Union is entitled to carry out actions to support, coordinate, and supplement the actions of the Member States in language-related matters and is not authorised to legislate or adopt legal acts binding upon the Member States in the area of languages. The Union, in particular the Commission, may take relevant actions falling within its remit to raise awareness in respect of multilingualism and to improve the coherence of actions taken at different levels. In practice, the European Union provides general law in the form of soft law,[87] with specific laws to be enacted by the Member States.

The confirmation of the general competence of the EU Member States to conduct their language policies can be found in the judgment in the *Groener*[88] (1989) case. The Court of Justice expressly ruled that competence in language matters is vested in the Member States, but at the same time it held that this competence must be exercised within the limits of the European Union law, in particular in compliance with the principles of non-discrimination and proportionality. Through the

85 OJ C 202/1, 7 June 2016.

86 Van der Jeught, *EU Language Law*, 103.

87 The non-exhaustive list includes: Communications from the Commission on making a European area of lifelong learning a reality COM(2001) 678; Promoting Language Learning and Linguistic Diversity. An Action Plan 2004–2006 COM (2003) 449; A New Framework Strategy for Multilingualism COM(2005) 596, Multilingualism: an asset for Europe and a shared commitment COM (2008) 566, Council Resolution on lifelong learning, OJ C 163, 2002; Opinion of the Committee of the Regions on A New Framework Strategy for Multilingualism OJ 2006/C 229/05, Opinion of the Economic and Social Committee on Multilingualism, OJ 2009/C 77/25; Code of Conduct on Multilingualism adopted by the Bureau of the European Parliament of 1 July 2019.

88 Judgment of the Court of 28 November 1989 in the case C-379/87 *Anita Groener v Minister for Education and the City of Dublin Vocational Educational Committee*, ECLI:EU:C:1989:599.

judgment, the Court put some limits on national competence in the field of languages by combining it with the internal market freedom of movement of Member State nationals. The Court specified that the implementation of language policy must not encroach upon a fundamental freedom of free movement of workers. It added that measures adopted by a Member State "must not be disproportionate in relation to the aim pursued, and the manner in which they are applied must not bring discrimination against nationals of other Member States".[89] Through the judgments in the cases decided when Union citizenship was in force,[90] the Court prevented Member States implementing their language policies from encroaching upon the rights vested in the Union citizen.

1.4.3.3 EU language policy vs minority language protection

EU law does not touch upon all the aspects of the EU language policy. One of its key legal dimensions where the EU is limited by international law includes the status of minority languages and minority protection. As the EU has no explicit jurisdiction in the field of minority language protection, the organization cannot guarantee diversity of minority and regional languages.[91] This constitutes an exclusive responsibility of the EU Member States which have competence to recognise minority languages on their territory and to ratify or not ratify relevant international law instruments. The EU is only entitled to promote and encourage respect for such languages through the fostering of a commitment to the promotion of minority culture as well as regional and minority languages in the EU Member States.[92] The lack of proper regulations in respect of minority languages and language rights of the persons belonging to minorities forces the Union to rely upon international treaties and agreements, in particular in the United Nations International Covenant on Civil and Political Rights,[93] the International Covenant on Economic, Social and Cultural Rights[94] and the Europe of Council instruments, in particular the European Convention for the Protection of Human Rights and

89 Judgment of the Court in the case 379/87, para. 19.

90 C-274/96 *Bickel and Franz,* C-85/96 *Martínez Sala,* C-281/98 *Angonese,* C-148/02 *Garcia Avello,* C-391/09 *Runevič-Vardyn and Wardyn.*

91 Iñigo Urrutia and Iñaki Lasagabaster, *Language Rights and Community Law,* European Integration online Papers, 2008, 6.

92 Van der Jeught, *EU Language Law,* 94.

93 International Covenant on Civil and Political Rights adopted by the UN General Assembly on 16 December 1966 by resolution No. 2200 A, entered into force on 23 March 1976. By 2020 ratified by 173 states.

94 International Covenant on Economic, Social and Cultural Rights adopted by the UN General Assembly on 16 December 1966 by resolution No. 2200 A, entered into force on 3 January 1976. By 2020 ratified by 171 states.

Fundamental Freedoms (ECHR),[95] the European Charter for Regional or Minority Languages[96] (ECRML), and the Framework Convention for the Protection of National Minorities[97] (FCNM).

As the EU language policy fails to regulate the issue of linguistic minorities, some experts question the very existence of an EU language policy, claiming that there are no formal and legal grounds for it.[98] Today, this is a minority opinion. The majority view[99] is that the European Union is an organization which pursues its own language policy separate from the language policies of its Member States. It is not a component of any other policy of the organization. The fact that the EU language policy is consistent with and supplemented by the policy of the Council of Europe does not question, but reinforces its existence.

1.4.4 Multilingualism strategy as a component of the EU language policy

1.4.4.1 Aims of the EU multilingualism strategy

Multilingualism strategy, also described as EU language learning policy, is an extensively developed component of the EU language policy focusing on the promotion of language learning and multilingualism. This component of the policy is based purely on soft law, having no binding force upon the Member States and their citizens. In this context, it is clear that this part of EU language policy has social and economic implications rather than legal. Nevertheless, the strategy is worth discussing for two major reasons. It is the part of the EU language policy most recognised by the EU Member State citizens. Owing to its enormous scale, it exerts a significant impact on the EU internal market. Actions initiated within the strategy by the Union institutions create an opportunity for a wide range of beneficiaries to participate in exchange and mobility programmes aimed at foreign language learning.

---

95 European Convention for the Protection of Human Rights and Fundamental Freedom signed on 4 November 1950, entered into force on 3 September 1953. By 2020 ratified by 47 states.

96 European Charter for Regional or Minority Languages opened for signature on 5 November 1992, entered into force on 1 March 1998. By 2020 ratified by 25 states.

97 Framework Convention for the Protection of National Minorities opened for signature on 1 February 1995, entered into force on 1 February 1998. By 2020 ratified by 39 states.

98 Hanna Komorowska, "Polska polityka językowa na tle innych krajów Unii Europejskiej", in: Hanna Komorowska (ed.), *Nauczanie języków obcych–Polska a Europa. Warszawa: Academica*, 2007, 13–55.

99 Coulmas (1991), Grucza (2002), Philipson (2003), Gazzola (2006, 2016), Łuczak (2010), Szpotowicz (2013).

The EU maintains its multilingualism strategy in order to raise its citizens' level of individual multilingualism and foster communication between them. The EU stresses the social benefits of knowing foreign languages and cultures, including better understanding, intercultural communication, social inclusion, tolerance, and enhanced mobility. Moreover, the EU underlines the growing importance of languages in the economic and commercial context. Higher economic competitiveness and labour market mobility require from entrepreneurs and employees a solid knowledge of foreign languages in order to be successful in the EU and the global market. Above that, the European Union promotes knowledge of languages as an asset for acquiring cross-sectoral key skills, for the improvement of performance in thinking, learning, problem-solving, and communicating, and as a resource for creative and innovative thinking.[100] Leonard Orban, European Commissioner for Multilingualism in the years 2007–2010, summarised the benefits of knowing foreign languages by saying that "the ability to communicate in several languages is a great benefit for individuals, organizations, and companies alike. It enhances creativity, breaks cultural stereotypes, encourages thinking 'outside the box', and can help develop innovative products and services".[101]

1.4.4.2 Legal basis for the EU multilingualism strategy

The EU multilingualism strategy is closely related to the EU education policy. Philipson even uses the term educational language policy in order to underline the aim of EU multilingualism which is ensuring the continued vitality of national languages, rights for minority languages, and diversification in foreign language learning.[102] The origins of the policy may be traced back to the Maastricht Treaty[103] which institutionalised its controversial education policy as one of the new policy areas in which the Community was granted the power of intervention. Articles 149 and 150 of the Treaty clearly conferred new competences on the Community in the fields of education and vocational training.[104] The adoption of the Lisbon Strategy by the Lisbon European Council of 23 and 24 March 2000 was the next important impulse in the development of the EU multilingualism strategy.[105] The Strategy exposed the economic aspects of language knowledge, and presented it as the key element of the dynamic knowledge-based economy. It strengthened the status of foreign language skills by incorporating them into key competences which should

---

100 A New Framework Strategy for Multilingualism COM(2005) 596.

101 Multilingualism: an asset for Europe and a shared commitment COM(2008) 566.

102 Robert Phillipson, *English-only Europe? Challenging Language Policy*, Routledge, 2004, 255.

103 OJ C 191, 29 July 1992.

104 Under the Lisbon Treaty competence in education and vocational training is granted in Article 165(2) TFEU.

105 Lisbon European Council 23 and 24 March 2000 Presidency Conclusions.

be mastered through lifelong learning. In order to pursue the goals of the Strategy, the strategic framework for European cooperation in education and training was established in form of 'Education and Training 2010'.[106] The cooperation primarily aimed at the improvement of national education and training systems by way of the development of complementary EU tools and the exchange of good practice based on an open method of coordination.[107]

Other landmark decisions in respect of the EU multilingualism strategy were made by the Barcelona European Council of March 2002. The Council set the goal to increase the level of individual multilingualism so that every citizen could speak at least two foreign languages in addition to their mother tongue ("2+1"). The Council called for further actions to improve basic skills, in particular by teaching two foreign languages from a very early age and the establishment of a linguistic competence indicator.[108] The consequence of that approach was the publication of the Commission's Communication of 24 July 2003 *Promoting Language Learning and Linguistic Diversity: an Action Plan 2004–2006* and the Commission's Communication of 22 November 2005 *A new Framework Strategy for Multilingualism*, which specified the areas of action in the field of language acquisition and promotion of multilingualism. Having implemented the first assumptions of the multilingualism strategy, in 2008 the European Commission published another Communication *Multilingualism: an asset for Europe and a shared commitment*, which not only reaffirmed the value of linguistic variety in a community or society, but also underlined the need for a broader and more complex policy to promote multilingualism through the development of curricula for interpreters and translators, enhanced student and worker mobility, creativity and innovation in language learning, the use of subtitles in television broadcasts, supporting projects involving language and communication technologies and cross-border administrative cooperation, and the promotion of European language in non-EU states.[109]

Multilingual education has also been accounted for in the 'Europe 2020' strategy for the advancement of the EU economy. Specifically, the Council Conclusions of 12 May 2009 on a strategic framework for European cooperation in education and training 'Education and Training 2020' introduced four strategic objectives. The

106 'Education & Training 2010' The Success of the Lisbon Strategy Hinges on Urgent Reforms – Joint Interim Report of the Council and the Commission on the Implementation, OJ 2004/C 104/1.

107 Jan Barcz, "Polityki społeczne w systematyce Traktatów stanowiących Unię Europejską", in: Jan Barcz (ed.), *Polityki Unii Europejskiej: polityki społeczne*. Vol. XXVII, Warszawa: Instytut Wydawniczy EuroPrawo, 2010, 13–5.

108 Presidency Conclusions. Barcelona European Council 15–16 March 2002, http://ec.europa.eu/invest-in-research/pdf/download_en/barcelona_european_council.pdf [retrieved on 14 March 2019].

109 Multilingualism: an asset for Europe and a shared commitment COM(2008) 566.

priority area of the second objective comprised language learning/teaching, i.e. enabling EU citizens to speak two foreign languages, promoting language teaching in Vocational Education and Training for adult learners, and providing migrants with opportunities to learn the language of the host Member State, as well as professional development for teachers and trainers.[110]

1.4.4.3 *Actions taken within the EU multilingualism strategy*

The history of the EU actions and programmes supporting foreign language learning can be traced back to the 1990s. New competences in the field of education given to the European Union under the Maastricht Treaty resulted in several programmes on language learning. The pioneering project *Leonardo da Vinci* was launched in 1995. It was intended to enhance the competitiveness of the European labour market through helping Europeans acquire new skills, including language skills. The project was designed to improve the quality and effectiveness of teaching through allowing teachers to be trained abroad, placing foreign language assistants in schools, funding class exchanges, and creating language courses on CDs and the Internet.[111]

Later, a series of actions and programmes to promote language learning was triggered by the Barcelona Council's commitments. The EU initiatives had two major goals:

1. to upgrade the language skills of the EU citizens ("2+1"), and
2. to introduce innovations and improvement to the Member State education systems.

As regards the first goal, in 2003 the European Commission committed itself to undertaking 45 actions to encourage national, regional, and local authorities to promote multilingualism. The major actions included *the Socrates/Comenius school language projects, Erasmus, Lifelong Language Learning, Comenius, and Culture.*[112] To continue, in 2005, in *A New Framework Strategy for Multilingualism,* the Commission identified key areas for action which would contribute to the improvement of citizens' language skills. These included a need to establish and implement national plans to promote multilingualism, the better training of foreign language

110 Council conclusions of 12 May 2009 on a strategic framework for European cooperation in education and training ('ET 2020'), Annex II, 28 May 2009.

111 Leonardo da Vinci Programme, https://eacea.ec.europa.eu/sites/2007-2013/llp/leonardo-da-vinci-programme_en [retrieved on 8 April 2019].

112 Promoting Language Learning and Linguistic Diversity. An Action Plan 2004–2006 COM (2003) 449.

teachers, teaching languages from an early age, and the development of Content and Language Integrated Learning (CLIL).[113]

The flagship EU programme for education, training, and sport for 2014–2020 is *Erasmus+*. It was initiated by the European Union in order to face the educational challenges of Europe caused by demographic changes, the need to adapt education systems to labour market needs, and the high unemployment rate among young and unskilled people. *Erasmus+* is also the Union's tool to meet 'Europe 2020' objectives and benchmarks concerning economic development, a higher level of employment, social justice, and social inclusion. This is a comprehensive programme built upon the experience of more than 25 years of European actions fostering language learning initiatives and replacing all previous education programmes. It covers various groups of beneficiaries, such as pupils, students, entrepreneurs, employees, and volunteers. The programme is divided into three main actions:

1) educational mobility,
2) cooperation and exchange of good practices as well as international initiatives, and
3) support of reforms in the area of education.

The first years of the programme implementation demonstrated both concrete results and a number of deficiencies both on the part of the EU and the Member States.[114] The example of Poland proves that *Erasmus+* has contributed to the increased mobility at higher education institutions. According to the Mobility tool + (IT tool of the European Commission), the mobility of students and academic teachers rose in Poland approximately threefold in the years 2014–2018 as compared with the period 2009–2013.[115] Nevertheless, the experience of the University of Warsaw proves that the programme implementation was not perfect. The early stages showed that there was much disorganization in respect of the requirements imposed on national educational institutions by the European Commission. On the one hand, the European Union required the fulfilment of strict conditions by the

113 A New Framework Strategy for Multilingualism COM(2005) 596.

114 Based on the research conducted by the author in 2016 on the example of the University of Warsaw. Aneta Skorupa-Wulczyńska, "Erasmus+ as the EU answer to the educational challenges faced by Europe", in: Istvan Tarrósy and Susan Milford (eds.), *Recent Political Changes and their Implications in the Danube Region*, Pecs, Hungary, 2016, 43–60.

115 The data is based on the presentations of Minister of Education and Minister of Higher Education at the meeting of the European Union Affairs Committee of the Sejm of the Republic of Poland held on 8 March 2019.

participating entities, while on the other hand, the EU officials did not comply with the rules and failed to provide fully developed and tested tools.[116]

With reference to the other goal – the improvement of the national education systems, the EU institutions initiated actions aimed at the development of common European instruments promoting quality, transparency, and mobility. Three main achievements should be noticed here, i.e. the Bologna Process, the Copenhagen Process, and the European Indicator of Language Competence. Firstly, the Bologna Process is the flagship EU initiative aimed to improve higher education cooperation. The Process took form of intergovernmental cooperation, initially gathering 29 and today 48 signatory states.[117] In the Bologna Declaration,[118] the ministers of education of signatory states expressed their willingness to enhance the competitiveness of the European education systems based on a voluntary harmonisation process. The Process has significantly contributed to the internationalisation of higher education through the introduction of the three-cycle system (bachelor/master/doctorate). It allowed easier recognition of qualifications and periods of study and strengthened quality assurance. The result of the Bologna Process is the establishment of the European Higher Education Area, which is an international forum of collaboration on higher education represented by the education ministers of its signatory states.[119]

Secondly, the Copenhagen Process became an integrated part of the Lisbon Strategy. It constitutes a telling example of an instrument aimed at the development of a common EU instrument for enhanced cooperation in the field of Vocational Education and Training (VET) between the EU Member States. According to the Copenhagen Declaration, which launched the Process, VET must play its active and key role in furthering lifelong learning policies and supplying the highly skilled workforce necessary to make Europe one of the most competitive and dynamic knowledge-based economies and societies.[120] The results of the Process included the creation of a single framework for transparency of qualification and competences *Europass,* and the identification and validation of non-formal and

116 Skorupa-Wulczyńska, "Erasmus+ as the EU answer to the educational challenges faced by Europe", 56.

117 The status as of October 2020.

118 Bologna Declaration of 19 June 1999. Joint Declaration of the European Ministers of Education. *The European Higher Education Area*, 6.

119 The Bologna Process and the European Higher Education Area, https://ec.europa.eu/education/policies/higher-education/bologna-process-and-european-higher-education-area_en [retrieved 20 May 2019].

120 Declaration of the European Ministers of Vocational Education and Training and the European Commission, 29–30 November 2002 on enhanced European cooperation in vocational education and training http://www.cedefop.europa.eu/files/copenahagen _declaration_en.pdf [retrieved on 20 May 2019].

informal learning as well as the publication of the Council Conclusions on Quality Assurance in Vocational Education and Training.[121]

Finally, the Barcelona European Council Conclusions of March 2002 and *A New Framework Strategy for Multilingualism*[122] called for the establishment of a European linguistic competence indicator. The indicator was achieved based on the European Survey on Language Competences (ESLC). The aim was to provide participating countries with comparative data, to give them insights into good practice in language learning, and to share experience. In the end, the common indicator was to allow all the Member States to measure overall foreign language competences according to the predetermined parameters, methods, and skills: reading, writing, and listening. All the measurements of the ESLC were based on the Council of Europe Common European Framework of Reference (CEFR) for Language and relied upon six language proficiency levels: A1 and A2, B1 and B2, C1, and C2.[123] The result was the establishment of the European Indicator of Language Competence (EILC). Since 2005 when the Member States were provided with a set of parameters and management arrangement for implementing the EILC,[124] the Indicator has been serving as a tool to provide Member States with hard data and comparisons on which any necessary adjustments to foreign language teaching can be based.[125]

1.4.5 Contradictions of the EU language policy

The European Union's respect for linguistic diversity and promotion of multilingualism are closely connected as they both constitute the two chief goals of the EU language policy.[126] The EU maintains its pluralist language policy in order to strike a balance between conflicting interests of official language users. On the one hand, the Union aims to respect and protect the linguistic diversity of its Member States by preventing the domination of one or more languages which would lead to linguistic discrimination. On the other hand, the policy strongly promotes multilingualism and aims to create conditions favourable for foreign language learning. Both goals seem to be complementary, as language learning is seen by the EU as the key to securing linguistic diversity. In fact, the growing tensions between

121 The Copenhagen Process – the European Vocational Education and Training policy – Frequently Asked Questions, 10 December 2004, https://ec.europa.eu/com mission/presscorner/detail/en /MEMO_04_293 [retrieved on 1 September 2020], 1–2.

122 A New Framework Strategy for Multilingualism COM(2005) 596.

123 A New Framework Strategy for Multilingualism COM(2005) 596.

124 Commission Communication of 1 August 2005 – The European Indicator of Language Competence COM(2005) 356 final. Not published in the Official Journal.

125 The European Indicator of Language Competence COM(2005) 356.

126 Philippe Van Parijs, "Linguistic diversity as curse and as by-product", in: Xabier Arzoz (ed.) *Respecting linguistic diversity in the European Union*, Amsterdam: John Benjamins Publishing,2008, 21.

the two prove that they are of a contradictory nature. The reason is that the EU undertakes a multitude of actions to promote multilingualism externally, but in fact it favours only a group of economically profitable languages. The LINEE Report confirms that the Union promotes those languages which are assessed highly through the prism of their usefulness in the labour market.[127] In fact, the spreading of a few languages, in particular English, unofficially considered to be the European *lingua franca*, contributes to a decline in the linguistic diversity of the continent.[128] Moreover, Sayers and Láncos (2017) assert that the very fact of promoting Member State national languages undermines linguistic diversity by creating pressure towards the greater linguistic homogeneity of the Member States.[129] At the same time, the EU speaks a lot about the value of nurturing all languages building up the diversity of the continent, yet not having much power to impose any laws in this regard.

The picture is complicated more by the fact that EU institutions often limit their internal multilingual communication, and unofficially practise linguistic pragmatism by allowing three working languages to be dominant. Such status of the policy is criticised by academics including Lenaerts (2001), Philipson (2003), Creech (2005), Ammon, Ricento (2006), Van Parijs (2008), Wright (2009), Williams and Williams (2016), and Sayers and Láncos (2017). For them, the EU language policy seems to be blind, unconscious of the outcome of conflicting aspirations, or pressure from the Member States, or interest groups. This causes growing chaos and disparity between theory and practice, i.e. between the declared attachment to multilingualism and the actual state of affairs.

The problems of the EU language policy are complex on a legal, political, and linguistic plane, and there is no solution which would be the cheapest, most effective, and egalitarian at the same time.[130] The sources of the problems are first and foremost assigned to the conflicting goals of the European Union itself. Its objectives to unify economically and politically favour the use of a single language or limited number of languages. Still, owing to the pressure coming from the Member States and their citizens, it preserves and promotes cultural and linguistic diversity, which, in turn, hampers efficient communication. To satisfy both, the Union attempts to maintain a language policy including the features of communication policy and identity policy at the same time. As a communication policy, it promotes multilingualism and language learning primarily aimed at better communication between EU citizens leading to the unity of a diverse EU. As an identity

127 Final report summary of the research project – Languages in a network of European excellence (LINEE), 25.

128 Van Parijs, 21.

129 Dave Sayers and Petra Lea Láncos, "(Re) defining linguistic diversity: What is being protected in European language policy?", *SKY Journal of Linguistics*, Vol. 30, 2017, 64.

130 Łuczak, 187–96.

policy, it protects the linguistic diversity of its Member States through a multilingual regime.[131]

Moreover, the challenges faced by the EU language policy go beyond its conflicting goals. Another key sensitive issue relates to the European Union's maintaining an affirmation of equal status only of national languages, thereby satisfying the national interests and sovereign considerations of the Member States without taking into account the relative size of each language and communicative needs of the EU citizens.[132] The proponents of the Union language policy claim that the policy is fair as every candidate state may in practice choose a language which is to be official for the purposes of the EU, and based on the principle of equality every Member State has one official language in the EU. This does not change the fact that the users of EU non-official languages have the right to feel neglected and marginalised, which goes against the primary assumptions of the EU language policy. Moreover, as stressed by Sayers and Láncos (2017), the EU's approach to linguistic diversity totally excludes numerous allochthonous languages (exceeding autochthonous languages around four to one). They note that EU linguistic diversity is more complicated and complex than the limited goals of its existing policies. They even indicate that the issue of linguistic diversity may ultimately fall outside the discourse of the EU contemporary language policy.[133]

1.5 Sources of language rights in the EU law

The contradictory nature of the EU language policy objectives raises a question on the scope and nature of language rights guaranteed to Member States' citizens. The specification of the scope of and legal grounds for language rights may be one of the European Union's tools to maintain a balanced language policy. The rights may be treated as a tool to measure linguistic diversity protection, and may indicate if the EU language policy is more a communication policy or an identity policy. The systematisation of language rights in the EU requires in the first place defining the sources of such rights, and in the second place, examining their nature and enforceability before the Court of Justice and national courts.

The above analysis proves the hypothesis that language rights are an integral part of the European Union language policy. They stem from the EU linguistic regime which constitutes the key legal dimension of the EU language policy. Under this regime, the languages of the EU Member States are classified into the treaty (authentic), official, and working language of the Union. The study also shows that

131 Łuczak, 128–30.

132 Creech, 153.

133 Dave Sayers and Petra Lea Láncos, "(Re)defining linguistic diversity: What is being protected in European language policy?" *SKY Journal of Linguistics*, Vol. 30, 2017, 64–5.

the policy is not the exclusive source of language rights. The investigation into the legal framework for the EU language policy demonstrates that the catalogue of language rights is complemented by the rights arising out of Union citizenship, as proved by the Court of Justice case-law.[134] The Court expressly combined language rights with the status of the Union citizen. Therefore, it may be asserted that the concept of Union citizenship is another major source of the language rights of Member State citizens. Finally, the European Union's lack of competence in the field of minority protection as well as the inclusion of the principle of respect for linguistic diversity in the Charter justify why language rights should also be examined as fundamental rights. A very close relationship between the protection of language rights and the protection of linguistic diversity in the EU has been underlined by Mancini and De Witte (2008). The relationship is so close that the protection of linguistic diversity has become an integral part of the agenda of fundamental rights protection in the European Union.[135]

All the three main categories of language rights – resulting from the EU linguistic regime, based on Union citizenship and constituting fundamental rights in the EU – need examination and systematisation.

1.6 Language policies of the United Nations and the Council of Europe

1.6.1 Language policy of the United Nations

1.6.1.1 Linguistic regime of the United Nations

The United Nations is a global organization that brings together 193 members to confront common challenges, manage shared responsibilities, and exercise collective actions in an enduring quest for a peaceful, inclusive, and sustainably developing world, in conformity with the principles of justice and international law.[136] As the United Nations has wide competences to promote international cooperation, maintain international peace, and develop friendly relations between the nations (Article 1 of the Charter of the United Nations),[137] from the very outset it considered languages to be a bridge for organised relations between the states. The use

134 C-186/87 *Cowan,* C-379/87 *Groener,* C-274/96 *Bickel and Franz,* C-85/96 *Martínez Sala,* C-281/98 *Angonese,* C-148/02 *Garcia Avello,* C-391/09 *Runevič-Vardyn and Wardyn.*

135 Susanna Mancini and Bruno De Witte, "Language rights as cultural rights: a European perspective", *International Studies in Human Rights,* Vol. 95, 2008, 247.

136 Overview, https://www.un.org/en/sections/about-un/overview/index.html [retrieved on 10 January 2020].

137 Charter of the United Nations signed on 26 June 1945, entered into force on 24 October 1945.

of several languages was considered not a matter of prestige for a ground-breaking international organization, but a matter of necessity. The United Nations General Assembly[138] consistently underlined the importance of a multilingual regime in achieving the goals of the organization, in particular in the area of human rights.[139] The UN multilingual regime affected the languages used in the organization's official documents and in agreements concluded under its auspices. It also became an important issue in the agenda of the UN organs.[140]

The grounds for the multilingual regime were incorporated in the UN founding treaty – the Charter of the United Nations. Article 111 of the Charter listed five authentic languages including English, Chinese, French, Russian, and Spanish. A new era of quinquilingualism in the conduct of multilateral affairs was initiated at the United Nations Conference on International Organization (San Francisco, 25 April to 26 June 1945), which by its decision set a precedent for linguistic practices at the United Nations. The Conference defined the organization's official languages and distinguished the status of working and official languages, with English and French serving as working ones. The distinction between two categories of languages was clearly visible in the day-to-day work of the UN organs, where only certain types of documents were published in all the official languages upon request. Interpretation and translation for the vast majority of documents, records, and the Journal of the United Nations were prepared only in two working languages.[141] With time, the UN linguistic regime evolved under the influence of the changing world and the shift of the world powers. The sweep of decolonisation greatly contributed to the inclusion of Spanish and Chinese in the UN working languages and made Arabic an official and working language of the General Assembly (GA) and of major diplomatic conferences. The case of the Arabic language clearly proved that the status of a language in the UN was regarded by its members as a matter of prestige and was a reflection of the state power.[142]

---

138 One of the six main organs of the UN which occupies a central position as the chief deliberative, policymaking, and representative organ, https://www.un.org/development /desa/dspd/united-nations-general-assembly.html [retrieved on 20 January 2020].

139 Multilingualism: Report of the Secretary-General. A/61/317, 6 September 2006, 1.

140 The UN organs include: the General Assembly, the Security Council, the Economic and Social Council, the Trusteeship Council, the International Court of Justice and the UN Secretariat.

141 Mala Tabory, *Multilingualism in international law and institutions*, Brill Archive, 1980, 7.

142 Tabory, *Multilingualism in international law and institutions*, 42.

1.6.1.2 UN's actions to promote multilingualism

UN language policy was shaped over many years. Initially, it was expressed solely through the organization's multilingual regime which, first and foremost, aimed to manifest the equality of its members.[143] In the 1990s, the United Nations expanded its language policy beyond the linguistic regime and began to promote multilingualism. A turning point in the UN language policy seems to have been the year 1995 when a landmark resolution on languages (Resolution No. 50/11[144]) was adopted by the GA. The Resolution classified all linguistic issues in the UN under the heading of 'multilingualism'. It outlined the framework for the UN language policy devoting a lot of attention to the equal treatment of all official languages, their promotion in the organization, and the provision of official documents in all the official languages. Moreover, the Resolution set out the scope of actions to be taken by the UN Secretary-General in respect of multilingualism. Accordingly, the Secretary General became obliged to provide the General Assembly with a biennial report on measures taken to promote multilingualism in the organs and specialised agencies of the United Nations and their members. The Resolution stressed the need for the external promotion of multilingualism, with the aim of informing and reaching out to the widest possible audience worldwide, not only in six official languages, but also in local languages. Since the adoption of Resolution No. 50/11, the GA has regularly passed resolutions on multilingualism and incorporated the issue into its two-year agenda.[145]

A crucial step in developing initiatives to promote multilingualism and linguistic equality in the UN was the appointment of Coordinator for Multilingualism in 2000 (Resolution No. 54/64),[146] a function held by Under-Secretary-General for General Assembly and Conference Management. The Coordinator's tasks included harmonising measures implemented in different UN organs and proposing strategies to ensure that the United Nations complies with the recommendations of the GA Resolution No. 50/11, as well as collecting proposals for actions in the area of multilingualism. The Coordinator is expected to act as a contact point for the concerns and queries of members' representatives, to serve as a facilitator to attain a coordinated, consistent, and coherent approach to multilingualism in the

---

143 Tabory, 2.

144 The resolution adopted by the General Assembly on 2 November 1995, A/RES/50/11.

145 The list of relevant resolutions on multilingualism is updated on https://digitallibrary.un.org/search?ln=en&as=1&m1=a&p1=multilingualism&f1=title&op1=a&m2=a&p2=&f2=&op2=a&m3=a&p3=&f3=&dt=&d1d=&d1m=&d1y=&d2d=&d2m=&d2y=&rm=&ln=en&sf=year&so=d&rg=50&c=United+Nations+Digital+Library+System&of=hb&fti=0&fct__1=Resolutions+and+Decisions&fti=0&fct__1=Resolutions+and+Decisions [retrieved on 20 January 2020].

146 The resolution adopted by the General Assembly on 21 January 2000, A/RES/54/64.

Secretariat, and to foster a culture conducive to multilingualism. The Coordinator is supported by a network of focal points representing all Secretariat Departments and Offices.[147]

One of the initiatives supervised by the Coordinator is *International Translation Day* celebrated annually on 30 September.[148] The aim of the initiative is to pay tribute to and promote the work of language professionals who through their work preserve clarity in international public discourse and interpersonal communication, as well as to stress the role of professional translation in connecting nations and fostering peace, understanding, and development.[149] Another initiative to recognise multilingualism as a core value of the organization was the proclamation of the *International Day of Sign Languages* celebrated annually on 23 September.[150] The Day falls within the ambit of the initiative 'With sign language, Everyone is included!' aiming to influence state governments to legally fulfil their obligations in the recognition of sign languages as equal to spoken languages.[151] Moreover, in order to show respect to languages as a repository for each person's unique identity, cultural history, traditions, and memory, the United Nations declared 2019 as the *Year of Indigenous Languages*.[152] The initiative aimed to benefit the people speaking indigenous languages, to raise awareness of others and to make them appreciate the important contribution they make to the world's rich cultural diversity.[153]

Notice should be taken of the fact that the UN has no uniform language policy throughout all its organs and agencies. The UN organs have the right to define their linguistic regimes in their internal regulations and specify their official and working languages. Significant differences also concern multilingualism strategies practised by the UN specialised agencies. Some of them have adopted an internal policy for multilingualism based on the Report of the Joint Inspection Unit of 2003 on the implementation of multilingualism in the United Nations system. The Report includes several recommendations for the UN organizations, including the review of the status of different languages in order to assure equal access of all

---

147 Coordination of Multilingualism, http://www.un.org/Depts/DGACM/ multilingualism.shtml [retrieved on 8 November 2018].

148 The resolution proclaimed by General Assembly on 24 May 2017, A/RES/71/288.

149 The resolution adopted by the General Assembly on 24 May 2017, A/71/L.68.

150 The resolution adopted by the General Assembly on 19 December 2017, A/RES/72/ 161.

151 International Day of Sign Languages and International Week of the Deaf 2018, http://wfdeaf.org/news/theme-for-international-day-of-sign-languages-and-international-week-of-the-deaf-2018/ [retrieved on 8 November 2018].

152 The resolution adopted by the General Assembly on 19 December 2017, A/RES/72/ 161.

153 Indigenous Languages, https://en.iyil2019.org/ [retrieved on 19 November 2018].

governments and all sectors of civil society to the documents, archives, and data banks, to disseminate information in all the UN official languages, and to provide interpretation and translation services at various types of meetings relating to multilingualism.[154] Agencies such as the United Nations Industrial Development Organization, the World Health Organization, and the World International Property Organization approached the Report as a source of inspiration for defining strategies to implement the policy of multilingualism.[155] There are also agencies without a defined multilingualism strategy. As a consequence, they do not take concrete steps to promote multilingualism and linguistic equality, as they focus on economic and financial aspects. These include the United Nations Economic Commission for Africa and the United Nations Economic Commission for Latin America and the Caribbean.[156]

1.6.1.3 United Nations Educational, Scientific and Cultural Organization (UNESCO)

Owing to its constitutional objectives, the United Nations Educational, Scientific and Cultural Organization (UNESCO) stands out against the background of the other UN specialised agencies in terms of its actions promoting multilingualism and active policies for language preservation throughout the world.[157] UNESCO pursues an active policy of promoting foreign language learning. It runs regular wide-ranging actions "to contribute to peace and security by promoting collaboration among the nations through education, science, and culture (...) without distinction of race, sex, language, and religion".[158] Within its mandate, UNESCO conducts a variety of projects and activities to cultivate awareness that languages play a vital role in developing and ensuring cultural diversity and intercultural dialogue, in building inclusive societies, and in preserving cultural heritage. The Organization promotes an interdisciplinary approach to multilingualism and

154 Report of the Joint Inspection Unit on the implementation of multilingualism in the United Nations System: note by the Secretary-General, A/58/251, 10 June 2003, 3.

155 Aneta Skorupa-Wulczyńska, "Polityka Językowa w Unii Europejskiej i Organizacji Narodów Zjednoczonych", *Sprawy Międzynarodowe*, No. 1, 2014, 119–35.

156 Papa Louis Fall and Yishan Zhang, *Multilingualism in the United Nations system organizations: Status of implementation*. JIU/REP/2011/4. Geneva: United Nations, 2011, 2.

157 Fall and Zhang, 2

158 Article 1 of the Constitution of the United Nations Educational, Scientific and Cultural Organization, signed on 16 November 1945, entered into force on 4 November 1946. By 2020 ratified by 193 states.

linguistic diversity involving sectors such as education, culture, communication, and information as well as social and human sciences.[159]

UNESCO takes both one-off actions and holds regular events of diverse outreach (local, regional or global). To give a few examples, it coordinated the actions related to the *International Year of Languages* 2008 declared by the General Assembly. UNESCO's actions included a variety of interdisciplinary projects taking the forms of building capacity, research and analysis, raising awareness, supporting projects, developing networks, and disseminating information.[160] One of the key recurring projects proclaimed by UNESCO is the *International Mother Language Day* (IMLD) celebrated annually on 21 February continuously since 2000. The Day aims to protect all native languages and serves to be an effective mobilisation for linguistic diversity.[161] UNESCO chooses a theme for each *International Mother Language Day* and sponsors related events at its Paris headquarters. On the IMLD, a number of prizes are announced or awarded. The Linguapax Institute in Barcelona awards the *Linguapax Prize*, which aims to recognise outstanding achievements in the preservation of linguistic diversity, the revitalisation of linguistic communities and the promotion of multilingualism.[162] Moreover, the annual *Ekushey Heritage Award* and the *Ekushey Youth Award* are granted. The former is awarded for outstanding achievements in the fields of education, social work, and community service, and the latter for inspiring youth in the fields of education, sport, literature, and community service.[163]

1.6.1.4 Language rights vs UN language policy

Based on the above, it may be contended that neither the linguistic regime of the UN, or of its specialised agencies, nor the linguistic regimes of individual UN organs exert much influence on the language rights of individuals. The lack of impact of the UN language policy on individuals results from the legal status of the organization. Apart from a few references to the word 'representatives' of the

159 Languages and Multilingualism, Languages matter! http://www.unesco.org/new/en/ culture/themes/cultural-diversity/languages-and-multilingualism/ [retrieved on 26 July 2018].

160 International Year of Languages, http://www.un.org/en/events/iyl//[retrieved on 26 July 2018].

161 Languages and Multilingualism, International Mother Language Day: 21 February 2011, http://www.unesco.org/new/en/culture/themes/cultural-diversity/langua ges-and-multilingualism/international-mother-language-day/ [retrieved on 26 July 2018].

162 International Linguapax Award, http://www.linguapax.org/en/linguapax-award/ [retrieved on 20 November 2018].

163 Ekushey Youth Awards, http://www.mjmf.org/index.php/about-us/ekushey-youth-awards [retrieved on 20 November 2018].

members, there are no express references to the language rights of individuals either in the UN Charter or in the rules of procedure of the UN organs. In fact, the citizen of a UN state party has no entitlement to claim any rights directly before the organization. Similarly, individuals have no right to address the UN's principal judicial organ – the International Court of Justice (ICJ) – directly. The major reason is that the ICJ has jurisdiction covering only the states, members of the UN, and parties to the Statute of the ICJ. As a result, the Court's decisions are binding upon them. In fact, the Court's limited jurisdiction, broad mandate, and procedures make its role insignificant in the field of the international protection of rights of individuals (human rights), including language rights of minority members.[164]

Notwithstanding the above, it must also be remembered that the UN takes actions aimed to protect linguistic diversity in order to prevent humanity from losses caused by the extinction of languages which leaves an irreparable gap in the cultural heritage of mankind.[165] Under the auspices of the organization, a number of important international treaties were concluded which aim to protect the language rights of national minorities in order to preserve their cultural identity. Such instruments include the Universal Declaration of Human Rights,[166] the International Covenant on Civil and Political Rights,[167] the International Covenant on Economic, Social, and Cultural Rights,[168] and the Declaration on the Rights of Persons Belonging to National and Ethnic or Religious Minorities.[169] Although the relevant provisions in various instruments differ in their scope and nature, they show that the protection of minority languages and their speakers is of importance in the UN agenda.[170] The relevant language rights of persons belonging to minorities entrenched in the treaties concluded under the UN will be analysed separately in chapter 4.

---

164 John R. Crook, "The International Court of Justice and Human Rights", *Northwestern University Journal of International Human Rights*, Vol. 1, 2003, 2.

165 Tove Skutnabb-Kangas and Robert Phillipson, "Wanted! Linguistic Human Rights", *ROLIG-papir*, No. 44, 1989, 2.

166 Universal Declaration of Human Rights adopted by the UN General Assembly on 10 December 1948 by resolution No. 217.

167 Vide supra 95.

168 Vide supra 96.

169 The Declaration on the Rights of Persons Belonging to National and Ethnic or Religious Minorities adopted by the UN General Assembly on 18 December 1992 by resolution No. 47/135.

170 Lauri Mälksoo, "Language Rights in International Law: Why the Phoenix is Still in the Ashes", *Florida Journal of International Law*, Vol. 12, 1998, 444.

1.6.2 Language policy of the Council of Europe

1.6.2.1 Linguistic regime of the Council of Europe

The Council of Europe (CoE) is the oldest intergovernmental organization in Europe founded in 1949. It brings together 47 states representing about 820 million Europeans.[171] The CoE principally aims to defend and set standards for human rights, including rights of persons belonging to minorities, the rule of law, and democracy in Europe. Under Article 1 of the Statute, the Council of Europe strives to achieve the greater unity of its members by safeguarding the principles and ideals which are their common heritage and by facilitating their economic and social progress.[172]

The CoE has its well established language policy characterised by multilingualism. The legal grounds for the organization's linguistic regime are specified in the Statute of the Council of Europe of 1949 (the Statute). Article 12 of the Statute stipulates that English and French are its official languages. The Council's organs[173] are bound by the regime established in the Statute. Moreover, the Article expressly states that the Committee of Ministers and the Parliamentary Assembly as statutory organs are entitled to set out their linguistic regimes in their rules of procedure where they may determine in what circumstances and under what conditions other languages may be used.

It is noteworthy that there have been a few attempts to extend a number of the Council's official languages, but no extension has occurred to date. The demand for additional languages did not seem to be in any sense the result of a desire for prestige, of pride, and of self-interest, but was related to the number of signatory states which has considerably grown since 1949.[174] In the light of the mounting pressure from the new signatory states, the Parliamentary Assembly decided to review the problem of the Council's official languages. The Committee on Political Affairs and Democracy considered three possibilities for the future Council's language policy:

1) retaining the present language system,
2) introducing either one or two more official languages,
3) adopting the official languages of all the signatory states as official languages.

---

171 The Council of Europe, https://www.eshre.eu/Europe/Council-of-Europe [retrieved on 10 January 2020].

172 Statute of the Council of Europe opened for signature on 5 May 1949, entered into force on 3 August 1949. By 2020 ratified by 47 states.

173 The Council's organs include: Committee of Ministers, Parliamentary Assembly, Congress of Local and Regional Authorities, Conference of International Non-governmental Organization, Secretary General.

174 Member States of the Council of Europe, https://www.coe.int/en/web/portal/47-members-states [retrieved on 11 May 2019].

In order to examine the question of official languages, the Assembly instructed the Secretary-General to address the representatives of the Parliamentary Assembly with the question in which languages they follow the debates and speak. Although some measures were taken, no decision on the extension of the number of official languages has been taken so far. The matter remains unresolved. Nevertheless, the third possibility was excluded straight away. The solution was regarded as impracticable, causing delays, complications, and high expenditure.[175]

1.6.2.2 Implementation of the CoE language policy

The Council of Europe's language policy comprises the organization's activities aimed both to promote language learning and plurilingualism as well as to protect linguistic diversity. The objectives of the policy include combating intolerance and xenophobia by improving communication and mutual understanding between individuals, protecting and developing the linguistic heritage and cultural diversity of Europe as a source of mutual enrichment, facilitating personal mobility and the exchange of ideas, developing a harmonious approach to language teaching based on common principles, and promoting large-scale plurilingualism.[176]

The implementation of the policy is entrusted to three Council's entities: the CoE's Education Department part of the Directorate General of Democracy in Strasbourg, the European Centre for Modern Languages (ECML) in Graz (Austria), and the secretariat of the European Charter for Regional or Minority Languages (ECRML) in Strasbourg. The Education Department and the ECML promote language learning and plurilingualism, and the secretariat of the ECRML is in charge of language protection. The promoting activities carried out by the Education Department and the ECML within the framework of the European Cultural Convention (1954)[177] have focused on the promotion of plurilingualism and pluriculturalism among the citizens of the CoE's state parties. The activities of the ECML and the Education Department are complementary. The Education Department pursues the CoE's language education policy. It designs and implements intergovernmental medium-term programmes (Language Policy Programmes) with a strong emphasis on the development and analysis of national language education policies aimed at promoting linguistic diversity and plurilingualism. The Department develops tools and standards to help the states develop transparent and coherent

175 Explanatory Memorandum on the official languages of the Council of Europe, Committee on Political Affairs and Democracy, doc. 1039, 14 September 1959.

176 ECML in the Council of Europe, https://archive.ecml.at/aboutus/aboutus.asp?t=council/ [retrieved on 11 May 2019].

177 European Cultural Convention opened for signature on 19 December 1954, entered into force on 5 May 1955. By 2020 ratified by 50 states.

language policies.[178] The ECML was founded on 8 April 1994 by eight members of the Council – Austria, France, Greece, Liechtenstein, Malta, the Netherlands, Slovenia, and Switzerland – as an "Enlarged Partial Agreement". The ECML Partial Agreement is 'enlarged', which means that states which are not members of the Council are also welcome to join the Centre.[179] Its mission is to encourage excellence and innovation in language teaching and increase efficiency in language education. A Partial Agreement admits such a form of co-operation as allows the pursuit of certain activities not supported by all members of the Council of Europe. Today, the ECML has 32 member countries. The activities of the Education Department and ECML are exceptionally diverse, yet none of the actions is binding upon the CoE members and their citizens. Still, many of them seem to be followed and implemented by the competent national authorities.[180]

One of the greatest achievements of the Council of Europe in the area of the promotion of language learning is the *Common European Framework of Reference for Languages: Learning, Teaching, Assessment* (CEFR),[181] published in 2003 after over twenty years of research. The Framework was designed to provide a transparent, coherent, and comprehensive basis for the elaboration of language syllabuses and curriculum guidelines, the design of teaching and learning materials, and the assessment of foreign language proficiency. The CEFR describes foreign language proficiency at six levels: A1 and A2, B1 and B2, C1 and C2. Although the CEFR is not a binding law, it is widely used in language education systems, the reform of foreign language curricula in signatory states, and the development of teaching materials (the results of a survey[182] carried out in 2006 among the Council of Europe's members).[183]

The protection of linguistic diversity within the CoE is entrusted to the secretariat of the ECRML.[184] The secretariat supervises the implementation of the

178 The Council of Europe and language education, https://www.coe.int/en/web/common-european-framework-reference-languages/language-policy-in-the-council-of-europe/ [retrieved on 19 May 2019].

179 ECML in the Council of Europe, https://www.ecml.at/Aboutus/ECMLintheCouncilof Europe/tabid/121/language/en-GB/Default.aspx [retrieved on 24 April 2018].

180 State countries of the ECML, https://www.ecml.at/Aboutus/ECMLMemberStates/tabid/ 149/language/en-GB/Default.aspx [retrieved on 20 January 2020].

181 Common European Framework of Reference for Languages: Learning, Teaching, Assessment (CEFR), Language Policy Unit, Strasbourg, https://rm.coe.int/16802fc1bf [retrieved on 1 September 2020].

182 Waldemar Martyniuk and José Noijons, *Executive summary of results of a survey on the use of the CEFR at national level in the Council of Europe Member States,* 2007, https://rm.coe.int/168069b7ad [retrieved on 10 January 2020].

183 Use of the CEFR, https://www.coe.int/en/web/common-european-framework-reference-languages/uses-and-objectives [retrieved on 11 May 2019].

184 Vide supra 98.

ECRML and aims to preserve linguistic diversity through the protection of regional and minority languages. It coordinates the actions intended to protect the languages in danger of extinction in order to enable their speakers to use them in the private and public spheres. The measures undertaken by the secretariat comprise the use of languages in education, in particular teaching in regional and minority languages, the use of regional or minority languages in the judiciary and in administration, the use of the languages in the media and the press, in cultural activities and establishments and in economic and social life.[185] Moreover, the secretariat sets out to protect and promote regional or minority languages as part of the European cultural heritage. Hence, it puts emphasis on the cultural dimension and the use of regional or minority languages in all the aspects of the life of their speakers. Clearly, the ECRML does not guarantee enforceable rights, either individual or collective, but it only encourages states to take measures to protect regional or minority languages.[186] For this reason, the secretariat does not represent or make claims for any individual or collective rights for the speakers of such languages.

1.6.2.3 Language rights vs CoE language policy

The final issue is whether the CoE language policy creates a legal basis for the language rights of the citizens of members of the organization. As regards the actions of the LPP, the ECML, and the secretariat of the ECRML, they are not established in order to directly affect individuals, but to influence the actions of their members (signatory states). As a result, individuals cannot be treated as direct beneficiaries of any rights. These depend on the implementing measures taken by the states. Next, the linguistic regime of the Council of Europe does not offer any special language rights to the citizens of the CoE members, as individuals are said not to be directly affected by language arrangements employed in the Council. The exception to this principle concerns the European Court of Human Rights (ECtHR) which can be addressed by individuals. Although the ECtHR is not the CoE organ, it is strictly related to its operation and activities. It ensures the enforcement and implementation of the ECHR[187] in the members of the Council of Europe. An application to the ECtHR may be lodged by an individual, a group of individuals, a company, or an NGO having a complaint about the violation of their rights, and by one state against another (inter-state applications). The judgments of the ECtHR

185 The Council of Europe, its European Convention for the Protection of Human Rights and Fundamental Freedoms and the most important treaties specifically dedicated to the minorities, https://www.minder heitensekretariat.de/en/legal-framework/council-of-europe/[retrieved 22 January 2020].

186 Explanatory Report to the Framework Convention for the Protection of National Minorities, Strasbourg, February 2005, https://rm.coe.int/16800c10cf [retrieved on 20 January 2020].

187 Vide supra 97.

are binding upon the states concerned which are obliged to execute them within the prescribed time limit. In fact, most applications before the Court are individual applications lodged by private persons, citizens of the CoE members. In the light of this, the linguistic regime of the ECtHR plays an important role in terms of the access of individual persons to justice. The analysis proves that an applicant may find on the website of the Court information in 36 languages on how to make a valid application, how to lodge it, what are the admissibility conditions, what is the flow of the legal process before the ECtHR, and other useful hints. The data provided is sufficient for the applicant to decide if the application has grounds and has a chance of being admitted by the Court.[188]

1.6.2.4 Language rights before the European Court of Human Rights

Details on the languages used in proceedings before the ECtHR are set out in the Rules of the Court.[189] The question to be answered is whether all the citizens of the CoE's members are granted equal language rights while pursuing a claim before the ECtHR. Rule 34(1) of the Rules of the Court sets out that English and French are the official languages of the Court. As a general rule, pleadings are filed in one of the two official languages, translated into the other official language and then published in two languages. Nevertheless, the procedure may be initiated by submitting an application in any non-official language. In a case when a non-official language is used in an application, the Court is obliged to communicate the notice of the application and any accompanying documents to the applicant in the language in which the application was lodged. Regardless of the language of the application, all the documents are also translated into English and French. Next, all communications following an application must be drawn up in one of the Court's official languages. The party may request the Court that a non-official language be used in the course of the proceedings. The President of the Chamber may grant leave to use any other language if this is in the interests of the proper conduct of the proceedings. In such a case, the requesting party is also obliged to file relevant translations into one of the official languages and bear the extra expenses of interpreting. Organizational and technical issues are arranged by the registrar who is responsible for making appropriate arrangements to ensure interpretation (Rule 34(3)(a)-(c)). The party may be required by the Court to provide a translation or a summary of all the submissions, of certain annexes thereto, or of any other documents or extracts therefrom. The same principles refer to the use of a non-official language by a third party. Rule 34(6) admits the use of any language by a witness, expert, or any other person appearing before the Court if a person does not have a sufficient knowledge of one of the Court's official languages. The Rule

188 Information documents for persons wishing to apply to the Court, https://www.echr.coe.int/Pages/home.aspx?p=applicants/ol&c= [retrieved on 24 April 2018].

189 Rules of the European Court of Human Rights of 1 January 2020.

guarantees that the Court will make the necessary arrangements for interpreting and translation in such a case. It is at the discretion of the Court which documents are to be translated and into which languages.

The admission by the ECtHR of any non-official languages does not affect the status of its official languages. Even if any other non-official language is admitted to be used in the course of the proceedings, all the ECtHR required documents must be published in French and English, and only in these languages do they constitute authentic texts. In principle, the Court's decisions and judgments are published in the official reports of the Court in both official languages. Under Rule 57, all decisions, and under Rule 76, all judgments of the Court may be issued in English and French. The Court each and every time designates which of the two texts shall be authentic. The choice of an authentic text depends on which language was used by the Court in the early draft of the judgment. In some cases both English and French are declared authentic.

In the years 2012–2016, the Court launched a case-law translation programme under which more than 21 000 texts including judgments, decisions and legal summaries were translated into thirty-one languages other than English and French. They were made available in the database of the ECtHR HUDOC.[190] The essential component of the programme was translating key case-law into twelve target languages, with beneficiary states including Albania, Armenia, Azerbaijan, Bosnia and Herzegovina, Georgia, Montenegro, the Republic of Moldova, Serbia, the former Yugoslav Republic of Macedonia, Turkey, and Ukraine. The objective of the project was to improve the understanding and domestic implementation of the ECHR standards and to ensure the dissemination of Court case-law to legal professionals and civil society in the developing states. Although the translations commissioned by the Court filled a significant gap in access to its decisions, still the linguistic problem remains when an individual does not have a command of an official language. In such a case, he or she is obliged to translate a decision or a judgment at his or her own expense to become familiar with the final decision of the Court. This determines the individuals' rights to have access to justice, making them dependent on knowledge of the Court's official language or the ability to cover the costs of translations. The issue of accessibility to the ECtHR case-law was raised at a conference on the future of the Court held in 2017 where the representatives of the state parties concluded that it was first and foremost the responsibility of the states to guarantee the application and implementation of the ECHR and other CoE treaties. They stressed the need to make the key case-law accessible to domestic courts, thereby reinforcing the principle of subsidiarity.[191]

---

190 Bringing the Convention closer to home, 2 February 2017, https://rm.coe.int/168070c5c7 [retrieved on 24 April 2018].

191 Bringing the Convention closer to home, 3.

Certainly, accessibility will be ensured when individuals have access to the Court's documents in their native languages. Individuals need to comply with the language rules prevailing in the Court. Only the application initiating the proceedings may be submitted in the Court's non-official language. Individuals need to use the Court's official languages in the course of the proceedings, or use their own language and bear the additional costs of translation and interpreting services throughout the entire process including the translation of the final decision of the Court. This state of affairs constitutes a deterrent factor for a significant number of individual applicants who do not speak English or French. They cannot exercise their right to use the language they know in order to pursue their claims before the Court without bearing a financial burden of translation and interpreting services.

1.6.3 EU language policy in comparison with the language policies of the UN and the CoE

The study of the language policies of the United Nations and the Council of Europe indicates that the organizations maintain their policies based on multilingualism. In this sense, their language policies are similar to that of the European Union. At the same time, multilingual policies in all the three organizations are practised in a different way. Their varying approaches towards multilingualism seem to be justified by a number of factors. The organizations differ in their legal nature, geographical scope, and objectives. Whereas the United Nations operates at a global level, the Council of Europe and the European Union are regional organizations. What makes a significant difference from the legal standpoint is the fact the UN (under the Charter of the United Nations) and the CoE (under the Statute of the Council of Europe) are intergovernmental organizations. This implies that the states, and not their citizens, may be granted rights and privileges and may incur obligations. In this respect, the EU is distinct, as it is the only international organization which exerts the direct effect of its law on the citizens of its Member States. It maintains a linguistic regime based on the equality of all the Member States in order to guarantee access to its legislation in all the EU official languages. Such an approach is compliant with the Union's aim to be "an ever closer union among the peoples of Europe",[192] which seems to be possible only if the citizens can use their own languages to communicate.

As noticed by Schilling (2008),[193] the language policies of traditional international organizations are quite different from those of the European Union in terms of its regime. In both the United Nations and the Council of Europe a small number of languages are made into official languages, English and French being among

192 OJ C 202, 7 June 2016.

193 Theodor Schilling, "Language rights in the European Union", *German Law Journal, Vol.* 9, 2008, 1123–4.

them. The United Nations with 193 members has only five Charter languages, and the Council of Europe with 47 members contents itself with the two official languages. The limited number of the official languages shapes them as clear communication policies. The EU with 27 Member States and 24 official languages[194] is the smallest and at the same time "most multilingual" organization in the world. This makes the EU linguistic regime the most complex as the obligations imposed on the EU institutions resulting from a multitude of official languages are incomparably wider than in the case of the UN or the CoE.

At the same time, it is also clear that all three organizations take measures to promote multilingualism and linguistic diversity. Through this, they implement the language policy's component of acquisition planning. The initiatives are not mandatory and do not generate any specific enforceable rights in any organization. The strategies differ in the types of actions and their intensity. The analysis proves that the CoE and EU actions in the field of acquisition planning affect the shape of the state education policies by harmonising the standards and increasing transparency. This is clearly evidenced by the Council of Europe's Common European Framework of Reference and the EU's Bologna Process, the Copenhagen Process, and the European Indicator of Language Competence.

Despite the growing complexity of the EU language policy, it still does not regulate the linguistic issues of persons belonging to national minorities. The Union's policy encourages respect for minority languages, but fails to protect minority and regional language users as the area of minority protection falls outside the scope of the European Union's powers. Moreover, the study demonstrates that the language policy is not the best medium to protect the languages of minority members. The reason is that the rights are categorised as human (fundamental) rights rather than the rights embedded in the linguistic regime of any organization. A legal gap seems to be filled by a number of international law instruments[195] concluded under the auspices of the UN and the CoE. The EU's lack of proper regulations in respect of minority languages forces the organization to rely upon these instruments ratified by most Member States and thus constituting the general principles of EU law. They regulate the major aspects of minority language rights. The rights will be analysed in chapter 4 which focuses on the languages rights having the status of fundamental rights entrenched in the Charter of Fundamental Rights of the European Union and relevant international human-rights treaties.[196]

The table below presents a summary of the EU, UN and CoE language policies.

---

194 The status as of 15 October 2020.

195 in particular: ECHR, FCNM, ECRML, ICCPR, CRC and ICESCR.

196 Van der Jeught, *EU Language Law*, 94.

	United Nations	*Council of Europe*	*European Union*
Number of official languages	6	2 (extension of languages is being considered)	24 (depends on the number of Member States)
Number of signatory/ member states	193	47	27
Legal basis for multilingual regime	Charter of the United Nations Rules of procedure of individual UN organs	- Statute of the Council of Europe	- Lisbon Treaty - Regulation No. 1/58 - Rules of Procedure of EU institutions
Legal basis for language rights	- International Covenant on Civil and Political Rights, - Convention on the Rights of the Child - Declaration on the Rights of Persons Belonging to National and Ethnic or Religious Minorities	- European Convention for the Protection of Human Rights and Fundamental Freedoms - European Charter for Regional or Minority Languages - Framework Convention for the Protection of National Minorities	- Lisbon Treaty - Charter of Fundamental Rights - secondary law - general principles of EU law
Legal basis for the promotion of multilingualism	Resolutions of the General Assembly	European Cultural Convention (1954)	Soft law issued by the EU institutions
Components of language policy	Status planning and acquisition planning	Status planning and acquisition planning	Status planning and acquisition planning

	United Nations	*Council of Europe*	*European Union*
Aims of multilingualism	communication policy promotion of linguistic diversity	communication policy protection and development of linguistic heritage and cultural diversity of Europe helping signatory states elaborate their coherent language policies protection of regional and minority languages	identity policy and communication policy protection of linguistic diversity promotion of multilingualism and foreign language learning respect for national identities
Bodies responsible for multilingualism policy	- UN Secretary General - Coordinator for Multilingualism	- Education Department - European Centre for Modern Languages - Secretariat of the European Charter for Regional and Minority Language	All EU institutions, in particular European Commission, Member States authorities

1.7 Conclusions

- Although Europe is the poorest continent in terms of languages, the EU makes the linguistic diversity of the continent an important aspect of its citizens' lives. The EU language arrangements which are deeply rooted in the principle of respect for linguistic diversity, respect for national identities of its Member States, and the principle of non-discrimination on the grounds of nationality have shaped the European Union as the international organization of extreme linguistic complexity. No other organization uses as many as 24 official languages, all of which are the national languages of its Member States.
- Owing to such a high number of official languages having equal legal status, the European Union maintains a complex language policy which attempts to keep a balance between the protection of linguistic diversity and the promotion of multilingualism. The protection of linguistic diversity of the EU Member States is provided through the protection of the state languages of the Member States. As a result, not all non-official languages are treated on an equal footing with the European Union official languages.

- The EU language policy's component of status planning implemented through the organization's multilingual regime guarantees language rights at two major levels. Firstly, the right to have free access to the EU law in one's own language. Secondly, the right to communicate directly with the EU institutions in one of the Union official languages.
- The EU language policy is not an exhaustive source of the citizen's language rights in the EU. The concept of Union citizenship fills the gap and shortcomings of legal protection in this regard. This is justified by the Court of Justice which puts some limits on national competence in the field of languages by combining it with the rights of the Union citizen. As a result, a Member State language policy must not encroach upon the rights and freedoms guaranteed by EU citizenship.
- Some language rights may be categorised as fundamental rights. They are entrenched both in the Charter of Fundamental Rights of the European Union and, owing to the lack of the European Union's competence in minority rights protection, in the relevant international law instruments, in particular those concluded under the UN and CoE auspices.
- The comparative study of the EU, UN, and CoE language policies demonstrates that only the EU language regime guarantees specific language rights to the citizens of its Member States. The UN and CoE language policies do not result in any particular rights related to language use to the citizens of their members, as justified by the legal nature of the organizations. The present findings confirm that the rules of procedure before the ECtHR do not provide an individual who may address the Court directly with the right to use his or her native language, if it is not English or French, without bearing the cost of translation and interpreting.
- Finally, respect for the national languages of all the EU Member States certainly classifies the EU language policy as an identity policy, where *ethnos* is more honoured than *demos*. The fact that all the Member States are linguistically represented in the Union by at least one Member State national language is an expression of the EU's respect for the national identities of the Member States. On the contrary, the UN and CoE policies, despite being multilingual, remain communication policies without any clear features of identity policy.

2. Language rights resulting from the European Union's linguistic regime

2.1 Opening remarks

The EU operates in a multilingual regime characterised by the formal principle of the equality of all the EU official languages.[1] Every Member State is linguistically represented at the European Union by its national language proposed by the candidate country prior to the accession. Such shape of the Union's linguistic regime aims to guarantee transparency, fairness, and non-discrimination in relation to any language(s) through equal access to the law, information, and procedures to all the Member States and their citizens. The equality of the Member State national languages is reflected in the EU multilingual law and in the multilingualism of the EU institutions. Legal and institutional multilingualism exposes two linguistic issues. On the one hand, languages are perceived as a source of difficulty owing to the existence of 24 equally authentic, but sometimes diverging texts, and on the other hand, as a source of the citizen's right to have free access to the law in their own language and to use their own language in the EU public sphere. Over time, these two roles have been raising mounting tension in the European Union. The organization attempts to deal with the issue by respecting one national language of every Member State and thus the rights of their users, and as a result diminishing the language-related obstacles.[2]

This chapter includes the key terminology related to the EU linguistic regime. The concept of 'linguistic regime' is used interchangeably with the term 'language system'. Next, 'EU legal multilingualism' is used with reference to EU multilingual law, and 'institutional multilingualism' refers to the multilingualism of the European Union institutions, including communication between them and third parties (external dimension) and communication inside them (internal dimension). Furthermore, the terms 'full linguistic regime' and 'restricted linguistic regime' are used in the context of institutional multilingualism. The former implies the obligatory use of the EU official languages and is in principle applied in the external dimension of institutional multilingualism. The latter refers to their limited number and is common for internal institutional communication. Although this is a general rule, there are cases when restricted language regimes are used in the

---

1 Theodor Schilling, "Multilingualism and Multijuralism: Assets of EU Legislation and Adjudication", *German Law Journal*, 2011, 1481–2.

2 Directorate-General for Translation EC, *Study on translation and multilingualism. Language and Translation in International Law and EU Law*, Publications Office of the European Union, 2013,65.

external communication of EU institutions. For this reason, external and internal institutional multilingualism cannot be understood as equivalent to full and restricted regimes respectively.

This chapter aims to examine the scope and nature of language rights entrenched in the EU linguistic regime. Owing to the extensive publications in the field, the author concentrates on such aspects of the EU linguistic regime are of importance for the main objective of the dissertation. The analysis is primarily focused on language rights arising from EU multilingual law based on the concept of authentic languages, and language rights attached to institutional multilingualism anchored in the notions of EU official and working languages. The chapter is divided into four major substantive subchapters. The first one distinguishes three categories of EU languages, such as treaty/authentic languages, official languages, and working languages. It discusses the status of each language category in order to determine their role in the context of the language rights resulting from the EU legal multilingualism and institutional multilingualism. This sub-chapter also analyses the concept of EU co-official language with a view to verifying whether the Union law grants any rights to the users of such languages. Moreover, it examines the status of English after Brexit and explores the proposal to introduce one EU official language. The following sub-chapter investigates the EU principles related to EU multilingual law in order to find out if the Union citizen has the right to be unilingual, i.e. rely only on one authentic language version of EU multilingual law and be guaranteed legal certainty. The study builds upon the analysis of three fundamental principles of EU law: the principle of legal multilingualism, the principle of equal authenticity, and the principle of the uniform interpretation and application of law which are collectively aimed to ensure legal certainty for EU law addressees. The fourth main sub-chapter studies the scope of language rights resulting from EU institutional multilingualism. It draws a line between its external and internal dimensions in order to present distinct categories of rights. The rights resulting from the external dimension include the right to communicate with EU institutions and the right of access to legal procedure before the Court of Justice in one of the EU official languages. The internal dimension of institutional multilingualism is discussed with a view to demonstrating limitations to the language rights of Union citizens resulting from the restricted internal linguistic regimes of individual institutions. The limitations appear in the context of the right to information about the EU and its activities, public consultations or recruitment procedures for the EU staff.

2.2 Status of languages

2.2.1 Treaty/authentic languages

Formally, three categories of languages may be distinguished in the context of the European Union: treaty/authentic languages, official languages, and working languages. The EU treaty languages are listed in Article 55(1) of the Treaty on

European Union (TEU),[3] and the European Union official and working languages are specified in Regulation No. 1 determining the languages to be used by the European Economic Community of 1958.[4]

Treaty languages are the languages in which the original texts of the founding treaties were drawn up. The concept of a treaty language was modelled upon the international law notion of an authentic language, which appeared together with the multilingual treaties after WWII. For the first time, multilingual treaties were analysed in Harvard Research[5] which advocated the search for a common meaning of the diverging authentic versions in the light of the 'intention of the treaty.' Next, the 1969 Vienna Convention on the Law of Treaties (the Vienna Convention)[6] was a milestone instrument in defining the instances in which authentic status should be conferred on different language versions. In fact, the Vienna Convention did not expressly refer to an authentic language, but it used the concept of an authentic text. Ergo, an authentic text of a treaty constitutes one unit consisting of one text including several language versions which are its integral parts, but not separate texts.[7] Based on this, the meaning of an authentic language may be deduced from the provisions of the Vienna Convention. Accordingly, an authentic language is the language in which an authentic text of an international law instrument is prepared. The issue of authenticity of international treaties and agreements drawn up in more than one language became a subject of extensive research and analysis following the Vienna Convention.[8]

In view of the above international law background, the term 'authentic language' can be transferred onto the EU context and can be used in place of 'treaty

3 OJ C 202, 7 June 2016.

4 Regulation No. 1 determining the languages to be used by the European Economic Community. OJ 017, 1 July 2013.

5 Harvard Law School, *Draft Convention* on the *Law* of *Treaties prepared as part of the Harvard Research in International Law*, Research in International Law under the Auspices of the Harvard Law School. 1935.

6 Vienna Convention on the Law of Treaties of 23 May 1969, entered into force on 27 January 1980. *United Nations Treaty Series*, Vol. 1155. By 2018 ratified by 116 states.

7 Mala Tabory, *Multilingualism in international law and institutions*, Brill Archive, 1980, 176–7.

8 To name a few important ones: Frankowska, "The Vienna Convention on the Law of Treaties before United States Courts", *Virginia Journal of International Law*, 1969, *Umowy międzynarodowe. Wprowadzenie do prawa traktatów*, 1972; Haraszti, *Some fundamental problems of the Law of Treaties*, 1973; Elias, *The Modern Law of Treaties*, 1974; Nahlik, *Kodeks Prawa traktatów*, 1976; Tabory, *Multilingualism in International Law and Institutions*, 1981; Sinclair, *The Vienna Convention on the Law of Treaties*, 1984; Rosenne, *Developments in the Law of Treaties, 1945–1986*, 1989; Reuter, *Introduction to the Law of Treaties*, 1989.

language' as a language in which the EU Treaties, as classical multilateral international instruments, are authentic and as such have authoritative force. Throughout the years, the number of treaty languages in the EU has been growing together with the accession of new Member States. The extension of treaty languages was intended to provide a true reflection of a changing number of the EU Member States whose languages were treated on an equal footing with the languages already used in the Community.

Historically, only the European Coal and Steel Community Treaty was authentic in a single language, i.e. in French. The Rome Treaties establishing the European Atomic Energy Community (EURATOM)[9] and the European Economic Community (EEC)[10] were a clear move away from a single authentic version. They were drawn up in four languages, i.e. French, German, Italian, and Dutch. The Treaty on European Union (1992) was prepared in 10 official languages: Danish, Dutch, English, French, German, Greek, Irish, Italian, Portuguese, and Spanish, with the texts of each language being equally authentic.[11] Finally, the Lisbon Treaty including the Treaty on European Union (TEU) and the Treaty on the Functioning of the European Union (TFEU) are drawn up in 24 EU official languages, with the texts in each language having equal status.[12] The TEU and the TFEU are unique in being authentic in all of the official languages of their contracting parties. Their peculiarity consists in the fact that they establish a supranational international organization based on the principle of linguistic equality.[13] The number of treaty languages is equal to the number of EU official languages.[14] Such a solution is intended to guarantee equal access to the provisions of the Treaty by the Member States and their citizens. This state of affairs confirms the formal equality of all Member States before the Treaties and is an expression of respect for the national identities of the Member States as enshrined in Article 4(2) TEU.

The concepts of 'authentic language' and 'authentic text' have acquired a new meaning in the context of the EU. Initially, the notion of 'authentic language' was used only with reference to the EU founding treaties, as implied by the term 'treaty language'. Such terminology resulted from the strong association of the term with

---

9 OJ C 326, 26 October 2012.

10 Treaty establishing the European Economic Community, Rome, 25 March 1957.

11 Treaty on European Union. OJ C 191, 29 July 1992.

12 OJ 2016 C 202, 7 June 2016. It is so provided in Article 55(1) TEU. Article 358 TFEU stipulates that the provisions of Article 55 TEU also apply to the TFEU.

13 Directorate-General for Translation EC, 17.

14 Until 2007, the number of treaty languages was not the same as the number of EU official languages. That state of affairs was caused by the status of Irish and Maltese which became treaty languages from the day of Ireland's and Malta's accession to the EU, yet not acquiring the official and working status at the same time. Irish and Maltese acquired the status of the fully-fledged EU official languages on 1 January 2007.

international treaties and agreements. The equal authentic status of all official language versions of EU secondary legislation was not straightforward, as neither Article 55 TEU nor Regulation No. 1/58 alluded to that issue. Only the Court of Justice in its ruling in *CILFIT*[15] (1982) upheld the view that all the EU official language versions of EU legislation were authentic.[16] Following *CILFIT*, the international law concepts of 'authentic language' and 'authentic text' began to be used with reference to the EU secondary law expressed in all the EU official languages with equal validity in the light of the law.[17]

It is worth noting that the EU has also embraced international law concepts of 'non-authentic language' and 'non-authentic text'. The former is defined as a language in which a text of a legal instrument has been drawn up, yet it does not carry a legal value equal to an authentic language version and can serve only for informative purposes. A non-authentic language version constitutes a non-authentic text. Wyrozumska (2006) notes that non-authentic texts are translations, which even if published in the state official journal are of no legal significance under international law.[18] As a consequence, neither official nor non-official translations are authoritative for the purposes of interpretation. Nevertheless, they may play a role at a national level and still affect the rights of individuals. Needless to say, national judges whose linguistic skills are often limited refer to such non-authentic texts, when authentic texts are not available. When the authentic text is not available and any doubts as to the law interpretation appear, the court is obliged to adjudicate in favour of an individual.[19]

The concept of a 'non-authentic text' appears in the EU in two contexts. First of all, it is used with reference to the texts of some international agreements entered into by the EU which were published in the Official Journal of the European Union (OJEU) in languages other than authentic. Such publications are often marked with the heading 'Translation' which warns the reader that the text is not an authentic one. An illustrative example of such publications is some bilateral agreements between the EU and the USA[20] originally prepared only in English. The agreements

---

15 Judgment of the Court of 6 October 1982 in the case 283/81 *Srl CILFIT and Lanificio di Gavardo SpA v Ministry of Health*, ECLI:EU:C:1982:335, para. 18.

16 Cornelis J. W. Baaij, *Legal Integration and Linguistic Diversity. Rethinking Translation in EU Lawmaking*, Oxford Studies in Language and Law, 2018.

17 Agnieszka Doczekalska, "Legal Multilingualism as a right to remain unilingual – fiction or reality?", *Comparative Lengilinguistics*, 2014, 12.

18 Anna Wyrozumska, *Umowy międzynarodowe: teoria i praktyka*, Prawo i Praktyka Gospodarcza, 2006, 359.

19 Wyrozumska, 362.

20 For instance Agreement between the European Union and the United States of America on the processing and transfer of Passenger Name Record (PNR) data by air carriers to the United States Department of Homeland Security (23 July 2007).

include relevant provisions according to which language versions other than English should be authentic upon approval by both parties. Until a particular language version is not approved by them, such a version remains a non-authentic text (translation).[21] The concept of 'non-authentic texts' is also used in the context of the publications made in the EU co-official languages.[22]

2.2.2 Official and working languages

The issue of the Community official languages has been a sensitive matter since the EEC and the EURATOM negotiations.[23] For this reason, at that time, rather than specifying the status of languages in primary law, the Treaties determined the procedure to establish language rules applicable at the Communities. The procedure was as follows: the linguistic regime of the EEC and EURATOM had to be established by the Council, whereas that of the Court of Justice had to be laid down in its Statute.[24] Article 217 of the Treaty establishing the European Economic Community (TEEC)[25] empowered the Council to act unanimously by means of regulations in matters concerning the use of official languages and to establish the official languages of the Community. The same principles have been applied to date.

Neither Article 217 TEEC (later Article 290 TEC) nor Article 342 TFEU have been a directly effective norm. *Ab initio* the norm has been implemented through Regulation No. 1/58. By way of the Regulation, the Council carried out its mandate by establishing the status of official and working languages. Accordingly, Regulation No. 1/58 was granted special power to regulate the EU language system. Such a solution allowed for a flexible approach which shifted the formal and factual basis of the EU linguistic regime to secondary law. The Regulation has been continuously applied since 1958, notwithstanding the increase in the number of official languages affecting the internal work of the institutions.[26] It was amended at every accession when relevant languages were added to the list of EU official languages.

The concept of the EU official language has always been based on the concept of 'state language', i.e. an official national language of a Member State used throughout its territory in dealings with public authorities and in legislative

21 Directorate-General for Translation EC, 40.

22 As of 6 June 2020, the EU co-official languages include Catalan, Basque, Galician.

23 At the Messina Conference held in June 1955 national delegations were reluctant to tackle the language issue and they decided that the Treaties should not include express provisions on language regime.

24 Statute of the Court of Justice of the European Economic Community, Publishing Services of the European Communities, 8012/5/XII/1962/5.

25 Article 217 TEEC became Article 290 TEC and is now Article 342 TFEU.

26 Theodor Schilling, "Language rights in the European Union", *German Law Journal*, 2008, 481–2.

procedure.[27] Regulation No. 1/58 had already established the equal status of the state languages of the Community Member States chosen by them to be official languages for the purposes of the Community. As a result, the EU official languages have always coincided with at least one official national language of every Member State. That solution was interpreted as a compromise among Member States which reflected their political and formal equality and became a symbol of the principles governing the European culture of integration.[28] Embracing a linguistic regime respecting the official languages of all Member States was also intended to be an expression of the Union's respect for Member States' national identities.[29]

The procedure of adding a language to the list of Union official languages is always initiated by an EU candidate country, which prior to the accession is obliged to propose a language which will have official status in the European Union. Once a relevant application has been submitted by a candidate country, the Council has to approve it unanimously in order for the language to acquire the EU official status. An initial decision on the choice of a language may be changed provided that all Member States agree to that.[30] It must be noted that not every language enjoying official status within a particular Member State has such as status in the EU (e.g. Luxembourgish in Luxembourg or Turkish in Cyprus). Article 8 of the Regulation prescribes that if a Member State has more than one official language, the state concerned selects the language to be used as official in the EU. The decision should be based on the general principles deriving from the legislation of that state. By referring to the national legislation, the provision of the Regulation does not unequivocally specify whether a given Member State may request the granting of official and working status to its two or more national languages.[31] Remarkably, so far no candidate country has ever requested an EU official status for more than one language.

The current version of Regulation No. 1/58[32] includes a complete list of 24 official languages and 24 working languages (Article 1) (as presented in the chart below).

---

27 Schilling, "Language rights in the European Union", 483; Davis and Stanley Dubinsky, 102.

28 Artur Nowak-Far, *Prawo Unii Europejskiej. Języki, struktury, działanie w praktyce*, C.H. Beck, 2020, 291.

29 Mary Dobbs, "The Shifting Battleground of Article 4 (2) TEU: Evolving National Identities and the corresponding need for EU management?", Vol. 21, No. 2, *European Journal of Current Legal Issues*, 2015.

30 Information available on the European Commission website: http://ec.europa.eu/dgs/ translation/translating/official languages/index_en.htm [retrieved on 5 November 2019].

31 Ewa Suwara, "Wyzwania prawno-proceduralne dla Unii Europejskiej związane z BREXIT-em", *Europejski Przegląd Sądowy*, 9/2016, 15.

32 The status as of 15 October 2020.

Official/working languages of the EU	since
French, Dutch, German, Italian	1958
Danish, English	1973
Greek	1981
Spanish, Portuguese	1986
Finnish, Swedish	1995
Czech, Estonian, Lithuanian, Latvian, Maltese, Polish, Slovak, Slovenian, Hungarian	2004
Bulgarian, Irish, Romanian	2007
Croatian	2013

Source: European Commission.[33]

The number of EU official languages is lower than the number of Member States as some languages are used in more than one state. Such languages include:

- **German** in Germany, Austria, Belgium, and Luxembourg,
- **French** in Belgium, France, and Luxembourg,
- **Swedish** in Sweden and Finland,
- **Dutch** in Belgium and the Netherlands,
- **Greek** in Greece and Cyprus.

The official status of such languages in the EU may generate some terminological problems. An illustrative example is German, notified both by Germany (1958) and Austria (1994) to have an official status for the purposes of the Community. As the language was already official when Austria acceded to the EU, the acceding state demanded that the terms specific for its national legal system must be accounted for in the EU terminology. As a result, the Accession Treaty of Austria was appended with the Protocol including a list of terms specific for Austrian German (Protocol

33 Information available on the European Commission website: http://ec.europa.eu/dgs/translation /translating/officiallanguages/ index_en.htm [retrieved on 16 September 2017].

No. 10). Under the Protocol, the Austrian terms were granted an equivalent legal status to the terms used in the German legal order.[34]

Apart from listing the EU official languages, Regulation No. 1/58 governs the rules on language use in the EU and grants a number of language rights. Firstly, the Regulation accords an express right to a Member State or a person subject to its jurisdiction to send to the EU institutions documents drafted in any one of the EU official languages (Article 2) and obliges the addressed EU institution to provide a reply in the same language (Article 3). Secondly, the Regulation obliges the EU to prepare regulations and other documents of general application in all the EU official languages (Article 4) and to publish them in the Official Journal of the European Union (Article 5). Next, the Regulation excludes the Court of Justice from the scope of Article 342 TFEU. Article 7 of the Regulation lays down that the language of proceedings before the Court of Justice is set out in the Rules of Procedure thereof.[35]

Apart from the official languages, Article 1 of the Regulation also lists 24 EU working languages, which are identical to the official ones. The Regulation grants the same status to both EU official and working languages.[36] Although some authors, including Labrie,[37] distinguish the concepts, the Regulation does not differentiate between the two terms. The question of the difference between official and working languages was investigated by the Council in the parliamentary inquiry in 1980.[38] In a response to the inquiry, the Council stated that neither the Treaty nor Regulation No. 1/58 provided an answer to that question, and on every occasion the matter should be solved by each institution on its own responsibility.[39] In practice, only a limited number of languages is used within the institutions. This possibility is provided for in Article 6 of Regulation No. 1/58 which allows each EU institution to set out its own rules of procedure for the use of languages for internal purposes. The institutions use the notion of 'working language'[40] to describe languages confined to the purely internal context as opposed to official languages

---

34 Accession Treaty of Austria, Finland, and Sweden, OJ C 241, 29 August 1994, 370.

35 OJ 017, 1 July 2013.

36 Robert Phillipson, *English-only Europe? Challenging Language Policy*, Routledge, 2004, 118.

37 Normand Labrie, *La construction linguistique de la Communauté européenne*, Honoré Champion, Vol. 1, 1993, 82.

38 Written question No. 1576/79 by Mr Patterson to the Council, OJ C 150, 18 June 1980.

39 Agnieszka Doczekalska, "Drafting or Translation – Production of Multilingual Legal Text", in: Frances Olsen, Alexander Lorz and Dieter Stein (eds.), T*ranslation Issues in Language and Law*, London, New York, Palgrave Macmillan Ltd, 2009.

40 The European Commission uses the term 'procedural language' instead, e.g. https://europa. eu/rapid/press-release_MEMO-13-825_en.htm [retrieved on 7 November 2019].

used while referring to the external communication between the institutions and Member States or their citizens. The notion of 'working language' is also used with reference to the language used in legislation drafting. Once a legislative act is published, a working language turns into an EU official language and, at the same time, an authentic language decisive for the interpretation purposes of a particular document.[41]

2.2.2.1 The concept of EU co-official language

The concept of an EU official language as a state language has triggered a debate on the status of other languages having an official status in some regions of a Member State or being its second official language. This group of languages includes Luxembourgish, having an official status in Luxembourg, and Catalan, Basque, and Galician being co-official languages in Spain, and Turkish with an official status in Cyprus. During the UK's membership in the European Union (1 January 1973 – 31 January 2020), the issue concerned also Welsh, having an official status in Wales, and Scottish Gaelic, officially recognised by the Scottish Parliament in Scotland. The users of the co-languages are not granted language rights similar to those granted to the official language users, making the issue very sensitive. As noted by Creech (2005), languages other than the official ones are left outside the system, regardless of the number of their speakers.[42] On the one hand, there is a large number of official languages spoken by proportionally few EU citizens (Maltese, Irish, Lithuanian, Latvian, Slovene, or Finnish) and, on the other hand, there are languages spoken by large numbers of people that cannot be granted an official status as they are not national official languages, in particular Catalan or Galician.[43] The matter is complicated even more as some languages, such as Irish or Maltese, enjoy the status of official languages although they are the second, after English, language of the state.[44]

---

41 Information on the Quality Legislation Team, http://ec.europa.eu/dgs/legal_service/legal _reviser_en.htm [retrieved on 19 May 2019].

42 Richard L. Creech, *Law and language in the European Union: the paradox of a Babel "United in Diversity"*, Groningen: Europa Law Publishing, 2005, 151.

43 Karolina Paluszek, "Institutional Multilingualism in the European Union – Policy, Rules and Practice", *Comparative Lengilinguistics,* 2015, 123.

44 Roman Szul, "Tożsamość europejska a kwestia językowa w Unii Europejskiej", *Studia regionalne i lokalne*, 2007, 70.

Language	Status in the EU	Number of speakers
Maltese	official	˜372 thousand
Irish	official	74 thousand
Estonian	official	1.1 million
Lithuanian	official	3.0 million
Latvian	official	1.8 million
Slovene	official	2.5 million
Finnish	official	5.4 million
Luxembourgish	non-official	400 thousand
Catalan	non-official	5.5 million
Basque	non-official	˜750 thousand
Galician	non-official	2.4 million
Welsh Gaelic	*after Brexit – non-EU language*	*˜700 thousand*
Scottish Gaelic	*after Brexit – non-EU language*	*˜60 thousand*

Figure 1. Author's own elaboration based on the https://www.ethnologue.com/browse/names. Status as of 17 February 2020.

EU official language status has never been acquired by Catalan, Galician, Basque, Welsh, or Scottish Gaelic as neither Spain nor the UK has ever filed a relevant application to the EU in this respect. Most probably the reason is that EU official status could not be granted to any of those languages as they are not used at a national but only at a regional level.[45] Although Spain sought the right for its citizens to use Catalan, Basque, and Galician in dealings with the EU institutions and bodies, including the use of these languages in speeches at the plenary sessions of the European Parliament and the Committee of the Regions as well as during Council meetings, the desired effect has not been achieved as national use of a language remains a precondition to be granted such a status.[46]

Despite fairly transparent conditions to be qualified as an EU official language, the debate on non-state languages of the EU Member States is still in progress. In recognition of the problems faced by minority and regional language speakers, the concept of EU co-official (also referred to as EU semi-official) language was

45 Stefaan Van der Jeught, *EU Language Law*, Europa Law Publishing, 2015, 109–11.

46 Council conclusion of 13 June 2005 on the official use of additional languages within the Council and possibly other institutions and bodies of the European Union. OJ C 148, 18 June 2005.

introduced.[47] The concept is not defined in any EU official documents. Its meaning may only be deduced from the literature in the field. It is understood as a language which enjoys official status in all or part of Member State territory[48] and is recognised in the Constitution of the Member State.[49] This is a feature which distinguishes co-official languages from any other languages used regionally and locally in a Member State. Such languages enjoy a better position than other regional languages in the EU, but still do not qualify as EU official languages. After Brexit, there have remained three languages which enjoy the status of the EU co-official languages. Interestingly, the issue concerns one Member State – Spain, and its co-official languages – Catalan, Galician, and Basque.[50]

The EU co-official languages are implicitly referred to by Article 55(2) TEU, according to which the Treaty may be translated into any other (than authentic) language determined by the Member State. In a case when a Member State wishes to have such a translation, it is expected to submit an already certified copy for deposit in the archives of the Council. The translation of the Treaty into any EU co-official language does not convert it into an authentic text of the Treaty, and does not result in any rights attached to it. Nevertheless, it is made publicly available and may be referred to by individuals if an authentic version has not been published in the language of a person concerned.[51] Accordingly, Article 55(2) TEU creates the possibility for the Union citizen to use an additional language which the Treaty is translated into to address the EU institutions. Such an enhanced use of the EU co-official languages may be implemented only through entering into an administrative arrangement with a particular EU institution.

In the Conclusion of 13 June 2005 on the official use of additional languages within the Council and possibly other institutions and bodies of the European Union, the Council specified the status of languages other than the languages referred to in Regulation No. 1/58 whose status was recognised in the constitution of a Member State on all or part of its territory or the use of which as a national language was authorised by law. Moreover, the Conclusion introduced the rules and circumstances for entering into an administrative arrangement between the requesting Member State and the Council. The Council does not specify the legal

---

47 Regional and minority languages in the European Union, http://www.europarl.europa.eu/ EPRS/EPRS-Briefing-589794-Regional-minority-languages-EU-FINAL.pdf [retrieved on 1 July 2019], 7.

48 Article 55(2) TEU, OJ 2016 C 202, 7 June 2016.

49 Paluszek, "Institutional Multilingualism in the European Union – Policy, Rules and Practice", 123.

50 Regional and minority languages in the European Union, http://www.europarl.europa.eu/ EPRS/EPRS-Briefing-589794-Regional-minority-languages-EU-FINAL.pdf, 7 [retrieved on 1 July 2019].

51 Anthony Aust, *Modern treaty law and practice*, Cambridge University Press, 2013, 226.

basis for such arrangements, but refers to the principle of respect for linguistic diversity and the EU's objective of bringing the Union closer to its citizens. The Conclusion sets out three situations when additional languages may be used. These include (1) making public acts adopted in co-decision by the European Parliament and the Council, (2) speeches to a meeting of the Council and possibly other institutions, and (3) written communications to Union institutions and bodies. At the end, the Council invites other EU institutions and bodies to conclude administrative arrangements on the basis of the Conclusion.[52]

Administrative arrangements were concluded between the Council and the Kingdom of Spain allowing "the official use at the Council of languages other than Castilian (Spanish) whose status is recognised by the Spanish Constitution",[53] and between the Council and the Government of the United Kingdom of Great Britain and Northern Ireland "allowing the official use at the Council of the languages whose status is recognised in the United Kingdom's constitutional system, by Acts of Parliament of the United Kingdom of Great Britain and Northern Ireland and/or legislative acts of the appropriate legislative body".[54] A similar arrangement was concluded between the European Commission and Spain.[55] It allowed legal and natural persons residing in Spain to write Catalan, Galician, and Basque in direct contacts with the EC, without the intervention of the Spanish administrative bodies, and to receive an answer in those languages.

One of the major benefits of an administrative arrangement between a Member State and the EU institution is that the citizen may have access to the EU legislative acts in a co-official language. To look critically, this access must be guaranteed by the Member State concerned which has to carry out translation at its own expense. Moreover, acts made public in the EU co-official languages have no legal effect equivalent to the documents drawn up in the EU official languages. They rather serve as a tool to make the acts available to a wider group of addressees. Next, an administrative arrangement seemingly grants the right to the citizens who wish to communicate in one of the languages not listed in Regulation No. 1/58. In fact, an arrangement creates only the grounds for the translation procedure rather than granting direct language rights. The procedure is that the citizen must address a competent national authority which sends the request to the addressed EU body or institution along with a certified translation. Next, the replies are addressed to the

52 OJ C 148/01, 18 June 2005.

53 Administrative Arrangement between the Kingdom of Spain and the Council of the European Union. OJ C 40/02, 17 February 2006.

54 Administrative Arrangement between the Government of the United Kingdom of Great Britain and Northern Ireland and the Council of the European Union. OJ C 194/04, 31 July 2008.

55 Administrative Arrangement between the European Commission and the Kingdom of Spain. OJ C 73/14, 25 March 2006.

national authority which provides a certified translation to a person concerned.[56] Last, but not least, the procedure itself does not always satisfy the person concerned as it lasts longer than a regular communication with the EU institution.[57] An administrative arrangement is conceived as a method to respect languages – other than Regulation No. 1/58 – and to guarantee their use while communicating with the EU, yet the analysis of the practical use of this method shows it is ineffective from the point of view of the protection of citizens' right in the area of language use. Moreover, the entire communication procedure is implemented at the expense of a Member State. Although there is no hard data on that, it may be assumed that a Member State may be unwilling to incur additional costs for communication of their citizens with the EU and may try to force them to use a state national language which is also an EU official language for this purpose.

2.2.3 The status of English after Brexit

The list of the EU official and working languages should be verified as a consequence of Brexit. The reason is that only the United Kingdom of Great Britain and Northern Ireland notified English as the official language for the purposes of the Union. Once the revision Treaty following Brexit enters into force, English may lose its official status if no steps are taken by the EU institutions and relevant Member States. From the formal point of view, the maintenance of English as an official language would require notification by another interested Member State, whose state language is English.[58] In this context, two scenarios are possible. Apart from the UK, English is also an official language in Ireland (according to Article 8.2 of the Irish Constitution of 1937, as amended)[59] and in Malta (Article 5 of the Maltese Constitution of 1964, as amended).[60] In order to keep the official status of English in the EU, one of these states will have to file a relevant application to the Council. Prior to their accession, Ireland and Malta notified their first official languages, i.e. Irish and Maltese, respectively. They did not refer to English, which had already been notified as the Community's official language by the UK.

From the procedural perspective, the UK's leaving the EU requires an update of Regulation No. 1/58. The result may be that English language will be deleted from the list of official and working languages and will possibly be re-granted the official status by virtue of an application made by either Ireland or Malta. Next, the application, would have to be examined and unanimously approved by the Council.

---

56 OJ C 148/01, 18 June 2005, para. 5(c).

57 Van der Jeught, *EU Language Law*, 115.

58 Suwara, 15.

59 Constitution of Ireland, http://www.irishstatutebook.ie/eli/cons/en/html#part2 [retrieved on 17 February 2020].

60 Constitution of Malta, https://www.constitution.org/cons/malta/chapt0.pdf [retrieved on 17 February 2020].

Although it is clear that such a procedure should be carried out swiftly after Brexit in order to minimise the negative impact on the decision-making procedure in the EU, so far, neither state has submitted a relevant application nor have such plans been revealed.[61]

In the aftermath of Brexit, Article 8 of Regulation No. 1/1958 acquires a special dimension. As it does not explicitly prohibit notification of more than one state language if a Member State respects more than one official language in its territory, it may occur that both Ireland and Malta may apply for the official and working status of English as their second official language. This would mean that neither Irish nor Maltese would have to be deleted from the list of EU official languages, and English would be added again to the list. Such a decision would be a precedent, as it could encourage other multilingual Member States to apply for adding their other official languages to the list of the EU official languages. If, however, the Council decided that a single-language principle must remain in force, the state filing an application would have to give up its existing official language status in favour of English.

The analysis leads to the conclusion that the case of Ireland seems to fully justify the reason why the state is most likely to apply for the official status of English. As the Eurobarometer survey shows, more than 97 per cent of the Irish speak English as their mother tongue.[62] In 2016, not even 40 per cent of the Irish declared that they could speak Irish Gaelic and only 4 per cent used the language on an everyday basis. If English was excluded from the EU official languages, more than 60 percent of the Irish would not have access to EU law.[63] It should also be recalled that although Ireland became a Community Member State in 1973, Irish became the EU official and working language in 2007 (based on Regulation No. 920/2005[64]) and until that time all its citizens were supposed to rely on English both in terms of access to law and in contacts with EU institutions. What happened following 2007 clearly showed that English was the preferred language in Ireland. The EU faced challenges with finding well-qualified Irish translators, so the Council released the EU institutions from an obligation to draft legislation in Irish. The Regulation provided for the derogation of 5 years in this respect with possible extension. Under the derogation, the EU institutions were not obliged to draft and publish all legislative acts in the Irish language, except for regulations adopted jointly by the European Parliament and the Council. This derogation was extended until 31 December

61 Suwara, 15.

62 Special Eurobarometer No. 386. Europeans and Languages. Report. Fieldwork: February-March 2012. Published in June 2012.

63 Agnieszka Doczekalska, "Angielski może w UE zostać po brexicie", 13 October 2018, https://www.prawo.pl/prawo/jezyk-angielski-w-ue-zostanie-po-brexicie,313073.html [retrieved on 1 July 2019].

64 OJ 2005 L 156/1, 18 June 2005.

2016 by Council Regulation (EU) No. 1257/2010[65] and re-extended by Council Regulation (EU, Euratom) 2015/2264.[66] It is to be gradually reduced in scope and eventually brought to an end by 31 December 2021. However, derogations still make Irish not a fully-fledged EU official language.

The history of Maltese in the EU was similar to Irish in a sense that the language did not become a complete EU official language following Malta's accession to the EU on 1 May 2004. The Council introduced a transitional period of 3 years, when the EU institutions were not obliged to draft all acts in Maltese (Regulation No. 930/2004[67]). Temporary derogation measures relating to the drafting of acts of the EU institutions in Maltese were caused by the shortage of sufficiently qualified linguists, translators, and interpreters. As a result, Maltese citizens were presumed to read EU legislation in English. After the expiry of the transitional period falling on 1 January 2007, Maltese became a fully-fledged EU official language. The backlog of all the legal acts that had to be published in Maltese caused the extension of publication time. Under Regulation No. 1738/2006[68] all the acts which were not published in Maltese by 30 April 2007 had to be made public in that language by 31 December 2008 at the latest".[69]

Notwithstanding the above formal argument, an important reason for maintaining English as the EU official language is that over the years it has gained a dominant position among Member State languages. Its deletion from the list of the EU official and working languages would strongly complicate the functioning of the EU institutions and the way the meetings would be organised. It

65 Council Regulation (EU) No. 1257/2010 of 20 December 2010 extending the temporary derogation measures from Regulation No. 1 of 15 April 1958 determining the languages to be used by the European Economic Community and Regulation No. 1 of 15 April 1958 determining the languages to be used by the European Atomic Energy Community introduced by Regulation (EC) No. 920/2005. OJ L 343, 29 December 2010, 5.

66 Council Regulation (EU, Euratom) No. 2015/2264 of 3 December 2015 extending and phasing out the temporary derogation measures from Regulation No 1 of 15 April 1958 determining the languages to be used by the European Economic Community and Regulation No. 1 of 15 April 1958 determining the languages to be used by the European Atomic Energy Community introduced by Regulation (EC) No. 920/2005. OJ L 322, 8 December 2015, 1.

67 Council Regulation (EC) No. 930/2004 of 1 May 2004 on temporary derogation measures relating to the drafting in Maltese of the acts of the institutions of the European Union. OJ L 169, 1 May 2004.

68 Council Regulation (EC) No. 1738/2006 of 23 November 2006 amending Regulation (EC) No 930/2004 on temporary derogation measures relating to the drafting in Maltese of the acts of the institutions of the European Union, OJ L 329, 25 November 2006.

69 Article 1 of Regulation No. 1738/2006.

is the most frequently chosen language by the EU institutions and the most popular foreign language in Member States.[70] Initially, the declaration of Brexit made francophones believe that French would regain its historical standing as Europe's language of diplomacy. Surprisingly, English was on the rise in the period from the UK's decision on Brexit to the actual withdrawal from the EU. The major reason was that officials from non-French speaking countries were more eager to see English as a 'neutral territory' and primary means of communication in the EU.[71] Some of the EU institutions took their official positions on the deletion of English from the list of EU official languages. In an answer to the question asked by Slator, the Language Industry Intelligence, the European Parliament Press Service gave its assurance that "the possibility that English will be abolished as an official language is virtually non-existent".[72] Next, the European Commission's communication on the budget for 2021–2027[73] clearly demonstrated that the UK's withdrawal from the EU would not affect the services of interpretation and translation from and into English. Despite comments and abundant press releases published in the Brexit negotiation period on the possible future of the English language in the EU, the status of English has not changed right after Brexit. Moreover, the State of the Union Address by President of the EC Ursula von der Leyen (16 September 2020) was in eighty percent delivered in English,[74] which confirmed the important role of the language in the political arena. Still, the issue remains unsolved from the procedural and legal point of view.

Half a year after Brexit, Regulation No. 1/58 has not been amended. The EU linguistic regime remains untouched, although the UK is not an EU Member State any more. The European Union websites, including europa.eu portal,[75] still list English as its official language. Moreover, the europa.eu website expressly indicates that

---

70 Special Eurobarometer No. 386. Europeans and Languages, Report. Fieldwork: February-March 2012, 5.

71 Maïa De La Baume, *As Britain leaves, English on rise in EU – to French horror*, 5 October 2018, https://www.politico.eu/article/french-english-language-brexit-european-parliament-ecj-commission-eu-next-waterloo/ [retrieved on 6 November 2019],

72 Esther Bond, *EU provides clarity on post-Brexit future for English language*, 2018, https://slator.com/demand-drivers/eu-provides-clarity-on-post-brexit-future-for-english-language/ [retrieved on 6 November 2019].

73 Communication from the Commission to the European Parliament, the European Council, the Council, the European Economic and Social Committee and the Committee of the Regions A Modern Budget for a Union that Protects, Empowers and Defends The Multiannual Financial Framework for 2021–2027 COM(2018) 321.

74 https://ec.europa.eu/commission/presscorner/detail/en/SPEECH_20_1655 [retrieved 17 September 2020]

75 EU languages, https://europa.eu/european-union/about-eu/eu-languages_en [retrieved on 11 May 2020].

even after the withdrawal of the United Kingdom from the EU, English remains one of the official languages in Ireland and Malta. Formally, this does not justify maintaining the official status of English in the EU. However, it indicates clearly that the EU notes the need to solve the unsettled status of English, but at the same time no formal procedure for approving English notified by either Ireland or Malta has been initiated.

2.2.4 The proposal to introduce one EU official language

The matter of a single EU official language is a multi-faceted, contested, and politically sensitive issue in the organization.[76] An idea of one universal language of the European Union was welcomed at the beginning of the twenty-first century in the context of further European integration, cross-border mobility, and cultural exchange.[77] As English became the most commonly spoken foreign language on the continent,[78] the debate focussed on this language as the European lingua franca. The matter had already appeared in the Commission's Communication of 2003 – *Promoting language learning and linguistic diversity*.[79] Although the Commission acknowledged that a European lingua franca had its limitations, as it did not permit any real understanding of other cultures and allowed for restricted business opportunities, it admitted that English had already become a European and world lingua franca. The Commission noted the advantages of these developments by stating that if English was spoken by a majority of Europeans, the language would be a shared medium for basic communication, commerce and travel between Member States.[80]

The proposal to introduce a single EU official language revived after the UK's declaration of exit from the EU. The predominant use of English in the EU institutions and in the law-making process together with the possible deletion of English from the catalogue of EU official languages owing to Brexit caused the issue to be extensively debated again. The issue of a European lingua franca was also discussed in the forum of the European Parliament in 2019, where a question to the Commission was asked on its approach towards English after Brexit,

---

76 Audrey Pariente (ed.), *Translation at the European Commission – a history*, Office for Official Publications of the European Communities, 2010, 57.

77 De Swaan, 2005; Salverda, 2002, 2; Philipson, 2003, 7.

78 Creech, *Law and language in the European Union: the paradox of a Babel "United in Diversity"*, 39.

79 Communication from the Commission to the Council, the European Parliament, the European Economic and Social Committee and the Committee of the Regions: Promoting Language Learning and Linguistic Diversity. An Action Plan 2004–2006 COM (2003) 449. 24 July 2003. Not published in the Official Journal.

80 Promoting Language Learning and Linguistic Diversity. An Action Plan 2004–2006 COM(2003) 449, 45.

and Latin as a lingua franca for Europe.[81] No answer has been provided to date. Modiano (2017) noted that UK's exit may give birth to a European English or Euro-English. This could be an official variety of English used by Europeans which is influenced by Standard English and by the native languages of speakers whose first language is not English.[82] Modiano's view is supported by Crystal[83] who claims that Brexit may help the development of Euro-English.[84] A strong argument raised in favour of English as a language of the EU is that approximately 95% of legislation adopted in the co-decision procedure is not only drafted in English,[85] but also debated, scrutinised, and revised in this language.[86]

Theoretically, if neither Ireland nor Malta notifies English as their official language, English could be proposed as a single EU official language, which would open the possibility of using a language, not notified by any Member State, but spoken by the largest number of Union citizens as a foreign language.[87] However, it must be noted that the policy of one EU language in place of the EU multilingualism has been proposed several times without success. So far, despite the excessively high costs and difficulties resulting from the extension of legal and institutional multilingualism, no effective steps have been taken which would result in a decrease in the number of EU official and authentic languages of EU law.[88] The scenario seems to be highly improbable as it remains in contrast to the EU policy of multilingualism which constitutes the cornerstone of European integration. As the linguistic equality of all Member States reflects the Union's respect for the national identities of the Member States, the introduction of a single EU official language

---

81 Question for written answer E-000517-19, http://www.europarl.europa.eu/doceo/document/E-8-2019-000517_EN.html [retrieved on 15 November 2019].

82 Marko Modiano, "English in a post-Brexit European Union", *World Englishes*, Vol. 36, 2017, 314–5.

83 David Crystal, "The future of new Euro-English", *World Englishes*, Vol. 36, 2017, 330–35.

84 However, it must be noted that not all linguists agree with that. Jenkins claims that Euro-English is a variety of standard English.

85 Dragone, 2006, 100; Frame, 2005, 22.

86 Cornelis J.W. Baaij, "The EU policy on institutional multilingualism: between principles and practicality", *JLL*, Vol. 1, 2012, 3.

87 According to Special Eurobarometer No. 386. Europeans and their languages: 38% of Europeans speak English, 12 % French, 11% German, 7% Spanish and 5% Russian.

88 On English hegemony: Pia Vanting Christiansen, "Language policy in the European Union: European/English/Elite/Equal/Esperanto Union?", *Language Problems and Language Planning*, 2006, 21–44; Jonathan Pool, *Optimal language regimes for the European Union*, 1996, 150–79, Esperanto: Florian Coulmas, *A language policy for the European Community*, 2013; Latin: Merike Ristikivi, "Latin: the common legal language of Europe", *Juridica International Journal*, 2005, 199–202.

would challenge the entire European identity policy. The Group of Intellectuals for Intercultural Dialogue[89] expressly stated that allowing *de facto* supremacy of one language over others in the daily operations of the EU would be contrary to the principle of respect for Europe's diversity of linguistic and cultural expression. Moreover, as Phillipson[90] and Forrest[91] argue, the danger of preparing new legislation in a single language is that those who speak English as their mother tongue would have an advantage over those for whom it is a foreign language.

At the same time, it is clear that the existing legal framework will trigger complexity of the EU multilingual law with every new accession.[92] Therefore, not only an option of a single EU official language[93] was considered, but the ideas of the bilingual system[94] and limited multilingualism were also submitted.[95] However, all the proposals to reduce the number of EU official languages have been rejected for one major legal reason – the direct effect of the EU acts of general application. Such direct applicability of EU law results in the Union's obligation to guarantee its Member State citizens certainty of the law they are expected to obey, and legal equality is implemented through linguistic equality. However, in the lack of growing legal certainty, the debate and mounting attacks on the EU multilingual

89 Directorate General for Education and Culture EC, *A Rewarding Challenge. How the Multiplicity of Languages could strengthen Europe: Proposals from the Group of Intellectuals for Intercultural Dialogue set up at the initiative of the European Commission*, Office for Official Publications of the European Union, 2008, 5.

90 Phillipson, *English-only Europe? Challenging Language Policy*, 21,131.

91 Alan Forrest, "The politics of language in the European Union", *European Review*, Vol. 6, No. 3, 299–319.

92 Colin D. Robertson, *Multilingual Law: A Framework for Analysis and Understanding*, Routledge, 2016. Robertson stresses that the growing complexity and multidisciplinary nature of EU law require a new discourse on areas such as policy formation, drafting, translation, revisions, terminology, and computer tools in connection with the legislative and judicial processes.

93 Schilling (2010, 65) proposes a one-authentic-text solution but acknowledges that it would probably be the most difficult to achieve politically.

94 C. and K. Lutterman (2004, 1008–10) propose that a European reference language model should be adopted, according to which two EU reference languages (English and German) would become consultation languages for other languages. The 'authenticity' of the other languages would be upheld insofar as they are in agreement with the two authentic languages.

95 Derlén (2011, 157) proposes the only option viable as it retains the legal basis of equal authenticity of all EU language versions. He calls for sweeping reforms in practice by making English and French consultation languages, which national courts would always be required to consult in addition to their own languages.

law-making are in progress, and some proposals maintaining the equal authenticity of all EU Member State languages have not been excluded.[96]

2.3 Language rights based on EU multilingual law

2.3.1 Principles related to EU multilingual law

2.3.1.1 The principle of legal certainty

Legal certainty[97] is an overarching requirement for the European Union and is therefore considered as the basis for other principles that ensure the proper functioning of the multilingual legal system. It is one of the general principles of EU law based on the presumption that the addressees of legal norms know them. The EU Treaties[98] include no explicit references to the principle. Nevertheless, respect for the principle of legal certainty was already acknowledged in the first judgments of the Court of Justice in the joined cases of *C-42* and *49/59 S.N.U.P.A.T*,[99] in *Bosch*,[100] *Defrenne*,[101] and *Azienda Colori Nazionali*.[102] The Court of Justice expressly held that legal certainty constitutes a legal norm affecting private and public interests

96 The proposals maintaining equal authenticity of all official language versions were submitted by Derlén (2011, vide supra 95) and Sarčević (2013). Sarčević proposes to determine future EU multilingualism through improving the reliability of all language versions. This can be achieved by combining efforts of maximum harmonisation of national laws, strict adherence to the drafting principles of the Joint Practical Guide and the use of plain language in legislative acts.

97 The principle of legal certainty in the EU has been the subject of extensive research. The most important entries relevant for the purposes of this thesis include: Raitio (2003); Tridimas (2007), Kalisz (2007); Derlén (2009); Baaji (2012); Paunio (2013); Paluszek (2014); Helios and Jedlecka (2018); Leszczyński (ed.) (2019); Doczekalska (2014,2019); Nowak-Far (2016, 2020), Kornobis-Romanowska (2018).

98 OJ C 2020/1, 7 June 2016.

99 Judgment of the Court of 22 March 1961 in the joined cases 42 and 49/59 *Société nouvelle des usines de Pontlieue – Aciéries du Temple (S.N.U.P.A.T.) v High Authority of the European Coal and Steel Community*, ECLI:EU:C:1961:5.

100 Judgment of the Court of 6 April 1962 in the case 13-61 *Kledingverkoopbedrijf de Geus en Uitdenbogerd v Robert Bosch GmbH and Maatschappij tot voortzetting van de zaken der Firma Willem van Rijn*, ECLI:EU:C:1962:11.

101 Judgment of the Court of 8 April 1976 in the case C-43/75 *Gabrielle Defrenne v Société anonyme belge de navigation aérienne Sabena*, ECLI:EU:C:1976:56.

102 Judgment of the Court of 14 July 1972 in the case 57-69 *Azienda Colori Nazionali – ACNA S.p.A. v Commission of the European Communities*, ECLI:EU:C:1972:78.

which must be obeyed while applying Union law.[103] This is a public law principle which must be applied by EU institutions and Member States while exercising their conferred powers.[104] The Court of Justice has employed the principle of legal certainty with creativity, invoking it in diverse contexts.[105] Primarily, the principle was used as an argumentative and interpretative tool which the Court adduced to justify a particular decision.[106] It was referred to in judgments connected with the protection of legitimate expectations towards Union legislation, the conduct of the EU institutions or national measures, the non-retroactivity of law, the recovery of unduly paid EU monies, and the recovery of unduly paid state aid.[107]

Legal certainty has a formal and substantive nature and both aspects aim to give law addressees legal security. The formal aspect is ensured when the law is published in an appropriate manner and satisfies the imperatives of clarity, stability, intelligibility, and predictability. The norms must be clearly formulated so that people can get to know their rights and obligations, calculate with relative accuracy the legal consequences of their actions, as well as predict the outcome of legal proceedings in the case of infringement (principle of legitimate expectations). The norms must govern factual circumstances in general terms and connect the factual circumstances with legal consequences so that it would be possible to apply the norm to all persons and to all comparable cases in the same way.[108] Through this, the law provides stability and legal peace. Tridimas[109] and Groussot[110] claim that the elements of clarity and predictability[111] as well as the effectiveness and stability of legal relations, may be deduced from the Court of Justice's jurisprudence.[112] The substantive aspect of the principle is related to the rational acceptability of legal rules. Therefore, it is not sufficient that laws are predictable. They

103 Judgment of the Court in the case C-43/75, para. 74.

104 Dagmara Kornobis-Romanowska, *Pewność prawa w Unii Europejskiej: pomiędzy autonomią jednostki a skutecznością prawa UE*, C.H. Beck, 2018, 9.

105 Takis Tridimas, *The General Principles of EU Law*, Oxford European Union Law Library, 2007, 243.

106 Juha Raitio, *The principle of legal certainty in EC law*, Kluwer Academic Publishers, 2003.

107 Raitio, 186–266.

108 Elina Paunio, *Legal certainty in multilingual EU law: language, discourse and reasoning at the European Court of Justice*, Routledge, 2016, 52.

109 Tridimas, 242.

110 Xavier Groussot, *General principles of community law*, Europa Law Publishing, 2006, 194.

111 Relevant case law: C-158/06 *Stichting ROM-projecten*, para 34; C-318/10 SIAT.

112 Relevant case law: C-508/04 *Commission v Austria*, para 79, C-158/06 *Stichting ROM-projecten*, para. 34; C-50/09 *Commission v Ireland*, para. 47, C-318/10 SIAT, C-284/11 *EMS-Bulgaria Transport*.

must also be reasonably justified and accepted by the community in question. That means that legal norms should correspond to the interests of citizens and society and comply with the rule of law. The substantive aspect of legal certainty includes an element of citizens' trust in respect of law interpretation and application.[113]

The multilingualism of the EU creates extraordinary conditions for the principle of legal certainty. On the one hand, multilingual law is a necessary corollary of the EU owing to its distinct legal nature, in particular the principle of direct effect and the doctrine of the supremacy of EU law over national laws. As the Union citizens are directly affected by EU legislation, they should have the law available in a language comprehensible to them. On the other hand, in the face of the growing number of EU official languages the assurance of citizens' trust in the EU legislation expressed in more than 20 languages has been growing increasingly difficult. That was caused mainly by the linguistic discrepancies between the equally authentic language versions. As the Union citizens have access to the law in all the EU official languages, the question arises whether the citizens in all Member States who rely on only one language version could trust that they enjoy the same rights as the citizens of the other Member States who learnt about the content of law based on another EU language version.

The implementation of the principle of legal certainty in the context of EU multilingualism is a challenge, both at the stage of law creation as well as in its phase of interpretation and application. Firstly, legal texts must be reproduced in a multitude of authentic language versions. Secondly, the interpretation of multilingual law connotes a deeper diversification of EU law in the inter-semiotic dimension, i.e. corresponding to the diversity of legal and social systems in which it is created. A multitude of authentic languages results in a situation where the same legal concepts may have other content and scope in individual Member States. This is caused, not only by linguistic differences, but also by the legal cultures of individual Member States.[114] This diversity makes the interpretative and executive model highly contextualised owing to the fact that to a high degree it is based on national mechanisms.[115] The principle of legal certainty in the EU context may be ensured only if the law is aimed to be equal at the stage of its drafting and in the process of interpretation in the case of linguistic discrepancies.[116] At the stage of drafting and law publication legal certainty is realised through the principle of

113 Kornobis-Romanowska, 10.

114 Anna Kalisz, *Wykładnia i stosowanie prawa wspólnotowego*, Wolters Kluwer, 2007, 330.

115 Artur Nowak-Far, "Co wielojęzyczność tekstów prawnych Unii Europejskiej mówi o naturze prawa?", in: Maciej Kłodawski, Alicja Witorska, and Mariusz Lachowski (eds.), *Legislacja czasu przemian, przemiany w legislacji. Księga jubileuszowa na XX-lecie Polskiego Towarzystwa Legislacji*, Wydawnictwo Sejmowe, 2016, 283.

116 Paunio, 34.

legal multilingualism and in the process of judicial interpretation and adjudication through the principle of equal authenticity and the principle of the uniform interpretation and application of law.[117]

2.3.1.2 *The principle of legal multilingualism*

2.3.1.2.1 *Drafting and publication of EU law*

The principle of legal multilingualism may be deduced from the Treaty and results directly from Article 4 of Regulation No. 1/58, which obliges the Community institutions to draft regulations and other documents of general application in all the Community official languages. The EU has developed an extreme case of legal multilingualism,[118] which has made law-making a complicated process involving a number of disciplines, such as law, languages, translation, and terminology.[119] Although the proposal of a legal act is usually presented in English or French (sometimes in German),[120] the proposal is usually immediately translated into the other official languages.[121] The EU law co-drafting process begins where drafting and legal translation intertwine. Legal drafting within EU institutions includes all the EU official languages which participate in all the drafting stages and influence each other. Although some elements of translation are involved in EU multilingual law drafting, by the end of the drafting process none of the language versions can be identified as a pure original, thus guaranteeing that the equality of all language versions throughout the drafting process is preserved.[122]

The equality of all official language versions of the EU acts requires, pursuant to Article 5 of Regulation No. 1/58, simultaneous publication in the Official Journal of the European Union (OJEU), which guarantees equal access to the laws in all the EU official languages. The EUR-Lex platform provides access to the OJEU, EU law (EU treaties, directives, regulations, decisions, consolidated legislation, etc.), preparatory acts (legislative proposals, reports, green and white papers, etc.), EU case-law, international agreements, EFTA documents, and other public documents.

---

117 Maciej Wojciechowski, "Wybrane aspekty problematyki pewności prawa", *Gdańskie Studia Prawnicze*, Vol. 24, 2010.

118 Doczekalska, "Legal Multilingualism as a right to remain unilingual – fiction or reality?", 10.

119 Cornelis J.W. Baaji, *Fifty Years of Multilingual Interpretation in the European Union*, The Oxford Handbook of Language and Law, 2012.

120 Nowak-Far (2020, 318) calls it a 'prototext'.

121 Karolina Paluszek, "The equal authenticity of official language versions of European legislation in light of their consideration by the Court of Justice of the European Union", *Comparative Legilinguistics*, 18/2014, 49.

122 Agnieszka Doczekalska, "Drafting or Translation – Production of Multilingual Legal Text", 116–35.

All the documents can be found through a quick, advanced, or expert search by using different criteria, such as by theme, by institutions, and by EuroVoc. The latter is the EU's multilingual and multidisciplinary thesaurus organised in 21 domains and 127 sub-domains used to describe the content of documents in EUR-Lex.[123] Moreover, the platform includes links to national law databases (N-Lex), the national transposition measures, national case law references concerning EU law and JURE collection giving access to relevant judgments given by national courts and by the Court of Justice.[124]

As all official language versions acquire equal legal status, the addressees of the norms should be offered the same level of protection.[125] The publication of a particular piece of legislation in the relevant language versions in the OJEU ensures an intrinsic element of the formal aspect of principle of legal certainty, i.e. predictability of law. However, this is only a minimum requirement as it does not account for any qualitative requirements of the law published. The qualitative aspects remain a separate issue which grows in importance in the process of law interpretation.[126] Nevertheless, already the proper publication of the EU legislation in the OJEU makes an act enforceable against the Union citizen.[127] The issue became apparent when acceding Member States had to face the linguistic challenge of translating the growing *acquis communautaire*[128] into their national languages. Although such an obligation is not entrenched explicitely in EU law, it constitutes a necessary precondition for the equal implementation of EU law for all Union citizens.[129] For instance, Poland managed to translate into Polish only the EU primary law and the Accession Treaty prior to its accession. The EU secondary law, under Article 58 of the Accession Treaty, had been gradually published in the OJEU by 22 March 2006. As a result, in the transitional period of almost two years there were

123 Information about access to European Union law through EUR-Lex, https://eur-lex.europa.eu/ content/welcome/about.html [retrieved on 26 June 2018].

124 National case-law, https://eur-lex.europa.eu/collection/n-law.html [retrieved on 26 June 2018].

125 Paunio, 57.

126 Paunio, 78.

127 Judgment of the Court in the case C-161/06, para. 46.

128 *Acquis communautaire* includes the entire law of the EU and the judicature of the Court of Justice. The legislative acquis includes the primary law, in particular treaties and secondary law, including regulations, directives, decisions, recommendations, opinions and *sui generis* acts. Source: Jan Barcz (ed.), *Prawo Unii Europejskiej. Zagadnienia systemowe. Prawo materialne i polityki*, Prawo i Praktyka Gospodarcza, 2006, 181–93.

129 Katarzyna Waszczuk, “Znaczenie przekładu aktów prawnych Unii Europejskiej dla polskiego kontekstu kulturowego i dyskursu społeczno-politycznego”, *Rocznik Przekładoznawczy*, 2008, 239–48.

EU legislative acts which were not available in the Polish language version. A similar situation concerned other new Member States.

The problem of the availability of a particular language version was analysed by the Court of Justice in the *Skoma-Lux*[130] (2007) case. It concerned a Czech wine-merchant and importer of wine who was penalised by the Czech customs authorities for infringing customs legislation by failing to comply with Article 199(1) of Regulation No. 2454/93.[131] Skoma-Lux filed for annulment based on the absence of publication in the Czech language of the relevant Community law by the customs authorities on the dates when the acts in dispute were committed.[132] In the preliminary ruling procedure, the Court of Justice was asked whether a regulation could be applied against an individual if it had not been published in the OJEU in the official language of the Member State in question at the relevant time. The Court justified that "the new Member States should take all the measures necessary to ensure that Community law is effective in their domestic legal systems: it would be *contra legem* (...) to require them to impose on individuals obligations contained in legislation of general application which is not published in the OJEU in the official language of those States".[133] Considering the above, the Member State national authority may reject applying binding EU law not yet published in a language of that State at the time of the case. The Court ruled that the lack of publication of a directly applicable regulation in the language of a new Member State meant that the regulation could not be enforced against individuals in that state even though they could have learned of the legislation by other means.[134] The Court based its decision on considerations reflecting its view on legal certainty which can be guaranteed only if those affected by the law can acquaint themselves with provisions conferring on them rights and imposing obligations.[135]

2.3.1.2.2 Legal acts subject to the principle of legal multilingualism

2.3.1.2.2.1 Regulations and other acts of general application

The entitlement of the EU institutions to adopt regulations, directives, decisions, recommendations, and opinions is granted in Article 288 TFEU.[136] Article 4 of

130 Judgment of the Court of 11 December 2007 in the case C-161/06 *Skoma-Lux sro v Celní ředitelství Olomouc*, ECLI:EU:C:2007:773.

131 Commission Regulation (EEC) No. 2454/93 of 2 July 1993 laying down provisions for the implementation of Council Regulation (EEC) No. 2913/92 establishing the Community Customs Code, OJ L 253, 11 October 1993.

132 Judgment of the Court in the case C-161/06, paras 12–14.

133 Judgment of the Court in the case C-161/06, para. 41.

134 Judgment of the Court in the case C-161/06, para. 51.

135 Judgment of the Court in the case C-161/06, para. 38.

136 OJ C 202, 7 June 2016.

Regulation No. 1/58 clearly sets out that the principle of legal multilingualism applies to regulations and other acts of general application. Firstly, regulations need to be drawn up in all the EU official languages. They exert legal effect against every person subject to the Member State jurisdiction. Once they are enacted and published in the OJEU, they enter into force and are directly applicable. Secondly, directives are also those acts which need to be prepared in all the EU official languages. The direct effect of directives recognised by the Court of Justice in *Van Gend en Loos*[137] enables individuals to immediately invoke a European provision before a national or EU court. This implies that only access to laws in one's own language ensures their effectiveness. Thus, the Union citizen can enforce rights conferred by a Union directive even if a Member State failed to translate this directive.[138] As regards decisions, further clarifications are required.[139] The issue of decisions is more complicated as these are the acts which may be either of general application or may have a specific addressee. Hence, if a decision is of general application, it needs to be drawn up in all the EU official languages. If the latter is the case, the decision may be addressed to specific addressees in the required languages. If the addressee is the EU Member State(s), then this is a language of the Member State(s) concerned. If one or several companies or individuals are the addressees, these are the languages of the entities or persons concerned. Other acts such as recommendations and opinions are excluded from the scope of acts which have to be drawn up in all the EU official languages as they are not of general application. As a result, they are not published in the OJEU and hence have no binding force.[140] Nevertheless, it should be noted that the lack of a particular language version of a recommendation or an opinion may encroach upon Member State citizens' rights to be involved in the activities of the EU institutions, including the right to address them or to access their documents.

The principle of legal multilingualism also refers to delegated acts adopted by the Commission. Under Article 290 TFEU, the Commission has the power to adopt non-legislative acts of general application to supplement or amend certain non-essential elements of a legislative act.[141] The availability of all the language versions of delegated acts stems, not only from Article 4 of Regulation No. 1/58, but is also a procedural requirement set out in Article 18 of the EC Rules of Procedure.

---

137 Judgment of the Court of 5 February 1963 in the case 26/62 NV *Algemene Transport- en Expeditie Onderneming van Gend en Loos v Nederlandseadministratie der belastingen*, ECLI:EU:C:1963:1.

138 How the EU works, https://www.europarl.europa.eu/unitedkingdom/en/education/teaching resources /howeuworks.html [retrieved on 1 July2019].

139 According to Article 288 TFEU.

140 How the EU works, http://www.europarl.europa.eu/unitedkingdom/en/education/teachingresources /howeuworks/legalsystem.html [retrieved on 1 July 2019].

141 Directorate-General for Translation EC, 30.

Hence, the drafting of a delegated act is made in all linguistic versions so as to guarantee legal certainty, and a breach of this gives rise to an action for annulment.[142] Contrary to delegated acts, the Commission's implementing acts set out in Article 291 TFEU are not co-drafted in all the EU official languages, although they are published in all language versions.

2.3.1.2.2.2 International agreements

The principle of legal multilingualism applies to international agreements entered into by the EU. This is justified by the fact that they constitute an integral part of the EU legal order and are binding upon the EU institutions and Member States and may contain provisions which are directly applicable by national courts. Thus, directly effective norms of international agreements may be relied on by individuals, in particular in the field of justice, the environment, and social affairs. Therefore, they should be available to them in their own language. The principle of legal multilingualism is conditional and its application depends on the types of agreements. It should be strictly followed in respect of these agreements which directly affect the rights of individuals. The exclusion of some official languages from authentic languages could lead to a violation of the principle of legal multilingualism and, as a consequence, challenge legal certainty. Moreover, it could result in a charge of discrimination on the basis of language.[143]

International agreements are common acts of the EU and the contracting parties, not separate acts of the Union. As such, they are not governed by Regulation No. 1/58 and an obligation to publish them in the OJEU is not expressly imposed. Nevertheless, the aspect of publication of international agreements concluded by the EU was mentioned in Regulation No. 1049/2001 regarding public access to the European Parliament, Council, and Commission documents. It states that international documents concluded by the EU are to be published in the OJEU, unless this would undermine the public interest, individual privacy, court proceedings etc.[144] According to the Court of Justice, the fact of non-publication of the agreement does not render it inapplicable *per se*.[145] However, it is a common practice that international treaties are published in the OJEU in every EU official language even in a case when the agreement was not drafted in all the languages and when not all the language versions are authentic. In such a case, the non-authentic text of

---

142 Rules of Procedure of the European Commission C(2000) 3614. OJ L 308, 8 December 2000.

143 Directorate-General for Translation EC, 37.

144 Regulation (EC) No. 1049/2001 of the European Parliament and of the Council of 30 May 2001 regarding public access to European Parliament, Council and Commission documents. OJ L 145, 31 May 2001, Articles 4 and 13.

145 Judgment of the Court of 23 November 1999 in the case C-149/96 *Portuguese Republic v Council of the European Union*, ECLI:EU:C:1999:574.

the publication is usually headed with the word 'translation'. It also happens that agreements are published only in authentic languages. In such a case, the Council's decision on the conclusion of a given agreement is published in all the EU official languages, but the text of the agreement is enclosed in the authentic language only.[146]

The EU attempts to acknowledge every EU official language as an authentic one. However, there are significant differences between the linguistic regimes of bilateral and multilateral agreements. Most bilateral international agreements concluded by the EU are authenticated in all the EU official languages and in the language of a contracting party if the latter is not an official language of the Union. In practice, a good deal of bilateral agreements are also drawn up in languages which are not EU official languages. In such cases, the EU has to accept the language of the contracting party as an authentic language, and the non-European contracting parties are obliged to accept all the EU official languages as authentic ones.[147] Although in principle the EU applies a full linguistic regime in this type of agreements, some derogations occur, but only if parties mutually agree to them. An example is the agreement on the security of classified information between the EU and the USA, where only the English language version was approved by the parties as authentic.[148]

The linguistic regime of multilateral international agreements with a large number of parties is more restrictive. Such agreements are often drafted within the existing linguistic framework, i.e. under the auspices of a particular international organization. For that reason, they are often authentic in the languages of the organization. Accordingly, agreements concluded under the United Nations are usually authentic in six working languages: Arabic, Chinese, English, French, Russian, and Spanish and within the framework of the Council of Europe in English and French. If no international linguistic regime prevails, the languages of multilateral

146 Examples include: Agreement between the Government of the United States of America and the Commission of the European Communities regarding the application of their competition laws, 23 September 1991, authentic and published only in English; European Convention for the Protection of Animals during International Transport, 25 January 2004, authentic and published in English and French; Convention for the strengthening of the Inter-American Tropical Tuna Commission established by the 1949 Convention between the United States of America and the Republic of Costa Rica, 13 December 2004, authentic and published in English, French and Spanish.

147 The example is the Trade, Development and Cooperation Agreement (TDCA) between the European Community and the Republic of South Africa. OJ L 311, 4 December 1999.

148 Agreement between the European Union and the government of the United States of America on the security of classified information. OJ L115, May 2007.

agreements tend to reflect the linguistic composition of the contracting parties. However, they are usually authenticated solely in the languages chosen by the parties by means of compromise acceptable for all of them. It is often the case that agreements which are authentic in several languages distinguish one language as authoritative in the case of any linguistic discrepancies. The selection of one authoritative version facilitates the process of agreement execution. A multitude of authentic versions always implies that all versions must be prepared for signature and be ready for publication at the same time. Irrespective of the nature of the agreement, whether bilateral or multilateral, the provisions of an agreement can impose direct obligations on individuals only if appropriately published, which implies publication in the languages understandable for the addressees.[149]

Upon the publication of an international agreement in the OJEU, its text, terminology, and the list of definitions are automatically integrated into the European legal language. Owing to the autonomy and independence of the EU legal system and its terminology, the EU has freedom as far as the extent of terminology implementation into its language regime is concerned. Still, the organization usually follows the terminology of international treaties to avoid terminological discrepancies. As a consequence, the EU takes over the majority of terminology used in international treaties in its implementing legislation, which, as a result, is further implemented in its secondary legislation and national laws.[150] In most cases, the terms applied in international agreements overlap with the terminology already used in the European Union legal instruments. In exceptional cases, international treaties create new terms or give strict definitions which diverge from those of the EU. Normally, the recitals of directives and regulations contain explicit reference to the international treaty with which they aim to align EU legislation. If the EU act does not define the relevant concept, its meaning will be deduced from the international treaty concerned. If any doubt as to the terminology arises, the Court of Justice is asked to interpret the meaning of the concepts of directives or regulations aiming to implement international obligations.[151]

2.3.1.3 The principle of equal authenticity

2.3.1.3.1 The principle of equal authenticity under international law

The concept of equal authenticity of multilingual law can be traced back to the 1969 Vienna Convention on the Laws of the Treaties (the Vienna Convention)[152] which is considered to constitute the basis for the principle of unity of a multilingual document and a blueprint for the interpretation of multilingual law. First

149 Directorate-General for Translation EC, 44–9.
150 Directorate-General for Translation EC, 55.
151 Directorate-General for Translation EC, 64.
152 Vide supra 6.

of all, the Convention made a presumption that the words used in all language versions have an equivalent meaning in all authentic texts.[153] Article 10 of the Convention described the authentication procedure and safeguarded the equal authority of all the authentic texts of multilingual treaties in the interpretation process. Moreover, Article 33 of the Convention outlined the interpretation methods of treaties authenticated in two or more languages. It prescribed that the wording of each authenticated text is intended to be equally authoritative in each language, and to have the same meaning. Such wording of the Convention results in a presumption that so long as a textual discrepancy does not arise, each authentic language version of the treaty is regarded as accurately rendering its content and meaning. Therefore, it is sufficient for an addressee to rely on any one authentic text. This approach, supported by Sir H. Waldock and Meinhard Hilf, was based on the assumption that each text alone comprises the content of the treaty and may therefore serve as the basis for its interpretation until or unless a lack of clarity or divergence is discovered. As a consequence, this approach rejected the suggestion of incorporating the comparison of texts as principal means of treaty interpretation. The absence of a legal obligation to consult every single version was also an adjustment of the law to practical considerations based on the inability of practitioners to master individually all the authentic languages.[154]

The interpretation of a multilingual treaty should be carried out against the background of Article 31 of the Convention, which stipulated that ordinary meanings of the terms at stake should be analysed, taking into account the object and purpose of the treaty (textual interpretation). Secondly, the features comprising the context should be interpreted (subjective interpretation). Finally, the interpretation of the text in the light of the purpose, values, social, and economic goals which may diverge from original intentions of the parties as expressed in the text should follow (teleological interpretation).[155] Under Article 31(4), a special meaning should be given to a term only if the parties so intended.

2.3.1.3.2 Interpretation of EU multilingual law by the Court of Justice

The principle of legal multilingualism is not sufficient to ensure legal certainty.[156] Article 4 of Regulation No. 1/58 does not expressly stipulate that all the EU official language versions are equally valid for the purposes of interpretation.[157] In order

153 Maria Frankowska, *Prawo traktatów,* Szkoła Główna Handlowa, 1997.

154 Tabory, *Multilingualism in international law and institutions*, 197.

155 Tabory, *Multilingualism in international law and institutions*, 202–3.

156 Agnieszka Doczekalska, "Zasada pewności prawa w wykładni wielojęzycznego prawa Unii Europejskiej", *Europejski Przegląd Sądowy,* Vol. 5, 2019, 12–18.

157 The principle of equal authenticity applies directly with regard to the Treaties. Article 55(1) TEU stipulates that all official language versions are authentic. There are also legal scholars who claim that with regard to secondary law the principle also

to ensure the equality, the principle of legal multilingualism must be accompanied by the principle of equal authenticity. The principle of equal authenticity of all EU official language versions creates the conditions for making uniform and just interpretation of the EU law for all the citizens of the Union.[158] It requires EU institutions to treat all official language versions as having the same legal force.[159] Moreover, it requires the Court of Justice to take all of them into account in the process of interpretation in the case of linguistic discrepancies.[160] The unprecedented number of more than twenty authentic languages applied in twenty-seven Member States[161] – each of them having its own specific legal system and legal language – makes the EU the most challenging legal forum in the world.[162]

Linguistic interpretation has always been applied by the Court of Justice. During the initial periods of its activity it was a primary method of interpretation.[163] As linguistic interpretation related to the analysis of semantic and syntactic layer of the text, the Court was supposed to determine the meaning of words by analysing all the authentic language versions.[164] Such an approach was consistent with the provisions of the Vienna Convention, which favoured textual interpretation. In one of its first judgments in *Stauder*[165] (1969), the Court of Justice decided that the equal authenticity of all language versions implied that one language version could not be relied on in the interpretation process and it required the analysis of all the language versions, hence a linguistic comparative method was required.[166] Since then, the comparison of all authentic language versions has become an intrinsic element of the linguistic method of interpretation by the Court of Justice. The

---

results from Article 4 of Regulation No. 1/58. Source: Brain McCluskey, "Respecting multilingualism in the enlargement of the European Union – the organizational challenge", *Termonologie et traduction*, 2/2001, 10.

158 Anastazja Gajda, "Wielojęzyczność Unii Europejskiej", *Socjolingwistyka*, 2013, 12.

159 Wioletta Jedlecka, "Reguły językowe wykładni prawa UE.", in: Leszek Leszczyński (ed.), *System Prawa Unii Europejskiej. Tom 3. Wykładnia prawa,* C.H.Beck, 2019, 144.

160 This has been confirmed in numerous CJEU judgments (C-372/88, C-64/95, C-72/95, C-375/97, C-498/03) and opinions of Advocates General (Stix-Hackl, Tizzano); as cited by Doczekalska [2009, 363].

161 The status as of 2 February 2020.

162 Agnieszka Doczekalska, "Legal Multilingualism as a right to remain unilingual – fiction or reality?", 10.

163 Jedlecka, 142.

164 Raitio, 308.

165 Judgment of the Court of 12 November 1969 in the case C 29-69 *Erich Stauder v City of Ulm – Sozialamt*, ECLI:EU:C:1969:57.

166 Joanna Helios and Wioletta Jedlecka, *Wykładnia prawa Unii Europejskiej ze stanowiska teorii prawa,* E-Wydawnictwo. Prawnicza i ekonomiczna Biblioteka Cyfrowa. 2018.

Court's ruling in *Stauder* posed other questions to the Court on how to deal with textual discrepancy of the equivalent authentic texts which was the outcome of the comparative method.[167] The Court referred to the interpretation of multilingual law and formulated the principle of the uniform interpretation and uniform application of law. The Court made it impossible to consider one version of the text in isolation. It required that interpretation must be based on the real intention of its author and the aim it sought to achieve, and in the light of the versions in all languages. The Court's reasoning showed that even if a decision concerned only one Member State, all the language versions had to be analysed to ensure the proper understanding of a decision. Such an approach was upheld in the judgments of *CILFIT*[168] (1982) and *EMU Tabac*[169] (1998) where the Court endorsed that the interpretation of a provision involved a comparison of different language versions, which was to ensure the principle of the uniform interpretation and application of law.

In the face of the growing complexity of EU law, the analysis of a legal text appeared to be insufficient to build a system of legal norms. The specific nature of EU law, and in particular its extraordinary multilingualism and the individual legal culture of the Member States, triggered a statement that no provision is 'clear'. Linguistic interpretation resulted only in finding a *sens littéral*. In order to fully reflect *sens clair*, it had to be combined with the non-linguistic context and other methods of interpretation.[170] As a result of necessity, the Court of Justice had to revalue the interpretation methods provided in the Vienna Convention.[171] Whereas international law preferred the linguistic analysis of the legal text, the growing importance of other interpretation methods was noted in the EU. This was caused by a number of factors. Firstly, a multitude of terms in the EU did not have established meanings which may have evolved and developed together with the entire system. Secondly, the linguistic layer of EU law was affected by the specific law-making process involving a number of institutions. This is the law of compromises and balance between interests of the EU Member States and pressure groups. Thirdly, the fact that law is created in a growing number of languages complicated the law-making and interpretation process. Many authentic languages imply that the same legal terms expressed in different languages may differ in their content and scope

167 Jedlecka, 148.

168 Judgment of the Court of 6 November 1982 in the case C 283/81 *Srl CILFIT and Lanificio di Gavardo SpA v Ministry of Health*, ECLI:EU:C:1982:335, paras 18–20.

169 Judgment of the Court of 2 April 1998 in the case C 296/95 *The Queen v Commissioners of Customs and Excise, ex parte EMU Tabac SARL, The Man in Black Ltd, John Cunningham*, ECLI:EU:C:1998:152.

170 Marta Szuniewicz, "Interpretacja prawa wspólnotowego – metody i moc wiążąca wykładni ETS", *Studia Prawnicze*, Vol. 1, 2006, 31.

171 Paunio, 28.

in different Member States. Finally, a good deal of the EU terms rooted in economic affect the sequence of interpretation methods used by the Court of Justice.[172]

In *Netherlands v Commission*[173] (1979), the Court of Justice, for the very first time, described the need to consider the context and purpose of legal provisions in the case of linguistic discrepancies.[174] Since then, the Court has been developing its own methods of interpretation of a multilingual text.[175] It is said to apply the dynamic "European model of interpretation". It begins with the text analysis and later the norm is decoded from the EU law,[176] it is "creatively developed by way of the legal discourse"[177] and by way of non-linguistic arguments related to a specific case.

Despite the vital role of non-linguistic methods of interpretation, the meaning of the linguistic comparative method cannot be undervalued. It still constitutes one of the equally important methods of interpretative findings applied by the Court of Justice.[178] Linguistic analysis is usually a starting point for interpreting the provisions at issue in the light of the purpose (telos) and general scheme (system) of the provision.[179] Moreover, the comparative method is also employed in order to confirm the divergences between language versions, and constitutes a useful tool to confirm an interpretation reached by other means. The omission of linguistic interpretation would stand for the rejection of the equal authenticity of all language versions. The results of research done by Baaij (2012) demonstrate that the rules and methods of linguistic interpretation are broadly applied in particular with regard to the more precise provisions developing the content of the primary law. Having analysed 246 cases of the Court of Justice handed down in the period between 1960 and 2010, Baaij noticed that 44 per cent of all examined judgments referred to interpretation discrepancies, where linguistic methods of interpretation were applied.[180] As noted by legal academics, despite its apparent complexity, the EU multilingual law must be perceived as linguistically superior to monolingual

---

172 Jedlecka, 142.

173 Judgment of the Court of 7 February 1979 in the case C-11/76 *Netherlands v Commission*, ECLI:EU:C:1979:28.

174 Nowak-Far, "Co wielojęzyczność tekstów prawnych Unii Europejskiej mówi o naturze prawa?", 290.

175 Paunio, 34.

176 Kalisz, 152–6.

177 Marek Zirk-Sadowski, "Wykładnia i rozumienie prawa w Polsce po akcesji do Unii Europejskiej", in: Sławomira Wronkowska (ed.) *Polska kultura prawna a proces integracji europejskiej*, Zakamycze Kantor Wydawniczy, 2005, 102.

178 Zirk-Sadowski, 21.

179 Paunio, 34.

180 Baaji, *Fifty Years of Multilingual Interpretation in the European Union*, 2012.

laws.[181] EU legal multilingualism is considered to facilitate the linguistic interpretation process by the Court of Justice. While analysing parallel texts in different languages, the Court must account for different contexts of the respective language versions and as a result bring the law closer to reality. Multilingual equally authentic law forces the Court of Justice to carry out in-depth analysis allowing linguistic triangulation. The Court must achieve the same interpretative outputs in all the language versions.[182]

The reality has changed dramatically since the *Stauder*[183] case in terms of the number of authentic texts. Nevertheless, the Court of Justice is still expected to consider all language versions and not to exclude any language versions in the process of interpretation even if it evidently diverges from other versions. Such an approach was confirmed by the judgments of the Court of Justice,[184] opinions of Advocates General,[185] and in the literature.[186] The same is not expected from national courts which encounter linguistic discrepancies.[187] As opposed to the Court of Justice, national courts do not have necessary resources to carry out comprehensive linguistic comparisons. They do not have at their disposal multilingual staff and lawyer linguists.[188] For this reason, the requirement to compare all the language versions to determine the meaning of an interpreted legal act and the actual abilities of national judges makes it unfeasible. This unfeasibility was also noticed by Advocates General who observed that the requirement would involve a disproportionate effort and put an overwhelmingly heavy burden on the national courts.[189] For the purposes of clarifying the meaning of legal provisions, national

181 Barbara Pozzo, "Multilingualism as a 'value' in the European Union", *The Multilanguage Complexity of European Law: Methodologies in Comparison*, European Press Academic Publishing, 133–4.

182 Schilling, "Multilingualism and Multijuralism: Assets of EU Legislation and Adjudication", 1463.

183 The comparison would include 24 languages not the 4 languages analysed in *Stauder*.

184 C-372/88, C-64/95, C-296/95, C-375/97, C-384/98, C-498/03, as cited by Doczekalska [2009, 363].

185 including the opinion of Advocate General Stix-Hackl in the case C-247/02 delivered on 1 July 2004, ECLI:EU:C:2004:399.

186 Including Doczekalska (2006, 16), Fryźlewicz (2008, 54).

187 Agnieszka Doczekalska, "Drafting and interpretation of EU law – paradoxes of legal multilingualism", 363–4.

188 Opinion of Advocate General Stix-Hackl in the case C -495/03 delivered on 12 April 2005, para. 9.

189 Following Doczekalska 2009, 364, opinion of Advocate General Jacobs in the case C-338/95 delivered on 10 July 1997, ECLI:EU:C:1997:352, and in the opinion of Advocate General Stix-Hackl in the case C-495/03 delivered on 12 April 2005, ECLI:EU:C:2005:215.

courts should address the Court of Justice for a preliminary ruling in cases concerning linguistic discrepancies between language versions. In this context, the Court of Justice is put in a position of a mediator between the text producer (EU legislator) and the text addressees (national courts, authorities applying EU law and Union citizens), thereby assuring proper application of EU law.

The presumption of examination of all official language versions is a formal condition for the implementation of the principle of equal authenticity.[190] In practice, the comparison of all the EU official language versions by the Court of Justice is rarely applied, as stated by Advocate General Jacobs.[191] That was confirmed in the study by Paluszek[192] who claims that the interpretation of all language versions is hardly ever employed. Out of 80 cases examined by the researcher, in 55 cases the number of examined language versions did not reach the level of 50%. In the light of these findings, it may be concluded that it is a wish expressed by legal scholars and the Court itself rather than a real judicial practice of the Court of Justice to compare all language versions. As some language versions are not even examined, there seems to be no equality. Moreover, the study by Paluszek showed that the choice of language versions to be examined in particular cases was not justified at all. Versions in the working languages of the Commission (English, French, and German) appeared to be most often examined (around 90% of the total number of relevant cases). The examination of a limited number of language versions is not compliant with the formal aspect of equal authenticity. This formal aspect is ensured when the Court chooses the meaning that remains in accordance with any of the official versions and any official version may have a potential influence on the final decision. If not all language versions are taken into account, those which are excluded from interpretation cannot anyhow affect the final decision of the Court.[193]

2.3.1.4 The principle of the uniform interpretation and application of law

The direct effect of EU law requires its uniform application in all the Member States. This is to be ascertained by the principle of the uniform interpretation and

---

190 Karolina Paluszek, *Komparatystyka językowa jako narzędzie interpretacyjne Trybunału Sprawiedliwości Unii Europejskiej*, Difin, 2019, 51.

191 Opinion of Advocate General Stix-Hackl in the case C -495/03 delivered on 12 April 2005, para. 9.

192 Paluszek, *Komparatystyka językowa jako narzędzie interpretacyjne Trybunału Sprawiedliwości Unii Europejskiej.*

193 Paluszek, *Komparatystyka językowa jako narzędzie interpretacyjne Trybunału Sprawiedliwości Unii Europejskiej*, 52–7.

application of EU law shaped by the Court of Justice.[194] In the *Stauder* case, the Court imposed on itself an obligation to compare language versions, with the aim of assuring uniform law interpretation and, as a result, guaranteeing legal certainty. The subsequent Court of Justice case-law leaves no doubt[195] that uniform interpretation is the only solution in the cases of discrepancies between the language versions. The parallel texts of all official language versions are expected to be interpreted and applied in the same way irrespective of the legal systemic context.[196] In order to ensure uniform law interpretation and application, the Court of Justice formulated the principle of purpose, according to which the provision in question must be interpreted by reference to the purpose and general scheme of the rules of which it forms a part.[197]

An essential tool to ensure the uniform interpretation and application of EU law is the autonomy of the Union legal system and its terminology (Community notions[198]). According to the principle of the EU legal order autonomy, the notions used in EU law are given separate meanings, independent of the meanings assigned to them in the legal systems of Member States.[199] Some terms used in EU law may seem to have the same meanings as those applied in individual Member States, but they may differ in their scope. Moreover, the EU law has also shaped a multitude of terms and concepts which do not exist in domestic legal systems. For this reason, they cannot be translated by the use of domestic law terminology.[200] In the context of EU law, system and culture-bound terminology can be perceived as a new variant of all official languages.[201] Even precise linguistic formulations do not always result in precise law: legal effects depend on the way how those linguistic formulations are interpreted in a particular factual situation under the constraints of case-law that conditions subsequent interpretations.[202]

---

194 Cemil Kaya, "The Role of the European Court of Justice in the Process of European Integration," *Annales de la Faculté de Droit d'Istanbul*, 2010, 215–29.

195 C- 283/81 *Srl CILFIT and Lanificio di Gavardo SpA v Ministry of Health*; C-261/09 *Gaetano Mantello*; C-458/08 *Commission v Portugal*.

196 Susan Šarčević, *New Approach to Legal Translation*, Kluwer Law International, 1997, 77.

197 Case C-144/10 *Berliner Verkehrsbetriebe (BVG)*, para. 28; Case C-341/01 *Plato Plastik Robert Frank*, para. 64; and Case C-340/08 *M and Others*, para. 44.

198 Jedlecka, 145.

199 Judgment of the Court of 7 December 1995 in the case *C-449/93 Rockfon A/S v Specialarbejderforbundet and Danmark*, ECLI:EU:C:1995:420.

200 Edward Seymour, "A common EU legal language?" *Perspectives: studies in translatology*, Vol. 10, 1/2002, 7–13.

201 Kaisa Koskinen, *Beyond ambivalence: Postmodernity and the ethics of translation*, Tampere University Press, 2000, 84.

202 Paunio, 13.

The autonomy of EU terminology was ascertained by the Court of Justice. In the *CILFIT*[203] (1982) case, the Court stressed that legal concepts did not necessarily have the same meaning under Community law and in the light of the laws of particular Member States. The autonomy of the EU legal order invariably restrains the Court from invoking any national legal systems. If interpretation was based on national legal systems, the law would be implemented differently in different Member States.[204] For this reason, every provision of Union law should be placed in its context and interpreted in the light of the provisions of Union law as a whole having regard to the purpose of the provision.[205] The conceptual autonomy of EU terminology is regularly referred to by the Court of Justice in those cases where there is a need to explain and define the meaning of disputed terms. The Court is in charge of providing uniform Community definitions of specialist terms, for instance in the case of *Ekro BV Vee- en Vleeshandel v Produktschap voor Vee en Vlees,*[206] it defined a term of 'thin flank' (the cut of meat) incorporated in the Community regulation. The Court is also obliged to shape autonomous definitions of the commonly used terms which often cause serious inconveniences. The examples include the *Rockfon*[207] case where the Court defined the term 'establishment' or the *Kingscrest and Montecello*[208] case containing an autonomous EU definition of the word 'charitable'.

The Court's effort to ensure uniform law interpretation is extremely difficult, still uniform application of Union law in all the Member States is even more challenging. The EU forms an amalgam of different systems that have evolved separately and are generally confined within national and linguistic boundaries.[209] The co-existence of a multitude of independent legal systems in the EU – called by Schilling (2011) 'multijuralism'[210] – constitutes an important pragmatic aspect of the EU multilingual law analysis. It allows the formulation of a general conclusion that even if the law is considered to be equivalent in all its official language

---

203 Judgment of the Court of 6 October 1982 in the case *C- 283/81 Srl CILFIT and Lanificio di Gavardo SpA v Ministry of Health.* ECLI:EU:C:1982:335.

204 Paunio, 13–6.

205 Judgment of the Court in the case C 283/81, paras 18–20.

206 Judgment of the Court of 18 January 1984 in the case C 327/82 *Ekro BV Vee- en Vleeshandel v Produktschap voor Vee en Vlees* ECLI:EU:C:1984:11.

207 Judgment of the Court of 7 December 1995 in the case C-449/93 *Rockfon A/S v Specialarbejderforbundet and Danmark*, ECLI:EU:C:1995:420.

208 Judgment of the Court of 26 May 2005 in the case C-498/03 *Kingscrest Associates Ltd and Montecello Ltd v Commissioners of Customs & Excise,* ECLI:EU:C:2005:322.

209 Anne Lise Kjaer, "Recontextualization of concepts in European legal discourse", in: Edda Weigand (ed.), *Dialogue and Rhetoric,* 2008, 257.

210 Schilling, "Multilingualism and Multijuralism: Assets of EU Legislation and Adjudication", 1463.

versions, the exact equivalence remains a fiction. It is difficult to achieve such equivalence owing to the very nature of natural languages, as living tools of communication.[211] Legrand (1998) claims that legal transplants are not conceptually equivalent owing to the divergence of legal cultures.[212] This difficulty results from different national procedural models affecting the law, and from the fact that EU law is produced in languages in which domestic laws are drafted. Hence, even if the law is drafted and translated to the best of the drafters' and translators' abilities, the provisions may not convey the same meaning to lawyers in different legal systems. Therefore, the law may not necessarily exert the same legal effect in different legal systems. What would be needed to achieve such an effect is a shared theory of regulatory matters.[213] To guarantee the uniformity of law at the executive level, procedural regulations would have to be harmonised and autonomous interpretation guidelines would have to be developed.[214]

2.3.2 The citizen's right to be unilingual in the light of EU multilingual law

The direct effect of the EU law and its supremacy over national laws of Member States impose on the EU institutions an obligation to draft and publish legislative acts in all the EU official languages in order to guarantee every Member State citizen the right of access to EU law. All of the official language versions are authentic texts which carry equal legal weight. As a result, regardless of the language version chosen by the law addressee, the law should produce the same legal effects. Hence, the law addressee should enjoy the right to rely on one official language version in order to acquaint himself or herself with content of law (the right to be unilingual). However, in the face of the academic debate challenging the uniform interpretation and, in particular, application of EU law towards all of its addressees, the question arises of whether such a right is actually guaranteed. As maintained by Derlén (2011) "[t]he right to rely on a single language version exists as long as this version is unambiguous and free from doubt".[215] In such cases, the

211 Neil MacCormick and Robert S. Summers, "Interpretation and Justification", *Interpreting statutes: a comparative study*, 1991, 517–18.

212 Pierre Legrand, "The Impossibility of 'Legal Transplants'", *Maastricht Journal of European and Comparative Law*, Vol. 4, 1997, 111–24.

213 Paunio, 9.

214 Nowak-Far, "Co wielojęzyczność tekstów prawnych Unii Europejskiej mówi o naturze prawa?", 306.

215 Mattias Derlén, "In defence of (limited) multilingualism", in: Kjær Anne Lise and Silvia Adamo (eds.), Linguistic Diversity and European Democracy, Ashgate Publishing, 2011, 145.

law is reliable and legitimate expectations based on a language version are satisfied.[216] As the Court of Justice case-law demonstrates, this is not always the case. Linguistic discrepancies between language versions may raise doubts as to the reliability of law and may challenge the citizen's legitimate expectations towards the equal authenticity of a particular language version.[217]

Šarčević (2013)[218] and Kornobis-Romanowska (2018)[219] maintain that the requirement to compare all language versions, when resolving divergences between authentic texts, is in conflict with the principle of legal certainty for individuals. Instead of promising the reliability of one's language version without the threat of discrimination, it sends the opposite messages. On the contrary, Doczekalska (2014) claims that the linguistic equality of all the official language versions of EU law guarantees the Union citizen the right to be unilingual.[220] She argues that the Court strives to guarantee uniform interpretation by employing appropriate methods of reconciling official language versions taking into consideration the general scheme and purpose of a given legislative act.[221] Even a language version which discloses discrepancies with other authentic language versions cannot be rejected *a priori*. The task of the Court of Justice is to make decisions about the intended meaning of language versions representing contradictory provisions in order to ensure the same interpretation of EU law for all its addressees. As a result, regardless of the language version chosen by the citizen to learn about the law, he or she may expect to be guaranteed the same rights and obligations as the citizens of the other Member States. The very fact that the Court of Justice omits to analyse all language versions cannot exert any impact on the citizen's right to rely on a version drawn up in a language he or she knows.

The analysis of the Court of Justice case-law proves that the right to rely on one language version has been challenged in respect of the public authorities transposing Union directives (*UAB Profisa*[222]) and in exceptional cases by the companies

216 Theodor Schilling, "Beyond Multilingualism: On Different Approaches to the Handling of Diverging Language Versions of a Community Law", *European Law Journal*, Vol. 16, No. 1, 2010, 61.

217 Schilling, "Beyond Multilingualism: On Different Approaches to the Handling of Diverging Language Versions of a Community Law", 53.

218 Šarčević, "Multilingual Lawmaking and Legal (Un)Certainty in the European Union", 13.

219 Dagmara Kornobis-Romanowska, *Pewność prawa w Unii Europejskiej: pomiędzy autonomią jednostki a skutecznością prawa UE*, C.H. Beck, 2018, 40–3.

220 Doczekalska, "Legal Multilingualism as a right to remain unilingual – fiction or reality?", 16.

221 Judgment of the General Court of 21 May 2014 in the case T-61/13 *Research and Production Company "Melt Water" UAB v OHIM*, ECLI:EU:T:2014:265, para. 34.

222 Judgment of the Court of 19 April 2007 in the case C-63/06 *UAB Profisa v Muitinės departamentas prie Lietuvos Respublikos finansų ministerijos*, ECLI:EU:C:2007:233.

(*Research*[223]), which may also be obliged to compare language versions.[224] However, the right seems to remain unaffected in respect of individuals – the citizens of the Union. The Court has in principle ruled in favour of persons who relied on a given disputable provision. Although some Court's rulings reveal that an individual's right to rely on one language version is not absolute,[225] no judgments issued by the Court of Justice has ever imposed an obligation of that kind on a natural person, and this seems to be objectively justified. Moreover, neither the principle of equal authenticity, nor the principle of uniform interpretation and application of law requires from the Union citizen to read EU law in more than one authentic language to understand its meaning. This does not change the fact that a citizen acting in reliance on one authentic language version, which later turns out to be contrary to the intention and purpose of the legislator, may subject himself or herself to acting against the law.

2.4 Language rights based on EU institutional multilingualism

2.4.1 External and internal dimension of EU institutional multilingualism

Institutional multilingualism is founded on the principles of respect for linguistic diversity and language equality. It comprises both the use of languages by the EU institutions in their internal operations and in outward communication.[226] An external dimension of institutional multilingualism, also referred to as the 'external linguistic regime', entails communication between the EU institutions and Member States as well as between the EU institutions and Member State citizens. The internal dimension of institutional multilingualism, also called the 'internal linguistic regime', entails the internal operations and procedures of various EU institutions. Both dimensions of institutional multilingualism reflect the distinction between the EU official and working languages. The EU official languages are used in the EU institutions' outward communication and working languages are employed at the institutions' internal level. A distinction between the external and internal linguistic regimes of the EU institutions seems to be proper to find out which language rights must be guaranteed and which may be denied in contacts with the EU public administration.[227]

223 Judgment of the General Court in the case T-61/13.

224 Doczekalska, "Zasada pewności prawa w wykładni wielojęzycznego prawa Unii Europejskiej", 17.

225 C 82/71 *Pubblico Ministero v Sail,* C 238/84 *Röser,* C 173/88 *Herinksen*, as cited by Šarčević (2013, 15–6).

226 Mamadouh (1999), Mamadouh (2002), Phillipson (2003), Baaij (2012).

227 Van der Jeught, *EU Language Law*, 117.

Institutional multilingualism is used by the EU as a tool to ensure democratic legitimacy. This democratic accountability has been invariably implemented despite an increasing number of official languages generating the growing financial burden of translation and interpreting services. The democratic entitlements of the Union citizen are exercised by the EU institutions through their external and internal linguistic regimes. The former aims to provide the citizens with equal access to the EU institutions and to information about the EU.[228] The latter should not limit the citizen's language rights resulting from the external linguistic regimes of institutions. Moreover, the internal linguistic regime rules should be non-discriminatory so that different Member State citizens may be represented within EU institutions on an equal basis, i.e. without language barriers.[229]

For the purposes of language rights analysis, both external and internal dimensions of institutional multilingualism must be investigated. With reference to the external one, the essential question must be answered as to whether the external linguistic regimes of the EU institutions amount to a full linguistic regime and, as a result, they guarantee the Union citizen the right to use any official language to contact them and to receive a reply in the same language. In respect of the internal linguistic regimes, the major question to be answered is whether the restricted internal regimes of particular institutions affect the scope of languages used for institutions' external communication and, as a consequence, the language rights of Member State citizens resulting from the external institutional multilingualism.

2.4.2 Language rights in the context of the external dimension of EU institutional multilingualism

2.4.2.1 The right to send documents to European Union institutions and receive a reply in one of the EU official languages

2.4.2.1.1 The EU institutions specified in Article 13 TEU

Regulation No. 1/58[230] imposes on the EU institutions the obligatory use of all the EU official languages in external contacts with Member State citizens. The institutions governed by Regulation No. 1/58 are listed in Article 13 TEU. These include the European Parliament, the European Council, the Council, the European Commission, the Court of Justice of the European Union, the European Central Bank, and the Court of Auditors.[231] The Treaty of Lisbon extends the catalogue

228 Schilling, "Multilingualism and Multijuralism: Assets of EU Legislation and Adjudication".

229 Cornelis J.W. Baaij, *Legal Integration and Linguistic Diversity. Rethinking Translation in EU Law*, Oxford Studies in language and Law, 2018, 2.

230 OJ L 17, 1 July 2013.

231 OJ C 202, 7 June 2016.

of the institutions governed by Regulation No. 1/58, and subject to the linguistic rules resulting therefrom, by adding the European Central Bank and the European Council. The special case is the Court of Justice which despite being mentioned in Article 13 TEU has always been governed by separate linguistic rules enshrined in its Statute and the Rules of Procedure. The Rules of Procedure provide the basis for initiating legal proceedings before the Court of Justice in one of the EU official languages.[232]

Under Regulation No. 1/58, both the EU Member States as well as legal and natural persons (Member State citizens) which are subject to their jurisdiction are entitled to freely choose one of the official languages to address any EU institution and to obtain a response in the same language. Article 2 of Regulation No. 1/58 states that "[d]ocuments which a Member State or a person subject to the jurisdiction of a Member State sends to institutions of the Community may be drafted in any one of the official languages selected by the sender. The reply shall be drafted in the same language". The language chosen does not have to be their native language. It might be any other EU official language. Likewise, under Article 3 of the Regulation, "[d]ocuments which an institution of the Community sends to a Member State or to a person subject to the jurisdiction of a Member State shall be drafted in the language of such State".[233] It is worth noting that Articles 2 and 3 regulate written communication with the EU institutions, not mentioning any oral communication, such as meetings or telephone calls. These are excluded from the scope of the provisions.

The right to communicate with the Union institutions in one of the EU official languages is an administrative entitlement which is a necessary precondition to make the European Union open and close to its citizens.[234] The full linguistic regime in communication with the EU major institutions seems to be a day-to-day reality which ensures a smooth flow of information between a given institution and an addressee. However, the fundamental question which arises is: what if such an entitlement is not respected and what are the legal consequences of such disrespect are. The infringement of rights to address the institutions must be divided into those which concern a Member State or a private company, and those which infringe the rights of individuals. In the former, the competent court is the Court of Justice which treats the infringement as a procedural irregularity. The latter are decided by the European Ombudsman and are categorised as a linguistic irregularity. Neither procedural nor linguistic irregularity automatically results in the annulment of any act ultimately adopted. In the case of a Member State or a company, the effects of procedural irregularities are assessed by the Court on a

232 Articles 36–38 of the Rules of Procedure of the Court of Justice of the European Union, OJ L 265/1, 29 September 2012.

233 OJ L 17, 1 July 2013.

234 Article 1 TEU, OJ C 202, 7 June 2016.

case-by-case basis.[235] A similar approach is taken by the European Ombudsman who perceives the infringement of the citizen's administrative language rights as maladministration.[236]

So far, the European Ombudsman has referred directly to Article 2 of Regulation No. 1/58 in several cases[237] concerning the EU institution's obligation to provide publications and communications to the public in the EU official languages. The landmark case in the area of individual's language rights based on institutional multilingualism was the *STÁDAS*[238] (2007) case. The complainant, a member of *STÁDAS* – an organization seeking to promote the Irish language in the European Union – in his individual capacity addressed the Council in Irish but received an answer in English. The complainant alleged that the failure to receive an answer in Irish was an infringement of his language rights. The Ombudsman noted that any failure to respect a fundamental right of citizens to correspond with the EU institutions in any of the treaty languages and to receive an answer in the same language impacts the dignity and individuality of every citizen. Therefore, according to the Ombudsman, any infringement of that kind constitutes an instance of maladministration.[239] The Ombudsman's decision did not result in any hard legal consequences owing to the lack of empowerment to take any other measures against the EU institution in such a case. The Ombudsman only urged the Council to take particular care to provide information to the public in all the EU official languages. As a matter of fact, the measures taken by the Ombudsman are reduced to the insistence on more transparency with regard to the information language policy of particular institutions, bodies, and agencies. The measures of the Ombudsman usually take the form of recommendations that the material intended for citizens should be published in all the EU official languages.[240]

2.4.2.1.2 The EU advisory bodies and agencies

The administrative right to address the EU bodies and agencies in one of the EU official languages is not guaranteed in all cases. The major reason is that the EU

---

235 Judgment of the Court of First Instance of 14 July 1994 in the case T-77/92 *Parker Pen Ltd v Commission of the European Communities*, ECLI:EU:T:1994:85.

236 Van der Jeught, *EU Law Language*, 123.

237 Including: European Ombudsman's decision of 23 March 2007 on complaint 259/2005 (PB)GG against the European Commission; European Ombudsman's decision of 22 November 2007 on complaint 3191/2006/(SAB)MHZ against the European Commission.

238 European Ombudsman's decision of 24 April 2007 on complaint 2580/2006/TN against the Council of the European Union.

239 European Ombudsman's decision on complaint 2580/2006/TN, para. 2.

240 European Ombudsman's decision of 22 November 2007 on complaint 3191/2006/(SAB)MHZ against the European Commission.

agencies[241] are characterised by heterogeneous language arrangements[242] distinct from Regulation No. 1/58. In view of their linguistic regimes, the agencies may be divided into four categories. The first group includes these bodies and agencies which comply with the language rules governed by Regulation No. 1/58. The founding instruments or the agencies' rules of procedure expressly provide that they are subject to the language rules enshrined in the Regulation. Such agencies include Europol,[243] the European Agency for Safety and Health at Work,[244] the European Union's Judicial Cooperation Unit (Eurojust),[245] the European Network and Information Society,[246] or the European Centre for the Development of Vocational Training (Cedefop).[247] Full multilingualism is also implemented in the Committee of the Regions. As a result, each individual member of the Committee receives information and assistance in his or her official language.[248] All official languages

241 The list of EU agencies can be found in: Van der Jeught, *EU Language Law*, 2015, 155–64.

242 Stefaan Van der Jeught, *What You Need To Know About EU Language Law*, 2016, https://slator.com/features/what-you-need-to-know-about-eu-language-law/ [retrieved on 26 June 2018].

243 Regulation (EU) No. 2016/794 of the European Parliament and of the Council of 11 May 2016 on the European Union Agency for Law Enforcement Cooperation (Europol) and replacing and repealing Council Decisions 2009/371/JHA, 2009/934/JHA, 2009/935/JHA, 2009/936/JHA and 2009/968/JHA. OJ L 135, 24 May 2016.

244 Council Regulation (EC) No. 2062/94 of 18 July 1994 establishing a European Agency for Safety and Health at Work. OJ L 216, 20 August 1994. Article 17 states that the language arrangements of the Community shall apply to the Agency.

245 Regulation (EU) No. 2018/1727 of the European Parliament and of the Council of 14 November 2018 on the European Union Agency for Criminal Justice Cooperation (Eurojust), and replacing and repealing Council Decision 2002/187/JHA. OJ L 295, 21 November 2018. Article 71 stipulates that Council Regulation No. 1 shall apply to Eurojust.

246 Regulation (EC) No. 460/2004 of the European Parliament and of the Council of 10 March 2004 establishing the European Network and Information Security Agency. OJ L 077, 13 March 2004. Article 22 expressly provides that the provisions laid down in Regulation No. 1 (...) shall apply to the Agency. The Member States and the other bodies appointed by them may address the Agency and receive a reply in the Community language of their choice.

247 Regulation (EEC) No. 337/75 of the Council of 10 February 1975 establishing a European Centre for the Development of Vocational Training. OJ L 39, 13 February 1975. Article 15 provides that the rules governing the languages of the European Communities shall apply to the centre.

248 Rules of Procedure of the Committee of the Regions of 31 January 2014. OJ L 65/41 5 March 2014, Rule 8(2).

may also be used in the Plenary Session, the committees, and in the Bureau.[249] The second group comprises the agencies without any formal language arrangements. Their constituting documents remain silent on linguistic issues. In principle, they establish rules for communication by means of their internal procedures.[250] The European Economic and Social Committee (EESC) is an apparent example here. Its Rules of Procedure[251] provide no details on linguistic regime, and language arrangements are made on a case-by-case basis by the Bureau of the President. In practice, the major working languages are English, French, and German. A full linguistic regime is limited only to the EESC's publications in the OJEU. Thirdly, there are agencies where the management board (or the Council) is entitled to lay down the language regime, including the European Centre for Disease Prevention and Control, the European Railway Agency,[252] and the European Data Protection Supervisor.[253] Finally, the special case of linguistic arrangements concerns the European Union Intellectual Property Office (EUIPO) (formerly: the Office for Harmonisation in the Internal Market (OHIM)).[254] The languages used by the EUIPO are restricted to English, French, German, Italian, and Spanish.[255]

In view of the above, it may be asserted that the right to communicate with Union agencies – excluding those governed by Regulation No. 1/58 – in all the EU official languages is not exercised. A clear example of the EU bodies left outside the umbrella of language rights protection guaranteed in Regulation No. 1/58 is the European Data Protection Supervisor (EDPS). The EDPS performs activities involving external communication, but its regime is limited to a few languages. Thereby the citizen's language entitlements are not satisfied. One of the most important documents from the perspective of a citizen seeking rightful protection,

249 Rule 80 of the Rules of Procedure of the Committee of the Regions.

250 Krystyna Kowalczyk-Bańczyk, "Komentarz do artykułu 24 TFEU", in: Andrzej Wróbel, Dawid Miąsik and Nina Półtorak (eds.), *Traktat o funkcjonowaniu Unii Europejskiej. Komentarz*, Vol. 1, Warszawa, 2012.

251 Rules of Procedure of the European Economic and Social Committee. OJ L 324/52, 9 December 2010.

252 Regulation (EC) No. 881/2004 of the European Parliament and of the Council of 29 April 2004 establishing a European railway agency. OJ L 220, 21 June 2004. The Regulation expressly provides that the Administrative Board shall decide on the linguistic arrangements for the Agency. At the request of a Member of the Administrative Board, this decision shall be taken by unanimity. The Member States may address the Agency in the Community language of their choice.

253 Complaints, https://secure.edps.europa.eu/EDPSWEB/edps/Supervision/Complaints [retrieved on 17 November 2019].

254 Council Regulation (EC) No. 40/94 of 20 December 1993 on the Community trade mark, OJ L 11, 14 January 1994.

255 Van der Jeught, *What You Need To Know About EU Language Law*, 2016.

namely the complaint submission form, is available only in English, French, and German.[256] The EDPS website is not available in all the EU official languages either.[257]

The EUIPO illustrates a peculiar example of the limited language rights in communication of the Union citizen with the EU agencies. Under Article 115 of Regulation No. 40/94[258] establishing the Office, an application for a Community trade mark must be filed in one of the five official languages of the Office. Moreover, the applicant is also obliged to indicate a second language which is one of the Office official languages as a possible language of procedure in opposition, revocation, and invalidity proceedings. If an application is filed in a language which is not one of the official languages of the Office, the Office must arrange to have the application translated into the language indicated by the applicant. Moreover, Article 115(4) of the Regulation expressly states that where the applicant for a Community trade mark is the sole party to the proceedings before the Office, the language of the proceedings should be the language of an application. If the application is made in a language other than the official languages of the Office, the Office may send written communications to the applicant in the second language indicated by the applicant in their application, which must be one of the five Office official languages.[259]

The best known case concerning the problem of communication language between an individual and the EU agency is the *Kik*[260] case. It concerned an application for a Community word trade mark (KIK) pursuant to Regulation No. 40/94. Christina Kik, an applicant in the case, drew up her application in Dutch and indicated this language as a second language. The application was dismissed on the formal grounds that the second language indicated was not one of the Office official languages. The case was analysed by the Court of First Instance which pointed out that Regulation No. 1/58, referred to as a legal basis by the applicant, was merely an act of secondary law and indicated that Member States did not lay down in the Treaty the rules governing language arrangements for particular institutions and bodies of the Community. The Court argued that Article 217 of the Treaty enabled the Council, acting unanimously, to define and amend

256 Complaints, https://secure.edps.europa.eu/EDPSWEB/edps/Supervision/Complaints [retrieved on 17 November 2019].
257 European Data Protection Supervisor, https://edps.europa.eu/ [retrieved on 18 March 2020].
258 Council Regulation (EC) No. 40/94 of 20 December 1993 on the Community trade mark. OJ L 011, 14 January 1994.
259 OJ L 011, 14 January 1994, Article 115(1)-(5).
260 Judgment of the Court of 9 September 2003 in the case C-361/01 P *Christina Kik v Office for Harmonisation in the Internal Market (Trade Marks and Designs) (OHIM)*, ECLI:EU:C:2003:434.

the rules governing the languages of the institutions and to establish different language rules. The Court concluded that the rules governing languages laid down by Regulation No. 1/58 could not be deemed to constitute a general principle of Community law. Accordingly, the applicant could not rely on Article 6 TEC in conjunction with Regulation No. 1/58 as a basis for demonstrating that Article 115 of Regulation No. 40/94 was illegal.[261]

The applicant lodged an appeal against the decision of the Court of First Instance with the Court of Justice.[262] She advanced two grounds of appeal: 1) incorrect interpretation of Article 115(4) of Regulation No. 40/94, and 2) infringement of Community law, more specifically Article 6 TEC, by not defining Article 115 of Regulation No. 40/94.[263] The Court of Justice considered the second ground of appeal to be inadmissible. As to the first ground, it stated that owing to the fact that the appellant failed to show damage resulting from the manner in which the Office applied the second sentence of Article 115(4) of Regulation No. 40/94, the argument was rejected.[264] The Court of Justice held that the limited use of Union official languages introduced by Regulation No. 40/94[265] was justified. The Court reasoned that it did not infringe the EU law, in particular Article 6 TEC, or any other Treaty provisions on application of the Member State official languages. The Court stated in justification that the references in the Treaty to the use of languages in the European Union cannot be regarded as conferring "a right on every citizen to have a version of anything that might affect his interests drawn up in his language in all circumstances".[266] "For an institution to address a citizen in his language does not therefore resolve all the linguistic difficulties encountered by citizens in the context of the activities of the EU's institutions and bodies".[267] The Court maintained that account must be taken of the fact that the Community trade mark was not created for the benefit of all citizens, but of economic operators, and that economic operators are not under any obligation to make use of it.[268] The Court added that the language regime of a body, such as the OHIM, was the result of a difficult process which sought to achieve the necessary balance between the interests of economic operators and the public interest in terms of the cost of proceedings, but also between the interests of applicants for Community trademarks and those of

261 Judgment of the Court of First Instance of 12 July 2001 in the case T-120/99 *Christina Kik v Office for Harmonisation in the Internal Market (OHIM)*, ECLI:EU:T:2001:189.
262 Judgment of the Court in the case C-361/01 P.
263 Judgment of the Court in the case C-361/01 P, para. 25.
264 Judgment of the Court in the case C-361/01 P, para. 49.
265 OJ L 011, 14 January 1994.
266 Judgment of the Court in the case C-361/01, para 82.
267 Judgment of the Court in the case C-361/01, para 86.
268 Judgment of the Court in the case C-361/01, para 88.

other economic operators in regard to access to translations of documents which confer rights, or proceedings involving more than one economic operator.[269]

The *Kik* judgment proves that restricted language regimes of the EU agencies are admitted in external communication, thereby limiting the right of citizens to contact them. Nevertheless, the specific nature of the EUIPO, as substantiated by the Court of Justice in its *Kik* judgment, seems to justify the limitations which aim to balance the interests of entities engaged.

The *Kik* argumentation was supported in similar cases decided by the Court of Justice. In the *Spain v Eurojust*[270](2005) case, Spain sought an annulment in seven calls for applications for the recruitment of temporary staff issued by Eurojust of the point concerning documents to be submitted in English by persons filing application forms in another language, and of the points concerning candidates' knowledge of languages. The Court found the application inadmissible.[271] The case was well explained by Advocate General Maduro in his opinion,[272] where he made a distinction between:

1) communication between the institutions and the citizens of the Union where respect for linguistic diversity deserves the highest level of protection, in particular access to legal acts and institutions producing them, and

2) contacts relating to administrative procedures, where the language rights of an individual are subject to restrictions based on administrative requirements. "The use of a language other than that of the persons concerned may be allowed in certain cases if it is clear that they have been put in a position where they can properly take note of the position of the institution concerned".[273] Maduro maintains that all-embracing linguistic pluralism is unworkable and economically intolerable.[274]

2.4.2.2 The right of access to legal proceedings before the Court of Justice of the European Union in one of the EU official languages

The Court of Justice of the European Union is the most multilingual international court in the world. No other court admits applications in as many as 24 languages. Article 7 of Regulation No. 1/58 makes reference to the languages used in the

269 Judgment of the Court in the case C-361/01, para 92.

270 Judgment of the Court of 15 March 2005 in the case C-160/03 *Kingdom of Spain v Eurojust,* ECLI:EU:C:2005:168.

271 Judgment of the Court in the case C-160/03, para. 1.

272 Opinion of Advocate General Maduro in the case C-160/03 delivered on 16 December 2004, ECLI:EU:C:2004:817.

273 Opinion of Advocate General Maduro in the case C-160/03, paras 43–44.

274 Opinion of Advocate General Maduro in the case C-160/03, para. 47.

proceedings of the Court of Justice by stating that they are laid down in its Rules of Procedure.[275] The Rules equip an applicant with the right to bring the case before the Court of Justice in any EU official language.[276] The language arrangements contained in the Rules may be amended upon the request of the Court addressed to the Commission and approved by the unanimous consent of the Council.[277]

The proceedings before the Court of Justice may be initiated both by a Member State and by an individual. The language of a case may be chosen by the applying Member State.[278] If an applicant is the EU citizen, he or she may use any EU official language for the application, and the language chosen does not have to be the native language of the applicant. If the case is brought by more than one applicant, the applicants must choose a common language or file separate applications. The principle is that the language in which an action is brought becomes the major language of the proceedings. However, the choice of the language of the case does not mean that this is the only language used in the course of the proceedings. The parties to the proceedings may request authorisation to use another language for all or part of the proceedings.[279] The President of the Court at its discretion decides on any possible derogations from the general linguistic rules. In each case, the President grants or refuses the request for the authorisation to use another language taking into account statement of reasons.[280]

In principle, the Court is reluctant to grant authorisations to use other languages than the language of the case. While considering an authorisation for the intervener, the Court verifies whether the procedure will not be delayed and the procedural rights of the main parties will not be prejudiced. The Court tends to grant the authorisation if the request relates to the oral procedure alone and the main parties bring no justified objections.[281] The Court also shows leniency when interveners who wish to use another language take part in the proceedings. If the Member State is an intervener, it may use its own language irrespective of the fact whether it intervenes in a direct action, in an appeal, or takes part in a preliminary ruling procedure.[282] In such a case, all its submissions have to be translated into the language of the case.[283] If other languages are admitted, the Court provides

---

275 OJ L 17, 1 July 2013.

276 Article 37(1) of the Rules of Procedure of the Court of Justice. OJ L 265/1, 29 September 2012.

277 Articles 36–38 of the Rules of Procedure of the Court of Justice.

278 The rules were introduced under the 2012 Court's Rules of Procedure. Prior to that, the applying EU Member State was obliged to use the language of the defendant Member State.

279 Article 37(1)(b) and (3) of the Rules of Procedure of the Court of Justice.

280 Article 37(4) of the Rules of Procedure of the Court of Justice.

281 Van der Jeught, *EU Language Law*, 2015, 186.

282 Article 38(3) and (6) of the Rules of Procedure of the Court of Justice.

283 Article 39 of the Rules of Procedure of the Court of Justice.

translations from and into the languages which are authorised for use during the proceedings. If the authorisation is not granted, the interveners are obliged to provide translations and attach them to their statement of intervention.[284] Moreover, neither Judges nor Advocates General are required to use the language of the case.[285] Under Article 38 of the Rules of Procedure, they are authorised to use any EU official language. In practice, Advocates General either use their native language or a language they know well, which is often not a language of the case. Practice shows that opinions are mostly delivered in one of the relay languages,[286] i.e. English, French, German, Italian, and Spanish. Advocates General may request a translation into a language of their choice of anything said and written in the course of the proceedings.[287] In the course of the hearing, simultaneous interpretation into the native language of every judge and Advocate General is provided.[288]

There are a few specific types of cases when language rules diverge from the general principles on the use of the EU official languages before the Court of Justice. The first category concerns infringement actions brought by the European Commission against a Member State. The language of the case is always the official language of the defendant State. The explanation for the exception originates from the necessity to safeguard the rights of defence and is justified by political sensitivity aimed to avoid the situation in which a Member State would have to defend itself in a language other than its official language.[289] Where the Member State has more than one official language, the applicant may choose the language for the legal action.[290] The second exclusion from the general language rules includes the national courts' requests for preliminary rulings. In such cases, specific language rules apply. The language of the case is normally that of the national court making a reference: such a language used before the national court is automatically the language of the case before the Court of Justice.[291] As the preliminary ruling proceedings are a sort of dialogue between the national and the EU court, the use of the same language in the national court proceedings and before the Court of Justice enables a national judge to explain intricate national provisions in a precise way and allows a party to the main proceedings to be represented by the same counsel. The problem arises when a minority language is used before the national court,

284 Van der Jeught, *EU Language Law*, 187.

285 Article 38(8) of the Rules of Procedure of the Court of Justice.

286 Relay language is a pivot language which is most widely used in order to use it as a medium to interpret into other less-known languages.

287 Article 39 of the Rules of Procedure of the Court of Justice.

288 Paluszek, "Komparatystyka językowa jako narzędzie interpretacyjne Trybunału Sprawiedliwości Unii Europejskiej", 49.

289 Van der Jeught, *EU Language Law*, 182.

290 Article 37(1) (a)-(c) of the Rules of Procedure of the Court of Justice.

291 Article 37(3) of the Rules of Procedure of the Court of Justice.

but it does not have official status in the EU. For instance, Welsh could be used in Welsh courts, but a judge could make a referral to the Court of Justice in English only.[292] Other cases concern Basque, Galician or Catalan. In such circumstances, a national judge is obliged to submit a request for a preliminary ruling in one of the EU official languages.[293] Next, if the party to the proceedings does not understand the language of the preliminary reference and the judgment in the preliminary ruling procedure published by the Court of Justice, the national court should provide a translation to the party to the national proceedings. The detailed rules on the provision of such translations should be established by the Member State.

2.4.2.2.1 Authenticity of the Court of Justice judgments

The Court of Justice pursues external multilingualism policy by maintaining its website in all the EU official languages and by publishing all judgments handed down by the Grand Chamber and chamber of five judges, opinions of Advocates General, notices, the Annual Reports, and information brochures in 24 official language versions. However, it must be noted that the increase in the number of official languages has made it impossible for the Court to apply full multilingualism in all of its publications. Hence, some of them, in particular orders and judgments of three judges, are published only in the language of the case and the language of the deliberation. This principle refers mainly to the judgments and orders which are less relevant for the development of EU law.[294]

Lack of publication of Court's decisions in all the languages may be justified by their limited authenticity. Contrary to EU legislation, judgments of the Court of Justice are not authentic in all the EU official languages. Under Article 41 of its Rules of Procedure, the judgments of the Court of Justice are authentic only in the language of the case or where applicable in another language authorised pursuant to Articles 37 and 38 of the Rules.[295] Accordingly, the texts of documents drawn up in the other EU languages may become authentic only if compared with the authentic language of the proceedings and judgment.

The problem of equal authenticity of the Court's judgments arose in the *European Commission v Republic of Poland*[296] (2019) case concerning the retirement age of the Polish Supreme Court judges. The Court of Justice based its reasoning on

292 Koen Lenaerts, Dirk Arts and Ignace Maselis, *Procedural law of the European Union*, Sweet and Maxwell, 2006, 499.

293 Van der Jeught, *EU Language Law*, 181.

294 Van der Jeught, *EU Language Law*, 191.

295 Articles 37, 38 and 41 of the Rules of Procedure of the Court of Justice.

296 Judgment of the Court of 24 June 2019 in the case C-619/18 *European Commission v Republic of Poland*, ECLI:EU:C:2019:531.

the *Associação Sindical dos Juízes Portugueses v Tribunal de Contas*[297] (2018) judgment. In the Portuguese case, the Court analysed judicial independence in Portugal and for the first time on this occasion referred to Article 19(1)(2) TEU concerning effective judicial protection. The problem arose as the English non-authentic version of the judgment differed from the authentic Portuguese language version. According to the literal interpretation of the Portuguese language version judgment, Article 19(1) TEU cannot be applied without a linking element with the EU law. The translations of the judgment in every EU official language except for English confirmed such interpretation and stated that the Court of Justice may control a national court only if the latter applies EU law or national law which falls within the areas covered by the EU law. This constitutes a precondition necessary to apply Article 19 TEU (dependent application). Only the English version of the judgment implied the contrary, i.e. an independent application of Article 19 TEU without the necessity of any other linking element with the EU law.[298]

The diverging English language version of Article 19 TEU in the *Associação Sindical dos Juízes Portugueses* against the EU legislator gave the right to its independent application. As a result, in the Polish case, the Court of Justice, Advocate General Tanchev[299] and the Polish court referring preliminary questions to the Court relied upon the mistranslated non-authentic English version of the *Associação Sindical dos Juízes Portugueses* judgment.[300] The matter was further complicated as the authentic text of the Advocate General's opinion was drawn up in English. As argued by Mr Gontarski, plenipotentiary of the Polish government, the Court of Justice must not rely on a mistranslated text of the judgment. Regardless of the subject matter of the dispute, the diverging language versions of the judgment triggered inequality of law. The Polish case exposes two important issues, firstly, the dominant use of English as a language used by Member State governments, national judges, and Advocates General, and, secondly, the serious legal consequences of relying on a non-authentic text of the judgment.

297 Judgment of the Court of 27 February 2018 in the case C-64/16 *Associação Sindical dos Juízes Portugueses v Tribunal de Contas*, ECLI:EU:C:2018:117.

298 Judgment of the Court in the case C-64/16, para. 29.

299 Opinion of Advocate General Tanchev in the case C-619/18 delivered on 11 April 2019, ECLI:EU:C:2019:325.

300 Waldemar Gontarski, *Karlsruhe blokuje Luksemburg i Brukselę – wyrok TSUE ws. Polski komentuje Waldemar Gontarski*, https://www.rp.pl/Rzecz-o-prawie/310019956-Karlsruhe-blokuje-Luksemburg-i-Bruksele---wyrok-TSUE-ws-Polski-komentuje-Waldemar-Gontarski.html [retrieved on 19 November 2019].

2.4.3 Language rights in the context of the internal dimension of EU institutional multilingualism

2.4.3.1 Internal linguistic regimes of the EU institutions

2.4.3.1.1 General remarks

Full multilingualism seems to be a day-to-day practice of the European Union institutions in their external communication.[301] On the contrary, a restricted linguistic regime is commonly used by EU institutions and agencies for the purposes of internal communication. Such a state of affairs found justification in the rulings of the EU courts which consistently held that communications between EU officials and the EU institutions were excluded from the scope of Articles 2 and 3 of Regulation No. 1/58.[302] Moreover, under Article 6 of Regulation No. 1/58, EU institutions may specify detailed rules for the internal use of languages in their rules of procedure or other internal instruments, such as resolutions or communications. Article 6 provides the legal basis for quite a large linguistic autonomy of the EU institutions. As a result, their linguistic regimes are limited to a number of languages informally used within EU institutions in a working mode.

The limited number of languages used by EU institutions for internal purposes is justified by pragmatic reasons. The selection of languages used in a working mode is affected by the conformity of officials, tradition, and political power, or engagement of the states which support the selected languages.[303] Such reasons have triggered a situation in which the EU administration works internally mostly in English. This is the language of the majority of the EU meetings. French, which at the outset of European integration was undoubtedly language number one, now places itself significantly behind English. German comes third despite being the mother tongue of the largest number of Member State citizens. The status of the German language in the EU may be objectively assessed as disproportionate to the demographic, economic, and political potential of the EU German-speaking Member States.[304]

2.4.3.1.2 The European Parliament

The European Parliament (EP, Parliament) proclaims its full internal multilingualism, and the institution is referred to as the most multilingual. It has the most detailed rules and procedures concerning language use. The procedures are

---

301 Krystyna Michałowska-Gorywoda, "Służby lingwistyczne Unii Europejskiej", *Studia Europejskie*, 2001, 81–9.

302 T-203/03 *Lars Bo Rasmussen v European Commission*; T-95/04 *Luciano Lavagnoli v European Commission.*

303 Szul, 69.

304 Gajda, "Wielojęzyczność Unii Europejskiej", 14.

included in the Rules of Procedure of the European Parliament,[305] which regulate parliamentary work. Under Rule 158, all the documents and debates must be translated and interpreted into the official languages of the EU. The EP emphasises that "the right of an elected representative to express himself and to work in his own language is an inalienable part of the rule of democracy and of his mandate".[306] Although translations in the EP are made based on relay languages including English, French, or German,[307] draft legislation or amendments thereto cannot be put to vote until they have been available in all the EU official languages.[308]

The Parliament is aware of the difficulties resulting from the application of full multilingualism in its administrative work. Therefore, it has adopted the Code of Conduct on Multilingualism (Code).[309] The Code refers to the concept of 'resource-efficient full multilingualism' as the means to limit the number of languages used in some instances justified by the President of the Parliament with the aim of keeping the costs of multilingualism within acceptable budgetary limits whilst maintaining equality between Member States and citizens. The measures introduced in the Code aim to allow more effective planning of requests for language facilities provided that the control of language resources is carried out in respect of the users' real needs.[310] The Code sets out the orders of priority for interpretation (Article 2) and translation (Article 3) and provides rules for managing requests for interpretation and translation, their scheduling and processing, as well as document circulation, and necessary deadlines for requests and their cancellation. The beneficiaries of the services (called 'users') are parliamentary governing bodies, committees and delegations.

Despite pragmatically justified arguments supporting the reduction of interpreting costs, the PE's solutions may result in unexpected complications as some languages are not represented at a committee meeting. This may cause absent members to be unable to follow the meetings online if they do not know the languages used by the participants.[311] The solutions were also criticised by some legal academics including Baaij. He claims that cost-cutting measures facilitate limited internal multilingualism which undermines the fundamental EU principle of equal democratic representation.[312] Despite the criticism, the acknowledgement

---

305 Rules of Procedure of the European Parliament, 2019–2024, 9th parliamentary term.

306 Resolution on the use of the official languages in the institutions of the European Union. OJ C 043, 20 February 1995, 91.

307 Suwara, "Wyzwania prawno-proceduralne dla Unii Europejskiej związane z BREXIT-em", 15.

308 Rules 158(1) and 169(6) of the Rules of Procedure of the European Parliament.

309 Code of Conduct on Multilingualism of 1 July 2029 adopted by the Bureau of the European Parliament.

310 Article 1 of the Code of Conduct on Multilingualism.

311 Van der Jeught, *EU Language Law*, 134.

312 Baaji, *Fifty Years of Multilingual Interpretation in the European Union.*

of practical limitations to multilingualism in the EP may be seen as a positive and reasonable solution. First of all, the introduced measures aim at better time-keeping, cost-saving, and the more efficient organization of day-to-day internal work. If applied without prejudice to the rights of the citizens, they could be treated as a model solution for other EU institutions where internal practical language arrangements remain largely unregulated.

2.4.3.1.3 The European Council and the Council of the European Union

Both the European Council and the Council of the European Union (Council) have always declared that they will apply full multilingualism only with regard to formal meetings.[313] Hence, informal meetings may be held in a restricted regime of languages selected by the hosting Member State. As regards the drafts of texts prepared in the Council, they have to be made available in the languages specified in the effective rules governing languages set out in Regulation No. 1/58. Only on the grounds of urgency and following a unanimous decision may the Council deviate from the general rules. Any member of the Council is entitled to oppose discussion if the proposed amendments are not drawn up in all the official languages.[314] Therefore, the Council's General Secretariat makes an effort to ensure that documents are available in all the required languages at the Council meetings.[315] In December 2003, the Committee of Permanent Representatives (COREPER) took a decision on a new approach to translation, which was later formalised by Decision No. 56/04 of the Council's Secretariat General.[316] Pursuant to the Decision, apart from the formal meetings of the European Council and the Council, interpretation into all the EU official languages will take place at the meetings of 20 preparatory groups for the Council and will be financed from its budget. The other meetings will be interpreted on "request" and interpretation services will be financed from budgetary envelopes allocated to each language and, if needed by a delegation.[317]

---

313 Article 9 of the Rules of Procedure of the European Council. OJ L 315, 2 December 2009. Article 14 of the Rules of Procedure of the Council of the European Union. OJ L 325, 11 December 2009.

314 Article 14(1)-(2) of the Rules of Procedure of the Council of the European Union.

315 Comments on the Council's Rules of Procedure, March 2016, https://www.consilium.europa.eu /media/29824/qc0415692enn.pdf [retrieved on 17 March 2020], 65.

316 Council's Secretariat General, *Interpreting in Council preparatory bodies*, No. 5149/10 of 11 January 2010, 2.

317 Council's Secretariat General, *Interpreting in Council preparatory bodies*, No. 5149/10 of 11 January 2010, 2.

2.4.3.1.4 The European Commission

The European Commission (EC, Commission) declares respect for full multilingualism, but at the same time it states that special language arrangements can be prescribed in certain situations. The Rules of Procedure of the European Commission[318] do not specify any language(s) as being used under preferential conditions compared to other official languages. Moreover, no legally binding instrument mentions some languages as "more" working than others. As the Rules do not set out which languages are to be used, in fact the EC restricts the number of languages in its internal work without the need for justification. The EC is also inconsistent in terms of terminology as its website includes both the terms 'working languages' and 'procedural languages' to refer to internal languages.[319] Practice shows that the languages used in the EC in a working mode include English, French, and German.[320] The other languages are needed later in order to communicate an act to the public and let it enter into force.[321] There is also an unwritten hierarchy between the three languages, with English and French being most frequently used and German playing a more subordinate role. The Commission uses the restricted language regime at regulatory committee meetings with EU Member States and at preparatory legislative meetings with national experts and officials. These are normally held in a few languages, sometimes only in English.[322]

The issue of the Commission's imbalance in treatment of various official languages in favour of English became the subject of a parliamentary question[323] addressed to Commission President Prodi in 2002. Spanish deputy Miguélez Ramos stressed that predomination of one language ran counter to the spirit of political integration and harmonious and balanced union among the peoples of Europe. She stressed that as a result of such predomination non-Anglo-Saxon officials were put at a disadvantage. In reply, President Prodi stated that the EC did not favour English over other official languages. He stressed that documents needed for the internal purposes of the EC were drafted in languages which corresponded to the actual needs of the Commission based on operational efficiency. His justification was that the rules implementing the Rules of Procedure provided that the documents

318 Rules of Procedure of the European Commission. OJ L 308, 8 December 2000.

319 Paluszek, "Institutional Multilingualism in the European Union – Policy, Rules and Practice", 132.

320 Traineeship, https://ec.europa.eu/stages/context/languages_en [retrieved on 18 March 2020].

321 Van der Jeught, *EU Language Law*, 137.

322 Van der Jeught, *EU Language Law*, 144.

323 Question raised by Rosa Miguélez Ramos as to the discriminatory treatment of languages, E-0615/02 of 5 March 2002, https://www.europarl.europa.eu/sides/getDoc.do?pubRef=-//EP//TEXT +WQ+E-2002-0615+0+DOC+XML+V0//EN [retrieved on 18 March 2020].

intended for use outside the EC were drawn up in the official languages in the case of instruments of general application, and that documents to be discussed at the Commission's meetings must be distributed to the Commissioners in the languages specified by the President in order to meet the minimum requirements.[324]

2.4.3.1.5 The Court of Justice of the European Union

Since the beginning of its existence, the Court of Justice has maintained a special internal language regime dominated by *de facto* one language, being French. This is the language of internal deliberations and general meetings carried out without interpretation. The tradition of using French in the Court in a working mode can be traced back to the European Coal and Steel Community Language Protocol of 1952 and is explained by historical reasons, yet no formal decision regarding the status of French has ever been taken. The internal status of French affects document circulation in the Court. If a pleading is submitted in a language other than French, it is translated into French for the Court's internal purposes. If the Advocate General drafts an opinion in any other official language, it is translated into French for the benefit of the judges and their deliberations.[325] The Court's traineeship application forms are available in French and English (recently added). The Court advises candidates that the Court's working environment requires a good knowledge of French.[326]

The internal status of French does not affect the rights of individuals to communicate with the Court in any EU official language [327] and to have the proceedings before the Court of Justice conducted in one of the EU official languages chosen by the applicant.

2.4.3.2 Impact of restricted internal linguistic regimes on external language use

2.4.3.2.1 Restricted language regimes vs the right of access to information

Philipson (2004) claims that the EU multilingualism confers upon the Union citizen the right to obtain information about the EU and its activities in all the EU official languages.[328] The failure to satisfy this right could result in 'democratic

---

324 Answer given by Mr Prodi to the question by Rosa Miguélez Ramos https://www.europarl. europa.eu/sides/getAllAnswers.do?reference=E-2002-0615&language=EN [retrieved on 18 March 2020].

325 Mathilde Cohen, "On the linguistic design of multinational courts", *International Journal of Constitutional Law*, Vol. 14, 2016, 498–517.

326 Court of Justice Traineeships, https://epso.europa.eu/job-opportunities/institutions-and-agencies/ 2088-court-justice_en [retrieved on 18 March 2020]

327 Van der Jeught, *EU Language Law*, 188.

328 Phillipson, *English-only Europe? Challenging Language Policy*, 129–31.

deficit'.[329] As the information may affect the life of every Union citizen, it should be published in all the EU official languages. As opposed to the right of access to the documents of the EU institutions, guaranteed under Article 15(3) TFEU,[330] the right of access to information about the Union in all the official languages is not expressly guaranteed under any EU legal instrument. It is a mere political declaration. Therefore, it raises questions as to what kind of information must be and what should be provided in all 24 languages. The right of access to information certainly includes publications made available on the internet websites of some EU institutions, invitations to tenders, relations with the media, public consultations, recruitment procedures, and calls for expression of interest/proposals.

The limited internal linguistic regimes of particular EU institutions affect the citizen's right of access to information about the EU in their languages. When the information is addressed to the public, it certainly falls within the scope of external communication of the EU institutions where full multilingualism in principle applies. The question is whether the limited use of languages to inform the Union citizens about EU activities infringes their language rights.

2.4.3.2.2 Information on the websites of the EU institutions

The EU institutions' websites are an essential element of the Union's information and multilingualism policy. The information disclosed on the websites provides transparency of the institutions' work and promotes good governance of the decision-making process.[331] Still, the institutions' websites often include publications only in selected EU official languages, mostly in English, French, and German.[332] In many instances, the homepages are available only in a few languages or in English only. Moreover, the further one digs for information, the more only an English version is available. The EU institutions also tend to use one or two languages in contacts with journalists. For instance, the Commission drafts press releases in English, French, and German and provides daily briefings in English

---

329 Annual Report of the European Ombudsman 2011, published on 13 February 2012, 8, https://www.ombudsman.europa.eu/pl/publication/en/11584 [retrieved on 12 July 2019].

330 The right of access to Union documents in one of the EU official languages is analysed in chapter 3, section 3.5.2.

331 The right of access to information in the European Union institutions and the role of the European Ombudsman in this process, https://idfi.ge/public/migrated/uploadedFiles/files/The%20right%20to% 20know%20in%20EU(1).pdf [retrieved on 12 July 2019].

332 Van der Jeught, *EU Language Law*, 140.

and French, except on Wednesdays, when translations of briefings into all the official languages are made available on the Commission's website.[333]

The issue of the publication of documents on the websites of the EU institutions, as a public service, was referred to by the European Ombudsman. One of the cases concerned the European Central Bank (ECB) information policy. The case was brought before the Ombudsman in 1999, when the ECB was not governed by Regulation No. 1/58.[334] According to the internal linguistic regime set out in its Rules of Procedure, the ECB applied the full language regime in respect of officially published acts, such as regulations, decisions, recommendations, and opinions.[335] As a consequence, the ECB's full linguistic regime was limited to the above acts. Other acts, such as guidelines and instructions, were notified to the Member States in the language of the State concerned. As English was used most frequently to draft the ECB's documents, it was also the language of most of the publications.[336] Only a few major regular publications, including the Monthly Bulletin and the Annual Report, were published simultaneously in all the EU official languages.[337] In the case before the Ombudsman, the complainant claimed that the Bank should comply with the same language rules as other Community institutions. Therefore, providing information on the website only in English was discriminatory. The Ombudsman held that publishing information on the website in a language in which it was drafted could not be considered maladministration by the ECB, as it was not the EU institution.[338] Nevertheless, in a similar case concerning the Commission, the Ombudsman took the same approach. It stated that the Commission was not obliged to translate booklets, newsletters, and brochures into all the EU official languages. It explained that the 'actual need' criterion should apply and financial reasons should be taken into consideration.[339]

The cases of publications made by the EU institutions on their websites analysed by the Ombudsman imply that internal documents can be published only in the language in which they were drafted or in a limited number of languages. Although in both cases mentioned above the Ombudsman referred to Article 2 of

333 European Commission, http://ec.europa.eu/dgs/translation/translating/officiallanguages/index_ en.htm [retrieved on 16 September 2017].

334 It acquired the status of the EU institution under the Lisbon Treaty and since then it has been governed by Regulation No. 1/58.

335 Article 17(8) of the Rules of Procedure of the European Central Bank. OJ L 338, 15 December 1998.

336 Article 17(2), (6) and (7) of the ECB Rules of Procedure.

337 Van der Jeught, *EU Language Law*, 141.

338 European Ombudsman's decision of 17 November 1999 on complaint 281/99/VK against the European Commission.

339 European Ombudsman's decision of 22 November 2007 on complaint 3191/2006/(SAB)MHZ against the European Commission.

Regulation No. 1/58 and urged the ECB and the EC to provide information to citizens in their own language in order to ensure effective communication, it took no effective measures. The Ombudsman was only competent to recommend that they should explain their information policies and provide all relevant material in all the EU languages. As a result, it may be concluded that the failure to provide information about the EU in all the EU official languages on the institutions' websites seems to result in no consequences for the institutions if a publication has non-binding force. Hence, if a citizen is not able to find information in his or her national language, he or she has no solid legal grounds for legal action concerning his or her disadvantage, except for the grounds of the Union's policy of openness and transparency. From the legal standpoint, the situation looks different in the case of a right of access to the EU documents entrenched in the Treaty.

2.4.3.2.3 Public consultations

The European Commission regularly seeks the views of Union citizens and stakeholders when it develops policies and legislation. Through this, citizens may participate in the EU's decision-making process and exercise their civic rights. The idea of public consultations seems to be fairly implemented if the consultation papers are available in all the EU official languages providing all interested citizens with an equal right to give their views. Otherwise, the process is limited by being addressed only to persons knowing English, French, and German. Practice shows that consultation announcements are very often available in the three languages or in English only.[340] The issue of a limited number of languages used during public consultations was analysed a number of times by the European Ombudsman. The Ombudsman held that in principle all the official languages should be used in the process as this is an essential precondition for participation by citizens in a decision-making process. The Ombudsman stressed that multilingualism is essential for the effective exercise of the citizens' democratic right to become informed about matters and issues that may lead to legislative action. Although it cannot be denied that citizens do not always have the right to obtain their language version of anything that might affect their interests, the cases when a particular language version is not available must be limited and justified on each occasion. Hence, unequal treatment is permitted only where there is reasonable and objective justification for it.[341]

In 2011 when the Commission launched a public consultation on financial sector taxation with a consultation paper available only in English, a Spanish lawyer lodged a complaint with the European Ombudsman based on discrimination on the

340 Public consultation on financial sector taxation, announcements published in English, French, and German and the consultation paper only in English.

341 European Ombudsman's decision of 4 October 2012 on complaint 640/2011/AN against the European Commission, paras 28–9.

grounds of language.[342] In defence, the Commission invoked time constraints. The Ombudsman doubted that the Commission had a clear language policy for public consultations as other examples of public consultations showed that different language combinations were used in public consultations and they did not follow a predictable pattern.[343] In view of the growing inconsistencies, the European Parliament in its resolution urged the Commission to make public consultations available in all the official EU languages.[344] Despite the resolution, the problem has not been fully resolved as members of federations and lobby groups use mostly English in their documents.[345]

2.4.3.2.4 Recruitment procedures for the EU staff

The internal language regimes of the EU institutions have a bearing on the linguistic requirements from candidates for the posts of EU officials and civil servants and the languages used in the recruitment procedures for the EU staff. In practice, the requirement of knowledge of a specific language mostly includes the institution's internal *de facto* working languages.[346] The language matters related to recruitment are governed by the Staff Regulations of Officials and the Conditions of Employment of Other Servants.[347] They include a general statement that a difference of treatment based on language cannot be permitted unless it is objectively and reasonably justified and meets legitimate objectives in the general interests of staff policy.[348] Language requirements from a candidate are considered to be formal job specifications, and as such they are not an issue. The legal discussions do not concern the linguistic requirements themselves, which are obvious in a multilingual organization. What is subjected to debate is the compatibility of the requirement of specific language knowledge with the real needs at a particular position. Hence, if command of a particular language is desired, it should be objectively justified and serve the attainment of duties pursued within the framework of the institution's

342 European Ombudsman's decision 640/2011/AN.

343 European Ombudsman's decision of 4 October 2012 on complaint 640/2006 against the Commission, para. 53.

344 Resolution of the European Parliament of 14 June 2012 on public consultations and their availability in all EU languages. OJ C 332 E/68 of 15 November 2013, para. 2.

345 Van der Jeught, *EU Language Law*, 2015, 144.

346 The EPSO website: http://europa.eu/epso [retrieved on 29 July 2019]. In most open competitions the language requirements are: a good command of two official languages of the EU (native language plus English, French, or German).

347 Regulation No. 31 (EEC), 11 (EAEC), laying down the Staff Regulations of Officials and the Conditions of Employment of Other Servants of the European Economic Community and the European Atomic Energy Community, OJ P 045 1 January 2020.

348 OJ P 045 1 January 2020, Article 1d (1)(6).

staff policy, and must be proportionate to the goals pursued within the interests of the service.

Initially, the Community courts were pragmatic about specific language requirements in the recruitment process.[349] In 1975, the Court of First Instance and the Court of Justice expressly held that specific language requirements were in principle compatible with EU law[350] if objectively justified by the interests of the service with the reservation that the required level of language command was proportionate to the genuine needs of the service.[351] As a result of a radical increase in a number of EU languages, and a growing number of judgments of the Court of First Instance/General Court of the EU in that area,[352] the Court of Justice imposed a general principle of strict respect for full multilingualism while conducting staff selection procedures.[353]

As regards the language used in the recruitment procedure for EU staff, the Court of First Instance clearly expressed its position in *T-185/05 Italy v Commission*[354] (2008). The case concerned the recruitment procedure for the Commission senior management staff announced only in English, French, and German. The Court held that the limitation of languages favoured candidates of particular nationalities whose mother tongue was one of the three languages, and it adversely affected candidates not knowing English, French, or German.[355] The Court adjudicated the infringement of Article 1(d)(6) of the Staff Regulations and annulled the vacancy notice on the grounds that the publication of notices in only three language was discriminatory and in the light of the fact that the Commission had failed to take any measures to enable those candidates who did not have command of these three languages to acquaint themselves with the precise content of that notice.[356]

349 Julain Currall, "Official languages inside and outside the institutions: An analysis of recent cases", *Georgia Journal of International & Comparative Law*, Vol. 39, 2010, 605.

350 Judgment of the Court of First Instance of 19 June 1975 in the case 79-74 *Berthold Küster v European Parliament*, ECLI:EU:C:1975:85, para. 16 and judgment of the Court of 29 October 1975 in the case 22-75 *Berthold Küster v European Parliament*, ECLI:EU:C:1975:140, para. 13.

351 Judgment of the Court of 27 November 2012 in the case C-566/10 P *Italian Republic v Commission*, ECLI:EU:C:2012:752; judgment of the Civil Service Tribunal of 29 June 2011in the case F-7/0 *Marie-Thérèse Angioi v Commission*, unreported.

352 Van der Jeught, *EU Language Law*, 146.

353 Judgment of the Court in the case C-556/10P.

354 Judgment of the Court of First Instance of 20 November 2008 in the case T-185/05 *Italian Republic v Commission*, ECLI:EU:T:2008:519, para. 117

355 Judgment of the Court of First Instance in the case T-185/05, para. 150.

356 Judgment of the Court of First Instance in the case T-185/05, para. 152.

C-566/10 P *Italy v Commission* (2012) was considered by the Court of Justice as an appeal of the Italian Republic against the judgment of the General Court entered in 2010.[357] Italy sought annulment of the notices of open competitions published in English, French, and German for Administrators (AD5) and Assistants (AST3) by the European Personnel Selection Office (EPSO). The appellant alleged *inter alia* the infringement of Articles 1, 4, 5 and 6 of Regulation No. 1/58. The Court of Justice admitted that the General Court had erred in law and set aside its judgment. It explained that if an institution has no specific regulations applicable to officials, no document existed on the basis of which it could be concluded that the relations between the institutions and their employees were completely excluded from the scope of Regulation No. 1/58.[358] The Court of Justice noted that a candidate was disadvantaged at two levels – firstly, with regard to the proper understanding of the competition notice and secondly, in respect of the period of time allowed to prepare and send an application to take part in the competition.[359] The Court concluded that such a difference in treatment of languages was disproportionate and amounted to discrimination on the grounds of language, as prohibited by Article 1(d) of the Staff Regulations.[360] In its judgment, the Court specified clear limits to the recruitment policies in three languages only. Accordingly, in principle the publication of the recruitment announcements should be carried out in all the EU official languages. In specific cases where limiting the number of languages in the job announcement has been restricted, the reasons must be proportionate and objectively justified by the interests of the service. Invariably, the institutions should also be able to justify such difference in treatment based on language by way of clear, objective, and foreseeable criteria enabling the candidates to understand the grounds for that difference in treatment.[361]

Also in the recent judgments in *Spain v Parliament*[362] and *Commission v Italy*[363] (2019), the Court of Justice upheld that differences in treatment based on language

357 Judgment of the General Court of the European Union of 13 September 2010 in joint cases T-166/07 and T-285/07 *Italian Republic v European Commission*, ECLI:EU:T:2010:393.

358 Judgment of the Court in the case C-566/10 P, para. 68. The Court followed the opinion by Advocate-General Kokott of 21 June 2012 who advised the Court of Justice to annul the judgment of the General Court. According to her, a notice of open competition must be drafted in all the EU official languages.

359 Judgment of the Court in the case C-566/10 P, para. 74.

360 Judgment of the Court in the case C-556/10 P, para. 77.

361 Van der Jeught, *EU Language Law*, 148.

362 Judgment of the Court of 26 March 2019 in the case C-377/16 *Kingdom of Spain v European Parliament*, ECLI:EU:C:2019:249.

363 Judgment of the Court of 26 March 2019 in the case C-621/16 P *European Commission v Italian Republic*, ECLI:EU:C:2019:251.

were in principle not allowed in the procedures for selecting staff for the EU institutions. In the former case, Spain asked the Court of Justice to annul, on the grounds of discrimination based on language, the European Parliament's call for applications launched in 2016 for the establishment of a database of candidates to work as drivers. As noted by Advocate General Sharpston, the language rights of candidates resulting from Articles 1 and 2 of Regulation No. 1/58 were infringed in two ways. Firstly, the application form was available only in English, French, and German, and, secondly, these were the languages of communication with the EPSO.[364] Sharpston maintained that discrimination based on language took place as candidates whose mother tongue was English, French, or German were better able to describe their positive aspects and less likely to include inexact information.[365] At the same time, Sharpston did not share the Spanish view that knowledge of these languages at B2 level would not be required in the performance of duties by selected candidates. The Court of Justice found that limitation to some languages is possible if properly justified. The Parliament declared that the restriction on the choice of 'language 2' served "the interests of the service, which required newly recruited staff to be immediately operational and able to communicate effectively in their daily work and by the fact that those three languages are the most widely used within the institution".[366] In its judgment, the Court of Justice annulled the call for expression of interest and declared the database to be void. According to the Court, the Parliament had failed to justify the restriction in relation to the specific language under Article 1d(6) of the Staff Regulations. The Parliament did not establish how each of those languages would be most useful for the performance of the duties in question and why that choice could not include other official languages which might be relevant to those duties.[367] Moreover, insofar as the Parliament had not adopted internal rules governing its language regime, it could not be affirmed that those three languages were, necessarily, the most useful languages for all the duties in that institution.[368]

Similarly, in the Italian case *C-621/16*, the Commission brought an appeal against the judgments of the General Court,[369] according to which two notices

364 Opinion by Advocate General Sharpston in the case C-377/16 delivered on 25 July 2018, ECLI:EU:C:2018:610.

365 Opinion by Advocate General Sharpston in the case C-377/16, para. 85

366 Judgment of the Court in the case C-377/16, para. 62.

367 Izabela Marcinkowska, "Poszanowanie różnorodności językowej w Unii Europejskiej", *Europejski Przegląd Sądowy*, 1/2020, 45.

368 Press release of the Court of Justice of the European Union No. 40/19, https://curia.europa.eu /jcms/upload/docs/application/pdf/2019-03/cp190040en.pdf [retrieved on 1 July 2019].

369 Judgment of the Court of First Instance of 15 September 2016 in joint cases T-353/14 *Italy v Commission* and T-17/15 *Italy v Commission*, ECLI:EU:T:2016:495.

of open competition of the EPSO were held unlawful for restricting the choice of 'language 2' in the competition to English, French, and German, as well as for restricting to those three languages the choice of language of communication between candidates and the EPSO. According to the Court of Justice, the General Court correctly held that a candidate's highest standards of ability, efficiency, and integrity were independent of language knowledge, the latter being the means of demonstrating the former. The Court noted that, while competition notices must be published in full in the OJEU in all the EU official languages, the EPSO is not obliged to communicate, in the context of a competition, with a candidate in a language freely chosen by the latter. However, the restriction on the choice of language of communication between candidates and the EPSO to a limited number of official languages indicated by the EPSO must be objectively justified. In this case, no such justification was provided.[370]

2.4.3.2.5 Invitations to tenders

The languages used in invitations to tenders and calls for proposals are affected by the internal language arrangements of individual EU institutions. Although there is no case of the EU courts in this field, the European Ombudsman has issued a number of decisions in such matters. In 2005, a complaint was brought to the Ombudsman against the Commission concerning a call for proposals concerning the rehabilitation of victims of torture.[371] Applicants were expected to apply in English, French, or Spanish. Moreover, certified translations of documents such as statutes, annual activity reports, accounts, and external audit reports had to be supplied. The applicant, a German association supporting treatment for victims of torture, alleged that all the official languages of the EU should be accepted in that call for proposals. In the applicant's opinion, the Commission's requirement concerning languages was discriminatory on the basis of Article 21(3) TEC and Regulation No. 1/58. In a decision closing the inquiry, the Ombudsman stated that Article 2 of Regulation No. 1/58 applied to calls for proposals and invitations to tenders contrary to what the Commission alleged.[372] Hence, any limitations to the right to send documents in all the EU official languages must be proportionate and based on valid reasons, necessary for the attainment of the legitimate aim pursued.[373] Having considered the Commission's grounds for restricting the number of languages in the call for proposals, the Ombudsman stated that the Commission

370 Differences of treatment based on language are, in principle, not allowed in the procedures for selecting staff for the EU institutions, https://curia.europa.eu/jcms/upload/docs/application/pdf/2019-03/cp190040en.pdf, 2 [retrieved on 1 July 2019].

371 European Ombudsman's decision of 30 April 2008 on compliant 259/2005(PB) GG against the European Commission.

372 European Ombudsman's decision 259/2005, para.5.

373 European Ombudsman's decision 259/2005, para. 7.

had failed to prove that there had been exceptional circumstances that would have made it impossible to deal with applications in other Community languages. Moreover, the Ombudsman acknowledged that the cost considerations might constitute a serious reason to limit the number of languages in calls for proposals. However, it also held that a general limitation of the languages that can be used when submitting proposals/tender bids would require a decision to that effect by the legislator. The Commission failed to prove that the rule was authorised by the Community legislator.[374]

2.5 Conclusions

- The EU principle of linguistic equality is a natural consequence of the formal equality of the Member States before the EU. The inclusion of one national language of every Member State into the corpus of EU official languages demonstrates respect for their languages and national identities. Moreover, it institutionalises the distribution of linguistic powers in the EU.
- The classification of languages into treaty (authentic), official, and working affects the rights granted to individuals:
- the treaty (authentic) language plays a key role in the EU multilingual law interpretation and affects language rights in this area,
- the official language is the key notion of the EU linguistic regime based on the criterion of a state language which strongly affects the language rights of the Union citizens who want to identify themselves with the law enacted on their behalf and therefore may wish to address the authorities/legislator in their own languages.
- the working language is used by the EU institutions for internal communication. However, it may affect the language rights of the Union citizen to the extent to which the internal regime of an institution affects the scope of languages used externally.
- EU co-official language users cannot enjoy the same rights as EU official language users, but may in particular circumstances claim the use of their languages in the EU public sphere.
- The EU linguistic regime aims to guarantee legal certainty and secure citizens' democratic rights. This is achieved through the EU multilingual law and institutional multilingualism.
- Within the framework of the EU linguistic regime, the right to use the EU official languages includes three fields: access to Union legislation, direct communication with the EU institutions, as well as access to EU legal proceedings.
- The Union citizen has the right to access EU legislation affecting him or her in his or her own language. The fact that all 24 authentic language versions of the

374 European Ombudsman's decision 259/2005, para. 11.

EU multilingual law (excluding the Court of Justice judgments) are considered to be equal in the light of the law results in the EU citizen's right to rely on any authentic language version of the text. This is safeguarded by:

- the principle of legal multilingualism which guarantees that all EU legislative acts of general application are published in the OJEU at the same time, and thereby the Union citizens have access to the law in their languages;
- the principle of equal authenticity which ensures that the Court of Justice is obliged to treat all authentic language versions equally and apply adequate interpretation methods which provide such equality;
- the principle of the uniform interpretation and application of EU law which is to be guaranteed by the autonomy of the EU legal order and terminology independent of the Member State legal systems. It constitutes the only available solution in the cases of linguistic discrepancies between the authentic language versions.
- The lack of real equivalence between all authentic language versions cannot challenge the EU citizen's right to rely on one official language version. This would question the functioning of the EU multilingual law.
- Institutional multilingualism guarantees that the EU citizen is in principle allowed to use every EU official language in the EU public sphere.
- The right to use one of the EU official languages by the Union citizen in direct communication with the EU institutions, bodies and agencies is not absolute:
- The citizen's right to send documents to the EU institutions and receive a reply in the same language includes the institutions specified in Article 13 TEU and the EU bodies and agencies subject to Regulation No. 1/58.
- As demonstrated in the *Kik* case, the limited use of languages in communication is justified when the beneficiaries do not act in the capacity of the citizens, but economic entities.
- In the *Eurojust* case, the citizen's right to communicate with the institutions/bodies was distinguished from contacts relating to administrative procedures. The language rights of an individual in the latter case are subject to restrictions based on administrative requirements.
- The citizen's access to proceedings before the Court of Justice in one of the EU official languages is guaranteed by the Court's Rules of Procedure and cannot be questioned on any grounds. Special language rules apply with respect to preliminary ruling procedures and proceedings against a Member State.
- The European Union's declarations on the equality of languages are inconsistent.[375] On the one hand, the principles of democracy and equality force the EU institutions to communicate and operate in the languages of EU citizens. On the other hand, the principles do not allow for the pragmatic and budgetary

375 Cornelis J.W. Baaij, "The EU policy on institutional multilingualism: between principles and practicality", *International Journal of Language and Law*, Vol. 1, 2012, 3.

arguments that the EU uses to justify the limited number of *de facto* working languages of its institutions.

- The internal use of a single or limited number of languages in EU institutions seems not to be in agreement with the EU's principle of equal treatment, however, it is allowed under Article 6 of Regulation No. 1/58.
- Internal institutional multilingualism is pragmatically limited to the predominant use of English. The EU institutions justify their limited multilingual practice by sober budgetary policy for translation and interpretation based on the arguments of efficiency and practicality.
- The internal linguistic regimes of the institutions in specific cases limit the language rights of EU citizens in the area of their access to information about the EU, public consultations, and calls for proposals/invitations to tenders favouring English, French, and German speaking users, and in some cases only English users.
- The internal linguistic regimes may be the grounds for different treatment based on language in the recruitment procedure for the EU institutions staff. However, such unequal treatment must be objectively and reasonably justified by the institution in question and must meet legitimate objectives in the general interest of staff policy (*T-185/05, C-566/10, C-377/16, C-621/16*). Otherwise, the procedure is deemed to be discriminatory and must be annulled.

3. Language rights resulting from citizenship of the Union

3.1 Opening remarks

At first sight, no clear linking between citizenship of the Union[1] and language rights exists. The rights granted to the Union citizen in the Lisbon Treaty[2] expressly refer to linguistic aspects only in the context of the citizen's communication with the EU institutions. This confirms the thesis that language rights are entrenched in the EU language policy, in particular in its linguistic regime. Nevertheless, this does not constitute the full picture of rights conferred upon the Union citizen in the area of languages. It is so because the EU language policy does not cover all aspects of linguistic issues falling within the scope of Union law which the Union citizen may encounter. A wide range of language-related matters falls beyond the scope of Regulation No. 1/58. The day-to-day life of the Union citizen who enjoys the right to move and reside freely may generate a multitude of situations concerning the use of one's own language. For this reason, it may be assumed that the rights granted to the Union citizen may entail language-related aspects which trigger language rights. According to Hilpold, Union citizenship fills a gap in the rights related to language use by the Member State citizens in the Union public sphere. He claims that the concept is highly relevant to the protection of linguistic diversity within the EU, and it harbours a great potential for the development of language rights within the organization.[3] Moreover, the rights based on citizenship reflect core elements of national identity,[4] expressed *inter alia* by language. The heavy dependence of language rights on the Union citizenship makes it advisable to analyse the concept and its impact on the language rights of the Union citizen. Accordingly, the primary objective of this chapter is to specify the scope and nature of such rights.

The chapter is structured as follows. Firstly, it analyses the concept of the citizenship of the Union and the principle of non-discrimination on the grounds of nationality in order to demonstrate a close link between the two. This connection resonates on the language rights resulting from the rights guaranteed to the Union

1 Also referred to as the Union citizenship and EU citizenship.

2 OJ 2016 C 202, 7 June 2016, Article 20 TFEU.

3 Peter Hilpold, "Union Citizenship and Language Rights", in: Xabier Arzoz (ed.) *Respecting Linguistic Diversity in the European Union*, Amsterdam: John Benjamins Publishing, 2008, 107.

4 Sandra Seubert, Oliver Eberl and Frans van Waarden, *Reconsidering EU Citizenship: Contradictions and Constraints*, Edward Elgar Publishing, 2018, 135.

citizen under the Lisbon Treaty, as presented in the third sub-section. Secondly, language rights attached to the right to move and reside freely read in conjunction with the principle of non-discrimination on the grounds of nationality are investigated. To introduce the background, the analysis includes a presentation of the right to move and reside freely, its limitations, and its relation with the internal market freedoms. Next, a number of particular language rights attached to the right of free movement and the principle of non-discrimination on the grounds of nationality are distinguished and discussed. These include the right of access to education in one's own language *(Commission v Belgium, Commission v Austria, Bressol v Chaverot)*, the right to use one one's own language before Member State courts *(Mutsch, Bickel and Franz, Rüffer)* and the right to choose one's name and surname (*Garcia Avello, Leonard Matthias, Sayn-Wittgenstein, Runevič-Vardyn and Wardyn)*. Following that, language rights of workers and self-employed persons are examined against the background of the free movement of persons *(Groener, Angonese, Haim, Hocsman)*. Subsequently, the analysis focuses on the language rights concerning citizen's contacts with the EU institutions. The right to petition the European Parliament, to apply to the European Ombudsman and to address the EU institutions and advisory bodies are analysed. Next, the linguistic aspects of the other rights attached to Union citizenship are explored. Three major rights have been selected: the right to diplomatic and consular protection of the Union citizen, the right of access to the Union documents, and the right to submit the European Citizens' Initiative. Finally, language rights of consumers are investigated against the background of the free movement of goods.

3.2 Citizenship of the Union

3.2.1 The concept of citizenship of the Union

The roots of citizenship of the Union can be traced back to the case of *Van Gend en Loos* (*Case 26/62NV).*[5] Through the judgment, the Court of Justice created a special relationship between Member State citizens and the Community. The Court expressly stated that the norms of the Community were directly applicable not only to its Member States but also towards their citizens. In the long-term perspective, the judgment in *Van Gend en Loos* had far-reaching consequences. Firstly, the principle of the direct effect of Community law on individuals resulted in the need to protect their fundamental rights. Secondly, creation of directly applicable law required democratic legitimisation in Community law. Thirdly, Member States had to grant the Community institutions competences in respect of their citizens,

5 Judgment of the Court of 5 February 1963 in the case 26/62NV *Algemene Transport- en Expeditie Onderneming van Gend en Loos v Nederlandseadministratie der belastingen*, ECLI:EU:C:1963:1.

which required the formulation of principles regulating the relations between the Community and citizens of Member States.[6]

Following the judgment in the *Case 26/62NV*, the increasing impact of Community actions on Member State citizens, the national nature of fundamental rights and citizens' willingness to participate in democratic processes triggered a widespread debate on how to confer specific rights upon Member State citizens by means of the Community law.[7] The idea of establishing European citizenship appeared in the Tindemans' report of 1975 *Towards a Europe of Citizens*.[8] The first general direct elections to the European Parliament held in 1976 were also considered to be a sign of strengthening the rights of Member State citizens.[9] The breakthrough in this area came in the late 1980s and early 1990s when the draft of the Maastricht Treaty[10] was prepared. Finally, the concept of citizenship of the Union was introduced into *acquis communautaire* by way of the Treaty establishing the European Community (TEC). The Treaty formed democratic legitimisation for the direct effect of the Union law created thirty years earlier. The final wording of the provisions on Union citizenship was the result of hard-won compromise.[11] Articles 17–22 TEC corresponded to the objective of the Treaty on European Union (TEU) to strengthen the protection of rights and interests of Member States citizens.[12]

Initially, citizenship of the Union was regarded as having a symbolic meaning not affecting the rights already granted by the Community law to the citizens of individual Member States.[13] However, the interpretation of Articles 17–22 TEC by the Court of Justice ignited some controversies.[14] By way of its judgments, the Court shaped citizenship of the Union as an institution actually strengthening the rights of individuals. It became an autonomous and fundamental status of Member State citizens.[15] In order to give an idea of the evolution of Union citizenship in

6 Izabela Skomerska-Muchowska and Anna Wyrozumska, *Obywatel Unii*, Vol. 6 No. 2, Instytut Wydawniczy EuroPrawo, 2010.

7 The citizens of the Union and their rights, http://www.europarl.europa.eu/factsheets/en/sheet/145 /the-citizens-of-the-union-and-their-rights [retrieved on 9 July 2019].

8 Bulletin of the European Communities, supplement 1975 (8) II.

9 Bulletin of the European Communities, 1975 (8) II.

10 OJ C 191, 29 July 1992.

11 Aleksander Gubrynowicz, "Obywatelstwo Unii Europejskiej – Stan Obecny i Perspektywy", *Obywatelstwo Unii Europejskiej. Zeszyty OIDE*, Wydawnictwo Sejmowe, 2008, 8.

12 Andrzej Wróbel, Dawid Miąsik and Nina Półtorak (eds.), *Traktat o Funkcjonowaniu Unii Europejskiej. Komentarz*, Vol. 1, Wolters Kluwer, Warszawa, 2012, 252.

13 Adam Bodnar, "Obywatelstwo UE a Ochrona Praw Podstawowych", *Obywatelstwo Unii Europejskiej, Zeszyty OIDE*, Wydawnictwo Sejmowe 2008, 50.

14 Gubrynowicz, 6.

15 Wróbel, Miąsik and Półtorak, 252.

the Court's case-law, a few landmark judgments need to be highlighted. In the cases of *Martínez Sala*[16] (1998) and *Bickel and Franz*[17] (1998), the Court of Justice laid the grounds for the fundamental status of Union citizenship. In *Martinez Sala*, it combined citizenship of the Union with the principle of non-discrimination on the grounds of nationality. In *Bickel and Franz*, the Court integrated the standards resulting from Union citizenship and internal market freedoms. In the case of *Grzelczyk*[18] (2001), the Court made a step forward and declared Union citizenship to be a fundamental status of a Member State citizen and ensured that individuals who are in similar situations should receive similar treatment. In *Zambrano*[19] (2011), the Court extended the scope of Union citizenship application to purely internal situations. All the above cases are discussed in-detail later in this chapter.

The development of Union citizenship shaped by the Court of Justice was recognised in the Lisbon Treaty (LT). The LT includes relevant provisions in the TEU and the Treaty on the Functioning of the European Union (TFEU).[20] Moreover, the Charter of Fundamental Rights of the European Union (Charter), incorporated into the EU primary law by way of the LT, raises the rights of the Union citizen to the status of fundamental rights.[21] The TEU comprises general provisions on citizenship of the Union, and the TFEU combines Union citizenship with the principle of non-discrimination on the grounds of nationality and contains a catalogue of rights granted to the Union citizen. Such a division of provisions seems to be justified by the lack of the TEU direct effect.[22] Accordingly, Article 9 TEU establishes citizenship of the Union and defines the Union citizen as an 'every national of a Member State'.[23] The Article states that Union citizenship is additional to national citizenship and does not replace it. This means that Union citizenship may be granted only to the citizens of EU Member States. According to Kadelbach (2013), citizenship of the Union creates a special relationship between the Union as an international organization and citizens of its Member States. However, as opposed to national citizenship, it imposes barely any obligations and offers a narrow catalogue of rights, listed in Article 20 TFEU.[24] Pudzianowska (2013) notices that

16 Judgment of the Court of 12 May 1998 in the case C-85/96 *María Martínez Sala v Freistaat Bayern*, ECLI:EU:C:1998:217.

17 Judgment of the Court of 24 November 1998 in the case C-274/96 *Criminal proceedings against Horst Otto Bickel and Urlich Franz*, ECLI:EU:C:1998:563.

18 Judgment of the Court of 20 September 2001in the case C-184/99 *Rudy Grzelczyk v Centre public d'aidesocialed' Ottignies-Louvain-la-Neuve*, ECLI:EU:C:2001:458.

19 Judgment of the Court of 8 March 2011 in the case C-34/09 *Gerardo Ruiz Zambrano v Office national de l'emploi (ONEm)*, ECLI:EU:C:2011:124.

20 OJ 2016 C 202, 7 June 2016.

21 Wróbel, Miąsik and Półtorak (eds.), 256.

22 Wróbel, Miąsik and Półtorak (eds.), 254.

23 The same is reaffirmed in Article 20(1) TFEU.

24 Stefan Kadelbach, *Union Citizenship*, New York University, School of Law, 2003, 15–8.

in the light of international law, Union citizenship does not establish any legal relationship between an individual and the EU. Outside the territory of the Union, an individual is not subject to citizenship of the Union, but it is invariably attached to national citizenship which creates the legal basis for the establishment of the rights and obligations of a state of citizenship towards other states and international organizations.[25]

Not all Member State citizens automatically qualify as Union citizens. The Member States hold an exclusive competence to grant national citizenship and, as a consequence, citizenship of the Union. A special Declaration No. 2 on nationality of a Member State was attached to the Maastricht Treaty, on the basis of which the States were granted power to declare who should be considered their nationals for Union purposes.[26] The States may withhold Union citizenship under some circumstances.[27] In principle, third-country nationals who are not family members of the Union citizen are not granted Union citizenship. Therefore, having the status of non-EU citizens, they are not entitled to enjoy the benefits reserved for the Union citizens. They may in relevant circumstances refer to the rights granted to long-term residents under Directive 2003/109/EC[28] and based on non-discrimination principles set out in Directive 2000/43/EC.[29] Another important case when a Member State may withhold Union citizenship concerns residents of overseas territories located outside the EU. For long years, this situation concerned large groups of British overseas residents. After Brexit, it affects the residents of French and Danish territories. French overseas territories include the French Southern and Antarctic Lands with no permanent population and overseas collectivities whose residents are considered to be Union citizens. The Danish policy is not coherent in this respect. To illustrate, the residents of the Faroe Islands of Denmark became expressly excluded from Union citizenship under the Danish Accession Treaty,[30] at the same time the residents of Greenland were not subject to such exclusion under the Treaty and enjoy the status of Union citizens.[31] It is also

25 Dorota Pudzianowska, *Obywatelstwo w Procesie Zmian*, Wolters Kluwer, 2013, 274.
26 Declaration on nationality of a Member State, OJ C 191, 29 July 1992.
27 Judgment of the Court of 17 September 2002 in the case C-413/99 *Baumbast and R v Secretary of State for the Home Department*, ECLI:EU:C:2002:493, para. 31.
28 Council Directive 2003/109/EC of 25 November 2003 concerning the status of third-country nationals who are long-term residents. OJ L 16, 20 May 2011.
29 Council Directive 2000/43/EC of 29 June 2000 implementing the principle of equal treatment between persons irrespective of racial or ethnic origin. OJ L 180, 19 July 2000.
30 Protocol No. 2 to the 1972 Accession Treaty.
31 Protocol No. 4 to the 1972 Accession Treaty.

worth noting that stateless persons[32] are treated as third-country nationals under Article 67(2) TFEU.

The Union citizen is only such a Member State citizen whose legal situation is covered by EU substantive law. A Member State national and his or her family members who enjoy the right to move and reside freely within the territories of the Member States for profit-making or other purposes are undoubtedly considered to be Union citizens (Directive 2004/38/EC).[33] In principle, a citizen of any EU Member State in a purely internal situation was initially not considered to be the citizen of the Union in a legal and institutional sense.[34] However, growing tensions which emerged as a result of the limited scope of application of the citizenship provisions only to those citizens defined by the Court and excluding those who found themselves in a purely internal situation necessitated a change in the Court's approach. In a few of its judgments, the Court of Justice accepted that some situations fell within the citizenship provisions despite the lack of a cross-border element.[35]

In the long-awaited judgment in *Zambrano*[36] (2011), the Court of Justice confirmed that Article 20 TFEU reached beyond the right to move and reside and Directive 2004/38/EC. The case concerned Ruiz Zambrano, a Colombian who together with his wife, also Colombian, unlawfully resided and worked in Belgium. Despite that, he was employed full time for an unlimited period.[37] Mr Zambrano attempted to legalise his residence a few times, including use of the Belgian procedures available to him for acquiring Belgian nationality for his child.[38] The dispute arose

32 At the end of 2018, the UNHCR estimated the total number of stateless persons in the EU and Norway at nearly 400 thousand individuals. The highest number of stateless persons was noted in Latvia (more than 250 thousand, 12% of the population) and in Estonia (around 82 thousand, 6% of the population) Source: Statelessness in the European Union, https://ec.europa.eu/home-affairs/sites/homeaffairs/ files/00_eu_inform_statelessness_en.pdf [retrieved on 20 July 2020].

33 Directive 2004/38/EC of the European Parliament and of the Council of 29 April 2004 on the right of citizens of the Union and their family members to move and reside freely within the territory of the Member States amending Regulation (EEC) No. 1612/68 and repealing Directives 64/221/EEC, 68/360/EEC, 72/194/EEC, 73/148/EEC, 75/34/EEC, 75/35/EEC, 90/364/EEC, 90/365/EEC and 93/96/EEC (Text with EEA relevance). OJ L 158, 30 April 2004.

34 Mateusz Żuk, *Relacja między obywatelem Unii Europejskiej a swobodami rynku wewnętrznego*, Wydawnictwo C.H. Beck, Warszawa 2013, 1.

35 Case C-212/06 *Government of the French Community and Walloon Government v Flemish Government*; C-200/02 *Kunqian Catherine Zhu and Man Lavette Chen v Secretary of State for the Home Department.*

36 Judgment of the Court in the case C-34/09.

37 Judgment of the Court in the case C-34/09, para. 18.

38 Judgment of the Court in the case C-34/09, paras 21 and 23.

when Mr Zambrano applied for unemployment benefits and was rejected. In the face of a negative decision, Mr Zambrano addressed the *Tribunal du travail de Bruxelles* (Employment Tribunal) claiming that he enjoyed the right of residence under the Treaty. The Tribunal referred to the Court of Justice in order to clarify if Union citizenship applied in the case of Mr Zambrano. The Court ruled that two of Mr Zambrano's children who possessed Belgian nationality enjoyed the status of the Union citizen. Therefore, it stated that refusal to grant a right of residence and a work permit to a third-country national with dependent minor children in the Member State where those are nationals and reside constitutes 'deprivation of enjoyment of the substance of the rights' conferred by citizenship of the Union. The lack of Mr Zambrano's right of residence and employment permit would force his children to leave the territory of the Union.[39] The Court decided to preclude Belgium from refusing Mr Zambrano the right of residence and a work permit in the Member State where his minor children – citizens of the Union – resided and exercised their rights as the Union citizens. The judgment was a milestone step forward as it made it possible to rely on Article 20 TFEU with reference to an internal situation of a Member State.

3.2.2 The principle of non-discrimination on the grounds of nationality and citizenship of the Union

The principle of non-discrimination on the grounds of nationality has been incorporated into EU primary law since Article 7 of the Treaty establishing European Economic Community (TEEC).[40] The principle has exerted a normative force within the scope of the Treaty application and beyond that scope the Member States have enjoyed freedom. The Court of Justice has interpreted the principle of non-discrimination on the grounds of nationality extensively and shaped the way how it should be applied. In the years of the European Communities, the general prohibition of discrimination based on nationality played a marginal role next to the non-discrimination principles resulting from the internal market freedoms. Nevertheless, already at that time the Court clearly stated that the principle constituted a special expression of the principle of equal treatment of Member State citizens (*Cowan, Rene Hochstrass, Pastoors*).[41]

In the *Cowan*[42](1989) case, the Court of Justice recognised the prohibition of discrimination laid down in Article 7 TEEC as the right to equal treatment conferred

39 Judgment of the Court in the case C-34/09, paras 42 and 44.

40 Article 7 TEEC, later in Article 6(1) of the TEC, after the Amsterdam Treaty Article 12 TEC and in the Lisbon Treaty as Article 18 TFEU and Article 21(2) of the Charter.

41 Susanne K. Schmidt and Michael Blauberger, "Free movement and equal treatment in an unequal Union," *Journal of European Public Policy*, Vol. 25, 2018, 1391–402.

42 Judgment of the Court of 2 February 1989 in the case 186/87 *Ian William Cowan v Trésor public*, ECLI:EU:C:1989:47.

directly by Community law. The case analysed in the procedure for preliminary ruling initiated by *Tribunal de grande instance de Paris* concerned a dispute between the French Treasury and a British tourist, Ian William Cowan. Mr Cowan claimed compensation for an injury resulting from a violent assault he suffered at the exit of a metro station during his holiday in Paris. The French code of criminal proceedings guaranteed such compensation only to French nationals or foreign nationals of those states that had concluded a reciprocal agreement with France for the application of such provisions and the holders of a residence permit.[43] The Court of Justice held that prohibiting discrimination on the grounds of nationality meant that in a situation governed by the Community law, nationals of the other Member States should be placed entirely on an equal footing with nationals of the host State. As a result, Member States were prevented from granting criminal compensation subject to holding a residence permit[44] or making it dependent on the existence of a reciprocal agreement between the states.[45] The Court found a way to protect a tourist on the grounds of the freedom of movement and treated him as a recipient of services. Relying on that, the Court handed down that a person going to another Member State should be protected from harm in the host State on the same basis as nationals and persons residing there.[46] The *Cowan* case was a signal of the direction the Court wished to go to protect the rights of Member State citizens.

The introduction of Union citizenship in the Maastricht Treaty created solid legal grounds to apply the principle of non-discrimination on the grounds of nationality separately from internal market rules. Since then, the Court of Justice has consistently linked the principle to the concept of Union citizenship, in particular the right to move and reside freely. The epochal judgment in this area was issued in the *Martínez Sala*[47] (1998) case. It concerned the discriminatory treatment of German authorities against Maria Martínez Sala, a Spanish national, authorised to reside in Germany. Ms Martínez Sala was required to produce a formal residence permit issued by the national authorities to achieve a child-raising allowance for her child. At the same time, the German authorities expected from German nationals only to be permanently or ordinarily resident in the state. When Ms Martínez Sala filed an application (January 1993), she was not professionally active. She had worked in Germany at intervals in the years between 1976 and 1989 and for one month in 1989. She was lawfully residing in Germany and, therefore, could invoke both Article 8(2) TEC and Article 6 TEC which guaranteed non-discrimination on the grounds of nationality. The Court considered two major legal

43 Judgment of the Court in the case 186/87, para. 4.
44 Judgment of the Court in the case 186/87, para. 10.
45 Judgment of the Court in the case 186/87, para. 12.
46 Judgment of the Court in the case 186/87, para. 17.
47 Judgment of the Court in the case C-85/96.

issues of the case. Firstly, it analysed whether the German authorities had been authorised to demand from Ms Martínez Sala a residence permit to apply for a child-raising allowance. Secondly, it reviewed whether she was entitled to receive a social benefit as the unemployed. The Court endorsed the reasoning that Union citizenship was of a fundamental nature and ruled that while moving to or residing in another Member State, the Union citizen should be in the same legal position as the nationals residing in their homeland (in this case Germans living in Germany). As regards the first question, the Court held that Community law precluded any Member State from requiring nationals of another Member State authorised to reside on their territory to produce a formal permit in order to receive a child-raising allowance.[48] As to the second question, the Court claimed to have insufficient information to decide in the matter. For this reason, it instructed the referring national court to determine whether Ms Martínez Sala fell within *ratione personae* of Article 48 TEC, and whether on the grounds of Regulation No. 1612/68[49] or Regulation No. 1408/71[50] she could enjoy the rights of a worker based on the fact that she used to work.[51] At the same time, the Court pointed out that Ms Martínez Sala should enjoy the status of an employed person once it was established that she was covered on a compulsory or an optional basis by German general or special social security.[52] The judgment in *Martínez Sala* was a breakthrough as for the first time, the Court of Justice combined the provisions on citizenship of the Union with the non-discrimination principle in order to combat the limitations imposed by the Member States on the citizens of other Member States.[53]

The Lisbon Treaty integrated the principle of non-discrimination on the grounds of nationality with the rights attached to Union citizenship. The principle of non-discrimination on the grounds of nationality is regulated in Article 18 TFEU. Above that, the norm permeates many other Treaty provisions constituting the normative and axiological basis for activities of every-day life performed by the Union citizen. Although the principle is not *expressis verbis* included in the catalogue of the rights entrenched in citizenship of the Union, Article 18 is directly

48 Judgment of the Court in the case C-85/96, para. 3 of the Operative Part.

49 Regulation (EEC) No. 1612/68 of the Council of 15 October 1968 on freedom of movement for workers within the Community. OJ L 257, 30 April 2004, in force until 15 June 2011.

50 Regulation (EEC) No. 1408/71 of the Council of 14 June 1971 on the application of social security schemes to employed persons and their families moving within the Community. OJ L 149, 1 May 2010.

51 Judgment of the Court in the case C-85/96, para. 2 of the Operative Part.

52 Judgment of the Court in the case C-85/96, para. 44.

53 Some of the cases included: C-184/99 *Grzelczyk, C-148/02,* C-158/07 *Förster,* C-103/08 *Arthur Gottwald.* Source: Wróbel, Miąsik and Półtorak (eds.), 254.

applicable, so, it can be adduced by the Union citizen before national courts.[54] The subjective scope of Article 18 TFEU may be determined only in conjunction with the provisions on Union citizenship. Article 20(2) TFEU stipulates that the rights granted to the Union citizen must be exercised in accordance with the conditions and limits defined by the Treaties and the measures adopted thereunder.[55] The integration of Article 18 TFEU and Article 20 TFEU excludes the application of non-discrimination on the grounds of nationality with reference to third-country nationals.

3.2.3 The rights of the Union citizen under the Lisbon Treaty

The TFEU includes the catalogue of rights granted to the Union citizen. The rights are listed in Article 20(2) TFEU and they include:

> "(a) the right to move and reside freely within the territory of the Member States;
> (b) the right to vote and to stand as candidates in elections to the European Parliament and in municipal elections in their Member State of residence, under the same conditions as nationals of that State;
> c) the right to enjoy, in the territory of a third country in which the Member State of which they are nationals is not represented, the protection of the diplomatic and consular authorities of any Member State on the same conditions as the nationals of that State;
> (d) the right to petition the European Parliament, to apply to the European Ombudsman, and to address the institutions and advisory bodies of the Union in any of the Treaty languages and to obtain a reply in the same language".[56]

Every citizen of the Union is entitled to rely on the rights listed in Article 20(2) TFEU as the norms directly applicable under the provision that the rights are subject to conditions and limitations defined by the Treaties or any measures adopted thereunder, in particular the guarantee of non-discrimination on the grounds of nationality (Article 18 TFEU).[57] The above rights are further developed in Articles 21–24 TFEU. Moreover, Article 25 TFEU clarifies that the above catalogue is non-exhaustive and open, which may be justified by the fact that citizenship of the Union is perceived as an evolving concept which may be extended or strengthened.[58]

---

54 Anna Zawidzka-Łojek, "Źródła prawa antydyskryminacyjnego", in: Anna Zawidzka-Łojek and Aleksandra Szczerba-Zawada (eds.), *Prawo antydyskryminacyjne Unii Europejskiej*, EuroPrawo, Warszawa, 45.

55 Wróbel, Miąsik and Półtorak (eds.), 255.

56 OJ C 202, 7 June 2016.

57 Wróbel, Miąsik and Półtorak (eds.), 254.

58 Wróbel, Miąsik and Półtorak (eds.), 266

A parallel catalogue of the Union citizen's rights entrenched in the TFEU is reflected in the Charter – Title V 'Citizen's rights' (Articles 36–46). Their inclusion in the Charter lifts the rights to the status of fundamental rights in the light of the Union law and extends their objective scope of some rights from the Union citizen onto every individual irrespective of their nationality. The analysis of language rights as fundamental rights set out in the Charter constitutes a separate matter investigated in chapter 4 of this dissertation.

Of rights enshrined in Article 20(2) TFEU, only subparagraph (d) grants the Union citizen specific rights in respect of language use. This is the right to use any Treaty language to petition the European Parliament, to apply to the European Ombudsman, and to address the Union institutions and to obtain a reply in the same language. The other rights granted to the Union citizen in Article 20(2) TFEU do not mention any linguistic aspects. However, it must be assumed that the rights granted may generate a multitude of situations related to the use of languages or language-related requirements for the Union citizen. By the same token, examination of such rights is certainly a good starting point for specifying the scope and nature of language rights attached to citizenship of the Union. Special attention must be directed to the right to move and reside freely. The right to enjoy diplomatic and consular protection of any Member State while staying in the territory of a third country implies some language rights, in particular the right for a translator. At the same time, it should be noted that the right to vote and to stand as candidates in elections to the European Parliament and in municipal elections in their Member State of residence under the same conditions as nationals of that State does not seem to include any linguistic aspects which may generate claims of individuals. Therefore, the right is omitted in the analysis within this dissertation.

Some rights of the Union citizen may also be derived from the TEU. These are the provisions aiming to make the Union as open and as close as possible to its communities and express the Union's respect for the principle of democracy. In view of linguistic aspects, notice should be taken of the right to participate in the Union's democratic life (Article 10 TEU), in particular the right of access to the EU documents (Article 15 TFEU), and the right to submit the European Citizens' Initiative (Article 11(4) TEU).

3.3 Language rights attached to the right to move and reside freely and the principle of non-discrimination on the grounds of nationality

3.3.1 The right to move and reside freely

3.3.1.1 The concept of the right to move and reside freely

The right to move and reside freely incorporated in Article 21 TFEU (formerly Article 18 TEC) implies that any domestic solutions of the Member States which would 'discourage' citizens from exercising the right should be excluded.[59] The right was characterised by Advocate General Colomer in his opinion to the *Commission v Belgium*[60] case as having four main features contributing to the privileged status of the Union citizen. Firstly, the right constitutes a personal guarantee which must be respected by all the Member States. Secondly, the right exerts a direct effect on the Union citizen and is therefore immediately applicable. Thirdly, the right is not an absolute one and, therefore, may be subject to some limitations and conditions resulting from the Treaty or relevant secondary law. Finally, the right should be interpreted broadly, which means a highly restrictive interpretation of its limitations. These should be confined to such conditions which do not undermine the freedoms and are exercised in the name of the principle of proportionality.[61]

The major aspects of the right were analysed by the Court of Justice in the landmark *Baumbast*[62] (2002) case. The case concerned the family of Baumbast: Mrs Baumbast, a Colombian national, and Mr Baumbast, a German national, and their two daughters, the elder, Maria Fernanda Sarmiento, Mrs Baumbast's natural daughter, a Colombian national and the younger, Idanella Baumbast, having dual German and Colombian nationality. The Baumbasts resided in the United Kingdom where Mr Baumbast first was employed and later pursued his own economic activity. His company failed and despite efforts to find employment in the UK, he did not succeed. He was employed by German companies in China and Lesotho. Mrs and Mr Baumbast owned a house in the UK and their daughters attended schools there. Mrs Baumbast applied for indefinite leave to remain in the UK for herself and for other members of her family but her application was refused by the British Secretary of State (1996). In 1998, the refusal was brought before the Immigration Adjudicator in the UK which found that pursuant to Directive 90/634/EEC[63] Mr Baumbast was neither a worker nor a person having general right of residence. As regards the children, the Adjudicator decided that they enjoyed an independent right of residence under Article 12 of Regulation No. 1612/68 governing the freedom of movement for workers, and that Mrs Baumbast enjoyed a right of residence for a period coterminous with that during which her children attended schools in the UK.[64]

---

59 Wróbel, Miąsik and Półtorak (eds.), 265.

60 Opinion of Advocate General Ruiz-Jarabo Colomer of 25 October 2005 in the case C-408/03, ECLI:EU:C:2005:638.

61 Opinion of Advocate General Ruiz-Jarabo Colomer in the case C-408/03, para. 33.

62 Judgment of the Court of 17 September 2002 in the case C-413/99 *Baumbast and R v Secretary of State for the Home Department*, ECLI:EU:C:2002:493.

63 Council Directive 90/364/EEC of 28 June 1990 on the right of residence. OJ L 180, 13 July 1990, in force until 29 April 2006.

64 Judgment of the Court in the case C-413/99, paras 16–21.

In its judgment, the Court dispelled doubts in respect of direct effect as well as limitations and conditions to the right to move and reside freely. By that time, the direct effect of Article 21 TFEU was not clear, mainly owing to the limitations and conditions attached to it and the fact that the Court referred to the Article directly only when no specific provision existed or when a specific provision could not be applied (*Bickel and Franz*). In *Baumbast* (later also in *Commission v Belgium*),[65] the Court held that the right was directly effective under the Treaty. Accordingly, Mr Baumbast as a citizen of the Union could rely on Article 18(1) TEC in a dispute before the Court of Justice and a national court (personal guarantee). Moreover, the Court admitted that the right to reside within the territory of another Member State was conferred subject to limitations and conditions laid down in the Treaty and the measures adopted to give them effect. Moreover, the Court formulated the principle that the imposed limitations and conditions must be applied highly restrictively in compliance with the general principles of Community law and collective values of its Member States as well as the principle of proportionality.[66] Moreover, such limitations and conditions should be interpreted in a broader context of general human rights, in particular the right to protect family (the same approach was also adopted in C-*200/02 Chen, C-215/03 Oulane, C-258/04 Ioannidis, C-1/05 Jia, C-50/06 Commission v the Netherlands*).[67]

3.3.1.2 Limitations to the right to move and reside freely

Limitations to the right to move and reside freely are set out in the Treaty and secondary law constituting measures adopted to give them effect.[68] Article 52(1) TFEU stipulates that Member States may exclude or limit the exercise of the right if it is justified on the grounds of Member State's public policy, public security, and public health.[69] In the case of *Grzelczyk*[70] and in the joint cases of *Orfanopoulos* and *Olivieri*,[71] the Court of Justice confirmed that limitations to the right to move and reside freely must be interpreted restrictively and with respect to the conditions specified in Article 52(1) TFEU. Specific criteria and conditions for exercising the

65 Judgment of the Court of 23 March 2006 in the case C-147/03 *Commission v Kingdom of Belgium*, ECLI:EU:C:2006:192.

66 Judgment of the Court in the case C-413/99, para. 15.

67 Wróbel, Miąsik and Półtorak (eds.), 66.

68 Freedom of establishment and freedom to provide services, http://www.europarl.europa.eu /factsheets/en/sheet/40/freedom-of-establishment-and-freedom-to-provide-services [retrieved on 27 August 2019].

69 OJ C 202, 7 June 2016.

70 Judgment of the Court in the case C-184/99, para.2.

71 Judgment of the Court of 29 April 2004 in joined cases C-482/01 *Georgios Orfanopoulos and Others* and C-493/01 *Raffaele Oliveri v Land Baden-Württemberg*, ECLI:EU:C:2004:262.

right to move and reside freely are enshrined in Directive 2004/38/EC (amending inter alia Directive 90/364/EEC),[72] which aimed to provide details on the right of the Union citizens and their families to move and reside freely within the territories of the Member States.[73] The Directive restricts the right in two particular cases: firstly, unreasonable burden on the social security system of the host Member State (Article 7) and secondly, subject to the Member State's public policy, public security or public health (Article 27).[74]

Article 7 of the Directive stipulates that the Union citizen has the right of residence on the territory of another Member State for a period longer than 3 months if he or she is a worker or a self-employed person, has sufficient resources not to become a social burden on the social assistance of the host Member State or has valid insurance cover.[75] This leaves no doubt that a distinction between economically active and inactive citizens remains in place, as the latter do not enjoy all the rights granted under Article 21 TFEU. In order to take full advantage of the right to move and reside freely, the Union citizen needs to comply with the conditions of self-sufficiency, which prevent him from burdening the social system of the host State. What should be noted is the fact that the burden of proof in respect of the self-sufficiency requirements falls upon the host State, not the citizen.[76] Such an approach implies that the norms of the Directive should be interpreted in line with the "civic-minded" understanding and enforcement.[77]

The issue of limitations to the right to move and reside freely in relation to the self-sufficiency condition was considered by the Court of Justice in the already mentioned *Baumbast* case. The Court relied on Article 1(1) of Directive 90/364/EEC which allowed a Member State to require from nationals of another Member State that they be covered by sickness insurance and have sufficient resources. Through this, they could avoid a situation in which other Member State citizens would become a burden on the social assistance system of the host Member State during the period of residence.[78] In the case of Mr Baumbast, it was clear for the Court that he had sufficient resources within the meaning of Directive. He worked and, therefore, lawfully resided in the UK as an employed person and later as a

72 OJ L 158/77, 30 April 2004.

73 Kadelbach, 466.

74 Solange Maslowski, "The Expulsion of European Union Citizens from the Host Member State: Legal Grounds and Practice", *Central and Eastern European Migration Review*, Vol. 4/2, 2015, 62.

75 OJ L 158/77, 29 April 2004, Article 7.

76 Alina Tryfonidou, *Impact of Union Citizenship on the EU's Market Freedoms*, Hart Publishing, 109–16.

77 Aleksander Cieśliński, *Konstrukcja Prawna Swobód Rynku Wewnętrznego Unii Europejskiej*, Prawnicza i Ekonomiczna Biblioteka Cyfrowa, 2013, 94–5.

78 Judgment of the Court in the case C-413/99, para. 87.

self-employed person. During that period, his family also resided in the UK and neither Mr Baumbast nor his family became a burden on the UK's public finances. Moreover, both Mr Baumbast and his family members had comprehensive sickness insurance in another Member State of the Union (i.e. in Germany).[79] The Court concluded that in those circumstances the fact that the UK refused to allow Mr Baumbast to exercise the right of residence only on the basis that his sickness insurance in Germany did not cover emergency treatment in the UK, as a host Member State, amounted to a disproportionate interference with the exercise of the right of residence and it was not an objectively justified limitation to the right to move and reside freely.[80]

Similarly to Article 7, Article 27 of Directive 2004/38 allows a Member State to restrict the free movement and residence of persons in the case of threat to public policy, public security, and public health. The measures taken by Member States must aim to ensure the stability of the state and its institutions, prevent disturbance of social order and preserve the territorial integrity of a Member State.[81] Any restrictions imposed by a Member State due to potential threats must be interpreted strictly.[82] The Court of Justice followed such reasoning in *Gaydarov*[83] (2012), where it restricted the right of the Union citizen, who was convicted of a criminal offence of narcotic drug trafficking in another State, based on the public security grounds. In joint cases of *C-331/16* and *C-366/16*,[84] the Court held that a Member State could automatically consider a Union citizen or his or her family member, who in the past was subject to a decision excluding him from refugee status, to create risk to the State. The mere presence of such an individual may justify the adoption by the Member States measures on the grounds of public policy and public security. Under its public policy, a Member State may reserve some areas for its nationals only. These in particular include the rights to vote and stand as a candidate in national elections, to be employed in the public service, and to

79 Judgment of the Court in the case C-413/99, para. 92.

80 Judgment of the Court in the case C-413/99, para. 93.

81 Communication from the Commission to the European Parliament and the Council on guidance for better transposition and application of Directive 2004/38/EC on the right of citizens of the Union and their family members to move and reside freely within the territory of the Member States COM(2009) 313, 10.

82 Judgment of the Court of 28 October 1975 in the case 36/75 *Roland Rutili v Ministre de l'intérieur*, 28 October 1975, para. 27, ECLI:EU:C:1975:137.

83 Judgment of the Court of 17 November 2011 in the case C-430/10 *Hristo Gaydarov v Direktor na Glavna direktsia 'Ohranitelna politsia' pri Ministerstvo na vatreshnite raboti*, ECLI:EU:C:2011:749.

84 Judgment of the Court of 2 May 2018 in joined cases of C-331/16 and C-366/16 *K. v Staatssecretaris van Veiligheid en Justitie (C-331/16), H.F v Belgische Staat (C-366/16).*

receive social assistance benefits without any limitation whatsoever.[85] Despite the limitations, Tryfonidou claims that the exclusion of some specific areas earmarked for the nationals does not change the fact that the Union citizen exercising the right to move and reside freely has been brought to a position very close to that enjoyed by the nationals of the host State.[86]

3.3.1.3 The right to move and reside freely vs internal market freedoms

Free movement of persons is the cornerstone of the EU internal market. The concept was introduced in the TEEC and could be enjoyed only by workers, service providers and self-employed persons conducting their business activity (freedom of establishment and freedom to provide services). The idea behind the freedom was to give Member State citizens an opportunity to live, work, study, and conduct their business, and eradicate barriers in free movement. The internal market freedom has guaranteed the rights of movement and residence for workers and self-employed persons, the rights of entry and residence for their family members, the right to work in another Member State and to be treated there on an equal footing with the host State nationals.[87] As the concept had only an economic dimension, an individual was perceived as *homo economicus* and was protected by the Community law only to the extent to which that served building the internal market and preventing from any discrimination and limitations related to the business activity.[88] In the 80s, the pure economic context of the internal market freedoms triggered the concepts of 'market citizenship' and 'market citizens'. 'Market citizens' were those individuals who were addressees and beneficiaries of the internal market freedoms. The concept of 'market citizenship' was deemed to be the only effective tool to build an internal market.[89]

---

85 Alina Tryfonidou, *Reconceptualising the EU's Market Freedoms as Union Citizenship Rights. Towards a Citizenship Right to Pursue an Economic Activity in a Cross-Border Context?,* 2011, 9, https://eustudies.org/assets/files/papers/Tryfonidou%20-%20EUSA%20 Paper%202011.pdf [retrieved on 21 July 2020].

86 Tryfonidou, *Reconceptualising the EU's Market Freedoms as Union Citizenship Rights. Towards a Citizenship Right to Pursue an Economic Activity in a Cross-Border Context?,* 9.

87 Zawidzka- Łojek, Anna and Adam Łazowski (eds.), *Podręcznik Prawa Unii Europejskiej. Instytucje i porządek prawny.* Prawo materialne, Instytut Wydawniczy EuroPrawo, 2017.

88 Amanda Root, *Market Citizenship: Experiments in Democracy and Globalization*, Sage, 2007, 85.

89 Robert Grzeszczak, "Dwie Narracje o Obywatelstwie Unijnym – Obywatel Rynku i Obywatel Unii Europejskiej", in: Andrzej Bator (et al.) *Współczesna Koncepcje*

The introduction of the notion of Union citizenship automatically enjoyed by every national of a Member State underpinned the legal status of persons enjoying the right to move and reside. As a result, the right to move and reside could be raised by every citizen of the Union, regardless of their professional status or economic activity.[90] Citizenship of the Union became a fundamental status constituting the basis for claiming specific rights by all the Union citizens. As elaborated on by Tryfonidou,[91] as a result of citizenship of the Union, internal market freedoms should be re-read and re-conceptualised. As the Union citizen status is of a fundamental nature, the internal market freedom of movement should be understood as a citizenship right in the economic sphere granted by virtue of holding nationality of one of the Member States. Construed in such a way, the internal market freedoms constitute one aspect of Union citizenship which includes the right to pursue any economic activity in the EU cross-border context.[92]

A need to re-interpret internal market freedoms in the light of Union citizenship has been manifested in a handful of cases considered by the Court of Justice. In *Bickel and Franz,* the Court combined the right to freely move and reside with the internal market free movement of persons.[93] Thereby, the Court integrated standards regarding the EU citizen's right to move and reside for non-profit purposes with the freedom of movement of service providers for profit purposes.[94] The Court adopted the same approach towards a lorry driver enjoying the status of a service provider protected under Article 56 TFEU (Mr Bickel) and a tourist (Mr Franz), both defendants in the case. The Court treated them equally as Union citizens exercising their right to freely more and reside arising out of Article 21 TFEU. The Court's ruling in the case proved that the status of the Union citizen strengthened the interpretation of internal market freedoms.[95] Such an approach clearly showed that Union citizenship expanded the scope of beneficiaries of the freedom of movement from a narrow group of 'market citizens' to all the Union citizens.[96]

Ochrony Wolności i Praw Podstawowych, Prawnicza i Ekonomiczna Biblioteka Cyfrowa, 2013, 82.

90 Making EU citizens' rights a reality: national courts enforcing freedom of movement and related rights, 2018, 9, https://fra.europa.eu/sites/default/files/fra_uploads/fra-2018-making-rights-a-reality-freedom-of-movement_en.pdf [retrieved on 4 February 2020].

91 Tryfonidou, *Reconceptualising the EU's Market Freedoms as Union Citizenship Rights. Towards a Citizenship Right to Pursue an Economic Activity in a Cross-Border Context?*, 1–35.

92 Tryfonidou, *Impact of Union Citizenship on the EU's Market Freedoms*, 11.

93 Judgment of the Court in the case C-274/96.

94 Żuk, 112–3.

95 Cieśliński, *Konstrukcja Prawna Swobód Rynku Wewnętrznego Unii Europejskiej*, 93.

96 Grzeszczak, 182.

Moreover, the concept enlarged the scope of application of non-discrimination on the grounds of nationality beyond workers.[97]

3.3.2 Language rights attached to the right to move and reside freely and the principle of non-discrimination on the grounds of nationality

3.3.2.1 The right of access to education in one's own language

The citizen's right to move and reside freely read jointly with the principle of non-discrimination on the grounds of nationality may generate a number of language rights for the Union citizen. The analyses of the Court of Justice case-law and the Union legislation make it possible to distinguish three specific language rights: the right of access to education in one's own language, the right to use one's own language before Member State courts, and the right to choose one's name and surname. Moreover, the right to move and reside in conjunction with non-discrimination on the grounds of nationality creates the legal basis for the language rights of workers and self-employed persons. This section focuses on the examination of the above rights and any limitations thereto.

Firstly, Union citizens and their family members should be entitled to move and reside under the objective conditions of freedom and dignity.[98] Such conditions may include the right of equal and non-discriminatory access to education. This equal access to education by the Union citizens may imply education in a language other than the official language of the host Member State, assuming that it is one of the EU official languages. Guaranteeing such a right in the Union multilingual context where the Union moving citizens speak a variety of languages is certainly not easy. This situation may certainly occur often, and whether the right may be satisfied or not in principle depends on the national regulations.

The right of equal access to education became an important component of the EU citizen's right to move and reside freely. As a result, the question arose whether the right, if analysed in conjunction with the principle of non-discrimination on the grounds of nationality, implies the right of access to education of the Union citizen in the official language of another Member State. Combining the right to education and the principle of non-discrimination resulted in a 'competence struggle' which arose between the Member States and the Commission.[99] It is clear that

97 European Union Agency for Fundamental Rights, *Making EU Citizens' Rights a Reality: National Courts Enforcing Freedom of Movement and Related Rights*, 2018, 15.

98 OJ L 158/77, 30 April 2004, Recital 5 in the Preamble.

99 Judgment of the Court of 1 July 2004 in the case C-65/03 *Commission v Belgium*, ECLI:EU:C:2004:402 and judgment of the Court of 7 July 2005 in the case C-147/03 *Commission v Austria*, ECLI:EU:C:2005:427.

the Union's powers in the area of education are only supportive. Article 6 TFEU stipulates that in the field of education and vocational training the Union has competence to carry out actions to support, coordinate, and supplement the actions of the Member States.[100] In addition, Articles 165 and 166 TFEU include the relevant provisions confirming the supportive role of the EU in this field. Pursuant to the subsidiarity principle, the EU Member States specify their education and training policies, and the Union may take measures in this area which must harmonise with the relevant Member State regulations. However, at the same time the Union is entitled to intervene into such areas of education which concern a moving Union citizen, in order to guarantee that he or she is not discriminated against on the grounds of nationality, and enjoys equal access to education.[101] The competence struggle has not been resolved yet, and it remains unclear who has the authority to regulate the right of access to education in the context of individuals who travel to another Member State to study and who exercises their right to free movement and residence with their families.[102]

There are no legal grounds either in the Treaties or in the secondary legislation supporting the statement that education must be provided in a particular language. A key secondary law instrument referring to the right of access to education is the Racial Quality Directive (Directive 2000/43/EC).[103] Importantly, the Directive does not refer to the concept of Union citizenship or the principle of non-discrimination on the grounds of nationality in any way whatsoever, but it implements the principle of equal treatment *inter alia* in education between persons irrespective of their racial and ethnic origin. The Directive refers to the principles of liberty, democracy, respect for human rights and fundamental freedoms and the Member States constitutional traditions rather than to the right of free movement and residence.[104] It should be noted that Article 3(1)(g) of the Directive obliges the public and private sectors of the Member States education systems to promote social inclusion so that the children of adults having different racial and ethnic origin can have equal access to a Member State education system and receive equal treatment in the course of the education process. The Directive is silent in respect of any guarantees concerning the language in which education should be provided.

100 OJ C202, 7 June 2016.

101 Urszula Stępkowska, "Edukacja, kształcenie zawodowe, młodzież i sport", in: Jan Barcz (ed.) *Polityki Unii Europejskiej: Polityki Społeczne Aspekty Prawne*, Vol. XXVII, 2010, 58–63.

102 Egle Dagilyte, *The Right to Education and Free Movement of Persons: Whose Right Is It and How Does the EU Protect It?*, https://www.academia.edu/1665538/The_Right_to_Education_and _Free_ Movement_of_Persons_Whose_Right_is_it_and _how_does_the_EU_Protect_it [retrieved on 10 July 2018], 2.

103 OJ L 180, 19 July 2000.

104 OJ L 180, 19 July 2000, para. 2 of the Preamble.

The tensions between the exercise of the right of equal access to education in the context of the right to move and reside freely and the principle of non-discrimination on the grounds of nationality have been examined in a handful of cases brought before the Court of Justice. In *Commission v Belgium,*[105] *Commission v Austria*[106] and *Bressol v Chaverot,*[107] the Court analysed only one aspect of the right of equal access to education. In all the three cases, non-nationals had to satisfy more difficult entrance conditions in order to be admitted to universities. Both Belgium and Austria limited access to free medical education by establishing quotas.[108] The Court of Justice held that different treatment of nationals of the host Member State and nationals of another Member State amounted to the infringement of the principle of non-discrimination on the grounds of nationality. All the three cases concerned financial aspects of the citizen's rights of equal access to education, not the right to be educated in a particular language.

Both the Union's lack of exclusive competence in the field of education and the case-law of the Court of Justice in the above cases have exposed a general question on the nature of linguistic aspects of the right of equal access to education in the EU. The question is whether the right to education in one's own language should be treated as a fundamental human right, or whether it should be treated as a right which is not absolute, binding only in the EU and conditional upon Union citizenship.[109] Certainly, the former seems to be the right answer. A human rights-based approach to the right to education is widely recognised in a number of international normative instruments elaborated by the UN[110] and the CoE.[111] It is based on the principle of non-discrimination which guarantees education without any discrimination, including discrimination based on language. Moreover, the fact that the right to education and the right to freely move and reside are equally protected in the Charter as the norms of the same value, supports the argument to analyse

---

105 Judgment of the Court in the case C-65/03.

106 Judgment of the Court in the case C-147/03.

107 Judgment of the Court of 13 April 2010 in the case C-73/08 *Nicolas Bressol and Others and Céline Chaverot and Others v Gouvernement de la Communautéfrançaise,* ECLI:EU:C:2010:181.

108 Dagilyte, 1–5.

109 Dagilyte, 9.

110 Universal Declaration of Human Rights (1948), UNESCO Discrimination against Discrimination in Education (1962), International Covenant on Economic, Social and Cultural Rights (1976), Convention on the Rights of the Child (1990).

111 European Convention for the Protection of Human Rights and Fundamental Freedom (1953) and Protocol to the Convention, the European Charter for Regional and Minority Languages, the Framework Convention for the Protection of National Minorities (1998).

the linguistic aspects of the right of access to education in one's own language as a fundamental right.[112]

3.3.2.2 *The right to use one's own language before Member State courts*

The issue of language use before Member State courts was analysed for the first time by the Court of Justice in the pre-Union citizenship era in the *Mutsch*[113] (1985) case. Mr Mutsch, a Luxembourg national residing in a German-speaking municipality of Belgium, was fined *in absentia* by the Belgian criminal court *Tribunal Correctionnel.* He applied to have the judgment set aside on the grounds that the proceedings should take place in German in compliance with the Belgian Law on the use of languages in the courts of 15 June 1935. The court of appeals *Cour D'Appel* was uncertain whether the right to use a German language in the criminal proceedings was granted only to Belgian citizens or it could be extended to persons enjoying the right of free movement of workers. It referred to the Court of Justice for a preliminary ruling. The Court held that Mr Mutsch should be treated on an equal footing with the nationals of Belgium who, if accused under Belgian Law, had the right to request that the proceedings before the criminal court be held in German.[114]

While analysing the right to use languages in criminal proceedings in the *Mutsch* case, the Court of Justice based its reasoning on the principle of free movement of workers, as laid down in Article 38 TEC and in Regulation No. 1612/68. The Court stated that "a worker who was a national of another Member State and habitually resided in another Member State was entitled, under the same conditions as a worker who was a national of the host Member State, to require that criminal proceedings against him take place in a language other than the language normally used in proceedings before the court which tries him".[115] The Court stressed that in a Community "based on the principles of free movement of persons and freedom of establishment, the protection of the linguistic rights and privileges of individuals is of particular importance".[116] It justified that the above right played an important role in the integration of a migrant worker and his family into the host State and thus in achieving the objective of free movement of workers.[117]

112 Dagilyte, 19–20.
113 Judgment of the Court of 11 July 1985 in the case C 37/84 *Criminal proceedings against Robert Heinrich Maria Mutsch*, ECLI:EU:C:1985:335.
114 Judgment of the Court in the case C 37/84, para. 3.
115 Judgment of the Court in the case C 37/84, para. 2 of the Summary.
116 Judgment of the Court in the case C 37/84, para. 11.
117 Judgment of the Court in the case C 37/84, para. 16.

It is important that, in its judgment, the Court classified the right to use a minority language in criminal proceedings before the court as a 'social advantage', within the meaning assigned in Article 7(2) of Regulation No. 1612/68. Social advantages comprised all such advantages which were generally granted to national workers primarily because of their objective status of workers and by virtue of the mere fact of their residence on the national territory. Although the right to use a given language in criminal proceedings was granted only to a person having the status of a worker, the Court's understanding of the right indicated the direction it wished to follow in this area. Moreover, such categorisation of the right was an impulse for inserting the right into the broader category of social rights which later became strongly affected by citizenship of the Union.[118]

More than a decade later when Union citizenship was already in force, in the *Bickel and Franz*[119] (1998) case, the Court had to decide on the right to use languages in criminal proceedings before the Member State court. Based on the Italian rules, Mr Bickel and Mr Franz, both of German nationality, were denied the right to have the criminal proceedings conducted in German in a German-speaking Italian region of Bolzano despite the fact that the competent Italian courts were in a position to conduct proceedings in German without additional complications and costs.[120] The reason was that they failed to satisfy the residence requirement. The District Magistrates' Court in Bolzano *Pretura Circondariale, Sezione Distaccata di Silandro* was not certain about the interpretation of the principle of non-discrimination on the grounds of nationality, the right of movement and residence and the freedom to provide services. It filed a reference for preliminary ruling to the Court of Justice and asked if another Member State national should be granted the right to have criminal proceedings conducted against him in another language if nationals of the host State enjoyed the right in the same circumstances. The Court of Justice ruled that the fundamental status of the Union citizen placed Mr Bickel, as a service provider, and Mr Franz, as a tourist visiting the Italian Province of Bolzano, in the same position as individuals exercising their right to move and reside freely. Regardless of their economic status, they both could rely upon their fundamental status of Union citizens and were entitled to treatment no less favourable than that accorded to nationals of the host State as far as the use of languages is concerned.[121]

The Court stated that "the right conferred by national rules to have criminal proceedings conducted in a language other than the principal language of the State falls within the scope of the Treaty and must comply with Article 6 TEC"[122] and

118 Bodnar, "Obywatelstwo UE a Ochrona Praw Podstawowych", 51.

119 Judgment of the Court of 24 November 1998 in the case C-274/96 *Criminal proceedings against Horst Otto Bickel and Ulrich Franz*. ECLI:EU:C:1998:563.

120 Judgment of the Court in the case C-274/96, para. 30.

121 Judgment of the Court in the case C-274/96, para. 16.

122 Judgment of the Court in the case C-274/96, Summary, para. 30.

freedom of movement of persons (Article 8A TEC). In the Court's judgment, the right could not be narrowed only to the nationals who were residents of the Province of Bolzano and members of its German-speaking community as this would go against Article 6 TEC.[123] At the same time, the Court admitted that, in principle, criminal legislation and the rules of criminal procedure "are matters for which the Member States are responsible, Community law sets limits to their powers in that respect. Accordingly, domestic legislative provisions may not discriminate against persons to whom Community law grants the right to equal treatment or restrict the fundamental freedoms guaranteed by Community law".[124] The Court pointed out that the right to have proceedings conducted in German was not conferred upon all Italians, but only upon a specific group. In fact, languages other than the official languages of Member States are admitted to court proceedings in those regions of Member States where other languages have official status. In order to know what the objective scope of non-discrimination on the grounds of nationality is, the national court must first determine whether the rules genuinely give rise to discrimination and identify the group of persons discriminated against. Finally, it has to find out whether such discrimination was justifiable by reference to objective references.[125]

A significant step forward in respect of the language rules applicable before Member State courts was made in the *Rüffer*[126] (2014) case, where the Court of Justice extended the right to use a minority language to the civil proceedings. The case concerned the civil lawsuit between Ms Rüffer, a German national injured in a skiing accident in a German-speaking Province of Bolzano in Italy and Ms Pokorná, a Czech national, sued for causing a harmful event. Ms Rüffer used German as a language of proceedings and Ms Pokorná submitted her defence in the same language and raised no objection as to the choice of German as a language of the case.[127] The competent national court in Bolzano *Landesgericht Bozen* raised an objection against the choice of the language and decided to stay the proceedings in order to refer to the Court of Justice for a preliminary ruling. The referring court asked if Articles 18 and 21 TFEU precluded the application of provisions of national law which granted the right to use the German language in civil proceedings only to Italian citizens domiciled in the Province of Bolzano, but not to nationals of other EU Member States.[128] In its reasoning, the Court of Justice invoked the *Bickel and Franz* judgment. The Court acknowledged that the

123 Judgment of the Court in the case C-274/96, para. 21.

124 Judgment of the Court in the case C-274/96, Summary, para. 5.

125 Judgment of the Court in the case C-274/96, para. 22.

126 Judgment of the Court of 27 March 2014 in the case C-322/13 *lrike Elfriede Grauel Rüffer v Katerina Pokorná*. ECLI:EU:C:2014:189.

127 Judgment of the Court in the case C-322/13, para.11.

128 Judgment of the Court in the case C-322/13, para.17.

same language rules must be applied in all judicial proceedings brought within the territorial entity concerned, in particular in the civil lawsuit.[129] The Court refused the Italian government's argument that conducting proceedings in German would be a burden to the court in terms of organization and time limits. In the face of the fact that judges in the Province of Bolzano were perfectly able to conduct the proceedings in either Italian or German and the use of German would not lead to higher costs, that argument was unfounded. Moreover, the Court argued that the settled case-law[130] showed that purely economic objectives could not constitute pressing reasons of public interest justifying a restriction of a fundamental nature guaranteed by the Treaty.[131]

3.3.2.3 The right to choose one's name and surname

The right to make choices about the language in which a name and surname is transcribed is considered to be an inseparable element of the human right to personal identity.[132] Personal identity conceptually falls within the broader right of respect for private and family life protected under Article 8 ECHR. The European sphere of the right is shaped by two major sources: the jurisprudence of the Court of Justice of the European Union and of the European Court of Human Rights (ECtHR). In addition, every EU Member State has its own domestic laws in this regard.

The ECtHR takes a conservative and rather resistant approach in matters concerning name and surname guarantees.[133] It is of the opinion that due to the variety of national systems referring to name and surname regimes and the procedures of making changes, signatories of the ECHR should be granted a wide margin of appreciation in this area.[134] Wide freedom allows the states to establish their own

---

129 Judgment of the Court in the case C-322/13, para. 20.

130 Case 352/85 *Bond van Adverteerders and Others* para. 34, Case C-288/89 *Collectieve Antennevoorziening Gouda*, para. 11, Case C-398/95 *SETTG*, para. 23, Case C-35/98 *Verkooijen*, para.48, and Case 388/01 *Commission v Italy*, para. 22.

131 Judgment of the Court in the case C-322/13, para. 25.

132 Iirs Goldner Lang, "Languages as a Barrier to Free Movement of Persons in the European Union", *Curriculum, Multilingualism and the Law*, Nakladni zavod Globus, 2009, 3.

133 Fernand De Varennes and Elżbieta Kuzborska, "Human Rights and a Person's Name: Legal Trends and Challenges", *Human Rights Quarterly*, Vol. 37, No. 4, 2015, 1022.

134 The problem of margin of appreciation was analysed by the Court in the following cases: *Burghartz v Switzerland*, No. 16213/90, judgment of 22 February 1994, Series A, No. 280-B; *Stjerna v Finland*, No. 18131/91, judgment of 15 November 1994, Series A, No. 299-B; *Guillot v France*, No. 22500/93, judgment of 24 October 1996, Reports of Judgments and Decisions 1996-V.

restrictions as to the naming regime. Based on the concept of Union citizenship and the principle of non-discrimination on the grounds of nationality, the Court of Justice aims to reduce the admissible margin of appreciation and create a higher standard of protection in respect of name and surname regimes in the EU.[135]

So far, the Court of Justice has considered a number of cases concerning the area of choosing a name and a surname. The first one was the case of *Konstantinidis* (1991).[136] Christos Konstantinidis, a Greek national residing in Altensteig in Germany, was a self-employed masseur and assistant hydro-therapist. According to his Greek birth certificate, his first name read Χρήστος and his surname Κωνσταντινίδης.[137] When he married in 1983 at the Registry Office in Altensteig, in the register of marriages his name was spelt as 'Christos Konsta*dini*dis'. In 1990, he applied to the Office to rectify his surname to 'Konstan*tini*dis' indicating that in such a way it was transcribed in Roman characters in his Greek passport.[138] Meanwhile, the issue got complicated by the fact that the court having jurisdiction to order rectification of entries (*Amtsgericht Tübingen*) obtained a translation of his birth certificate where his surname was transcribed as 'Hréstos Konstantinidés'. Mr Konstantinidis objected to the change in transcription. In that situation, *Amtsgericht Tübingen* raised problems of interpreting Community law and referred to the Court of Justice for a preliminary ruling. It asked whether the change of the Greek name 'Christos Konstantinidis' into 'Hréstos Konstantinidés' constituted an encroachment against Community law.[139]

The Court of Justice analysed whether it was contrary to Article 52 TEEC regulating the freedom of establishment to enter the misspelt surname of a person pursuing an occupation in another Member State into the registers of civil status of that State. The Court ruled that nothing in the Treaty precluded the transcription of a Greek name in Roman characters in the registers of civil status of a Member State which uses the Roman alphabet. Therefore, a Member State should adopt such legislative and administrative measures as provided detailed rules for such transcription. Such rules might be regarded to be contrary to Article 52 TEEC only when their application caused inconvenience which interfered with the freedom to exercise the right of establishment.[140] The Court concluded that it was incompatible with Article 52 of the Treaty for Mr Konstantinidis to use a distorted pronunciation of his surname while pursuing his occupation because it exposed him to a

135 Bodnar, "Obywatelstwo UE a Ochrona Praw Podstawowych", 65–6.

136 Judgment of the Court of 30 May 1993 in the case C-168/91 *Christos Konstantinidis v Stadt Altensteig – Standesamt and Landratsamt Calw- Ordnungsamt,* ECLI:EU:C:1993:115.

137 Judgment of the Court in the case C-168/91, para. 3.

138 Judgment of the Court in the case C-168/91, para. 4.

139 Judgment of the Court in the case C-168/91, para. 8(1).

140 Judgment of the Court in the case C-168/91, para.14.

risk that potential clients might confuse him with other persons.[141] As a result, he could lose his clients.

More than ten years later in the case of *Garcia Avello*[142] (2003), the Court of Justice combined the EU naming regime with Union citizenship and the principle of non-discrimination on the grounds of nationality. The case concerned the surnames of children from a mixed-nationality couple residing in Belgium. Carlos Garcia Avello was Spanish, Isabelle Weber was Belgian and their children had dual citizenship. The parents registered their children – Esmeralda and Diego – at the Spanish embassy according to the Spanish pattern, giving them the compound surname 'Garcia Weber'. They applied to the Belgian civil registry office to register them under such a surname. The office failed to satisfy the Spanish tradition of surnames emerging from both parental and maternal elements. The children were listed under the father's name 'Garcia Avello' in compliance with the Western European system according to which children born in wedlock receive their fathers' last name. The office argued that having a single paternally-derived surname was essential to the social order in the country, and that the absence of it would retard assimilation into the nation for immigrants and dual nationals.[143]

In the judgment, the Court of Justice expressly admitted that the rules governing a person's surname did not fall within the Treaty's *ratione materiae* if applied internally.[144] However, if combined with the right to move and reside freely on the territory of the Member States, they fall within the matters regulated by Community law.[145] The very fact that children had dual nationality was a sufficient element linking the facts with Community law. Following the opinion of Advocate General Jacobs,[146] the Court held that the principle of non-discrimination on the grounds of nationality in that context must also be applied. In the judgment, the Court established the so-called 'serious-inconvenience test'.[147] It ruled that children's surnames written according to the Belgian law were likely to cause serious inconvenience for them both at professional and private levels.[148] The confusion about the actual name of the child could cause considerable difficulties later

141 Judgment of the Court in the case C-168/91, para. 17.

142 Judgment of the Court of 2 October 2003 in the case C-148/02 *Carlos Garcia Avello v Belgian State*. ECLI:EU:C:2003:539.

143 Judgment of the Court in the case C-168/91.

144 Judgment of the Court in the case C-148/02, para. 26.

145 Judgment of the Court in the case C-148/02, para. 25.

146 Opinion of Advocate General Jacobs delivered on 22 May 2003 in the case C-148/02, ECLI:EU:C:2005:419.

147 Aistė Mickonytė, "The Right to a Name Versus National Identity in the Context of EU Law: The Case of Lithuania", *Review of Central and East European Law, Vol.* 42, No. 4, 2017, 345.

148 Judgment of the Court in the case C-148/02, para. 36.

in life, where identity documents, diplomas or certificates would be needed. It concluded that the Belgian authorities' refusal to grant a surname 'Garcia Weber' was against Articles 12 and 17 TEC. As a result, the children were entitled to use a surname according to law and tradition of another Member State (Spain).

The Court's decision was abundantly commented on and criticised, mainly owing to Court's interference into the domain of Member States. Despite the criticism, the ruling in *Garcia Avello* was a signal to Member States that the naming regime based on a traditional approach had to be verified and adapted to the requirements of Community law. Through the case, the Court showed that, first of all, the European integration of diverse cultures made the Member States adjust their regulations to respect linguistic diversity, and, secondly, that the Union citizen's rights should be given priority. As a result, an individual should be granted the right to decide about the surname for himself or herself as well as names and surnames for his/her children.[149]

In *Leonhard Matthias*[150](2006), the Court of Justice again faced the matter of conflicting national and Community regulations in the area of naming regime. The case concerned the spelling of surname of a child of two German nationals residing in Denmark – Mr Grunkin and Ms Paul. They registered their son Leonard Matthias as Grunkin-Paul, in accordance with the Danish law. When Mr Grunkin and Ms Paul sought recognition of the child's double-barrelled surname in Germany, the German registry office refused it on the grounds that the name must be determined under the laws of the state of nationality, i.e. under German law. The German civil code does not allow for hyphenated surnames composed of both parents names. As a result of the parents' complaints, the office referred to the Court of Justice for a preliminary ruling. It was rejected owing to the lack of the office competence to file such questions. Later, a similar question was referred by the competent German administrative court.[151] Having considered the case on its merits in *Grunkin-Paul*, the Court of Justice admitted that the principle of non-discrimination on the grounds of nationality was not at stake as both parents were German nationals. Moreover, the Court found that no discrimination had occurred because the child was German and was treated by German authorities in the same way as any other German citizen.[152] However, as noted by Advocate General Jacobs, in practice the situation of Leonhard Matthias was similar to that of Gracia Avello. Moreover, Jacobs stressed that name and surname constituted a

149 Bodnar, "Obywatelstwo UE a Ochrona Praw Podstawowych", 64.

150 Judgment of the Court of 27 April 2006 in the case C-96/04 *Standesamt Stadt Niebüll*. ECLI:EU:C:2006:254.

151 Reference for a preliminary ruling from the Amtsgericht Flenburg (Germany) filed on 28 August 2006, C 281.

152 Judgment of the Court 14 October 2008 in the case C-353/06 *Grunkin-Paul v Standesamt Niebüll*, ECLI:EU:C:2008:559.

fundamental element of person's identity and his or her private life.[153] Following Jacobs' opinion, the Court ruled that using one set of surnames in the Member State of nationality and a different set in the Member State of birth and residence is liable to hamper the exercise of the right to move and reside freely.[154] It required the German authorities to accept the surname given to Leonard Matthias in Denmark (Grunkin-Paul) arguing that different surnames in different Member States would certainly raise doubts concerning person's identity and suspicions of misrepresentation caused by different surnames in Danish official documents, including his birth certificate, his German passport and the surname used by Leonhard Matthias on day-to-day basis.[155]

In 2010, in the case of *Sayn-Wittgenstein*,[156] the Court of Justice applied 'the serious-inconvenience test'. Nevertheless, the results were different from those in *Garcia Avello* and *Grunkin-Paul.* Ms Ilonka Sayn-Wittgenstein, an Austrian citizen residing in Germany, received the noble title of Fürstin von Sayn-Wittgenstein having been adopted by Mr Lothar Fürst von Sayn-Wittgenstein. The title was a part of her surname and was entered into the Austrian civil register.[157] In 2003, the Constitutional Court of Austria precluded Austrian citizens from holding a surname entailing a noble title.[158] As a result "Fürstin von" was removed by the Austrian authorities from the civil register. The applicant alleged violation of Article 21 TFEU. Ms Syan-Wittgenstein claimed that her noble title was an asset in her business in the luxury real estate sector. Therefore, changing her surname would cause her personal and professional inconvenience.[159] The Austrian government argued that Ms Sayn-Wittgenstein could keep her name except from the part indicating her noble title[160] and called for maintaining balance between the free movement right and state constitutional values. The government stressed that satisfying the applicant's requests would have led to a grave impairment of such values in Austria.[161] The Court of Justice accepted those arguments and justified acceptance

153 Opinion of Advocate General Francis Jacobs in the case C-96/04 delivered on 30 June 2005, ECLI:EU:C:2005:419.

154 Judgment of the Court in the case C-353/06, para. 22.

155 Judgment of the Court in the case C-353/06, para. 26.

156 Judgment of the Court of 22 December 2012 in the case C-208/09 *Ilonka Sayn-Wittgenstein v Landeshauptmann von Wien*, ECLI:EU:C:2010:806.

157 Judgment of the Court in the case C-208/09, para. 22.

158 Judgment of the Austrian Constitutional Court Verfassungsgerichtshof (VfGH), B 557/03, 27 November 2003, available at https://www.ris.bka.gv.at/VfghEntscheidung.wxe?Abfrage=Vfgh&Dok umentnummer=JFT_09968873_03B00557_2_00&IncludeSelf=True [retrieved on 29 January 2020].

159 Judgment of the Court in the case C-208/09, para. 21.

160 Judgment of the Court in the case C-208/09, para. 32.

161 Mickonytė, 346.

on the grounds that the Law on the abolition of nobility constituted an element of Austrian national identity.[162] In its argumentation, the Court relied on Article 4(2) TEU and explained that the national measure on the abolition of noble titles introduced in Austria was deemed consistent with the principle of proportionality and, therefore, was compatible with Article 21 TFEU.[163] Moreover, the Court agreed that the Austrian law pursued the aim of equal treatment, also recognised in the EU law under Article 20 of the Charter.[164]

Naming regimes are of utmost importance in Latvia and Lithuania where the state official languages enjoy special constitutional status. Constitutional courts in Lithuania[165] and Latvia[166] held that national languages are an expression of national identity which unites the nation and manifests its sovereignty.[167] As a consequence, foreign surnames in both states must be adjusted to the national spelling rules. That state of affairs stood in contrast with the existing case-law of the Court of Justice (*Konstantinidis, Garcia Avello, Grunkin-Paul*), which stressed the need to maintain the original spelling of surnames of the Union citizens enjoying the right to move and reside freely. The problem of spelling surnames according to the Lithuanian language rules is faced by many Poles entering into marriages with Lithuanians as well as Lithuanian women marrying the EU citizens. Their names and surnames in the civil status documents are often distorted and differ from original spelling. For many years, the scale of the problem has been of such significance that it has been one of the most sensitive issues in Polish-Lithuanian relations.[168]

162 Judgment of the Court in the case C-208/09, para. 83.

163 Judgment of the Court in the case C-208/09, para. 94.

164 Judgment of the Court in the case C-208/09, para. 92.

165 Ruling on the compliance of the 31 January 1991 Supreme Council of the Republic of Lithuania Resolution "On Writing Names and Family Names in Passports of Citizens of the Republic of Lithuania" with the Constitution of the Republic of Lithuania. Judgment of the Constitutional Court of Lithuania of 21 October 1999, No. 14/98, https://www.lrkt.lt/en/court-acts/search/170/ta1147/ summary [retrieved on 24 October 2019].

166 Judgment in the name of the Republic of Latvia on Compliance with Article 19 of the Language Law and the Cabinet of Ministers August 22, 2000 Regulations No. 295 "Regulations on Spelling and Identification of Names and Surnames" with Article 86 and 116 of the Satversme (Constitution). Judgment of the Constitutional Court of Latvia of 21 December 2001, No. 2001-04-0103, http://www.satv.tiesa.gov.lv/upl oad/2001-04-0103E.rtf [retrieved on 24 October 2019].

167 Anneli Albi, "Europe Articles in the Constitutions of Central and Eastern European Countries", *Common Market Law Review, Vol.* 42, No. 2, 2005, 421–2.

168 More on the issue: Kuzborska (2012), Kuzborska and Wardyn (2014).

The dispute concerning the spelling of names and surnames under Lithuanian law was considered by the Court of Justice in *Runevič-Vardyn and Wardyn*[169] (2011). It arose when the Lithuanian Civil Registry Division refused to modify several civil status documents of Malgožata Runevič-Vardyn, a Lithuanian national of Polish origin, and Łukasz Paweł Wardyn, a Polish national, according to the rules of the Polish alphabet. In the national court *Vilniaus miesto savivaldybės administracija* in Lithuania, Ms Runevič-Vardyn applied for her name to be written as "Małgorzata Runiewicz Wardyn" as it was required by the Polish spelling rules, and her husband Mr Wardyn applied for changing the transcription of his names in the marriage certificate from "Lukasz Pawel" to "Łukasz Paweł". The applicants in the main proceedings maintained that the competent Polish authorities issued a marriage certificate on which their surnames and forenames were entered in accordance with Polish spelling rules.[170] Mr Wardyn claimed that the fact that the Lithuanian authorities refused to transcribe his forenames on the marriage certificate in a form which complied with the rules governing Polish spelling constituted discrimination against a citizen of the Union who entered into a marriage in a State other than his State of origin. The fact of entering into marriage with a person of another nationality affected the original spelling of his forenames but not the surname. Mr Wardyn wished to know why the original spelling of his surname was retained, although the letter 'W' does not exist in the Lithuanian alphabet, whilst that of his forenames was changed.[171] The First District Court of the City of Vilnius *Vilniaus miesto 1 apylinkės teismas* was unable to provide clear answers to the questions raised in the dispute, hence, it stayed the proceedings and referred to the Court of Justice for a preliminary ruling. It asked whether the national rules which imposed on the authorities an obligation to spell forenames and surnames on certificates of civil status only by use of the national language letters were against Article 2(2)(b) of the Racial Equality Directive[172] and were contrary to Articles 18 and 21 TFEU.[173]

In order to answer the questions, the Court of Justice considered the relevant Lithuanian national law including the Lithuanian Constitution (Article 14), Article 2.20(1) of the Lithuanian Civil Code which guaranteed every person the right to a name and a surname, and Article 3.282 which expressly stipulated that "entries on certificates of civil status must be made in Lithuanian. Forenames, surnames, and place names must be written in accordance with the rules of the Lithuanian

169 Judgment of the Court of 12 May 2011 in the case C-391/09 *Malgožata Runevič-Vardyn and Łukasz Paweł Wardyn. Vilniaus miesto savivaldybės administracija and Others.* ECLI:EU:C:2011:291.

170 Judgment of the Court in the case C-391/09, para. 19.

171 Judgment of the Court in the case C-391/09, para. 25.

172 OJ L 180, 19 July 2000, para. 22.

173 Judgment of the Court in the case C-391/09, para. 28(1).

language".[174] Finally, the Court relied upon the Lithuanian civil registration rules[175] providing that "entries made on certificates of civil status must be in Lithuanian".[176]

The Court of Justice held that national rules regulating the spelling of person's forenames and surnames entered on the certificates of civil status fell beyond the scope of the Racial Equality Directive and confirmed that Articles 18 and 21 TFEU were applicable to the situation. The Court of Justice held that Article 21 TFEU does not preclude Member State authorities from refusing to amend the joint surname of a married couple who are citizens of the Union, as it appears on the certificates of civil status issued by the Member State of origin of one of those citizens, in such a form as makes the spelling compliant with the national language rules of the host State.[177] However, the Court specified clear conditions when a national court may deem a change in one's name and surname to be in breach of the Union law. The Court gave the national court a prerogative to carry out 'the serious inconvenience test' and determine if the refusal to amend the name gave rise to serious inconvenience at administrative, professional, and private levels,[178] for instance by "giv[ing] rise to doubts as to [the citizen's] identity and the authenticity of the documents".[179] If the answer is in the affirmative, the national court should determine whether the refusal was necessary for the protection of the interests which the national rules are designed to secure and was proportionate to the legitimate aim pursued.[180] The Court of Justice agreed that the national norms examined in the case could restrict the rights stemming from Article 21 TFEU as the restrictions aimed to protect a state official language constituting a fundamental element of Member State national identity.[181] As a result, the Court of Justice did not oblige the Lithuania authorities to amend the surnames in a form which would comply with the spelling rules of the Member State of origin. As a result, the Lithuanian marriage certificate of Ms Runevič-Vardyn and Mr Wardyn did not include Polish letters and diacritical marks as entered on the certificates issued by Polish authorities.[182] However, the case has not finished at this stage. According to the applicant, different spellings in Polish and in Lithuanian could result in serious inconvenience. The Lithuanian competent court – the Vilnus District Court – in its decision of 7 November 2016 allowed Malgožata Runevič-Vardyn to change her surname

174 Judgment of the Court in the case C-391/09, paras 8 and 11.

175 Decree No. IR-294 of the Minister for Justice of 22 July 2008 confirming the civil registration rules (Žin., 2008, No. 88–3541).

176 Judgment of the Court in the case C-391/09, para. 14.

177 Judgment of the Court in the case C-391/09, Summary of the judgment, para. 3.

178 Judgment of the Court in the case C-391/09, para. 76.

179 Judgment of the Court in the case C-391/09, para. 81.

180 Judgment of the Court in the case C-391/09, para. 3.

181 Judgment of the Court in the case C-391/09, paras 86–87.

182 Judgment of the Court in the case C-391/09, Operative part.

into Wardyn and in its decision of 23 October 2019 to change her forename into Małgorzata.[183] This is the first case in Lithuania where the court admitted the right to transcribe the forename of the Lithuanian citizen of the Polish origin in original form. As a consequence of the judgments, the marriage certificate had to be appropriately changed.

The cases of *Sayn-Wittgenstein* and *Runevič-Vardyn and Wardyn* exposed the relationship between the right to a name and respect for the national identity of a Member State. They imply that Article 4(2) TEU may be a legitimate basis for justifying a restriction to Article 21 TFEU as long as the principle of proportionality is complied with[184] and subject to 'the serious-inconvenience test' carried out by national courts which aims to check the excessiveness of a domestic measure".[185] The Court of Justice sees national courts to be in the best position to determine whether national measures strike a balance between an individual right to move and reside and public interest reflected in state language policy.[186] Notice should be taken of the fact that the results of the test may differ in different Member States as the national courts' assessments of the excessiveness of national measures may depend on the constitutional status of a language.

3.3.2.4 Language rights of workers and self-employed persons and their limitations

As Union citizenship is a fundamental status of the Union citizen, the workers and self-employed persons in the EU internal market should be defined as those Union citizens who exercise the right to move and reside freely for economic purposes. The rights of workers and their families as well as limitations to the rights are set out in Article 45 TFEU and Regulation No. 492/2011.[187] The Regulation codifies the rights of workers to move and access employment in another Member State without unjustified discrimination. It prevents a Member State from engaging in direct discrimination against foreign nationals or from pursuing policies that result in indirect discrimination against foreign nationals who wish to get employed

183 Vilnus City District Court allows for original spelling of Malgorzata, http://en.efhr.eu/2019/11/20/ vilnius-city-district-court-allows-for-original-spelling-of-malgorzata/ [retrieved on 22 July 2020].

184 Hanneke Van Eijken, "Case Note on C-391/09, Malgožata Runevič-Vardyn and Łukasz Paweł Wardyn v Vilniaus Miesto Savivaldybės Administracija and Others", *Common Market Law Review*, 2012, 809.

185 Mickonytė, 357.

186 Mickonytė, 357.

187 Regulation (EU) No. 492/2011 of the European Parliament and of the Council of 5 April 2011 on freedom of movement for workers within the Union Text with EEA relevance. OJ L141/1, 27 May 2011.

in another Member State. As a result, Member States are banned from laying down their own regulations or adopting practices which in fact make access to employment or internal market more difficult for foreign nationals. That ban includes linguistic discrimination in the recruitment procedure and in the course of the employment relationship. Distinct treatment of workers or work seekers due to their inability to speak a language of an accepting state, if unjustified, amounts to discrimination on the grounds of nationality.[188]

In this context, it must be assumed that the Union citizen cannot be discriminated against on the basis of language, an intrinsic element of one's nationality. Further, it may be asserted that a worker or a self-employed person is entitled to know only his or her native language and participate in the EU internal market. The lack of knowledge of the other EU official language cannot be the underlying reason for exclusion from the market. However, the right is subject to limitations which may affect the scope of rights of economically active citizens in the area of languages. The language entitlements may be limited by objectively justified requirements resulting from the Member State national regulations. They may constitute the grounds for justified requirement of language knowledge and skills which are necessary to practise some professions or to be recruited for particular positions, as they are considered to determine someone's ability to work adequately to the expectations of an employer or may be one of the *sine qua non* conditions which has to be met to be employed.[189]

Based on Article 45 TFEU and Regulation No. 492/2011, three groups of justified language requirements applied to workers and self-employed persons may be distinguished:

1) language skills required by law, regulation and administrative action or practice (Article 3(1) of Regulation No. 492/2011),[190] or by collective or individual agreement or any other collective regulation (Article 7(4) of Regulation No. 492/2011),
2) language skills required in relation to workers or self-employed persons exercising regulated professions (Article 53 of Directive 2005/36/EC),[191] and
3) language skills required by private entities (Article 45 TFEU).[192]

---

188 Wróbel, Miąsik and Półtorak (eds.), 595–6.

189 Wróbel, Miąsik and Półtorak (eds.), 595–6.

190 Formerly Article 3 of Regulation No. 1612/68.

191 Directive 2005/36/EC of the European Parliament and of the Council of 7 September 2005 on the recognition of professional qualifications. OJ L 255, 30 September 2005.

192 Ulla Iben Jensen, *Analytical Note for 2013. The Language Requirements under EU Law on Free Movement of Workers*, https://ec.europa.eu/social/keyDocuments.jsp?type=0&policyArea=25&sub Category=475&country=0&year=0&advSearchKey=FMWthematic&mode=advancedSubmit&langId =en [retrieved on 10 May 2017], 20.

In all three instances, language requirements towards workers are perceived as exceptions rather than a general rule. If imposed, they must be applied in a non-discriminatory and proportionate manner in order to be justified.[193] The first group of linguistic requirements results from Article 3 of Regulation No. 492/2011. The Article provides a linguistic exception to the principle of equal treatment in employment. It allows a certain level of language command to be required from migrant workers in relation to specific posts. The requirements are based on a Member State clear policy to maintain and promote the use of national languages as a means of expressing national identity and culture, where the constraints of proportionality are satisfied. This category includes language requirements regulated by domestic legislation of a general nature, both in the public and private sector (e.g. State Language Acts in Estonia, Latvia and Lithuania) or only in the public sector (the other Member States).[194] Moreover, specific language requirements imposed on workers in any form of individual agreement or collective regulation concerning employment, remuneration, and other conditions of work or dismissal must be compliant with Article 7(4) of Regulation No. 492/2011, which prohibits the national authorities from imposing any discriminatory conditions in respect of workers who are nationals of another Member State.

Groener[195] (1989) was the first case considered by the Court of Justice in the area of language requirements imposed by national law on an employee. Anita Groener, a Dutch national, was refused a permanent teaching post at a Dublin design college for lacking knowledge of Irish. Irish is the first Irish national language, but is not spoken by the whole Irish population. It was a public policy of the state to promote the language in order to propagate Irish as a means of expressing national identity and culture. For that reason, Irish courses were compulsory for children receiving primary education and optional for those receiving secondary education. The obligation of Irish knowledge imposed on lecturers in public vocational education schools constituted yet another measure adopted by the Irish government in furtherance of the Irish language promotion policy.[196] Miss Groener argued that this was a restriction on her right to the free movement of workers. The High Court on Dublin referred to the Court of Justice for a preliminary ruling. It asked whether the condition of having knowledge of Irish was compliant with Article 3 of Regulation No. 1612/68,[197] (later replaced by Regulation No. 492/2011). The Court of Justice noted that "the EEC Treaty does not prohibit the adoption of

---

193 Goldner Lang, 175–91.

194 Iben Jensen, 47.

195 Judgment of the Court of 28 November 1989 in the case C-379/87 *Anita Groener v Minister for Education and the City of Dublin Vocational Educational Committee*, ECLI:EU:C:1989:599.

196 Judgment of the Court in the case 379/87, para. 18.

197 Judgment of the Court in the case 379/87, para. 10.

a policy for the protection and promotion of a language of a Member State which is both the national language and the first official language. However, the implementation of such a policy must not encroach upon a fundamental freedom such as that of the free movement of workers".[198] Therefore, a policy must not in any circumstance be disproportionate in relation to the aim pursued and the manner in which it is applied must not bring about discrimination against nationals of other Member States.[199] Accordingly, Member States are not allowed to impose any requirement on an individual to acquire linguistic skills or force foreign nationals to retake national language examination in the Member State, as it would violate the principle of non-discrimination on the grounds of nationality.[200] With reference to Ms Groener, the Court stated that a permanent full-time post of lecturer in public vocational education institutions was a post which justified the requirement of command of Irish. According to the Court, the requirement imposed on her was applied in a proportionate and non-discriminatory manner.[201]

Language requirements may also be imposed on regulated professions governed by Directive 2005/36/EC (amended by Directive 2013/55/EU).[202] A profession is considered to be regulated when access to it and its exercise are subject to the possession of a specific professional qualification.[203] Article 53 of the Directive stipulates that "persons benefiting from the recognition of professional qualifications shall have knowledge of language *necessary* for practising the profession in the host Member State". Any language requirement must be proportionate and objectively justified by the real needs. Article 53 creates the grounds for language testing in order to verify language knowledge. However, the Group of Coordinators for the Directive notes that the proportionality principle excludes any systemic and standardised check of language skills. On the contrary, it requires case-by-case analysis. A few important points should be made here. Firstly, language testing is not part of recognition procedure[204] but relates to the exercise of a profession

198 Judgment of the Court in the case 379/87, para. 19.
199 Judgment of the Court in the case 379/87, para. 19.
200 Judgment of the Court in the case 379/87, para. 23.
201 Judgment of the Court in the case 379/87, Operative Part.
202 Directive 2013/55/EU of the European Parliament and of the Council of 20 November 2013 amending Directive 2005/36/EC on the recognition of professional qualifications and Regulation (EU) No 1024/2012 on administrative cooperation through the Internal Market Information System ('the IMI Regulation'). OJ L 354, 28 December 2013.
203 Regulated professions by country, https://ec.europa.eu/growth/ tools-databases/ regprof/index.cfm? action=regprofs [retrieved on 30 January 2020].
204 The Directive recognises three systems for the recognition of professional qualifications: *the automatic recognition of 7 sectoral professions*, where the minimum training conditions are harmonised: architects, dental practitioners, nurses, doctors, veterinary surgeons, midwives and pharmacists. *the general system*, where

in another Member State. This means that the host Member State may only check the language knowledge of migrant professional after recognition has taken place. Such an approach is reflected in the application procedure for the European Professional Card (EPC).[205] Article 13 of the Commission Implementing Regulation expressly states that a Member State may require documents proving knowledge of language, but such documentary proof "shall not be part of the documents required for issuing EPC".[206] Secondly, there are exceptional cases where linguistic knowledge may be required in the process of recognition. There are derogations which concern language-related industries, where linguistic knowledge conditions the pursuit of a profession, such as speech therapists or language teachers. Still, even in such professions sometimes language requirements of a foreign language may not be objectively justified if for instance the training provided is addressed only to the nationals of the trainer and command of the host Member State language is not necessary. This may occur especially where a large group of migrants reside in neighbouring localities of one host State. Finally, the general rule is that in the course of language skills verification, migrant professionals cannot be compelled to hold a specific certificate of language knowledge delivered by a particular institution as this would be considered discriminatory.[207]

The findings of an analytical study on the language requirements related to workers in the EU internal market prepared for the European Commission in 2013 showed that different language requirements were imposed on particular groups of regulated professions. The majority of Member States (Austria, Bulgaria, Croatia, Cyprus, Czech Republic, Denmark, Finland, Germany, Hungary, Ireland, Lithuania, Poland, Slovakia, Slovenia, Sweden, the Netherlands and United Kingdom) require a certain level of linguistic ability for workers within the medical sector. Language proficiency is required for the employment of or self-employment by legal professionals (Croatia, Denmark, Germany, Slovakia, Spain and the Netherlands), certified auditors (Hungary and Poland), members of management boards in certain institutions and patent counsels (Poland and Romania), notaries (Croatia, Lithuania, Romania and the Netherlands), insurance brokers (Cyprus) or real estate agents engineers and interior designers (Cyprus and Luxembourg).[208]

---

the minimum training conditions are harmonised and a Member State may impose compensation measures for the applicant for passing an aptitude test or to complete an adaptation period, *recognition either through automatic recognition or on the basis of the general system* within craft, commerce and industry sector.

205 Article 4 of Directive 2005/36/EU as amended by Directive 2013/55/EU.

206 Commission Implementing Regulation (EU) No. 2015/983 of 24 June 2015 on the procedure for issuance of the European Professional Card and the application of the alert mechanism pursuant to Directive 2005/36/EC of the European Parliament and of the Council. OJ L 159/27, 25 June 2015.

207 Iben Jensen, 130–5.

208 Iben Jensen, 136.

On various occasions, the Court of Justice dealt with linguistic requirements towards Member State citizens pursuing regulated professions in another Member State. In the case of *Haim*[209] (2000), the Court examined the compatibility of language requirements towards a professional of a medical sector with the freedom of establishment. The proceedings were raised by Salomone Haim, an Italian national, who claimed for compensation for the loss of earnings which he maintained to have suffered as a result of the breach of Community law by the Association of Dental Practitioners of Social Security Schemes in Nordrhein. Mr Haim, held a diploma in dentistry awarded in 1946 by the University of Istanbul, Turkey, where he had practised until 1980. Later, he obtained permission (approbation) to practise as a self-employed dentist in the Federal Republic of Germany. Subsequently, he pursued his profession in Brussels. When he came back to Germany to be enrolled on the register of dental practitioners, he was refused for the lack of preparatory training. The national court *Landesgericht Düsseldorf* argued that one of the arguments was that he failed to have a sufficient command of German. *Landesgericht Düsseldorf* referred to the Court of Justice for a preliminary ruling. It asked if the competent authorities of a Member State may make the appointment of a dental practitioner conditional upon his having linguistic knowledge which he needed for the exercise for his professional activity in the host State.[210] The Court held that the need to communicate with patients and administrative authorities and bodies, as well as to comply with the rules of professional conduct in the Member State of establishment required from Mr Haim an appropriate knowledge of the host State language. Language skills in Mr Haim's case guaranteed his reliability which constituted an overriding reason of general interest.[211] The Court added that the imposed language requirements should not go beyond what is necessary to attain the professional objectives of a dentist. In this respect, the Court stressed that it might also be in the interests of some patients whose mother tongue was not the national language of the State that there exist a certain number of dental practitioners who were also capable of communicating with such persons in their own language. Taking this into consideration, the Court concluded that the competent authorities of a Member State may make the appointment of a medical practitioner conditional upon his having linguistic knowledge.[212]

The linguistic skills of a dental professional were also analysed in the opinion of Advocate General Jacobs in the *Hocsman*[213] (2000) case. The Advocate General

---

209 Judgment of the Court of 4 July 2000 in the case C-424/97 *Salomone Haim v Kassenzahnärztliche Vereinigung Nordrhein*, ECLI:EU:C:2000:357.

210 Judgment of the Court of 4 July 2000 in the case C-424/97, para. 24(3).

211 Judgment of the Court of 4 July 2000 in the case C-424/97, para. 59.

212 Judgment of the Court of 4 July 2000 in the case C-424/97, para. 3 of the Operative Part and paras 59–61.

213 Opinion of Advocate General Jacobs delivered on 16 September 1999 in the case C-238/98, ECLI:EU:C:1999:426.

took a similar approach in respect of language requirements towards medical professionals to the one expressed in *Haim*. Jacobs analysed the linguistic question raised by Dr Hocsman, an Argentinian and Spanish national, who held a diploma of doctor of medicine awarded in 1976 by the University of Buenos Aires, Argentina, and a diploma of specialist in urology awarded in 1982 by the University of Barcelona, Spain (i.e. when Spain was not the member of the Community).[214] In the period between 1990 and 1995, he practised his profession as a hospital doctor in France on the basis of a series of fixed-term contracts under the rules which allowed public establishments to engage medical staff who obtained their qualification outside the Community. The rules were repealed in 1995 and Dr Hocsman's contract could no longer be renewed.[215] When he applied for a position of a doctor in 1997, he was required to sit an examination in general medicine in French. The French Minister for Employment and Solidarity refused to grant Dr Hocsman authorisation to practise medicine in France on the grounds that he did not meet requirements.[216] In this context, Jacobs fully agreed with the view that any assessment of linguistic abilities of a person concerned must comply with the principle of proportionality. Following the opinion delivered earlier in the *Haim* case by Advocate General Mischo,[217] Jacobs distinguished three aspects that must be taken into account while considering the linguistic requirements towards professionals practising medicine abroad:

1) the ability to communicate with patients,
2) the ability to cope with administrative work entailed by the social security system, and
3) the ability to communicate accurately and effectively with professional colleagues.[218]

Further, Jacobs stressed that submission to any linguistic tests requiring language knowledge going beyond a regular doctor's work might be discriminatory or disproportionate. The Member State authorities and court should assess whether the criteria tested are proportionate and appropriate. Advocate General Mischo concluded that owing to the fact that Dr Hocsman already practised in France for a number of years without displaying linguistic inadequacy, a language test on the basis of which he could be disqualified might infringe the principle of proportionality.[219] Interestingly, in its judgment in

214 Judgment of the Court of 14 September 2000 in the case C-238/98 *Hugo Fernando Hocsman v Ministre de l'Emploi et de la Solidarité*, ECLI:EU:C:2000:440, para. 12.

215 Opinion of Advocate General Jacobs in the case C-238/98, para. 6.

216 Opinion of Advocate General Jacobs in the case C-238/98, para. 9.

217 Opinion of Advocate General Mischo delivered on 19 May 1999 in the case C-424/97, ECLI:EU:C:1999:253.

218 Opinion of Advocate General Mischo in the case C-424/97, para. 56.

219 Opinion of Advocate General Mischo in the case C-424/97, para. 57.

Hocsman,[220] the Court did not refer to the linguistic requirements towards Dr Hocsman. That was not the subject of the reference for a preliminary ruling filed by *Tribunal Administratif de Châlons-en-Champagne*. The Court was asked whether under Article 52 TEC (Article 49 TFEU) experience and qualifications evidenced by another Member State corresponded to those required for the award of national diplomas and formal qualification.[221] The Court concluded that the other Member State national may access a profession if he or she has a relevant diploma certificate of professional qualification or periods of practical experience. It added that the verifying Member State is obliged to take into consideration all the diplomas, certificates or other evidence and experience by comparing specialised knowledge and abilities with the knowledge and qualifications required by the national rules.[222] The Court left the decision for the French authorities to decide in the light of the evidence submitted by the applicant whether Dr Hocsman's diplomas corresponded to the French one.[223]

The third category of linguistic requirements imposed on workers concern language skills required by private entities subject to the conditions specified in Article 45 TFEU. Language requirements in the private sector are in general justified by communication skills and the nature of the job, for instance contact with customers and responsibility for correspondence with business partners or the necessity to understand written instructions or safety codes.[224] The compliance of language requirement with EU law was analysed by the Court of Justice in *Angonese*[225] (2000). A dispute arose between Roman Angonese, an Italian national whose mother tongue was German, and a private bank, Cassa di Risparmio. In August 1997, Mr Angonese returned to Italy from Austria where he has been studying. He applied for a job with the bank. One condition for the post was possession of a type-B certificate of bilingualism (in Italian or German), which could only be obtained by taking an exam in Italy. Although Mr Angonese had no certificate, he was perfectly bilingual and produced evidence to this effect. In spite of that, his application was rejected on the grounds that he did not possess the relevant certificate. Mr Angonese challenged the need to evidence bilingualism by the requirement of a certificate under Article 39 TEC (Article 45 TFEU). The bank argued that Article 39 TEC was not applicable. However, in an answer to a question addressed by the *Pretura Circondariale di Bolzano* in the preliminary ruling procedure, the Court of Justice ruled that prohibition of discrimination applied

220 Judgment of the Court in the case C-238/98.
221 Judgment of the Court in the case C-238/98, para. 19.
222 Judgment of the Court in the case C-238/98, para. 40.
223 Judgment of the Court in the case C-238/98, para. 39.
224 Iben Jensen, 124.
225 Judgment of the Court of 6 June 2000 in the case C-281/98 *Angonese v Cassa di Risparimo di Bolzano SpA*, ECLI:EU:C:2000:296.

to the case, as it was applicable both to public authorities as well as private entities. The Court of Justice considered language requirements imposed by the bank as indirectly discriminatory and precluded "an employer from requiring persons applying to take part in a recruitment competition to provide evidence of their linguistic knowledge exclusively by means of one particular diploma issued only in one particular province of a Member State".[226] The Court held that the recruitment competition organised by Cassa di Risparmio constituted discrimination on the grounds of nationality, which was contrary to Article 39 TEC.[227]

3.4 Language rights in communication with the EU institutions

3.4.1 The right to petition the European Parliament in one of the Treaty languages

The establishment of Union citizenship was combined with introducing democratic communication mechanisms between the Member State citizens and the EU institutions. By incorporating the right to communicate with the EU institution into the Treaty, the language rights already acknowledged in Regulation No. 1/58 establishing the EU linguistic regime were elevated to the status of primary law rights. As a result, they strengthened the democratic legitimacy for communication with the EU institutions in 24 languages. Article 24 TFEU expressly guarantees the right to petition the European Parliament, to apply to the European Ombudsman and to address the Union institutions and advisory bodies of the Union in any of the Treaty languages and to obtain a reply in the same language. The Article has two functions: to control the operations of the EU institutions and to guarantee the transparency of the EU functioning. Firstly, Article 24 provides the legal basis for the out-of-court mechanisms of EU institutions' control and as such it constitutes a technical supplement to Article 11 TEU specifying the citizen's rights to make legislative initiative. Secondly, it exercises the citizens' right of access to information in recognition of the principle of openness aiming to meet the Union's objective specified in Article 1 TEU to be as closely as possible to the citizens.[228] Article 24 TFEU regulates the issue of written communications between the Union citizens and the EU institutions. The language used in communication is a Treaty language,[229] not an official language. Such a solution triggers legal implications. It means that Regulation No. 1/58 cannot be changed to reduce the number of languages used for written communication with the EU institutions, as the reduction

---

226 Judgment of the Court in the case C-281/98, para. 45
227 Judgment of the Court in the case C-281/98, Operative part.
228 Wróbel, Miąsik and Półtorak (eds.), 284.
229 Indicated in Article 55(1) TEU.

of languages would require the revision of the Treaty. Article 24 TFEU does not specify the issue of language use in respect to the oral contacts.

The rights listed in Article 24 TEFU should be analysed separately as they differ in scope. The right to petition the European Parliament (EP) is also specified in Article 227 TFEU and the Rules of Procedure of the European Parliament (the Rules).[230] Article 227 TFEU sets out the subjective and objective scope of the right to petition. As to the objective scope, the right to petition the European Parliament is vested in any Union citizen, natural, and legal person residing or having its registered office in the Member State acting individually or in association with other citizens or persons. The subjective scope includes matters which come within the Union's fields of activity and affect the person(s) filing petition directly.[231] The Rules lay down the procedure for dealing with petitions. One of the formal requirements for the right to petition to be exercised is that it must be prepared in one of the EU official languages, as expressly stated in Rule 226(6). Notice should be taken that the Rules refer to EU official, not treaty, languages. Petitions drawn up in any other language are considered only if they are accompanied by a translation into one of the EU official languages. In such a case, in the course of correspondence with the petitioner, the EP uses a language of translation. The Bureau of the European Parliament is authorised to decide about accepting petitions and correspondence with the petitioner to be conducted in a language other than EU official languages which according to the constitution of a given Member State is an official language on its entire territory or a part of it.[232]

3.4.2 The right to apply to the European Ombudsman in one of the Treaty languages

The right to apply to the European Ombudsman, specified in Article 228 TFEU, is straightforward. The right has the same objective scope as the right of petition to the EP. It comprises any Union citizen, natural and legal person residing or having its registered office in a Member State. The subjective scope of the application is considerably narrower. As the role of the Ombudsman is to safeguard the fundamental rights of Union citizens living in Europe by ensuring open and accountable administration in the EU, the Ombudsman accepts complaints concerning instances of maladministration in the activities of the Union institutions, bodies, offices or agencies, with the exception of the Court of Justice.[233] Instances

230 Rule 226 of the Rules of Procedure of the European Parliament.

231 OJ C 202, 7 June 2016.

232 Adam Łazowski, "Obywatelstwo Unii Europejskiej – Uwagi Teoretyczne i Praktyczne w Dziesięć Lat Po Wejściu w Życie Traktatu z Maastricht", in: Eugeniusz Piontek and Anna Zawidzka (eds.), *Szkice z Prawa Unii Europejskiej*, Kraków, 2003.

233 OJ C 202, 7 June 2016.

of maladministration may include administrative irregularities, unfairness, discrimination, abuse of power, lack of information, refusal of information and unnecessary delay. All complaints addressed to the European Ombudsman may be filed and will be answered in one of the Treaty languages. In order to make it possible, the Ombudsman's website is available in 24 EU official languages, including the electronic compliant form and interactive guide. The Ombudsman's recommendations and decisions are published on the website in the language of the complainant as well as in English. Summaries of cases of a wider public interest are published in all the EU official languages.[234]

3.4.3 The right to address the Union institutions in one of the Treaty languages

The right to address the Union institutions aims to implement citizens' right to control the institutions and obtain the information relevant for them in their own language. On the one hand, this certainly seems to increase the transparency of the Union functioning, while on the other, it falls within the broader context of the right to good administration enshrined in Article 41(4) of the Charter.[235] The right to address EU institutions and agencies has important limitations: 1) it is granted to the Union citizens and 2) includes the institutions listed in Article 13 TEU i.e. European Parliament, European Council, Council, European Commission, Court of Justice, European Central Bank and Court of Auditors, and two advisory bodies: Economic and Social Committee and Committee of Regions.[236]

3.5 Other language rights attached to the rights of the Union citizen

3.5.1 Language rights resulting from diplomatic and consular protection

Article 23 TFEU stipulates that the Union citizen who stays on the territory of any third country where his or her Member State does not have its representative office or embassy is entitled to take advantage of diplomatic and consular protection of any other EU Member State on the same conditions as the citizens of the assisting Member State. The Member States are obliged to adopt the necessary provisions and start international negotiations with an aim to securing protection for such a

234 The European Ombudsman's language policy, https://www.ombudsman.europa.eu/pl/language policy/pl [retrieved on 29 August 2019].

235 Artur Nowak-Far, *Prawo Unii Europejskiej. Języki, struktury, działanie w praktyce*, C.H. Beck, 2020, 314.

236 Wróbel, Miąsik and Półtorak (eds.), 288.

citizen. Based on the Article concerned, Directive 2015/637 was adopted in order to provide further details on the right. It establishes cooperation and coordination measures necessary to facilitate consular protection.[237] The Directive stresses that the essence of the right to consular protection of an unrepresented citizen is derived from citizenship of the Union. First of all, it defines the notion of an unrepresented citizen of the Union. It sets out that the citizens of the Union should be considered unrepresented in a third country if their Member State of nationality has no embassy, consulate or honorary consulate established there on a permanent basis, or if the embassy, consulate or honorary consul is not in a position for any reason to provide assistance in a given case. Moreover, accessibility and proximity should also be taken into account.[238] Directive 2015/637 took effect from 1 January 2018, and by far no data have been published demonstrating the actual benefits for unrepresented citizens.

Neither the Treaty nor Directive 2015/637 includes clear provisions on the language-related aspects of consular protection. Nevertheless, some relevant rules may be deduced. The right to consular protection relies on the principle of non-discrimination on the grounds of nationality. Therefore, a Member State is obliged to grant protection to an unrepresented citizen to the extent to which the citizens of that State would be entitled to.[239] For instance, if a German citizen is provided consular assistance by the Polish consular authority on a territory of a third country, he or she is entitled to the same extent of assistance which would be provided to a Polish citizen.

The Directive expressly refers to the language matters only in one place. Article 14(3) stipulates that arrest and detention may generate high translation costs for the consular and diplomatic authorities of the assisting Member State. In such a case, the Member State of an unrepresented citizen should be informed of possible costs and arrangements concerning the reimbursement. The Directive also clearly states that according to the non-discrimination principle, the Member State of nationality cannot ask its citizens to reimburse high translation costs if nationals of the assisting Member State would not be required to repay.[240] Moreover, under the general rules on financial procedures specified in Article 14(1), the costs imposed on an unrepresented citizen should be the same as in the case of the national of the assisting Member State. Therefore, it may be assumed that an embassy or

237 Council Directive (EU) 2015/637 of 20 April 2015 on the coordination and cooperation measures to facilitate consular protection for unrepresented citizens of the Union in third countries and repealing Decision 95/553/EC. OJ L 106, 24 April 2015.

238 OJ L 106, 24 April 2015, para. 8 of the Preamble and Article 6.

239 Marta de Bazelaire de Ruppierre and Katarzyna Frączak, "Ochrona Konsularna Niereprezentowanych Obywateli Unii Europejskiej w Państwach Trzecich (Art. 23 TFEU)", *Przegląd Legislacyjny*, 2016, 25–48.

240 OJ L 106, 24 April 2015, para. 25 of the Preamble.

consular authority which provides linguistic assistance to an unrepresented citizen is allowed to charge for any certified or consular translations[241] in accordance with the same fees as for the citizens of the Member State whose consular authority provided assistance. From the practical point of view, the Union citizen who speaks any Union official language should search for the embassy or consular authority of the state whose language he or she speaks in order to avoid language barriers and potential costs. In the other case, he or she may contact any EU Member State embassy or consular post which will then contact the nearest diplomatic mission or consular authority of that person's Member State.

The linguistic aspects of the Union consular protection are affected by the international consular law, in particular by the Vienna Convention on Consular Relations of 24 April 1963,[242] and bilateral international agreements. The Vienna Convention includes general guarantees in this regard. It states that the consular functions include protecting the interests of nationals of the sending State as well as helping and assisting them.[243] Such general formulations of the consul's obligations have been implemented in the national legal orders and give some leeway to the national authorities also in the area of language-related matters. Based on the example of Poland, the consul is obliged to provide assistance to the Polish citizen within the necessary scope in order to protect his or her essential rights and interests.[244] The same scope of protection should be offered to any other Union unrepresented citizen. Accordingly, the consul is obliged to provide the citizen in need with language assistance to such extent as their essential rights and interests are protected. There is no case-law concerning the interpretation of essential rights and interests. Under no legal act, the consul is obliged to provide specific activities to ensure linguistic assistance. Such assistance may be provided at the consul's discretion. The general principle is that any translation and interpretation services must be ensured by the person concerned. The costs for translation and interpreting services provided by the consul or certified translator are specified in the internal domestic regulations.[245]

241 Consular translations are considered to have the same legal force as translations made by certified translators.

242 Vienna Convention on Consular Relations of 24 April 1963, Treaty Series, Vol. 596, in force since 19 March 1967. By 2020 ratified by 180 states.

243 Vienna Convention on Consular Relations, Article 5(a) and (e).

244 Act of the Polish Parliament of 25 June 2015 Consular Law, Journal of Laws 2015, item 1274.

245 Under the Polish legal system, such fees are established in the Ordinance of the Minister of Foreign Affairs of 18 December 2015 on consular fees.

3.5.2 The right of access to Union documents in one of the EU official languages

The right of access to Union documents is governed by the principles regulating publication of documents by the EU institutions and the principles of access to the documents not made available to the public.[246] The right of access to documents constitutes an important element of the EU's policy of openness and transparency. Openness and transparency have always been at the centre of European integration as they allow the citizens of the Member States to follow the actions of the Union institutions and control them. Providing information to the public makes it possible for citizens to express their approval or disapproval of decisions made. The policy of openness aims to enable citizens to participate more closely in the decision-making process and guarantees that public administration enjoys greater legitimacy and is more effective and more accountable to the citizens in a democratic system.[247] As noted by Frost, openness in the EU is not an aim *per se,* but it aims to engage the citizens of the Member States in the Union affairs and leads to their direct participation in the EU's decision-making process.[248] Indeed, openness, transparency, and access to information are perceived as actions aiming to remove shortage of democratic legitimacy of the EU institutions.[249] The Lisbon Treaty includes a number of provisions supporting the policy of openness. Article 10(3) TEU states that "every citizen shall have the right to participate in the democratic life of the Union". Article 11(2) TEU stipulates that "the institutions shall maintain an open, transparent and regular dialogues with representative associations and civil society". The right to address the Union institutions (guaranteed in Article 24 TFEU) also implements the elements of the openness policy.[250]

---

246 Izabela Budzyńska and Bartosz Pawłowski, "Polityka Jawności i Przejrzystości Unii Europejskiej Ze Szczególnym Uwzględnieniem Dostępu Do Dokumentów Publicznych", *Informacja BSE*, No. 731, Warszawa: KS Biuro Studiów i Ekspertyz, 2000, 13.

247 Regulation (EC) No. 1049/2001 of the European Parliament and of the Council of 30 May 2001 regarding public access to European Parliament, Council and Commission documents. OJ L 145, 31 May 2001, para. 2 of the Preamble.

248 Amanda Frost, "Restoring Faith in Government: Transparency Reform in the United States and the European Union", *European Public Law,* Vol. 9, No. 1, 2003, 87–104.

249 Anna Ogonowska, "Dostęp Do Dokumentów Unii Europejskiej", *Źródła Informacji o Unii Europejskiej. Zarys Problematyki.* Wydawnictwo Sejmowe, Warszawa, 2006, 44–5.

250 Anna Wyrozumska, "Jednostka w Unii Europejskiej", in: Jan Barcz (ed.) *Prawo Unii Europejskiej. Zagadnienia Systemowe, Prawo materialne i polityki,* Warszawa: Wydawnictwo Prawo i Praktyka Gospodarcza, 2006, 416.

The right of access to the Union documents was expressly granted for the first time in the Treaty of Amsterdam.[251] The Treaty obliged the EP, the Council, and the Commission to disclose their documents according to the rules established by the Council.[252] Under the Lisbon Treaty, Article 15(3) TFEU clearly formulates the right of any citizen of the Union to have access to documents of the Union institutions, bodies, offices, and agencies[253] whatever their medium, subject to the principles and the conditions, including limits determined by the European Parliament and the Council by means of regulations and the Rules of Procedure of particular institutions, bodies and agencies.[254]

The Treaty-based right of public access to the documents of the European Parliament, the Council and the Commission was developed in Regulation No. 1049/2001.[255] The Regulation introduced uniform principles, conditions, and limits on access to documents and provided for two types of access: direct, and based on application. Pursuant to Article 12 of the Regulation, the institutions should as far as possible make documents accessible directly to the public in electronic form or through a register in accordance with the rules of the institution concerned. Access based on application concerns such documents as those which, for some reasons, were not disclosed to the public in the full text.[256] Under the principle of linguistic equality and the principle of non-discrimination, the right of access to documents should be provided in all the Union official languages. As proved by experience, the access to the documents of the EU institutions in languages other than English and French is not common.[257] As the widespread knowledge of English (even more so French and German) is rather a myth than reality, the exercise of the right of access to documents is very often impossible owing to language barriers.

The direct access is provided by means of seven major registers of documents kept by the relevant institution or body.[258] The registers demonstrate significant

---

251 OJ C 340, 10 November 1997, Article 255 TEC.

252 Anna Ogonowska, "Dostęp Do Dokumentów Rady Unii Europejskiej", *Unia Europejska Istota Szanse Wyzwania*, CeDeWu, 2018, 92.

253 The institutions include: the European Commission, the European Parliament, and the Council of the European Union – as well as other offices, bodies, and agencies. The European Central Bank, the Court of Justice of the European Union, and the European Investment Bank also fall within the obligation to grant access to their documents only when exercising their administrative tasks.

254 Wróbel, Miąsik and Półtorak (eds.), 163.

255 OJ L 145, 31 May 2001.

256 Ogonowska, "Dostęp Do Dokumentów Unii Europejskiej", 49.

257 Ogonowska, "Dostęp Do Dokumentów Rady Unii Europejskiej", 65.

258 The registers of the Council, Commission, Parliament, Committee of the Regions, Social and Economic Committee. The Commission administers three registers: a register of the Commission's documents, interinstitutional register of delegated acts

differences among institutions in understanding the principle of openness and transparency and in the scope of documents to be disclosed.[259] They also differ in terms of the number of available language versions. The registers of the Council, the EP, and the basic register of the Commission's documents are maintained in all the EU official languages. This does not mean that all the documents are available in all language versions. The descriptions of documents include information about the available language versions. In fact, only some documents are available in all the EU official languages, and the majority can be read only in English and French. As regards the register of the Committee of the Regions, the number of languages is limited to 11 languages and the Social and Economic Committee maintains its register only in English and French.[260]

The indirect access to documents carried out upon an application also shows linguistic deficiencies. Article 6(1) of Regulation No. 1049/2001 allows the Union citizen to submit a written application, including in electronic form, to the institution for access to documents drawn up in one of the Union official languages. However, the Regulation does not guarantee that the answers to applications will be provided in the same language. This right may only be deduced from the rules of the EU linguistic regime under Article 3 of Regulation No. 1/58. [261] Since the entry into force of Regulation No. 1049/2001, there has been an increase in the number of requests for documents almost year by year. In 2018, nearly seven thousand applications were filed, which was a striking increase by nearly ten per cent when compared with 2017. The Report of 2019 on the application of Regulation No. 1049/2001 shows a higher demand for increased transparency in the area of public access to documents. At the same time, it reveals lack of sufficient resources allocated to the Commission to efficiently handle access. The Report remains silent on languages used in the answers provided by the institutions.[262]

3.5.3 The right to submit European Citizens' Initiative in one of the EU official languages

The European Citizens' Initiative (ECI) is a participatory democracy instrument derived from Union citizenship which was introduced in the LT. The legal basis

---

and the comitology register, http://oide.sejm.gov.pl/oide/en/index.php?option=com_content&view=article&id=14441&Itemid=367 [retrieved on 31 July 2019].

259 The issue is not governed by Regulation No. 1049/2001 and hence every institution independently specifies the scope of such documents.

260 Ogonowska, "Dostęp Do Dokumentów Unii Europejskiej", 65.

261 OJ 17, 1 July 2013.

262 European Commission, Report from the Commission on the Application in 2018 of Regulation (EC) No. 1049/2001 Regarding Public Access to European Parliament, Council and Commission Documents COM(2019) 356 Final, 29 July 2019.

for the right to submit a citizens' initiative is enshrined within the provisions on democratic principles. The right to submit an ECI is clearly separated from the right to submit a petition, as it is ultimately addressed to the Commission, not to the EP. Article 11(4) TEU establishes the basic framework for the right. It states that "not less than one million citizens who are nationals of a significant number of Member States may take the initiative of inviting the European Commission (...) to submit any appropriate proposal on matters where citizens consider that a legal act is required for the purpose of implementing the Treaties." The procedures and conditions for the citizens' initiative were set out in Regulation No. 211/2011 (ECI Regulation).[263] The instruments functioning under the Regulation raised significant concerns. Such a state of affairs gave rise to the Commission's legislative proposal to revise the ECI Regulation. The new Regulation No. 2019/788[264] was adopted and has been in force since 1 January 2020. The new ECI Regulation aims to introduce easier registration of activities and simplify the rules for signatories.[265]

The ECI incudes clear linguistic aspects, and it poses the question of what language rights for the Union citizens arise from the initiative. The analysis of provisions referring to the use of languages enshrined in Regulation No. 211/2011 and Regulation No. 2019/788 proves that a number of significant changes have been introduced in the area of language use. Regulation No. 211/2011 referred to the use of languages only in the context of the registration of a proposed citizens' initiative. Article 4 stipulated that information on the subject matter and objectives of the proposed citizens' initiative must be provided by the organisers of the initiative in one of the EU official languages. Reservation was made that, upon registration, the organisers could provide the proposed citizens' initiative in other official languages of the Union for inclusion in the register. However, the translation of the proposed citizens' initiative into other official languages of the Union was the responsibility and at the expense of the organisers.[266] Regulation No. 2019/788 is more specific in respect of language use. The Preamble reads that "in order to make European citizens' initiatives more inclusive and visible, organisers can use for their own promotion and communication languages other than the official languages of the institutions of the Union which, in accordance with the Member States' constitutional orders, have official status in all or part of their territory".[267] Through this, the range of the persons entitled is extended onto the users of the

263 Regulation (EU) No. 211/2011 of the European Parliament and of the Council of 16 February 2011 on the citizens' initiative. OJ L 65, 11 March 2011.

264 Regulation (EU) No. 2019/788 of the European Parliament and of the Council of 17 April 2019 on the European citizens' initiative. OJ L 130, 17 May 2019.

265 New Regulation on the European citizens' initiative, https://ec.europa.eu/citizens-initiative/public /regulation-review [retrieved on 2 August 2019].

266 OJ L 65, 11 March 2011

267 OJ L 130, 17 May 2019, para. 11 of the Preamble.

Union co-official languages[268] who are granted the right to rely upon their own regional language while submitting the initiative. Article 4 requires the Commission to make a guide on the European Citizens' Initiative publicly available in all the official languages of the Union institutions. When compared to Regulation No. 2011/211, the new Regulation guarantees that upon the registration of the initiative, the Commission will provide the translation of the content of that initiative[269] into all the official languages of the Union institutions and obliges the group of organisers to provide translation of additional information on the initiative.

As of 6 November 2020, seventy-five initiatives have been submitted, out of which only six have been successfully approved. The others were either rejected or withdrawn after being approved. Eleven initiatives are active ones. This means that the signatures of supporters are being collected.[270] One of the successful initiatives in the area of languages is Minority SafePack which was submitted to the Commission for examination on 10 January 2020, after more than 1.1 million valid signatures had been collected.[271] Minority SafePack promoted by the Federal Union of European Nationalities called the EU to adopt a set of legal acts to improve the protection of persons belonging to linguistic and national minorities and to strengthen cultural and linguistic diversity in the Union. The initiative exposes the need for policy actions concerning regional and minority languages, in particular in the field of education and culture, regional policy as well as audiovisual and media content.[272] The initiative manifests the citizens' need for a pact between minorities and majorities. Such a pact should contribute to creating conditions favourable for linguistic and cultural diversity, as well as for preserving and promoting the identity of the minority communities.[273] The public hearing on the Minority SafePack at the European Parliament held on 15 October 2020 displayed the initiative as a method to peacefully safeguard the rights of minority members within the existing EU legal framework. The Minority SafePack does not aim to establish the supranational system of minority protection but endeavours to prevent the existing policies from adversely affecting such protection.[274]

268 Catalan, Basque and Galician.

269 The content is specified in Annex II to the Regulation.

270 https://europa.eu/citizens-initiative/ [retrieved on 6 November 2020]

271 https://europa.eu/citizens-initiative/initiatives/details/2017/000004_en [retrieved on 2 February 2020].

272 Minority SafePack Initiative, http://www.minority-safepack.eu/assets/downloads/booklet/ MSPI_brochure_EN.pdf [retrieved on 2 February 2020].

273 Look! We have a pact! between minority and majority, http://www.minority-safepack.eu/ [retrieved on 2 February 2020].

274 Public hearing on European Citizens' Initiative – Minority safepack https://www.europarl. europa.eu/committees/pl/public-hearing-on-european-citizens-init/product-etails/20201013CAN57884 [retrieved on 16 October 2020].

3.6 Language rights of consumers

3.6.1 Free movement of goods vs consumer protection

Consumer rights are the rights of individuals including their right to be informed, to terminate contracts or to receive compensation.[275] The protection of consumers is essential for the functioning of the market in the interests of the Union citizens. The EU consumer policy needs sensible and efficient regulation to ensure it works for approximately 450 million consumers. The rights granted to the EU internal market consumers include linguistic aspects. Such specific rights may be called the language rights of consumers. As product recipients, consumers are entitled to understand labels, safety instructions or manuals of the product they buy. The protection of consumers is difficult not only to numbers, but also to the existing internal market conditions. The EU was founded as an economic community and its internal market represents the very essence of it. At the same time, the EU has always preserved the linguistic diversity as its fundamental right and one of its objectives. In this context, the EU internal market exposes two equally important aims of the organization – preserving linguistic diversity of EU Member States on the one hand, and smooth functioning of the internal market, on the other. The EU's challenge is to strike a balance between those two equally important principles, which means maintaining the equilibrium between the interests of traders, employers, workers and consumers.[276]

The EU multilingual regime based on respect for linguistic diversity causes the exercise of internal market freedoms to be strictly related to the issue of language use. Languages in this context may be perceived as sources of rights and requirements at the same time. Internal market rules impose particular language requirements on entrepreneurs operating at a cross-border level. The EU market is fragmented into linguistic territories which require traders to modify products to be in conformity with the language requirements of individual Member States. Thus, goods must be re-labelled in a particular language, business and consumer contracts must be drawn up in a certain language, and official documents issued by the Member State authorities must be presented in the language of the host Member State.[277] The above requirements are deemed to hinder the free movement[278] and are seen as a "soft barrier" to the exercise the free movement of goods mainly due to the need for translations. The same language rules which create obstacles for entrepreneurs at the same time eliminate such barriers for consumers and constitute their rights.[279]

---

275 Seubert, Eberl and Van Waarden, 136.

276 Directorate-General for Translation EC, 7.

277 Directorate-General for Translation EC, 84.

278 C-51/93 *Meyhui v Schott Zwiesel Glaswerke*, para. 13; C-33/97 *Colim NV v Bigg's Continent Noord NV*, para. 36.

279 Directorate-General for Translation EC, 7 and 84.

The linguistic regime defined by Regulation No. 1/58 does not regulate language use in trade. As a general rule, the Union and Member States share competences, both the fields of internal market and consumer protection.[280] By virtue of the subsidiarity principle, the EU should legislate only where it can be proved that Member States cannot effectively regulate the subject-matter concerned on their own, and the objective pursued can be attained by EU wide measures.[281] The Commission Communication of 1993 on language use for the information of consumers in the Community[282] confirms that languages in the area of consumer protection naturally fall within the competence of Member States. This approach is reinforced by a number of secondary legislative acts. The major directives in the area of consumer protection, including the Directive on the protection of consumers in respect of distance contracts,[283] the Directive on consumer rights[284] and the Directive to protect the consumer in respect of contracts negotiated away from business premises[285] indicate, that the language of consumer contracts is a matter for the Member States which are free to set requirements concerning the use of languages in their own national legislation.

From the legal point of view, language requirements imposed on producers or traders may be regarded as rules which hinder, directly or indirectly, trade within the EU (*Procureur du Roi).*[286] Under Article 34 TFEU, they would be qualified as measures having an effect equivalent to quantitative restrictions. However, Article 36 TFEU expressly lists the exceptions to such rules, which include the restrictions justified on the grounds of the protection of health and life of humans, including the protection of consumers. Moreover, Article 169(1) TFEU guarantees the protection of consumer's safety, health and economic interests. The Court of Justice has

280 OJ 2016 C 202, 7 June 2016, Article 4 TFEU.

281 Zawidzka-Łojek and Łazowski (eds.), 35–6.

282 Communication from the Commission to the Council and the European Parliament concerning language use in the information of consumers in the Community COM (93) 456 final, 10 November 1993, para. 2.

283 Directive 97/7/EC of the European Parliament and of the Council of 20 May 1997 on the protection of consumers in respect of distance contracts. OJ L 144, 4 June 1997.

284 Directive 2011/83/EU of the European Parliament and of the Council of 25 October 2011 on consumer rights, amending Council Directive 93/13/EEC and Directive 1999/44/EC of the European Parliament and of the Council and repealing Council Directive 85/577/EEC and Directive 97/7/EC of the European Parliament and of the Council. OJ L 304, 22 November 2011.

285 Council Directive 85/577/EEC of 20 December 1985 to protect the consumer in respect of contracts negotiated away from business premises. OJ L 372, 31 December 1985.

286 Judgment of the Court of 11 July 1974 in the case 8/74 *Procureur du Roi v Benoît and Gustave Dassonville*, ECLI:EU:C:1974:82, para. 5.

developed certain grounds that may justify a restriction on the free movement of goods for reasons justified by consumer protection. The judgment in the landmark case of *Cassis de Dijon*[287] defined the general principle that the goods legally produced and marketed in one EU Member State should be admitted to the markets of the other Member States. In the same judgment, the Court established a linguistic restriction substantiated by the fact that consumers were entitled to be informed of the characteristics of the product in the required language.[288] As a result, linguistic labelling provisions could not qualify as a measure having equivalent effect to quantitative restrictions. The Court of Justice also dealt with another issue related to the language rights of consumers. It analysed the meaning of the phrase 'use of a language easily understood'.[289] In *Piageme I*[290] (1991) and *Piageme II*[291] (1995), the Court held that the concept did not automatically mean the use of an official language of the State, as the requirement for an exclusive use of a particular language may constitute a measure having equivalent effect to quantitative restrictions on imports. The Court stressed that the aim is to ensure that the consumer is provided with necessary information rather than impose a specific language use. Instead, a national court must examine on a case-by-case basis whether the information provided in a language other than the main language of the state or region can be easily understood by affected consumers.[292]

Within its competences, the Union aims to protect consumers by granting them the right to receive necessary information from labelling in their own language. The Directive on general product safety[293] does not provide a general obligation to translate instructions or warnings into the language of the Member State, but authorises the Member State to set such requirements. Moreover, the Directive stipulates that national authorities might require that the product be marked with

287 Judgment of the Court of 20 February 1979 in the case C-120/78 *Rewe-Zentral AG vs Bundesmonopolverwaltung Für Branntwein*, ECLI:EU:C:1979:42.

288 Judgment of the Court in the case C-120/78, para. 8.

289 Including the Old Foodstuffs Directive (Article 14), the Aromatised Wine Regulation (Article 8(5)-(8)), the Spirt Drinks Regulation (Article 14(1)-(4)), the Lactoprotein Directive (Article 4(2)), the Extraction Solvents Directive (Article 7(4)).

290 Judgment of the Court of 18 June 1991 in the case C-369/89 *Piageme and others v BVBA Peeters*, ECLI:EU:C:1991:256.

291 Judgment of the Court of 12 October 1995 in the case C-85/94 *Groupement des Producteurs, Importateurs et Agents Généraux d'Eaux Minérales Etrangères VZW (Piageme) and others v Peeters NV*, ECLI: EU: C: 1995: 312.

292 Judgment of the Court of 12 October 1995 in the case C-85/94 *Groupement des Producteurs, Importateurs et Agents Généraux d'Eaux Minérales Etrangères VZW (Piageme) and others v Peeters NV*, ECLI: EU: C: 1995: 312.

293 Directive 2001/95/EC of the European Parliament and of the Council of 3 December 2001 on general product safety. OJ L 11, 15 January 2002.

suitable, clearly worded, and easily comprehensible warnings on the risk it may present. This must be done in the official language(s) of the Member State in which the product is marketed. At the same time, it is certain that complete elimination of language barriers for the consumers would result in excessively high translation costs for the producers and traders. As a general rule, the burden of translation falls upon the producer or the trader.[294] Well-translated instructions and manuals may boost the company's image in other Member States. On the contrary, translation errors in manuals and instructions might be embarrassing and lead customers to question the quality of a product, thereby decreasing their trust in the company. Moreover, missing translations or bad translations may cause legal and factual consequences.[295]

3.6.2 Language use in consumer contracts and disputes

EU legislation provides for certain provisions on the use of language in only specific circumstances. The EU intervenes if language use provisions are necessary to ensure an adequate level of protection for the consumer and such adequate protection cannot be guaranteed by the Member State. The aim of linguistic provisions is to set common harmonised safeguards that Union citizens can access on the territory of the EU.[296] The scope and necessity of Union legal intervention must be thoroughly considered in each case. In practice, this occurs when such provisions are necessary for the functioning of the internal market and dictated by higher rank objectives of consumer protection. Such objectives would include the protection of the consumer as a weaker party to a contractual relation or the protection of consumer health and safety.

One of the higher rank objectives justifying language requirements is the protection of a consumer language rights in cross-border consumer contracts and disputes. In order to protect consumers in a contractual relationship, the EU has adopted a series of directives including explicit references to language use, yet not prejudicing the right of the Member States to regulate the languages used in contracts. These instruments lay down language requirements either in respect of the accessibility of information or the actual use of a language. To name a few examples:

294 Directorate-General for Translation EC, 91.

295 A survey carried out by the German Institute for Standardisation (DIN) demonstrates that the most frequently used remedy in mistranslation of consumer instruction is the correction (50%) followed by legal consequences (37%) and action for damages (12%). Missing translation is in every case remedied by re-translation. Source: *Studie des Verbraucherrates des DIN: Folgen fehlerhafter Anleitungen am Markt und Lösungsansätze zur Verbesserung technischer Anleitungen*, 2010, 84.

296 Directorate-General for Translation EC, 86.

- *the Directive on timeshare and long-term holidays*[297] contains provisions on both the language used in pre-contractual information and that of the contract. Both must be drawn up in a language of the Member State in which the consumer is a resident or of which he is a national. The only condition is that it has to be an official language of the EU.[298] An evaluation study on the Directive application shows that, since the application of the Directive, only 7 % of surveyed consumers received pre-contractual information in a language they did not understand.[299] From a consumer's perspective, this issue does not appear to be a cause for concern.
- *the Directive on certain aspects of the sale of consumer goods and associated guarantees*[300] contains provisions on language requirements with regard to guarantees. Accordingly, the guarantee must be drafted in one or more languages which shall be determined from among the official languages of the EU.[301]
- *the Directive on electronic commerce*[302] stipulates that the service provider must give information about the language used before the order is placed by the service recipient. Such information embraces languages offered for the conclusion of the contract. Moreover, the Directive provides grounds for the codes of conduct drawn up by trade, professional and consumer associations or organizations which should be accessible by electronic means in all the EU official languages.
- *the Unfair Commercial Practices Directive*[303] provides that the misleading and abusive use of languages is considered to be an unfair commercial

---

297 Directive 2008/122/EC of the European Parliament and of the Council of 14 January 2009 on the protection of consumers in respect of certain aspects of timeshare, long-term holiday product, resale and exchange contracts. OJ L 33, 3 February 2009.

298 OJ L 33, 3 February 2009, Article 4(3).

299 Evaluation Study on the Application of the Timeshare Directive 2008/122/EC by the Centre for Strategy and Evaluation Services (CSES), Table 4.3, 41, http://ec.europa.eu/consumers/consumer_ rights/travel/timeshare/index_en.htm [retrieved on 25 October 2019].

300 Directive 1999/44/EC of the European Parliament and of the Council of 25 May 1999 on certain aspects of the sale of consumer goods and associated guarantees. OJ L 171, 7 July 1999.

301 OJ L 171, 7 July 1999, Article 6(5).

302 Directive 2000/31/EC of the European Parliament and of the Council of 8 June 2000 on certain legal aspects of information society services, in particular electronic commerce, in the Internal Market. OJ L 178, 17 July 2000.

303 Directive 2005/29/EC of the European Parliament and of the Council of 11 May 2005 concerning unfair business-to-consumer commercial practices in the internal market and amending Council Directive 84/450/EEC, Directives 97/7/EC, 98/27/EC and 2002/65/EC of the European Parliament and of the Council and Regulation (EC)

practice.[304] Annex I to the Directive states that a misleading commercial practice also takes place when a trader provides after-sales service to consumers with whom he communicated before a transaction in a language which is not an official language of the Member State, but in another language not known to the consumer, if the consumer was not informed of that fact.[305]

Specific compulsory language rules in particular contexts do not prejudice the right of the Member States from regulating the language used for consumer contracts and the law applicable to it. The Member States may set more stringent rules regarding the use of languages than those imposed by the Union if this is justified by consumer protection.[306]

According to the Eurobarometer 2006,[307] 2011,[308] and 2015[309] and the study of the European Parliament Research Service of 2017,[310] language barriers have been seen as the major obstacles in cross-border trade. Consumers often refrain from buying abroad for fear that they will have major difficulties in making their claims successful *inter alia* due to language problems. This fact is justified as consumers cannot effectively enforce their rights before the national authorities or courts of another Member State if they do not have a command of that state's language.

In order to assist consumers in cross-border complaints and disputes by providing them with information and translation, the Commission set up the European Consumer Centres' Network (ECC-Net).[311] Since 2005, a European Consumer Centre (ECC) has been founded in every Member State, as well as in Iceland and Norway. The ECCs are jointly financed by the European Commission and the Member States. They are hosted by either the national consumer protection authority or a consumer association. A consumer confronted by a cross-border dispute, who has contacted the trader in the other country directly in order to solve the problem, but failed to do this, is entitled to address the national ECC and request help. In the next step, the national ECC contacts the ECC of the trader's country,

No. 2006/2004 of the European Parliament and of the Council ('Unfair Commercial Practices Directive'). OJ L 149, 11 June 2005.

304 OJ L 149, 11 June 2005, Article 9(b).

305 OJ L 149, 11 June 2005, Annex I, para. 8.

306 Directorate-General for Translation EC, 87.

307 Flash Eurobarometer Series 186: Business attitudes towards cross-border sales and consumer protection, 2006.

308 Flash Eurobarometer Series 321: B2C on the European contract law, 2011.

309 Flash Eurobarometer 397: Consumer attitudes towards cross-border trade and consumer protection, 2015.

310 Language Equality in the Digital Age. Towards a Human Language Project, 2017, https://www.europarl.europa.eu/RegData/etudes/STUD/2017/598621/EPRS_STU(2017)598621_EN.pdf [retrieved on 22 July 2020].

311 Directorate-General for Translation EC, 96.

which then contacts the trader to find an amicable solution.[312] As languages play a role in this type of claims and disputes, the ECCs also provide translation assistance. Regulation No. 764/2008[313] was adopted in order to facilitate the work of ECCs and to foster the effective functioning of the principle of mutual recognition. This was of particular importance for those products which did not fall under harmonisation, and where the information on technical product requirements was of special importance.

The EU does not have powers to impose an obligation upon a Member State to guarantee the availability of such information in all the official languages as this would constitute an excessive burden. Recital (30) of the Preamble to the Regulation contains recommendations for the Member States according to which Product Contact Points (PCPs) operating with the ECC-Net – in charge of proving information on national product requirements – should be adequately equipped and resourced to make the information available to consumers through their website and in a multitude of Community languages. The Anniversary Report on the ECC-Net operation 2005–2015[314] evidenced that approximately 100000 consumers contact the ECCs annually and the Net handles approximately 2000 consumer complaints. The number of queries has been rising systematically, with the dramatic increase noted as an impact of coronavirus. In order to cope with the queries and warn consumers about fraudulent medical products, a dedicated multilingual website was created by the Commission.[315]

A similar solution in respect of services was adopted in the Service Directive 2006/123[316] which entrusts the task of providing information on applicable national requirements concerning services to the Points of Single Contact (PSCs) operating under the EUGO Network. The PSCs have been established in all the Member States as well as in Iceland, Lichtenstein and Norway. The Points function in form of an electronic portal which provides information on formalities and procedures,

312 Quality charter, https://konsument.gov.pl/en/quality-charter/ [retrieved on 3 February 2020].

313 Regulation (EC) No. 764/2008 of the European Parliament and of the Council of 9 July 2008 laying down procedures relating to the application of certain national technical rules to products lawfully marketed in another Member State and repealing Decision No. 3052/95/EC, OJ L 218, 13 August 2008.

314 The European Consumer Centres Network. 10 years serving Europe's consumers. Anniversary Report, 2005–2015, https://ec.europa.eu/info/sites/info/files/ecc_net_-_anniversary_report_2015 _en.pdf [retrieved on 22 July 2020].

315 https://ec.europa.eu/info/live-work-travel-eu/consumers/resolve-your-consumer-complaint/europ ean- consumer-centres-network-ecc-net/ecc-net-and-covid-19_en [retrieved on 22 July 2020].

316 Directive 2006/123/EC of the European Parliament and of the Council of 12 December 2006 on services in the internal market. OJ L 376, 27 December 2006.

available databases or public registers. They aim to increase transparency and make it easier for consumers to use services offered in the internal market. As to the languages of such information, the Directive goes further than the Regulation on Product Contact Points. Although it includes no strict obligation to display information in other languages, Article 7(5) of the Directive states that the Member States and the Commission shall take necessary measures to encourage PSCs to make the information available to the public in other EU languages. Still, most PCS websites are available only in the national language and English. The exceptions are websites of the Czech Republic (6 languages), Belgium (4 languages), Finland, Luxembourg, Spain, Estonia, Romania and Latvia (3 languages).[317] In view of the above, it may certainly be concluded that the right to obtain information by a consumer in their language through the PCPs and PSCs depends on a Member State and is limited to the languages offered by particular Member State.

3.6.3 Language use when health and safety are at stake

Another overriding reason substantiating the Union's intervention into the language matters occurs when the consumer's health and safety are at stake. Three major types of products may be distinguished in this category: medical devices, toys and cosmetic products. The protection measures include labelling requirements, and the language used in instructions for use or safety instructions of a product placed on the internal market. The burden of translation falls on the producer or trader placing the product on the market. In the case of medical devices, the requirements are the most stringent. Annex II to Regulation No. 2017/745 on medical devices determines that labels on the device and on its packaging as well as instructions for use must be provided in the languages accepted by the Member States where the device is envisaged to be sold.[318] The Directive on the Community code relating to medicinal products for human use imposes an obligation to provide the entire package leaflet of such product in the official language or language where the product is marketed.[319] In order to ensure high quality translation the European Medicines Agency introduced a multi-step linguistic review process in all the EU official languages.[320]

---

317 Points of Single Contact, https://ec.europa.eu/growth/single-market/services/services-directive/in-practice/contact_en [retrieved on 7 September 2019].

318 Regulation (EU) No. 2017/745 of the European Parliament and of the Council of 5 April 2017 on medical devices, amending Directive 2001/83/EC, Regulation (EC) No. 178/2002 and Regulation (EC) No 1223/2009 and repealing Council Directives 90/385/EEC and 93/42/EEC. OJ L 117, 5 May 2017.

319 Directive 2001/83/EC of the European Parliament and the Council of 6 November 2001 on the Community code relating to medicinal products for human use. OJ L 311, 28 November 2001, Article 63.

320 Directorate-General for Translation EC, 91.

Less stringent rules are applied in respect of toys. Here, the EU provisions are not so specific.[321] The Directive on the safety of toys[322] establishes a sort of a mixed system, wherein Member States' competence to regulate language requirements is limited by the provisions of the Directive imposing certain obligations on producers and traders. The instructions and safety information must be prepared by the producer or the importer in an intelligible language, the language itself being determined by the Member State concerned.[323] The linguistic requirements in relation to cosmetic products seem to be the most flexible. Article 19(5) of Regulation No. 1223/2009 states that the language of the information provided on the label should be determined by the law of the Member State in which the product is made available to the end user".[324] Moreover, producers and importers of a certain cosmetic product are obliged to demonstrate, at the request of the national authority and in a language that is understood by the authority, that the product is compatible with the market requirements.[325]

3.7 Conclusions

- The language rights attached to the concept of Union citizenship are varied in nature and scope. They include rights of a social, personal and political nature. Firstly, social rights comprise the right to use one's own language before a Member State court, the right not to be discriminated against as a worker or self-employed person on the basis of language skills, or the consumer's right to have product labels and instructions available in their own language. Secondly, personal rights entail the right to choose one's own name and surname. Finally, political rights embrace the right to petition the EP, to apply to the Ombudsman and to address the Union institutions in any Treaty language and to obtain a reply in the same language and the right to enjoy consular and diplomatic protection of any Member State while being in a third country.
- The introduction of Union citizenship into the EU law contributed to building a more advanced system of individual rights protection, including language rights. The system was developed by the Court of Justice which consistently linked the right to move and reside freely with the principle of non-discrimination on the grounds of nationality (*Martinez Sala, Bickel and Franz, Grzelczyk*).

---

321 Directorate-General for Translation EC, 84.

322 Directive 2009/48/EC of the European Parliament and of the Council of 18 June 2009 on the safety of toys. OJ L 170, 30 June 2009.

323 OJ L 170, 30 June 2009, Articles 4 and 6.

324 Regulation (EC) No. 1223/2009 of the European Parliament and of the Council of 30 November 2009 on cosmetic products. OJ L 342, 22 December 2009.

325 OJ L 342, 22 December 2009, Article 5(3).

- The jurisprudence of the Court of Justice evidences that the rights granted to the Union citizen in Article 20(2) TFEU and developed in Articles 21–24 TFEU include linguistic aspects which are covered by the scope of Community law.
- The analysis of the right to move and reside freely read in conjunction with the principle of non-discrimination on the grounds of nationality leads to the following conclusions in respect of language rights:
  - o The right of equal access to education constitutes an important element of the right to move and reside freely and the principle of non-discrimination on the grounds of nationality. This is the area where the Union has competence to intervene in order to ensure free-of-charge education on non-discriminatory basis. However, the Union's lack of general competence in the area of education does not allow the EU to regulate the language of education in particular Member States.
  - o The Union citizen is granted the right to have judicial proceedings, both criminal and civil *(Bickel and Franz* and *Rüffer),* conducted by the Member State court in a language other than the one habitually used if such a right is granted to the nationals of that State. The right is not absolute as it is conditional upon the treatment which a Member State accords to its own nationals.
  - o The right to choose one's name and surname remains an evolving matter in the EU. The judgments of the Court of Justice in *Konstantinidis, Garcia Avello, Leonard Matthias* and *Grunkin-Paul, Sayn-Wittgenstein* as well as *Runevič-Vardyn and Wardyn* prove that the rules governing a person's name and surname fall within the Union's competence if combined with the right to move and reside freely. Such a state of affairs has forced a change in the traditional approach to forename and surname spelling in the EU Member States. Different spellings can hamper the exercise of the right by raising doubts concerning person's identity and, as a result, may trigger serious inconveniences at administrative, private, or professional level. In such a case, different spelling should be forbidden unless it is justified by legitimate aims pursued by the Member State. Therefore, the right to a name and surname may be confronted by the Union's respect for the national identity of a Member State expressed though respect for its constitutional values (*Sayn-Wittgenstein*) and respect for the national language rules (*Runevič-Vardyn and Wardyn).* These may constitute the basis which may justify the restriction to the right on condition that the restrictions are compliant with the principle of proportionality and do not cause serious inconvenience for the person concerned. The competence to verify the proportionality of a domestic measure against the right to move and reside freely is granted to Member State national courts.
  - o The analysis of language rights of the Union citizen against the background of the EU internal market freedoms leads to the conclusion that the status of the Union citizen is fundamental (*Grzelczyk*) and, therefore, the rights of economically active and inactive citizens are in principle equal (*Bickel and Franz*). In justified cases, the rights for economically inactive citizens may be

limited by the principles of the internal market as long as the adopted measures are proportionate and non-discriminatory (*Baumbast*).
- o Language rights of economically active citizens entrenched in the right to move and reside freely may be limited by way of imposing specific language requirements, which if objectively justified, do not infringe EU law.
  - Firstly, language requirements imposed on workers by national legislation are justified if they do not violate the principle of non-discrimination on the grounds of nationality and the principle of proportionality *(Groener).*
  - Secondly, a Member State may define linguistic requirements towards a professional (e.g. a dental professional) practising on its territory if language knowledge and skills are needed to perform his or her duties, i.e. to communicate with patients and professional colleagues as well as to arrange one's administrative work. Nevertheless, the requirements should not go beyond what is necessary to attain professional objectives, otherwise the requirements are deemed to be unlawful (*Haim, Hocsman*).
  - Finally, the requirement to prove one's linguistic knowledge in a recruitment procedure by means of one particular diploma constitutes discrimination on grounds of nationality (*Angonese).*

- The right to use any Treaty language while submitting a petition to the EP, applying to the European Ombudsman and addressing the Union institutions enshrined in Article 24 TFEU strengthens the rights based on the Union linguistic regime and raises the status of the Union citizen's right to control the EU institution operations and receive relevant information in their own language.
- The Union citizen who has the status of an unrepresented citizen within the meaning of Directive 2015/637 has the right to be provided with the same diplomatic and consular protection as is ensured to the citizen of the assisting Member State. This is compliant with the principle of non-discrimination on the grounds of nationality. The language-related assistance to the unrepresented citizen is ensured to the extent which guarantees protection of the essential rights and interests of the citizens. In principle, the consul is not obliged to provide specific language assistance. If he or she provides such a service, the fees imposed on an unrepresented citizen are charged on the same principles as in the case of the citizens of the assisting Member State.
- The Union citizen's language rights attached to the right of access to Union documents are limited to the availability of particular documents disclosed through a register or upon application in a given language version.
- The European Citizens' Initiative is a significant step forward in implementing citizens' language rights within the framework of democratic participation in the Union's life and the EU's policy of openness and transparency. Moreover, the entry into force of Regulation No. 2019/788 indicates the development in the area of language use. Having met the necessary conditions, the Union citizens are authorised to submit the initiative is any official or co-official language of the EU and the EU guarantees translation of an application.

- Language rights of consumers constitute a special category of consumer rights. The EU aims to grant consumers the right to receive necessary information about the product in their own language. Nevertheless, the specific requirements depend on the product category and are determined by the Member States. In justified cases, language rights of consumers may restrict free movement of goods (*Cassis de Dijion*). The EU is authorised to intervene into consumer protection and grant language rights to consumers if it is justified by higher rank objectives, in the case when:
  - o there is a need to adequately protect the consumer as a weaker party to a cross-border consumer contract. Consumers are entitled to receive consumer contracts in a language understandable by them, including timeshare and long-term holiday contracts, contracts for e-commerce services or guarantees attached to the contracts.
  - o consumer's health and safety are at stake. In this area, three categories of products are distinguished: medical devices, toys, and cosmetic products. In the case of medical devices, on the basis of EU law, consumers have the right to have labels and any other relevant information, including safety and health warnings, available in their own language. In the case of toys, the language of instructions and safety information may be determined by the Member State. For cosmetic products, there is no clear obligation to provide information in a given language unless the national authorities require that from the producer or importer.

4. Language rights resulting from the protection of fundamental rights in the European Union

4.1 Opening remarks

The introduction of Union citizenship into the Union law coincided with the development of the European Communities towards protection of fundamental rights. On the one hand, Union citizenship contributed to the expansion of the scope of right holders based on the principle of non-discrimination on the grounds of nationality, thereby aiming to eliminate any provisions discriminatory towards the Union citizen. On the other hand, the EU took actions to strengthen fundamental rights protection by introducing relevant provisions to the Treaties.[1] The parallel development of Union citizenship and fundamental rights placed the rights of individuals in the spotlight of Union activities. The rights based on Union citizenship differ from the fundamental rights in their subjective and objective scope. Union citizenship has created a number of extraordinary civil rights, while the fundamental rights comprise a wide spectrum of personal rights, political rights as well as social, economic and cultural rights. Whereas Union citizenship is a source of rights for the citizens of the Member States of a political organization, the protection of fundamental rights in the Union results in a wider range of rights granted to any individual, regardless of nationality.

Language-related guarantees play an important role in the context of the Union's commitment to linguistic pluralism, making the organization a good forum for language claims based on their fundamental status.[2] In order to create the exhaustive catalogue of fundamental language rights, one needs to analyse the sources of such rights. Certainly, the major source is the Charter of Fundamental Rights of the European Union (the Charter)[3] which constitutes the key human rights instrument in the EU. As the Charter includes both direct and indirect references to language-related rights, freedoms, and principles, the analysis of all the fundamental rights which entail linguistic aspects should be carried out. Still, the Charter does not cover all the linguistic fundamental guarantees which could be invoked by individuals in the EU. Moreover, owing to its limited scope and the lack of the direct effect

---

1 Adam Bodnar, "Obywatelstwo UE a ochrona praw podstawowych", *Obywatelstwo Unii Europejskiej. Zeszyty OIDE*, Wydawnictwo Sejmowe, 2008, 50.

2 Stefaan Van der Jeught. *EU Language Law*, Europa Law Publishing, Groningen, 2015, 97.

3 OJ C 202/2, 7 June 2016.

of its provisions, the sources of language rights must also be sought in the general principles of Union law entrenched in the extensive case-law of the Court of Justice, constitutional traditions of the Member States and international human rights instruments, in particular in the Convention for the Protection of Human Rights and Fundamental Freedoms (ECHR).[4] The general principles of law refer primarily to the language rights of persons belonging to national and linguistic minorities, which is an area falling beyond the EU's explicit powers.[5]

The concept of 'fundamental rights' is the key term used in this chapter. It should be understood as autonomous inalienable rights which are inherent in all human beings, regardless of their nation, location, language, religion, ethnic origin, or any other status. As noted by Marshall, fundamental rights are human rights which are reflected in the norms of a constitutional rank.[6] The term 'fundamental right' dominates over the notion of 'human right' in the frequency of use, when referred to the EU legal order. It is justified by the fact that the term, also 'fundamental human rights',[7] has been consistently used by the Court of Justice[8] in order to underline the autonomous nature of the Union legal order, and the fact that the concept entered into the legal language by way of the Charter. The notion of 'human rights' is used in the chapter with reference to international law instruments and on some occasions with reference to the EU legal order, when this results from the original wording of the EU institutions documents.[9] 'National minority' is another key concept used in the chapter. It was coined in the Council of Europe Framework Convention for the Protection of National Minorities (FCNM),[10] yet it is not clearly

4 Convention for the Protection of Human Rights and Fundamental Freedoms signed on 4 November 1950, entered into force on 3 September 1953. By 2020 ratified by 47 states.

5 Van der Jeught, *EU Language Law*, 95.

6 Thomas H. Marshall, "Citizenship and Social Class", in: Jeff Manza and Michael Sauder (eds.) *Inequality and Society*, New York, 2009, 8.

7 Judgment of the Court of 12 November 1969 in the case C 29-69 *Erich Stauder v City of Ulm – Sozialamt*, ECLI:EU:C:1969:57.

8 C-11/70 *Internationale Handelsgesellschaft mbH v Einfuhr- und Vorratsstelle für Getreide und Futtermittel;* C-4/73 *J. Nold, Kohlen- und Baustoffgroßhandlung v Ruhrkohle Aktiengesellschaft*; C-377/16 *Kingdom of Spain v European Parliament*; C-414/16 *Vera Egenberger v Evangelisches Werk für Diakonie und Entwicklung e.V*; C-193/17 *Cresco Investigation GmbH v Markus Achatzi.*

9 Agnieszka Płachta, "Zasada Ochrony Praw Podstawowych", in: Andrzej Wróbel (ed.), *Stosowanie prawa Unii Europejskiej przez sądy*, Kraków, 2005, 342.

10 Framework Convention for the Protection of National Minorities opened for signature on 1 February 1995, entered into force on 1 February 1998. By 2020 ratified by 39 states.

defined there.[11] Based on the provisions of the FCNM and specialised literature,[12] for the purposes of this chapter 'national minority' is understood as a community which is compactly or dispersedly settled on the territory of a state, and which is smaller in number than the rest of the state population and has ethnic, linguistic, or cultural features different from those of the rest of the state population. 'National minority' is a non-dominant community which has a desire to retain its distinctive identity. The notion of 'linguistic minority' also appears in the chapter mainly in the context of the international law instruments. The concept is used in Article 27 of the International Covenant on Civil and Political Rights (ICCPR),[13] Article 30 of the Convention on the Rights of the Child (CRC),[14] as well as in the Declaration on the Rights of Persons Belonging to National or Ethnic, Religious, and Linguistic Minorities.[15] Although none of the instruments provides a transparent definition of 'linguistic minority', it seems obvious that such minority has its linguistic identity which makes it different from others. The concept of 'national minority' differs in scope from the notion of 'linguistic minority'. The former is embodied by belonging to one state, the latter is characterised mainly by the language. The analysis proves that the United Nations instruments refer to both national and linguistic minorities, while the Council of Europe relies on national minorities while protecting and promoting languages. The EU has not taken an explicit stance on what it considers to be a minority in a particular Member State. This is justified by the fact that the groups are qualified as 'minorities' at a Member State level and increasingly also at a sub-state level. The EU appears to follow

---

11 The FCNM does not contain a definition of 'national minority' as there is no definition agreed upon by all Council of Europe members. Each party to the Framework Convention is therefore left with a margin of appreciation to assess which groups are to be covered by the Convention within their territory. This decision must be made in good faith and in accordance with general principles of international law. However, their decision must be based on objective criteria connected with their identity, such as their religion, language, traditions and cultural heritage.

12 Kristin Henrard, "An EU Perspective on New versus Traditional Minorities: On Semi-Inclusive Socio-Economic Integration and Expanding Visions of European Culture and Identity", *Columbia Journal of European Law*, Vol. 17, 2010, 57.

13 International Covenant on Civil and Political Rights adopted by the UN General Assembly on 16 December 1966 by resolution No. 2200 A, entered into force on 23 March 1976. By 2020 ratified by 173 states.

14 Convention on the Rights of the Child adopted by the UN General Assembly on 20 November 1989 by resolution No. 45/25, entered into force on 2 September 1990. By 2020 ratified by 196 states.

15 Declaration on the Rights of Persons Belonging to National or Ethnic, Religious and Linguistic Minorities adopted by the UN General Assembly on 18 December 1992 by resolution No. 47/135.

international trends in adopting inclusive definitions of both concepts.[16] At the same time, Member States tend to define the concepts and apply them accordingly within their domestic legal framework. For instance, the Republic of Poland clearly defined the concept of national minority in an Act of Parliament.[17]

This chapter focuses on the analysis of language rights as fundamental rights in the light of the EU law. It consists of four major sections. The first section presents the international law context for language rights. It is of importance owing to the fact that the international human rights instruments constitute general principles of EU law. Moreover, international law creates the background to the conceptual categories and terminology. The section begins with the analysis of the aims and scope of language rights protection. To visualise the analysis, the scope of language rights protection is presented in the form of concentric circles. Next, the concept of collective and individual language rights, the exercise of rights in private and public spheres, as well as positive and negative obligations of the state related to the exercise of rights are presented. Thereafter, language rights qualified as universal human rights are selected and examined. These include freedom of expression in one's own language, the right of non-discrimination on the grounds of language, and procedural linguistic rights. Finally, the enforcement of these rights is analysed. The second section scrutinises the fundamental nature of language rights in the EU, including language rights as general principles of EU law and the rights entrenched in the Charter. The third section focuses on a one-by-one examination of the language rights enshrined in the Charter. First and foremost, the investigation goes into the analysis of rights having clear linguistic references, such as the right to non-discrimination on the grounds of nationality and language, as well as respect for linguistic diversity. Following that, the linguistic aspects of the other fundamental rights are examined, including the right to education, citizens' rights, in particular the right to good administration, as well as the rights related to the enforcement of justice such as the right to a fair trial and the right of defence. Finally, the chapter highlights the impact of the EU accession to the ECHR

---

16 Henrard, 63, 66.

17 Act of the Polish Parliament of 6 January 2005 on national and ethnic minorities and on national language (Journal of Laws 17, item, 141, as amended). Article 2 stipulates that "national minority shall be a group of Polish citizens who jointly fulfil the following conditions: 1) is smaller in number than the rest of the population in the Republic of Poland, 2) significantly differs from remaining citizens by language, culture or tradition, 3) strives to preserve their language, culture or tradition, 4) is aware of their own historical national community and is oriented towards its expression and protection, 5) its ancestors have been living on the present territory of the Republic of Poland for at least one hundred years, 6) identifies themselves with the nation having its own state." *(author's translation)*

on the fundamental rights protection in the Union, including language rights of fundamental status.

4.2 Language rights in the light of international law

4.2.1 Aims and scope of language rights protection

International law has explicitly dealt with language rights since the early 1990s of the twentieth century by granting them at different levels and for different purposes.[18] So far, the law has offered no comprehensive, overarching framework for the protection of language rights, and there is no international treaty dedicated to language rights. Moreover, it remains a matter of dispute among academics whether international law is an appropriate tool to use in language conflicts. As Patten and Kymlicka argued "[a]ny attempt to define a set of rights that applies to all linguistic groups, no matter how small and dispersed, is likely to end up focusing on relatively modest claims".[19] Such a state of affairs is the result of the fact that international law does not recognise language rights in a clear and codified form. Owing to that, language rights are barely protected by universally binding international law instruments. Notwithstanding the lack of an internationally accepted definition of language rights, much attention has been devoted to the analysis of the aims, nature, and scope of such rights. Toscano Méndez (2012) notes that the analysis should include four aspects: 1) who is or can be the right holder, 2) what is the right's content, 3) who is the addressee of the claim-right, or who bears the correlative duty, and 4) what is the degree of stringency of the right, that is, what is its weighing force as compared to other considerations.[20] The examination of all the determinants helps specify the nature of the right and legal implications it bears for the right holder and the obligated entities.

The history of language rights in international law reveals three main purposes of their protection: 1) preservation of peace and security, 2) promotion of fair treatment of individuals and 3) preservation of linguistic diversity.[21] All three may both compete with and contradict each other. Firstly, the idea that language rights

---

18 Directorate-General for Translation EC, *Study on translation and multilingualism. Language and Translation in International Law and EU Law*, Office for Official Publications of the European Union, 2012, 6.

19 Alan Patten and Will Kymlicka, "Introduction: Language Rights and Political Theory: Context, Issues, and Approaches", in: Allan Patten and Will Kymlicka (eds.), *Language Rights and Political Theory*, Oxford University Press, 2003, 35.

20 Manuel Toscano Méndez, "Language Rights as Collective Rights: Some Conceptual Considerations on Language Rights", *Res Publica: Revista de Filosofía Política, Vol.* 12, 2012, 113.

21 Lauri Mälksoo, "The Language Rights in International Law: Why the Phoenix is still in the Ashes?", *Florida Journal of International Law*, Vol. 12, 1998, 431–4.

should serve as a tool to preserve peace and security was developed based on the United Nations Declaration on the Rights of Persons Belonging to National, Ethnic, Religious and Linguistic Minorities adopted by the General Assembly in 1992.[22] The purpose of the Declaration was to promote more effective implementation of the human rights of persons belonging to minorities, and to contribute to the realisation of human rights instruments adopted at the universal and regional level. The Declaration was inspired by Article 27 of the binding ICCPR, but it is more specific as it clearly recognises explicit rights and the state's obligation to take positive measures.[23] The Preamble of the Declaration sets forth that the "promotion and protection of rights of persons belonging to national, ethnic, religious, and linguistic minorities contributed to the political and social stability of the states in which they live" and "to the strengthening of friendship and cooperation among peoples and States".[24] This theory equated the problem of language rights in international law with the linguistic rights of minorities. The Declaration expressly stipulated that persons belonging to linguistic minorities should have the right to use their own language, both in private and in public, freely without interference of any discrimination. Prohibiting discrimination and intolerance against linguistic minorities corresponded with most states' interests, in so far as it helped avoid the outbreak of internal conflicts that could affect other states' international security. Noting that the rights protected in international and national laws are generally interpreted subject to national interests such as security, the dominant argument in the literature on language rights was that granting minority language rights in fact contributed to peace and stability by improving state relations with aggrieved minorities.[25]

Another important step in this area was taken as a reaction to the breakup of Yugoslavia. In 1990 the Copenhagen Document establishing the mandate of the Higher Commissioner on National Minorities was signed, and in 1998 the Oslo Recommendations were adopted by the Organization for Security and Cooperation in Europe.[26] The Oslo Recommendations constitute one of the key measures

---

22 Vide supra 15.

23 Commentary of the Working Group on minorities to the United nations Declaration on the Rights of Persons Belonging to National or Ethnic, Religious and Linguistic Minorities, E/CN.4/Sub.2/AC.5/2005/2, 4 April 2005, paras 1 and 6.

24 Paras 5 and 6 of the Declaration.

25 Mälksoo, 435.

26 Fernand De Varennes and Elżbieta Kuzborska, "Continued Relevance of an 'Oslo' Language Policy in a Changing World", in: Iryna Ulasiuk, Laurenţiu Hadîrcă and William Romans (eds.), *Language Policy and Conflict Prevention,* 2018, Brill Nijhoff, 125. De Varennes and Kuzborska elaborate on the relevance of the Oslo Recommendations in the twenty-first century and conclude that the universal recognition and respect for the rights of minorities is more urgent and pressing rather than relevant. The

taken to protect the language rights of national minorities with an aim of preserving peace and security. The Recommendations stressed the need to avoid ethnic tensions and achieve appropriate balance between dominant and minority languages.[27] Nevertheless, the idea of the language rights protection of certain group members collectively became a contentious matter and was challenged with reference to Central and Eastern Europe where, instead of enhancing security, the measure aiming to protect linguistic minorities in a way threatened and damaged security. As a result, it is still argued whether granting language rights to a minority as a group reduces or actually creates or escalates potential conflicts. This also poses the question of what is the status of such language rights if they are granted collectively.[28]

The other major aim of the language rights protection is to ensure fair treatment of individuals. According to this approach, the potential for conflicts between the majority and minority is not ultimate rationale for the protection. The theory was developed on the basis of justice for individuals as decisive for language rights. Some academics also call this justice 'human dignity', but the idea remains the same.[29] Freedom to use one's language is seen inherent in the dignity of a human person.[30] An individual is placed in the spotlight of protection and should be granted specific language prerogatives and guarantees in this respect. The motivation behind this approach was the principal universal norm of international law on language rights, i.e. Article 27 ICCPR[31] which, according to its narrow binding interpretation, guarantees rights to persons belonging to minorities, but not to a minority as a whole.[32]

The third approach to language rights had close links to the broader concept of the cultural diversity of mankind. It proclaimed that preserving linguistic diversity necessitated the protection of language rights to avoid language death. Kloss argued that, with the death of a language, a unique way of seeing the world vanishes.[33] Although international law does not offer ultimate models or a set of

---

relevance of the Oslo Recommendations has not faded away in any way. On the contrary, it has grown.

27 The Oslo Recommendations regarding the Linguistic Rights of National Minorities and Explanatory Note, OSCE, February 1998.

28 Directorate-General for Translation EC, 66.

29 Tove Skutnabb-Kangas and Robert Philipson, "Linguistic Human Rights, Past and Present", in: Tove Skutnabb-Kangas and Robert Philipson (eds.), *Language Rights*, Routledge, 2017.

30 Moria Paz, "The Tower of Babel: Human Rights and the Paradox of Language", *European Journal of International Law*, 25/2, 2014, 475.

31 Vide supra 13.

32 Directorate-General for Translation EC, 66

33 Heinz Kloss, "Language Rights of Immigrant Groups", *International Migration Review*, Vol. 5, No. 2, 1971.

unambiguous principles and rules to accommodate linguistic diversity, the underlying idea is that humanity suffers losses with the extinction of a language and a lost language leaves an irreparable gap in the cultural heritage of all mankind.[34] Moreover, loss of diversity diminishes the range of options for development (economic, cultural, intellectual, and spiritual). Hence, "the present generations should take care to preserve the cultural diversity of humankind".[35] In Mälksoo's view, the recognition of the need to protect endangered languages inevitably leads to the recognition of language rights as collective rights of a linguistic group. He argues that minorities speak a language different from the majority and these groups deserve special protection so as to preserve their cultural identity.[36] The theory has been challenged by an argument that the idea of "endangered languages" is often a subjective criterion as in the era of globalisation even the speakers of major languages may feel endangered in the global competition of language use under free-market conditions.[37]

4.2.1.1 Language rights protection in the concentric circles

The key language rights are anchored in international law instruments entered into under the auspices of the United Nations and the Council of Europe, such as the Universal Declaration of Human Rights (UDHR, UN Declaration),[38] the International Covenant on Civil and Political Rights,[39] the International Covenant on Economic, Social and Cultural Rights (ICESCR),[40] the Convention on the Rights of the Child,[41] and the International Convention on the Protection of the Rights of All Migrant Workers and Members of Their Families,[42] the European Convention

---

34 Tove Skutnabb-Kangas and Robert Phillipson, "Wanted! Linguistic Human Rights", *ROLIG-papir*, No. 44, 1989, 3.

35 Article 7 of the Declaration on the Responsibilities of the Present Generations Towards Future Generations, adopted on 12 November 1997 by the General Conference of UNESCO.

36 Mälksoo, 444–5.

37 Directorate-General for Translation EC, 67.

38 Universal Declaration of Human Rights proclaimed by the United Nations General Assembly in Paris on 10 December 1948 in resolution 217 A.

39 Vide supra 13.

40 International Covenant on Economic, Social and Cultural Rights signed on 16 December 1966, entered into force on 3 January 1976. By 2020 ratified by 171 states.

41 Vide supra 14.

42 International Convention on the Protection of the Rights of All Migrant Workers and Members of Their Families signed on 18 December 1990, entered into force on 1 July 2003, by 2020 ratified by 25 states.

for the Protection of Human Rights and Fundamental Freedoms,[43] the European Charter for Regional and Minority Languages (ECRML),[44] and the Framework Convention for the Protection of National Minorities.[45] The instruments listed above illustrate various areas where the language-related claims may occur, including civil, political, economic, social and cultural rights as well as the right to education and employment.

The protection of language rights under international law can be described as a system of concentric circles, where individual circles provide different protection. The larger is the circle, the broader, but also the weaker, the protection is. The first circle constitutes the core of international language rights. These are the rights which are not primarily concerned with languages, but imply the right to use a language by an individual right holder in particular circumstances. Most often, they stem from classic human rights aiming to protect human identity and dignity. Such rights include the prohibition of discrimination on the grounds of language, freedom of expression in respect of the choice of language, as well as procedural linguistic human rights, in particular the linguistic aspects of the right to liberty and security, and the right to a fair trial and defence.

The broader circle refers to the protection of minority languages and the language rights of persons belonging to minorities. The primary source of rights in this area is Article 27 ICCPR. Finally, the broadest circle includes a good deal of soft law instruments which create a framework for the protection of minority language rights.[46] Soft law instruments guarantee the weakest protection as they do not lead to a formal obligation on the part of the states, which is why they often contain more far-reaching provisions than binding sources of law. Moreover, they contain numerous provisions on promoting minority languages.

The focus of the analysis will be given to the legally binding instruments, in particular the ICCPR, the ECHR, the ECRML, and the FCNM, which are complementary to the ECHR in respect of language rights.

43 Vide supra 4.

44 European Charter for Regional and Minority Languages signed on 5 November 1992, entered into force on 1 March 1998. By 2020 ratified by 25 states.

45 Vide supra 10.

46 Directorate-General for Translation EC, 68

Figure 1. The system of concentric circles – own elaboration of the author

4.2.2 Individual vs collective nature of language rights

4.2.2.1 Language rights as collective rights

4.2.2.1.1 Corporate and collective conceptions

The three objectives of language rights protection reveal that language rights may be perceived as individual rights and collective rights. Such categorisation leads to a question on the legal status and scope of such rights, whether granted individually and collectively. There are academics in the field, including Foucher,[47] Tabory,[48] and Mälksoo,[49] who maintain that language rights have a collective nature. They admit that, indeed, the right to language preservation may be crucially

47 Pierre Foucher, "Le Droit et La Langue Française Au Canada: Évolution et Perspectives", *Francophonies d'Amérique*, No. 26, 2008, 63–78.

48 Already in 1980 Mala Tabory claimed that language rights were collective rights. Source: Mala Tabory, "Language Rights as Human Rights", *Israel Yearbook on Human Rights*, Vol. 10, 1980, 167, 208

49 Mälksoo, 443.

important for an individual in order for him or her to use a language, but it cannot be secured through individual rights only. They claim that language rights always involve some collectivity mainly due to the fact that linguistic and ethnic minorities are usually tightly interrelated. As a result, the approach, where solely individual rights are recognised and the aspect of collectivity is avoided, does not solve the problem and represents only one side of the issue.[50] As stated by Foucher, language rights may be formulated in individual terms or accorded to individuals, but they have a collective dimension that should bear consequences for their scope and interpretation.[51]

The collective nature of language rights must be explained as it may be understood twofold – in line with a corporate conception, and with a collective conception. Under the corporate view, collective rights are defined according to the right holder and are assigned to a group and not to the individual members of the group. In that sense, a group is seen as a single, integral entity, like a collective agent having legal personality separate from its members. In contrast, according to the collective conception, collective rights are defined by a type of good to which individuals are entitled, not by a right holder. The holders of the collective right are always individual human beings inasmuch as they share a common interest in a collective good, which is a language. According to the collective conception, a language right is a right to a public good and only individuals are entitled to that public good. As linguistic minorities typically lack the legal personality of corporations and, more importantly, they should not be considered as legal persons with rights of their own, the collective conception appears proper for considering language rights as collective rights.[52]

The above seems to be sufficient justification for understanding language rights as rights of individual members of a minority. However, the debate on the nature of language rights has not been finished. The voices of linguists, who maintain that language rights may be considered in some cases both as individual and collective rights, including both conceptions, have added additional layers to the debate. May (2011) coined the term 'group-differentiated rights' in order to reflect different possibilities concerning the right holders. In his view, the rights may be conferred on individual members of a group, on a group as a whole, or even on a federal state or a province where the group forms a majority.[53] Skutnabb-Kangas and Philipson (2017) take note of the fact that the notion of collective rights is easily

50 Toscano Méndez, 113–5.

51 Foucher, 64.

52 Toscano Méndez, 114–5.

53 Stephen May, "Language Rights: The "Cinderella" Human Right", *Journal of Human Rights*, Vol. 10, No. 3, 2011, 268.

misunderstood,[54] which results from the misinterpretation of Article 27 ICCPR. Wrong understanding of corporate and collective conception of language rights may cause broad interpretation benefiting both individuals and groups.[55] Regardless of the diverging voices, the dominant view is that the right holders are individuals, which defends itself in the light of Article 27 ICCPR and was also approved in the 1992 Declaration on the Rights of Persons Belonging to National and Ethnic or Religious Minorities, which stipulated that "persons belonging to (...) linguistic minorities have the right (...) to use their own language".[56] As maintained by De Varennes (1996), a narrow interpretation of Article 27 must be applied as it was never an intention of the drafters to provide concessions to linguistic minorities as such. The debate on the interpretation of Article 27 ICCPR made language rights first and foremost individual in nature, despite having features of collectivity.[57] As a result of such understanding, the term 'collective rights' has been used with reference to the rights of individuals, who are members of a minority (both national and linguistic).

4.2.2.2 Language rights as individual rights

4.2.2.2.1 Human rights-based approach to language rights

It has been established under Article 27 ICCPR and the academic literature that language rights are primarily the domain of individuals. Still, the scope of the concept is far from clear. The merits of individual language rights must be explained on the basis of the theory and development of the idea. The concept of 'individual language rights' was coined by Heinz Kloss, a German linguist and authority on minority rights, in 1971.[58] Kloss divided individual language rights into 'tolerance-oriented language rights' and 'promotion-oriented language rights'. The former stood for the rights of individuals to preserve their language(s) in the private sphere. The key principle of such rights was that the state could not interfere in the private domain of language rights. Therefore, the rights should be perceived as inviolable and the minimum standard in a democratic state. The latter referred to the rights recognised within all formal domains of the nation-state, thus allowing

54 Tove Skutnabb-Kangas and Robert Philipson, "Linguistic Human Rights, Past and Present", in: Tove Skutnabb-Kangas and Robert Philipson (eds.) *Language Rights*, Routledge, 2017, 2.

55 Fernand De Varennes, *Language, Minorities and Human Rights (International Studies in Human Right)*, Brill Nijhoff, 1996, 217–8.

56 Vide supra 13.

57 Fernand De Varennes, "Language Rights as an Integral Part of Human Rights", *International Journal on Multicultural Societies*, 2001, vol.3, No. 1, 15.

58 Heinz Kloss, "Language Rights of Immigrant Groups", *International Migration Review* Vol. 5, No. 2, 1971, 250–68.

a member of the minority to care for its internal affairs through the public authorities. The aim of the promotion-oriented language rights is to improve access to public institutions, such as courts, state schools, and public services. International law instruments impose on the states obligations to guarantee 'tolerance-oriented language rights'.[59] 'Promotion-oriented language rights' are not guaranteed *a priori* and the scope of their protection is continuously evolving. Nevertheless, these developments are uneven, delimited, and remain at the mercy of the nation-states for their effective implementation. Moreover, the question of who should be eligible for them still remains unanswered. It might be noticed that persons belonging to national minorities and indigenous people are gaining ground here, with migrants remaining largely excluded despite growing trends of transmigration and increasing linguistic diversity.[60]

The issue of language rights as individual human rights was elaborated on by Skutnabb-Kangas and Philipson. As enthusiastic advocates of human rights-based approach to individual language rights, they claimed that such rights should be accorded to every human being by virtue of the mere fact that they are human and ought to be recognised by the states and international organizations. Skutnabb-Kangas and Philipson coined and defined the term 'linguistic human rights'. They narrowed its scope to educational rights for minority members. They justified it by the fact that formal education plays a decisive role in the maintenance and development of languages. They distinguished two types of linguistic rights: 'necessary linguistic rights' and 'enrichment-oriented linguistic rights'. The former include the rights to use and learn one's mother tongue and to learn one of the official languages of the state of residence in a standard form. They should be considered inalienable linguistic human rights. Their inalienable nature is justified by the fact that they guarantee an individual the right to build up his or her linguistic repertoire satisfying hir/her emotional, psychological as well as social, political, and economic needs. The latter entail the right to learn foreign languages. As such they are not inalienable as they do not predetermine someone's survival, but can be important for personal or professional purposes. They are perceived a privilege rather than human rights.[61]

A more rigorous characterisation of language rights as human rights was presented by Arzoz (2007). He argued that the general assimilation or equation between language rights and human rights was erroneous. According to him, language rights are an issue devolved to the political process and they create a distorted image of the relationship between law and politics. He touched upon an

59 Mälksoo, 431, 441.

60 Stephen May, "Language, Imperialism, and the Modern Nation-State System", in: Nelson Flores, Ofelia Garcia and Massimiliano Spotti (eds.), *The Oxford Handbook of Language and Society*, Oxford Handbooks Online, 2016, 47–8.

61 Skutnabb-Kangas and Philipson, "Linguistic Human Rights, Past and Present", 21–2.

important discussion on the fundamental character of language rights as a particular category of domestic constitutional rights. He presented three approaches towards language rights as fundamental (human) rights:

1) the approach which resorts to the minimal position of language rights as fundamental rights where linguistic aspects of fundamental rights are explicitly or implicitly recognised as a universal right accorded to everyone; such rights include freedom of expression, the right of respect for private and family life, the right to a fair trial, or the right to education. Any linguistic intolerance and repression of non-dominant languages should regarded as inconsistent with fundamental rights of an individual.
2) a relativist approach according to which language rights are fundamental rights only when they are constitutionally entrenched as such. As a result, their status depends on a domestic legal order.
3) a genuine language rights approach whose aim is to protect the freedom and equality of all individuals and groups. The aim of this approach is to recognise language rights in the organization of social areas and public services through the medium of a designated language, including education, relation with authorities, and the publication of legislation. In line with this approach, language rights may be formulated in individual terms as fundamental rights, but they have a collective dimension that should bear consequences for their scope and interpretation.[62]

Foucher (2008) notes that the recognition of language rights in state constitutions is based primarily on contingent historical reasons.[63] Constitutions and national legal orders illustrate a diversity of solutions, approaches, and regulatory models, which demonstrate that language rights are not at the heart of human rights. The widely diverging approaches to language rights adopted by states in their legislation on the use or recognition of languages other than official language(s) reveal the difficulty of establishing common principles on human rights and could not be comprehensively reflected in international law instruments. Moreover, one should keep in mind the difference between the rights which are actually characterised as human or constitutional rights and the aspirations which one believes also ought to be characterised as such.[64]

4.2.3 Negative and positive language rights

The literature dedicated to language rights distinguishes between the concepts of negative and positive language rights. The notions clearly draw on the Kloss's

62 Xabier Arzoz, "The Nature of Language Rights", *JEMIE* 6, 2007, 25–31.
63 Foucher, 83.
64 Arzoz, "The Nature of Language Rights", 3.

theory on 'tolerance-oriented' and 'promotion-oriented' languages rights. Accordingly, negative language rights require the lack of state interference, and positive language rights impose on the state particular obligations with the objective of protecting individual language rights. The negative rights aim to ensure the regime of linguistic tolerance and include the rights that protect speakers of minority languages against discrimination. The state must prevent any discrimination related to minority languages in a case when individuals are entitled to benefit from specific services. Positive language rights seek to provide the regime of linguistic promotion. As such, they require actions from the state and generate rights of access to key public services, such as education, relationships with public power (government, courts, etc.) and public media in a specific minority language. As a result, granting positive language rights to individuals implies assuming duties on the part of the government to provide the personnel who will facilitate linguistic services in administration, education or justice.[65]

The demarcation between negative and positive language rights was criticised by Patten and Kymlicka (2003) as making untrue implications. For instance, protecting individual spaces of linguistic freedom through state non-interference could result in affecting cultural and linguistic expression as their inevitable corollary. The main criticism seems to be that the state cannot guarantee perfect linguistic neutrality as it must designate a certain language for providing social services.[66] However, Arzoz claims that the distinction between negative freedoms and positive rights is still justified for the purposes of a law-based discussion on language rights. The fact that language rights belong to two different categories affects their enforceable nature. There is a clear correlation between negative and positive language rights with the rights accorded to individuals in the private and public sphere. On the one hand, negative language rights should be immediately applicable as they are free of state interference and as a result fall into one's private sphere. On the other hand, positive language rights include specific rights to receive public services in a particular minority language. The degree of enforceability of such rights differs depending on domestic state constitutional and statutory provisions, ranging from self-executing to programmatic provisions. Positive language rights tend to be drafted as programmatic provisions which imply that the state is under a duty to make individuals benefit from the constitutionally guaranteed rights.[67]

The distinction between negative and positive language rights is clearly differentiated in the light of international law instruments. In principle, the negative rights provide a basic regime of linguistic tolerance by imposing on the states

65 Robert Dunbar, "Minority Language Rights in International Law", *International & Comparative Law Quarterly*, Vol. 50, No. 1, 2001, 91–2.

66 Patten and Kymlicka, 27–8.

67 Arzoz, "The Nature of Language Rights", 6–7.

a general obligation to comply with a principle of non-discrimination and various forms of assimilation (compulsory, degrading etc.). They aim to prevent, in all areas of state involvement and conduct, unjustified disadvantage suffered by a minority member due to the use of a certain language. The protection of negative language rights is granted through universal human rights such as the right to non-discrimination, freedom of expression, and the right of respect for private and family life. Notably, these are the protective measures granted to any individual, whether a minority member or not. In the area of promotion, international law relies mostly on non-binding instruments where the obligations imposed on the states are scarce and lack legal bite. As a matter of fact, Article 27 ICCPR is the only one isolated provision which may be interpreted as obliging the states to positively support minority language maintenance and revitalisation. Some authors, including De Varennes[68] and Tomuschat,[69] object to such interpretation and even authors interpreting the provision in such a way acknowledge that states are not required to give effect to any specific activity or measure.[70]

4.2.4 Language rights in the private and public sphere

Both international law instruments and the literature in the field distinguish two major spheres where language rights may be exercised, i.e. the private sphere and the public sphere. The rights in the private sphere stand for the rights to use a minority language in one's private life, and those in the public sphere imply the right to use a minority language in one's public life. The ECRML in the Preamble provides that "the right to use a regional and minority language in private and public life is an inalienable right".[71] The distinction between the private use of language and the use of a minority language in contact with public authorities results in different types of rights. The main distinctive feature of the private use of language is that such rights manifest fundamental individual rights which are unconditional, and as such they cannot be arbitrarily or unlawfully affected by public authorities. State may be in breach of existing international human rights. The catalogue of fundamental language rights in the private sphere often demonstrates the existing fundamental human rights such as freedom of expression, the right to non-discrimination or the right to private and family life. To give a few more precise examples, the right to have one's name and surname recognised in one's own

68 De Varennes, *Language, Minorities and Human Rights (International Studies in Human Rights)*, 151–7.

69 Christian Tomuschat, "Protection of Minorities under Article 27 CCPR", in: Rudolf Bernhardt [et al.] (eds.), *Völkerrecht als Rechtsordnung, Internationale Gerichtsbarkeit, Menschenrechte*, Spinger, 1983, 949, 970.

70 Patrick Thornberry, *International Law and the Rights of Minorities*, Oxford University Press, 1992, 387.

71 Vide supra 39.

language may be called a language right, but at the same time it is also a universal human right recognised under international law as an inseparable part of the right to private life.[72] As names and surnames are a means of identifying persons within their families and the community, a state cannot prevent an individual from not having them spelt in an official language. Another example of infringement would be a state's ban on the private use of a language in public areas, such as a private conversation between minority members in public streets or parks. This language right is a manifestation of an existing fundamental right – freedom of expression. De Varennes notes that universal human rights such as freedom of expression, the right to non-discrimination or the right to private life cannot be made conditional upon belonging to a national or linguistic minority. Every individual should be guaranteed the right to use his or her language in communication with other members of his or her linguistic group.[73]

On the contrary, the right to the public use of a minority language is not always regarded as fundamental. It is not absolute as it depends on how the state organises its communication with minorities. De Varennes makes a distinction between two categories of language use in the public sphere:

1) language rights in relation to the fairness of judicial proceedings, and
2) language rights resulting from the general use of minority languages by state public officials.

Similarly to the right to use a language in the private sphere, the first category of rights does not depend on any factors. They are directly linked to the right to a fair trial and entrenched in most treaties dealing with human rights, in particular the ICCPR and the ECHR. The result is that an accused is entitled to translation and interpretation support in the course of criminal proceedings. This area of language rights in the public sphere is well regulated. The other area of concern involves the general principles on the use of a minority language by public authorities, including using a minority language in public education, public radio and television broadcasting, as well as providing public services, cultural, and musical expression or designation of localities and topography in a minority language. The general use of a minority language in public is regulated by the state authorities, and it usually depends on numbers and geographic concentration of minority language speakers. The right to have a minority language used by public officials is variable. It is not

72 Communication No. 453/1991 of the United Nations Human Rights Committee in the case *Coeriel and Aurik v Netherlands*, U.N. Doc. CCPR/C/52/D/453/1991 (1994); judgment of the ECtHR of 22 February 1994 in the case *Burghartz v Switzerland*, 18 E.H.R.R. 101. More on the issue: Fernand De Varennes and Elżbieta Kuzborska, "Human Rights and a Person's Name: Legal Trends and Challenges", *Human Rights Quarterly*, Vol. 37, No. 4, 2015, 977–1023.

73 De Varennes, "Language Rights as an Integral Part of Human Rights", 17–8.

satisfied every time. A demand to use a minority language usually arises when a sufficient number of minority language speakers request a particular type of a public service in their language. In the case when the number of minority language speakers constitutes a very high percentage, a sufficient number of public officials who will be able to respond in a minority language will have to be ensured. All activities pertaining to administrative and public authorities and all areas of state involvement, including the judiciary, state education, state-provided health services, or public broadcasting will also be provided in a minority language. As a result, when a number of speakers is too low, and it is too onerous to use a minority language in a certain type of public service, the right to use a minority language is not considered to be violated.[74]

An example of non-absolute language rights in the public sphere is the right to use a minority language during civil ceremonies. The right is not imposed by any legally binding international law instrument. This is the state authorities which decide on appropriate circumstances for providing this public service in a language of a specific minority. If circumstances are defined by the state as appropriate, then the state must respond to the needs of the minority in respect of language rights in civil ceremonies. In principle, appropriate circumstances for the state authorities are defined as a particular minimum number and geographic concentration of the speakers of a minority language which make it reasonable or justified for the state to use that minority language in the civil ceremonies.[75]

As noted by Kuzborska (2015), the world today is facing the problem of a growing number of persons excluded from meaningful participation in the economic, social and political life of their communities because of language barriers resulting from the states' policies. Certainly, appropriate legislation respecting the language and identity of minorities reflecting their needs and reality would be an advisable approach.[76] In fact, one can observe the deterioration of minority language rights protection in the public sphere in a number of EU Member States, including Lithuania and Slovakia.[77] Following their accession, they have decreased

74 De Varennes, "Language Rights as an Integral Part of Human Rights", 19–20.

75 Fernand De Varennes, "The Existing Rights of Minorities in International Law", in: Mikl¢s Kontra [et al.] (eds.), *Language: a Right and a resource*, Central European University Press, 1999, 121–7.

76 Elzbieta Kuzborska, "The Protection of Language Rights of Minorities in Lithuania", in: Elżbieta Kuzborska (ed.), *Integration and Exclusion. Linguistic rights of national minorities in Europe*, Vilnus 2015, 133–6.

77 Outside the EU, a flagrant example of diminishing language rights of minority members includes Ukraine. Under the Ukrainian Constitution, Ukrainian is a state language, but the status of Russian has always been privileged as a minority language. The new Law on Languages finally adopted in 2018 aims to significantly limit the use of Russian in the public sphere. The Law has been criticized for many contradictions, gaps and unclear provisions. Source: Tadeusz A. Olszański, *Ukraincy*

their level of protecting minority languages. The case study of Lithuania carried out by Wardyn illustrates examples where the regression was noted in the period 2010–2013. Public TV and radio broadcast in minority languages was reduced, bilingual street signs in area highly populated by national minorities were eliminated and access to schools in a minority language was significantly limited.[78] Moreover, the reform of the educational system of minorities in Lithuania of 2011 which mainly consisted in increasing the number of subjects or hours taught in the official language of the State and a unified exam for all school graduates was introduced against the will of the affected minorities (mainly Polish and Russian), with no effective consultations[79] and resulted in massive protest campaigns.[80] As regards Slovakia, the amendment to the language law in 2009 also limited the use of minority languages in the public sphere by increasing the circle of persons and organs bound to use the state language in official communications, allowing the use of minority languages only in municipalities where minorities constitute at least 20% of the population.[81]

4.2.5 Language rights as universal human rights

4.2.5.1 Freedom of expression

Freedom of expression, also known as freedom of speech, is a universal human right recognised in all the major human rights instruments. It is enshrined in Article 10 ECHR, Article 19 UDHR, and Article 19 ICCPR. To begin with, Article 10(1) ECHR states that "(e)veryone has the right to freedom of expression. The

---

nie gęsi... Ustawa o języku państwowym Ukrainy, https://www.osw.waw.pl/pl/publikacje/komentarze-osw/2019-06-11/ukraincy-nie-gesi-ustawa-o-jezyku-panstwowym-ukrainy [retrieved on 28 October 2020].

78 Łukasz Wardyn, "The Observance of national minorities from the perspective of the European Union: selected aspects", in: Elżbieta Kuzborska (ed.), *Integration and Exclusion. Linguistic rights of national minorities in Europe*, Vilnus, 2015, 238.

79 The analysis of the conclusions and recommendations of the UN Committee on the Elimination of Racial Discrimination and the Committee on Economic, Social and Cultural Rights on education of national minorities in the states including Moldova, Israel, Latvia carried out by De Varennes prove that any changes to the education system should be introduced after consultations with the minorities concerned. Source: Fernand De Varennes, *Discrimination and the Right to Education and language in main documents and conclusions from UN mechanisms*, Reference Document – Education and Language, 20 October 2014.

80 Kuzborska, "The Protection of Language Rights of Minorities in Lithuania", 139.

81 Łukasz Wardyn and Jan Fiala, "The 2009 Amendment of the Slovakian State Language Law and Its Impact on Minority Rights", *XXIX Polish Yearbook of International Law*, 2009, 157–9.

right includes freedom to hold opinions and to receive and impart information and ideas without interference by public authority and regardless of frontiers". Article 10 ECHR does not expressly refer to linguistic aspects of the freedom of expression. Nevertheless, one may clearly see that formulation of the Article aims at protecting a tolerance regime where public authority should not interfere, also in terms of language-related aspects. Freedom of expression is also protected under Article 19(2) ICCPR, which reads that "(e)veryone shall have the right to freedom of expression; this right shall include freedom to seek, receive, and impart information and ideas of all kinds, regardless of frontiers, either orally, in writing or in print, in the form of art, or through any other media of his choice". The linguistic aspects of the freedom of expression were dealt by the United Nations Human Rights Committee (UNHRC) in the *Ballantyne*[82] case in the context of commercial advertising in the Canadian francophone region of Quebec. The problem concerned the free use of English by English-speaking citizens in different commercial signs. According to the local law, the public communication should take place solely in French. The Committee noted that Article 19(2) ICCPR must be interpreted in such a way that "the commercial element in an expression taking the form of outdoor advertising cannot have the effect of removing this expression from the scope of protected freedom".[83] Moreover, the Committee noted that there were no grounds to lawfully limit the commercial free speech of the petitioners. It was justified by the fact that such free speech did not infringe the rights of the French language users. As a result, the Committee concluded that a state may choose one or more official languages, but it must not exclude, outside the spheres of public life, the freedom to express oneself in a language of one's choice.[84]

The *Ballantyne* case is one of not many cases where language rights were considered against the background of freedom of expression. The freedom of expression is considered to have a limited reach in respect of language rights protection. It is only deemed to protect private communications between persons using the same (minority) language in a hostile environment.[85] Hence, freedom to express oneself in a minority language in the public sphere is breached when the authority prevents one from the private use of a minority language in public areas. In cases when a person is not allowed to use a minority language publicly, the authorities' decision would be analysed by judicial bodies in terms of discrimination based on language rather than violation against freedom of expression. De Varennes maintains that there is a direct link between freedom of expression and the right

---

82 Communications of the UN Human Rights Committee, Nos. 359/1989 and 385/1989 in the case *Ballantyne, Davidson, McIntyre v Canada,* U.N. Doc. CCPR/C/47/D/359/1989 and 385/1989/Rev1 (1993).

83 *Ballantyne, Davidson, McIntyre v Canada,* para. 11.3.

84 *Ballantyne, Davidson, McIntyre v Canada,* para. 11.4.

85 Directorate General for Translation EC, 71.

of non-discrimination as there should be no discrimination between speakers of a language that dominates on a territory and speakers of other languages who should be granted the right to express themselves in their languages in the public sphere.[86]

4.2.5.2 *The right to non-discrimination on the grounds of language*

4.2.5.2.1 *Overview of key binding international law instruments on the right to non-discrimination on the grounds of language*

The right to non-discrimination on the grounds of language plays a pivotal role in respect of language rights protection in international law. It is considered to constitute the basis for the regime of linguistic tolerance and the entire catalogue of negative language rights. Green (1991) maintained that that the principle of non-discrimination might serve as the most powerful right for individuals who seek more just and responsive conduct from public authorities in language matters.[87] Paz (2013) contended that language rights promoted as universal human rights should be combined with the prohibition of discrimination on the grounds of language.[88] When properly understood and applied, non-discrimination offers a balanced mechanism according to which the state may have legitimate reason to favour one or a few languages in carrying out its affairs.[89] There is also a broad consensus that the prohibition of discrimination constitutes one of the two major strands of an adequate system of minority protection, which is 'non-minority-specific'. The other strand includes those rights which are explicitly granted to persons belonging to minorities ('minority specific'). Despite being non-minority-specific, prohibition of discrimination is, nevertheless, of special relevance for minority members in respect of rights which protect expression and manifestation of a minority identity, freedom of expression or the right to education.[90]

To give the background, Article 27 ICCPR read in conjunction with Article 2 ICCPR[91] constitutes the basis for the enforcement of the right of non-discrimination

86 De Varennes, "The Existing Rights of Minorities in International Law", 117–46.

87 Leslie Green, "Freedom of Expression and Choice of Language", *Law & Policy*, Vol. 13, issue 3, 1991, 215–29.

88 Moria Paz, "The Failed Promise of Language Rights: A Critique of the International Language Rights Regime: A Critique of the International Language Rights Regime", *Harvard International Law Journal*, Vol. 54, 2013, 171.

89 De Varennes, "Language Rights as an Integral Part of Human Rights", 15–7.

90 Henrard, 58–9.

91 Article 2(1) reads: "Each State Party to the present Covenant undertakes to respect and to ensure to all individuals within its territory and subject to its jurisdiction the rights recognized in the present Covenant, without distinction of any kind, such

on the grounds of language. Championed by legal scholars as a crown jewel in the protection of national minority members, Article 27 is the most widely accepted legally binding provision on language rights. It reads that "[i]n those States in which ethnic, religious or linguistic minorities exist, persons belonging to such minorities shall not be denied the right, in community with the other members of their group, to enjoy their own culture, to profess and practise their own religion, or to use their own language". Whereas the interpretation of Article 27 ICCPR does not leave doubt that its addressees are individuals, it still remains a matter of discussion if the rights granted by the Article are exclusively of a negative nature (protection against interference) or they include a state obligation to take positive measures on behalf of the members of minority groups.[92] There are authors who claim that the Article imposes obligations on the state to positively support minority language maintenance and to specify the measures necessary to comply with broad commitments with respect to cultural and linguistic preservation. Paz notes that Article 27 calls for positive legislative, judicial and administrative commitments on the part of the states to protect of the identity of minorities.[93] However, it remains clear that the Article leaves the states a leeway on the modalities of its application.[94] Article 27 identifies the priorities but it requires signatory states to articulate the policy to fulfil that obligation.[95]

Next, the right of non-discrimination is set out in Article 14 ECHR reading that "[t]he enjoyment of the rights and freedoms set forth in this Convention shall be secured without discrimination on any ground such as sex, race, colour, language, religion, political or other opinion, national or social origin, association with a national minority, property, birth or other status". Although the Article may be invoked by any individual, in fact it is mostly adduced by minority group members. In the light of the law, the Article is considered problematic due to its ambivalent nature. It remains unclear whether the ECHR anti-discrimination clause provided in the Article covers linguistic and cultural preservation of the collective rights or it only protects individual members of a minority group. Scholars unanimously claim that the ECHR shows deficiencies as it lacks a direct language privilege.[96]

---

as race, colour, sex, language, religion, political or other opinion, national or social origin, property, birth or other status."

92 Dunbar, 107.

93 Paz, Moria, "The Tower of Babel: Human Rights and the Paradox of Language", *European Journal of International Law*, 25/2, 2014, 478.

94 Patrick Thornberry, *International Law and the Rights of Minorities*, Oxford University Press, 1992, 387.

95 Dieter Kugelmann, "Minderheitenschutz Als Menschenrechtsschutz", *Archiv Des Völkerrechts*, Vol. 39, No. 3, 2001, 233.

96 Paz, "The Failed Promise of Language Rights: A Critique of the International Language Rights Regime", 171.

As opposed to Article 27 ICCPR, Article 14 ECHR offers no rights to the use of minority languages when interacting with the state. Since the right to use one's language in dealing with public authorities is not protected by any other provision of the Convention, Article 14 cannot be used to challenge the unequal application of state regulations concerning public language use. As a result, minority members have no direct way to claim language rights before the ECtHR. This is the reason why the ECtHR tends to quickly dismiss applications that raise such violation.[97] In *Mentzen v Latvia*, the ECtHR stated that "[l]inguistic freedom as such is not one of the rights and freedoms governed by the Convention (...) [but] the fact remains that, with the exception of the specific rights stated in Articles 5(2) and 6(3) (a) and (e),[98] the Convention does not *per se* guarantee the right to use a particular language in communications with public authorities or the right to receive information in a language of one's choice".[99] The above ruling confirms that the ECHR lacks a direct language privilege and, furthermore, includes no substantive right to communication with the government that would enable a claim to non-discrimination under Article 14. As a result, Article 14 ECHR has only an accessory nature, as the prohibition of discrimination must be invoked in combination with other rights enshrined in the Convention. Paz claims that, as opposed to the ICCPR, the ECHR provides no non-discrimination guarantee, but only functional guarantees, which in practice result in the language rights related to the proceedings in court.[100]

Despite the gaps in Article 14 ECHR, for long Europe has been perceived to be at the forefront of developments in the area of minority language rights mainly owing to the European Charter for Regional or Minority Languages[101] and the Framework Convention for the Protection of National Minorities[102] claimed by some academics to represent the most advanced notion of international minority protection available in the world.[103] Actually, their genesis lies in the observed

---

97 Paz, "The Failed Promise of Language Rights: A Critique of the International Language Rights Regime", 196.

98 Article 5(2) ECHR guarantees everyone who is arrested the right to be informed in a language which he understands of the reasons for his arrest and free assistance of an interpreter if he or she cannot understand or speak the language used in court. Article 6(3) (a) and (e) ECHR guarantee the same rights to a person charged with a criminal offence.

99 Judgment of the ECtHR of 7 December 2004 in the case *Mentzen v Latvia* (application No. 71074/01), para. 2(b).

100 Paz, "The Failed Promise of Language Rights: A Critique of the International Language Rights Regime", 191.

101 Vide supra 39.

102 Vide supra 10.

103 Arzoz, "The Nature of Language Rights", 15.

shortcomings within the ECHR system with regard to safeguarding the rights of minorities to use their own language on a non-discriminatory basis. The instruments seem to complement each other. Firstly, the ECRML sets out to protect and promote regional or minority languages as an integral part of the European cultural heritage. It places emphasis on the cultural dimension of the use of a regional or minority language in all the aspects of the life of its speakers. Accordingly, the aim of the ECRML is not to guarantee human rights *per se*, but to protect languages. As a result, the Charter does not guarantee enforceable rights for the speakers of regional or minority languages, but it only encourages the states to take adequate measures to protect them.[73] The ECRML allows each state that ratifies the instrument to specify which minority or regional language it wants to incorporate into the scope of protection. Every signatory state can choose under an *à la carte system* which paragraphs or subparagraphs it intends to apply. A signatory state is obliged to choose a minimum number of 35 paragraphs or subparagraphs out of 97 options to be complied with. The context-based varying standards established by the ECRML allow the states to adjust them to the needs of each particular language.[104]

As opposed to the ECRML, the FCNM attempts to extend the language rights of persons belonging to national minorities, which are considered part of the universal human rights. It is the first legally binding multilateral instrument in the world devoted to the protection of persons belonging to national minorities. The signatory parties to the FCNM undertake to promote the full and effective equality of minority members in all areas of economic, social, political, public, and cultural life, together with conditions that will allow them to express, preserve, and develop their culture, religion, language, and traditions. They have to ensure their freedom of assembly, association, expression, thought, conscience, religion, and their access to and use of media. The FCNM also provides guidelines for the linguistic freedoms and rights regarding education. The compliance with the FCNM is monitored by the Council of Europe Committee of Ministers assisted by the Advisory Committee. The Committee adopts conclusions and resolutions in respect of the state concerned.[105]

Both the ECRML and the FCNM are criticised mainly for giving the possibility for the signatory states to 'opt out' from some clauses and nominate certain minorities for protection, as well as to have a monitoring rather than enforcement mechanism. Another aspect subjected to criticism concerned the fact that both instruments recognised a gradation that must be respected as to the degree to

---

104 Explanatory Report to the European Charter for Regional and Minority Languages, Strasbourg, 5 November 1992, https://rm.coe.int/16800cb5e5 [retrieved on 19 October 2020], para. 35

105 Factsheet on the Framework Convention for the Protection of National Minorities, https://www.coe.int/en/web/ minorities/fcnm-factsheet [retrieved on 7 May 2020].

which public authorities must use a minority language. As a result, the signatories refer to a model based on the state's resources and an ability to respond in a reasonable way (a sliding-scale model) which accounts for disadvantages affecting persons belonging to a minority.[106] Last but not least, the limited scope of use of the instruments was underlined by critics. They noticed that the effects of both the ECRML and the FCNM are not satisfactory, as only a small number of states signed and ratified both the ECRML (ratified by 25 states) and the FCNM (ratified by 39 states). Moreover, the parties may treat the provisions of the ECRML and FCNM, at their discretion, as moral and political principles which are not part of international law. As a consequence, they are desired but not legally required.

4.2.5.3 The right to education

One of the most important aspects of the right to non-discrimination on the grounds of language entails education in a minority language. The legal point of view of the right to be educated in one's own language at the international level is not straightforward. Most international treaties are ambiguous about the actual education in state schools, proposing, for example, that a minority language can simply be taught as a subject or used as a language of instruction in schools (to an unspecified degree), in compliance with national laws.[107] There have been numerous political and non-binding developments in the field. Although they create an impressive foundation acknowledging the validity of education in a minority language, they cannot alone form the basis for such a right. While not providing express references to education in minority languages, international law instruments connected the right to education of persons belonging to minorities with the right to non-discrimination on the grounds of language. The UNSECO Convention against Discrimination in Education of 1960[108] states that discrimination in education includes language matters and refers to the access to education, the standard and the quality of education. Accordingly, persons belonging to national minorities should be given the right to learn free-of charge the official language of the state of residence to a reasonable degree of fluency as the absence of such instruction would in the long run exclude minority members from

106 De Varennes, "The Existing Rights of Minorities in International Law", 130.

107 The ICCPR does not include any educational clauses. The ICESCR omits any references to language in the right to education (Article 13). The ICESCR expressly refers to "racial, ethnic, and religious" groups in education, but not to national or linguistic minorities. The UN Convention on the Rights of the Child does not mention language in its general article on education (Article 28). Article 29 CRC mentions that child's education should express respect for his or her cultural identity and language.

108 UNESCO Convention against Discrimination in Education adopted on 14 December 1960, entered into force 22 May 1962. By 2019 ratified by 104 states.

employment or educational opportunities and would constitute discriminatory treatment under international human rights law.[109]

De Varennes divides the main developments in tminority language education into two parts: those truly global and those developed at the regional level of the Council of Europe. He claims that at the global level the legal instruments dealing with education in minority languages are limited to Article 27 ICCPR and Article 29 CRC. Although Article 27 ICCPR *prima facie* is silent on education, it is widely believed to protect at least private minority schools.[110] Article 29 CRC asserts that education of a child should be directed to the development of respect for child's parents and his or her own identity, language, and values. Here again, the CRC does not require directly any use of a minority language as a medium of education or even any suggestion that it should be taught. The limitations and vague wording of Article 27 ICCPR and Article 29 CRC fail to provide a general, unambiguous and legally binding obligation to comply with the right. As a result, there is still some difficulty in getting the broad international consensus as to the status of the right to education in a minority language.[111]

Developments in the Council of Europe realised mainly though Article 14(1) FCNM[112] and Article 8 ECRML[113] offer a more solid basis for education in minority languages from a strictly legal point of view. The FCNM indicates that 'bilingual education', i.e. education in a state official language and a minority language, is one of the methods to guarantee the right to be educated in a minority language without prejudice to the learning of the official language.[114] Both treaties set out that "in appropriate circumstances" states must make available teaching of or in a minority language at schools. Education in a minority language is not automatic and is limited to situations where it is justified and reasonable or where the

---

109 De Varennes, "The Existing Rights of Minorities in International Law", 131.

110 Fernand de Varennes and Elżbieta Kuzborska, "International Law and Language Minority Education", *Language Policy and Political Issues in Education*, 2016, 5.

111 De Varennes and Kuzborska, "International Law and Language Minority Education", 6.

112 "The Parties undertake to recognise that every person belonging to a national minority has the right to learn his or her minority language."

113 "With regard to education, the Parties undertake, within the territory in which such languages are used, according to the situation of each of these languages, and without prejudice to the teaching of the official language(s) of the State: (…) to make available pre-school education (…) primary education (…) secondary education (…) and technical and vocational education in the relevant regional or minority languages."

114 Explanatory Report to the Framework Convention for the Protection of National Minorities, Strasbourg, H (95)10, https://rm.coe.int/16800c10cf, [retrieved on 19 October 2020], para. 77.

number of students in part of a territory is substantial or sufficient. Neither treaty stipulates that all languages should be treated the same. In fact, the smaller the language in terms of the number of speakers, the less it is entitled to be used in the area of education.[115]

The formative judgment of the ECtHR in this field is the *Belgian Linguistic Case*.[116] It demonstrated the limited reach of the prohibition of discrimination on the grounds of language with regard to the right to education in a minority language. The ECtHR appeared to have been reluctant to derive rights from the prohibition of discrimination. The contrary would create a positive obligation on the state to establish and finance education facilities in respect of education in minority languages. The applicant in the case claimed that the Belgian legislation which stated that the language of education shall be Dutch in the Dutch-speaking region, French in the French-speaking region and German in the German-speaking region, infringed the prohibition of discrimination set out in Article 14 ECHR. Moreover, the applicant claimed the infringement of the right to state education in a minority language under Article 2 of Protocol 1 to the ECHR. The Belgian government argued that the right to education in one's own language was not included in the ECHR or the Protocol, and the applicants did not belong to a national minority within the meaning of Article 14. The ECtHR found that Article 14 ECHR read in conjunction with Article 2 of the Protocol had not been breached. The ECtHR added that the ECHR laid down no specific obligations concerning the organization or subsidisation of an official educational system of the state. The right to education enshrined in Article 2 of the Protocol guarantees access to educational establishments existing in a given state and by its nature calls for the regulation by the state, which implies that the regulations in this respect may vary depending on the needs and state's resources. Further, Article 2 of Protocol 1 does not include any linguistic requirements and does not specify the language in which education must be conducted in order for the right to education to be respected and satisfied. However, the ECtHR found it discriminatory that some children were denied education solely on the basis of their parents' place of residence, preventing certain children from having access to the French-language schools existing in the six communes on the periphery of Brussels.[117] As a result, the Court gave the state the right to decide what language education should be offered and added that for the right to education to be effective, it was necessary that the individual who is

115 De Varennes and Kuzborska, "International Law and Language Minority Education", 6.

116 Judgment of the ECtHR of 23 July 1968 in the case *Belgian Linguistic Case v Belgium* (applications No. 1474/62; 1677/62; 1691/62; 1769/63; 1994/63; 2126/64).

117 Judgment of the ECtHR of 23 July 1968 (applications no 1474/62; 1677/62; 1691/62; 1769/63; 1994/63; 2126/64), III.90.

the beneficiary should have the possibility of drawing profit from the education received.[118]

The ECtHR's decision in the *Belgian Linguistic Case* ran against the human rights-based approach to languages.[119] The case was decided more than forty years ago, since when some international treaties, in particular the ECRML and the FCNM, have been opened for signature. Still, no instrument provides solid legal grounds for education in a minority language. Most legally binding treaties appear to leave the powers to decide on the use of a minority language as a medium of instruction in state schools to the state authorities. Some bilateral agreements between the states fill the gap here and constitute another important means of guaranteeing the right to education in a minority language. For instance, the 1946 Treaty of Peace with Italy which guaranteed the right of the German-speaking minority in the province of Bolzano to "elementary and secondary teaching in the mother tongue",[120] or the Treaty of 26 April 1994 between the Republic of Lithuania and the Republic of Poland on good neighbourhood and cooperation.[121]

At the same time, it should be noted that the developments in the ECtHR case-law have demonstrated that the ECtHR more often acknowledges that the language of education may not simply be left to a state's determination or discretion. In *Cyprus v Turkey*[122] (2001) the ECtHR contradicted traditional views and stated that the linguistic policies of Northern Cyprus in the area of public education were inadequate and violated Article 2 of Protocol 1 to the ECHR. The case concerned the right of children of Greek-speaking parents residing in Northern Cyprus who wished to pursue a secondary education in Greek. They were obliged by the authorities to be transferred to schools to the south although they were able to continue education in English and Turkish in the north. The ECtHR ruled that the children should be granted the right to continue their education in Greek at the higher levels in view of the fact that they received primary education in a Greek-Cypriot school. In the ECtHR's view, offering them education in English or Turkish constituted a denial of the effective right to education. The basis for the Court's decision was not absolutely clear as, on the one hand, it admitted that the right of education in state schools did not have any linguistic components, but on the other hand, it

118 Judgment of the ECtHR of 23 July 1968 applications no 1474/62; 1677/62; 1691/62; 1769/63; 1994/63; 2126/64), para. 4 of the Operative Part.

119 Skutnabb-Kangas and Philipson, "Linguistic Human Rights, Past and Present", 11.

120 De Varennes and Kuzborska, "International Law and Language Minority Education", 3.

121 The Treaty between the Republic of Poland and the Republic of Lithuania on Good Neighbourhood and Friendly Cooperation of 26 April 1994 (Journal of Laws of 1995, No. 15, item. 71).

122 Judgment of the ECtHR of 10 May 2001 in the case *Cyprus v Turkey* (application No. 25781/94).

indicated that the right entailed a linguistic component for secondary education because the authorities in Northern Cyprus already provided primary education in Greek. Therefore, the fact that Cypriot authorities stopped offering it after primary school 'negated' the right to education.[123]

In this context, it is worth noting that the UN Committees[124] competent to consider whether it is possible to have an exercisable right to education in a minority language in public educational institutions have also changed their approach recently. The analysis made by De Varennes and Kuzborska (2016) indicate that the Committees gave interpretations favourable to a possible general claim to education in one's mother tongue. In practice, the four UN Committees in their own interpretation of various treaty obligations have increasingly recognised a qualified right to education in one's language under certain conditions.[125]

The developments in the application of the right to education and non-discrimination in international law as well as the changing views of the ECtHR and UN Committees on the language dimension of the right to education suggest that the legal relationship between education and minority languages is still evolving. This state of affairs combined with the lack of parameters for a linguistic component of the right in international law to education makes the right to education in a minority language far from crystal clear. One of the major problems faced by jurists is that it is not easy to require the use of a minority language in education if it is not permitted under a state's official language legislation. Certainly, more adjudications on the right to education and non-discrimination may breathe new life into existing legal standards and make the right more transparent from the legal point of view. What is known is that the right to education in a minority language is not absolute. It depends on the number of speakers and any other considerations of feasibility. The evolution signals that where appropriate and practicable, a number of human rights standards should accommodate the use of minority languages as a medium of instruction in public schools.[126]

4.2.5.4 *Procedural linguistic human rights*

Procedural linguistic human rights are fundamental human rights which are the cornerstone of a just society. They aim to prohibit arbitrary detention and guarantee

---

123 De Varennes and Kuzborska, "International Law and Language Minority Education", 8.

124 The competent UN Committees include: the Human Rights Committee, the Committee on the Rights of the Child, the Committee on Economic, Social and Cultural Rights and the Committee on the Elimination of Racial Discrimination.

125 De Varennes and Kuzborska, "International Law and Language Minority Education", 9.

126 De Varennes and Kuzborska, "International Law and Language Minority Education", 9–10.

fair and certain legal process for individuals. Procedural linguistic human rights are derivative from the other procedural human rights, such as the right to liberty and security and the right to a fair trial. Both entail negative and positive aspects, as they prevent abuses of the state and put an obligation on the state to provide actively for the right implementation. The right to liberty and security and the right to a fair trial have a long history starting with the UN Declaration.[127] It recognised these rights as a response to the horrors of the WWII. Although the Declaration exerted no legally binding force, it affected a number of binding human rights instruments in terms of language matters. The right to liberty and security protected in Article 9 UDHR which prohibited arbitrary arrest, detention, or exile was a model provision for Article 9 of the legally binding ICCPR. Article 9(2) ICCPR guarantees the right for the arrested or detained to be promptly informed of the reasons for arrest or charges. It requires immediate actoion on the part of the state in respect of access to a translator/interpreter. Next, the right to a fair trial enshrined in Article 10 UDHR was also incorporated into Article 14 ICCPR. Specifically, language aspects are referred to in Article 14(3)(f) ICCPR which guarantees free assistance of an interpreter if a person charged cannot understand or speak the language used in court. Both Articles 9 and 14 ICCPR grant the right of equality, fairness and lack of arbitrariness at the stage of detention and the legal process itself, which also implies the right to understand the language in which the charges, rights, and obligations are pronounced. As a result, the provisions result in the right to interpretation and translation. The fact that the language rights are included in the ICCPR as components of the right to liberty and security and the right to a fair trial makes them legally enforceable.

The provisions of the UN Declaration also exerted an impact on the linguistic aspects of the right to liberty and security and the right to a fair trial set out in Articles 5 and 6 ECHR. They guarantee the right of an arrested and accused person to a translator and/or interpreter at different stages of criminal proceedings, including arrest, police custody, investigation, and trial. Firstly, Article 5(2) ECHR stipulates that "everyone who is arrested shall be informed promptly, in a language which he understands, of the reasons for his arrest and of any charge against him". Next, Article 6(3)(a) ECHR makes clear reference to languages by stating that "everyone charged with a criminal offence has to be informed promptly, in a language which he understands and in detail, of the nature and cause of the accusation against him" and Article 6(3)(e) guarantees for those charged with a criminal offence "to have the free assistance of an interpreter if he or she cannot understand or speak the language used in court".

The ECtHR has extensively referred to the linguistic aspects of the right to liberty and security and the right to a fair trial, such s the right to language assistance[128]

127 Vide supra 36.

128 James Brannan, *ECHR Case-Law on the Right to Language Assistance in Criminal Proceedings and the EU Response,* a seminar Organised by the AIIC Committee for

or the right for interpretation and translation in criminal proceedings.[129] The overview of the ECtHR case-law proves that establishing the existence of the right itself is not a problem as the protection against arbitrary deprivation of liberty is an elementary safeguard of any arrested person. The ECtHR often refers to section 1 of Article 6 which includes a general statement that "everyone is entitled to a fair trial and public hearing within a reasonable time by an independent and impartial tribunal". In this mode, the arrested should know why he or she is deprived of his or her liberty in a language he or she understands. Such an approach was approved in *Delcourt v Belgium*[130] where the Court ruled that when the person deprived of liberty does not understand an official language of the state, the explanation must be provided in a language the person understands, including Braille or sign language, and the explanation needs to be given at the initial moment of apprehension by a person who can speak the language of the detained. The protection of the right to free assistance from an interpreter exercised under the right to a fair trial was expanded by the ECtHR in its case law. Over time, the ECtHR extended the right beyond procedures qualified as criminal onto a procedure aimed at finding a regulatory offence. In *Öztürk v Germany*,[131] the Court stated that the causing of an accident as a result of careless driving by Mr Öztürk constituted a regulatory offence which substantiated the criminal nature of the sanction and application of Article 6(3)(e) ECHR. As a consequence, the right to receive free assistance from an interpreter was vested in anyone who could not speak or understand the language used in court both in criminal proceedings and proceedings relating to regulatory offences.[132]

The challenge related to the right to language assistance lies in various aspects of the practical implementation of the right. There are three main categories of legal problems considered by the ECtHR in this respect: 1) When may language assistance be refused? *(Bozicek v Italy)*, 2) Should such assistance be free of charge? *(Luedicke, Belkacem & Koç v Germany, Isyar v Bulgaria)*, and 3) What is the extent of the authorities' duty in respect of language assistance? *(Kamasinski v Austria, Hermi v Italy)*. Moreover, the ECtHR has also dealt with an issue of the translator/interpreter choice *(Cuscani v the United Kingdom)*, translation/interpretation

Court and Legal Interpreting at the European Court of Human Rights: Droits de l'Homme En Europe et Interprétation Juridique, Strasbourg, 2010.

129 Evert-Jan van der Vlis, "The right to interpretation and translation in criminal proceedings", *The Journal of Specialised Translation*, no 14, 2010.

130 Judgment of the ECtHR of 17 January 1970 in the case *Delcourt v Belgium* (application No. 2689/65).

131 Judgment of the ECtHR of 21 February 1984 in the case *Öztürk v Germany* (application No. 8544/79).

132 General-Directorate for Translation EC, 72.

quality control *(Panasenko v Portugal)* and impartiality and independence of a translator/an interpreter *(Ucak v the United Kingdom).*[133]

Firstly, the refusal of language assistance was examined by the ECtHR in *Brozicek v Italy.*[134] The problem was that the applicant was not informed of the charges in a language he understood. The letter sent to Mr Brozicek, Czechoslovakian citizen, by the Italian Public Prosecutor's office was prepared in Italian. The applicant was convicted *in absentia* despite the fact that he responded indicating that he did not speak Italian. He claimed that he had not been given an opportunity to participate in a trial in order to defend himself against the charges brought against him. The ECtHR ruled that the judicial notification of charges against Mr Brozicek did not satisfy necessary linguistic requirements and, therefore, the trial was not fair within the meaning of Article 6(1)[135] and (3)(a) ECHR. The lack of written translation of the indictment may have put the accused in a disadvantaged position and prevented him from effective defence.

Secondly, the coverage of costs for language support is another key linguistic aspect of the right to a fair trial considered by the ECtHR. The landmark case which exposed the problem was *Luedicke, Belkacem and Koç v Germany.*[136] Since the accused were not sufficiently familiar with the language of the country, they were assisted by an interpreter in accordance with German law. After conviction, they were ordered, amongst other things, to pay the costs of the proceedings, including the interpretation costs.[137] Notably, the German court rested on the supposition that the free assistance of an interpreter covered only the costs resulting from the interpretation at the trial hearing but not at earlier stages of the criminal proceedings. As a result, Mr Leudicke had to cover the costs of translation and interpretation. The ECtHR examined the possible violation of Article 6(3)(e) ECHR in

133 Brannan, *ECHR Case-Law on the Right to Language Assistance in Criminal Proceedings and the EU Response,* 1.

134 Judgment of the ECtHR of 19 December 1989 in the case *Brozicek v Italy* (application No. 10964/84).

135 Article 6(1) reads: "In the determination of his civil rights and obligations or of any criminal charge against him, everyone is entitled to a fair and public hearing within a reasonable time by an independent and impartial tribunal established by law. Judgment shall be pronounced publicly but the press and public may be excluded from all or part of the trial in the interests of morals, public order or national security in a democratic society, where the interests of juveniles or the protection of the private life of the parties so require, or to the extent strictly necessary in the opinion of the court in special circumstances where publicity would prejudice the interests of justice".

136 Judgment of the ECtHR of 28 November 1978 in the case *Luedicke, Belkacem and Koç v Germany* (application No. 6210/73, 6877/75, 7132/75).

137 Judgment in the case *Luedicke, Belkacem and Koç v Germany*, para.10.

the context of the translation or interpretation of all the documents or statements in the proceedings which were necessary to have the benefit of a fair trial. The ECtHR ruled that the state had an obligation to act in order to comply with the language rights of an individual. The court held unanimously that Article 6(3)(e) ECHR had been breached and that the Federal Republic of Germany should reimburse the interpretation costs of the trial hearing to Mr Luedicke. The Court did not determine whether the right stated in Article 6(3)(e) ECHR extended to the costs that the German court awarded against Mr Belkacem. The reason was that the request made in his name was not well-founded and no reimbursement of costs was claimed.[138] As regards Mr Koç, he accepted the offer of the German authorities which proposed to recover the costs, and, as a result, the case was struck out of the list.[139]

Thirdly, the extent of the authorities' duty in respect of language assistance is yet another important linguistic dimension of the right to a fair trial examined by the ECtHR. The Strasbourg case-law proves that the authorities have a duty to provide the accused with language support if requested, unless it is evidenced that the request is not justified. In the case when the right is refused, this is the government which bears the burden of proof before the court to demonstrate that language services are not essential. When the accused is provided with language assistance, but complains about its quality or the impartiality of a translator/interpreter, they will have to show before court that they were adversely affected by these grounds.[140] The issues of free assistance of an interpreter and the scope of the authorities' support were also raised in the *Kamasinski v Austria*[141] case. The ECtHR decided that the right to language assistance applied not only to oral statements made at the hearing, but also to documentary material and the pre-trial proceedings. In this case, the applicant's (Mr Kamasinski) principal grievance derived from his inability to understand or speak the language used in the criminal proceedings brought against him in Austria. He complained of inadequate interpretation of oral statements and the lack of written translation of official documents in the criminal proceedings, as a result of which a defendant did not have enough evidence to allow him to defend himself and protect his interests during adjudication. Mr Kamasinski maintained discrimination in the enjoyment of the fundamental rights protected by Article 6 ECHR. The ECtHR decided unanimously that Article 6(1) ECHR was violated because the factual inquiry carried

138 Barbara Mensah, *European Human Rights Case Summaries*, Routledge-Cavendish, 2002.
139 Judgment of the case *Luedicke, Belkacem and Koç v Germany*, para. 5.
140 James Brannan, "Identifying written translation in criminal proceedings as a separate rights: scope and supervision under European law", *The Journal of Specialised Translation*, https://jostrans.org/ issue27/art_brannan.php [retrieved on 20 October 2020].
141 Judgment of the ECtHR of 9 December 1989 in the case *Kamasinski v Austria* (application No. 9783/82).

by the Austrian courts was unilateral in nature, and the applicant was not able to effectively participate in proceedings and protect his interests. In the same judgment, the ECtHR held that there was no violation of Article 6(3)(e). The court demonstrated that the requirements of Article 6(3)(e) ECHR were not met in the case, as the accused could, though roughly, understand the language of the criminal proceedings. Under such circumstances, the accused was not vested with the right to free interpretation/translation services as according to the Court he was able to understand the language of the proceedings. This approach was also expressed in the case of *Cuscani v Italy*.[142]

A similar approach was confirmed in the case *Shamayev and 12 Others v Georgia and Russia*,[143] where the ECtHR held the violation of Article 5(2) ECHR and ruled that the applicants had not received sufficient information about their detention in a language understandable to them. In the light of that finding, the Court stated that well-qualified translators should be used for the purpose of translating the warrant of arrest and for interrogation of the applicant, and it was incumbent on the authorities to ensure that requests for translation are formulated with precision.[144]

4.2.5.5 Enforcement of language rights

Human rights scholars maintain that there is a gap between the promise of language rights protection entrenched in the key international human rights instruments and the judicial meanings of these rights developed by competent courts. The UNHRC and the ECtHR are the most significant international human rights enforcement bodies which create judicially enforceable rights that lead to decisions of general application.[145] The analysis carried out by Paz demonstrates that there is a striking discrepancy between the announced declarations and the actual decisions of transnational bodies of the Council of Europe and the United Nations. This results in a situation that language interests irrespective of how valid and worthy they may be, they cannot be defended in practice under the rubric of human rights. Paz claims that by advocating the human rights-based approach to linguistic conflicts between minorities and majorities academic scholars transform political questions into legal questions, and then transform legal questions into questions of universal abstract language rights, or human rights more generally.

---

142 Judgment of the ECtHR of 24 September 2002 in the case *Cuscani v Italy* (application No. 32771/96).

143 Judgment of the ECtHR of 12 April 2005 in the case *Shamayev and 12 Others v Georgia and Russia* (application No. 36378/02).

144 Guide on Article 5 of the Convention. Right to Liberty and Security, available at: *http*://www.echr.coe.int/Documents/Guide_Art_5_ENG.pdf [retrieved on 17 July 2017], 23.

145 Paz, "The Tower of Babel: Human Rights and the Paradox of Language", 477.

With this movement, they promise a solution the law cannot deliver.[146] Moreover, as stressed by Arzoz the problems with the human rights-based approach to language rights lie in the sharp contrast between excessive expectations and the demands of state positive laws. He claims that linguistic human rights need the reinterpreting of entitlements already recognised by international binding rules and their effective implementation by the states.[147]

The UNHRC and the ECtHR regimes are very closely aligned regarding the language rights of persons belonging to minorities in respect of non-discrimination. Legal entitlements in relation to linguistic minorities enshrined in Article 27 ICCPR and Article 14 ECHR prove that, in principle, there is convergence between the UNHRC and the ECtHR in handling claims bearing on language use in the public sphere. Both the UNHRC and the ECtHR demonstrate the limited pragmatic model of language protection. They take a narrowly utilitarian approach to language by accommodating non-majority language speakers in the public realm only insofar as is needed to prevent irreparable harm from discrimination based on linguistic status, and to the extent to which the use of a minority language facilitates communication with the majority and with the official bodies of the state. The aim is to avoid situations where a non-dominant language becomes a barrier to realising certain other universally accepted human rights that are not specific to culture. Here, the UNHRC and the ECtHR interpretation of language rights tends to emphasise procedural issues. Instead of strong language guarantees, only transitional accommodations are offered in the public realm for those individuals or groups who are unable to speak the majority language. Case-law has consistently favoured linguistic assimilation rather than the protection of linguistic diversity.[148]

In terms of the enforcement of procedural linguistic rights, the ECtHR and the UNHRC adopted a similar approach. Both supranational bodies treat language rights as part of a right to liberty and security and the right to a fair trial (due process guarantee). They focus on individual procedural fairness and have developed a utilitarian test for what constitutes a sufficient level of language knowledge. According to the test, the accused should be able "to have knowledge of the case against him and to defend himself".[149] In this respect, both institutions have been criticised for being unfair. The point is that, on the one hand, a person charged in a criminal trial who belongs to a non-dominant linguistic group, but has assimilated enough into the state to possess "sufficient knowledge" in the dominant language

146 Paz, "The Failed Promise of Language Rights: A Critique of the International Language Rights Regime", 163–9, 213.

147 Arzoz, "The Nature of Language Rights", 2–3.

148 Paz, "The Failed Promise of Language Rights: A Critique of the International Language Rights Regime", 163.

149 Judgment of the ECtHR of 14 January 2003 in the case *Lagerblom v Sweden* (application No. 26891/95).

is forced to speak this language, even if he or she feels that his or her knowledge of that language is not "sufficient for a successful pursuit of his/her claim".[150] On the other hand, if the same accused had never learnt the state language (again either by choice, by necessity, or otherwise), he or she would be allowed to use the language of his or her choice in court sessions, and would have the costs of an interpreter covered by the state. Procedurally, this means that those who do not participate in the state activities are more privileged by the international legal regime than those who do. In fact, it seems that the international regulations protect claimants who are completely ignorant of the procedural language and thus cannot respond to the charges against them, but fail to provide protection to those who made an effort to assimilate themselves and are engaged in social life.[151]

The decisions of the members of the UNHRC and the judges of the ECtHR have been criticised by human rights scholars who claim that language rights protection is politically driven. They maintain that the UNHRC and the ECtHR are likely to prioritise state interests and provide only nominal accommodation of language-related claims over the demands for maximal interpretation of the rights. Their final decisions are a far cry from adopting a human rights-based approach to the linguistic conflicts. They prove that language disputes may be considered as demands for new distributions of power.[152]

4.3 Language rights as fundamental rights in the EU

4.3.1 Classification of language rights as fundamental rights

The classification of language rights as fundamental rights in the EU was not straightforward to all experts in the field when the debate began in the first decade of the twenty-first century. Different voices exposed diverging views and justifications in the matter. The intense debate on that issue was initiated by Arzoz (2007) who claimed that international organizations contributed to creating a false image of an extended level of language rights protection. He maintained that one might have an impression that language rights constituted a consolidated category of fundamental rights with a sound basis in contemporary international law.[153]

In 2008, other researchers in the field took their position. Mancini and De Witte stated that language rights should be treated as fundamental rights when they protect language-related values and are entrenched in the state constitution or in an international treaty binding on that state. As noted by Mancini and De Witte,

150 Judgment of the ECtHR of 8 June 1976 in the case *Isop v Austria* (application No. 808/60).

151 Paz, "The Failed Promise of Language Rights: A Critique of the International Language Rights Regime", 191–5.

152 Arzoz (2007), Paz (2013, 2014),

153 Arzoz, "The Nature of Language Rights", 1.

the EU fundamental rights can also be found in European law, comprising both the Council of Europe and European Union norms. They increasingly set limits to national language policies with an aim of protecting the language rights of individuals at a transnational level. The European standards binding upon the EU Member States which are the parties to the ECHR limit the previously complete discretion of the states in regulating language matters.[154]

Urrutia and Lasagabaster (2007, 2008[155]) endorsed the position of Mancini and De Witte and maintained that there was sufficient legal basis to assert that language rights constituted fundamental rights in the EU. They contended that the EU was obliged to comply with the international regulations which guaranteed language rights to linguistic minority members, and adhere to constitutional traditions common for the Member States if they treated language rights as fundamental rights.[156] In their view, the fact that the language rights of minorities wer recognised in international law, in particular in the ECHR and the FCNM, made the fundamental rights form a part of the general principles of EU law. Moreover, they asserted that the protection of persons belonging to minorities was an inherent part of the EU policy on human rights, and respect for human rights was a common value to the Member States. In their opinion, categorising language rights as human rights does not result in the extension of competences of the Union institutions in the field of minority language protection as the rights would only apply in the areas where the Union law had authority conferred upon it by the Treaties.[157]

On the contrary, Schilling (2008) claimed that there was no scope for language rights as general principles of law.[158] He argued that language rights granted under EU law came from different levels of multilingualism for which different criteria applied. Firstly, he distinguished the language rights of Union citizens in administrative and court proceedings vis-à-vis the EU institutions. Secondly, he indicated a wide range of linguistic aspects of parliamentary and inter-governmental proceedings, multilingual publication of authentic legal texts, education and the maintenance of linguistic diversity. According to Schilling, most language rights in the EU originate from the organization's well-developed system of language rules, based on the principle of language equality, which concern various aspects of the citizen's access to the EU institutions, and the deliberations of the European Parliament and

154 Susanna Mancini and Bruno De Witte, "Language rights as cultural rights: a European perspective", *International Studies in Human Rights*, Vol. 95, 2008, 247.

155 Iñigo Urrutia and Iñaki Lasagabaster, "Language Rights and Community Law", *European Integration online Papers*, Vol. 14, 2008.

156 Urrutia and Lasagabaster, "Language Rights and Community Law", 7.

157 Urrutia and Lasagabaster, "Language Rights and Community Law", 8 and 13.

158 Theodor Schilling, "Language Rights in the European Union", *German Law Journal*, Vol. 9, 2008, 1242.

the Council, possibly with the assistance of a translator or interpreter. As to the fundamental nature of language rights, Schilling asserted that freedom of language was not mentioned in most human rights catalogues by name. In his view, the freedom of one's own language should be considered as an individual human right forming part of the right to respect one's private life protected under the ECHR and as an essential part of human dignity protected expressly under Article 1 of the Charter of Fundamental Rights. He stated that protection of minority language rights should be left for a decision of the states which, under the ECRML and the FCNM, were given a wide leeway to define the terms for the use of minority and regional languages.[159]

The debate was affected by the entry into force of the Charter of Fundamental Rights of the European Union, which strengthened the status of language rights expressly included in the catalogue or intrinsically related to more general rights. Thus, Schilling's argument of limiting language rights to the Union citizen and, thus not being universal, may be challenged based on the Charter, which made the principle of equality one of the fundamental rights in the EU. The requirements flowing from the protection of equality as a fundamental right in the EU are binding upon the Union institutions and Member States implementing EU rules or acting within the EU law towards any individual. Moreover, the principle of equality became closely related to the principle of non-discrimination entrenched in the constitutional traditions of Member States, EU law, and international human rights law invoked by the Court of Justice. The argument of the absence of Union's competence in minority issues may also be questioned based on the fact that the fundamental language rights can deduced from a number of sources. Firstly, Article 2 TEU explicitly enshrines respect for the rights of persons belonging to minorities as a foundational value of the EU. Indeed, there is no explicit minority policy for internal purposes, but it is possible to identify the gradual emergence of a minority-conscious implementation of non-minority-specific EU policies which allow minorities to benefit from them. Although the EU lacks competences to impose on the Member States an obligation to subscribe to particular minority rights, several non-minority-specific policies maintained within the Union competences actually contribute to minority protection within the Member States. In particular, this concerns the right of non-discrimination, social inclusion, integration, respect for human rights, and cultural diversity. The socio-economic policies remain the Union's dominant focus, which apparently works as a catalyst for integration in the field of cultural identity.[160] EU minority consciousness may also be traced in the Court of Justice judgments which are supported by reference to the ECHR and its interpretation by the ECtHR.[161]

159 Schilling, "Language Rights in the European Union", 1220–6.
160 Henrard, 60–2.
161 Henrard, 82.

Taking into consideration the EU system of fundamental rights protection, the Union's competence in language matters and the voices in the debate on the status of language rights in the EU, it is safe to conclude that there are language rights which may be classified under the Union legal order as fundamental rights. As such they should be investigated from the perspective of two major sources: 1) language rights as general principles of European Union law anchored in international human rights instruments, and 2) language rights enshrined in the Charter. It is reasonable to begin with analysis with binding international human rights instruments recognising language rights, in particular the ECHR, the FCNM, the ECRML, and the ICCPR. Despite the fact that some Member States have failed to ratify certain international law minority rights instruments,[162] these instruments may be deemed to exert a strong impact on the EU Member States laws on language rights protection, including the rights of persons belonging to minorities.

4.3.2 Language rights as general principles of EU law

The Treaties establishing the Economic Communities did not include any catalogue of fundamental rights or references to human rights, and the Court of Justice did not analyse the cases in view of their compliance with fundamental rights. At the initial stages of European integration, human rights protection in Europe was the domain of the Council of Europe. The first clear sign for the need to protect such rights within the Community was the Court's ruling in *Van Gend en Loos*[163] (1963) which conferred the direct effect of the Community law on individuals. It stated that the Community constituted the new legal order in international law which affected not only the Member States, but also their citizens. By combining the Community integration with human rights protection, the Court of Justice had to guarantee the effective protection of rights by means of the Community law. The Court did it through the principle of Community law supremacy, the principle of direct effect, and by acknowledging fundamental rights as general principles of

162 The ECRML has been ratified by 16 EU Member States, The 11 Members State which have not ratified the ECRML include: Belgium, Bulgaria, Estonia, France, Greece, Ireland, Italy, Latvia, Lithuania, Malta and Portugal. The French Conseil Constitutionnel declared the ECRML incompatible with the constitutional principles of the indivisibility of the Republic, equality under the law, and uniqueness of the French people. The FCNM has been ratified by all Member States except for Belgium, France, Greece and Luxembourg.

163 Judgment of the Court of 5 February 1963 in the case 26/62 NV *Algemene Transport- en Expeditie Onderneming van Gend en Loos v Nederlandseadministratie der belastingen,* ECLI:EU:C:1963:1.

Community law.[164] For many years, the case-law of the Court of Justice was the basic mechanism for the protection of fundamental rights in the Community. The history of human rights in the Court of Justice jurisprudence is considered to have begun with the judgment in *Stauder*[165] when the Court acknowledged that fundamental human rights formed an integral part of the general principles of Community law, and as such they constituted the primary source of law. In the following cases, the Court formulated the principles according to which the sources of such fundamental rights should be sought in the Member State constitutional orders (*Internationale Handelsgesellschaft mbH)*[166] and international law instruments on human rights protection (*Nold, Kohlen- und Baustoffgroßhandlung*),[167] in particular in the ECHR (*Roland Rutili*).[168]

Every reform of the Treaties reflected the strengthening of human rights protection in the Community. The Single European Act in its Preamble exposed the attachment to fundamental rights recognised in the constitutions and laws of the Member States, in the ECHR, and the European Social Charter.[169] Fundamental rights as general principles of EU law were entered into the Treaty on European Union of 1993 which in Article F(2) read that "the Union shall respect fundamental rights, as guaranteed by the European Convention for the Protection of Human Rights and Fundamental Freedoms signed in Rome on 4 November 1950, and as they result from the constitutional traditions common to the Member States, as general principles of Community law".[170] The Treaty of Amsterdam provided the Union with a legal basis to take actions to combat discrimination based on any grounds protected by law.[171] The Lisbon Treaty was a breakthrough in respect of human rights protection in the EU, as upon its entry into force, the EU Charter of Fundamental Rights acquired the status of the Union's primary law.

---

164 Aleksandra Szczerba-Zawada, "Ochrona praw człowieka w Unii Europejskiej", in: Ewa Latoszek [et al.] (eds.), *Unia Europejska. Istota, Szanse, Wyzwania*, CeDeWu, 2018, 115.

165 Judgment of the Court of 12 November 1969 in the case C 29-69 *Erich Stauder v City of Ulm – Sozialamt*, ECLI:EU:C:1969:57.

166 Judgment of the Court of 17 December 1970 in the case C 11/70 *Internationale Handelsgesellschaft mbH v Einfuhr- und Vorratsstelle für Getreide und Futtermittel*, ECLI:EU:C:1970:114.

167 Judgment of the Court of 14 May 1974 in the case C 4/73 *J. Nold, Kohlen- und Baustoffgroßhandlung v Ruhrkohle Aktiengesellschaft*, ECLI:EU:C:1974:151.

168 Judgment of the Court of 28 October 1975 in the case C 36/75 *Roland Rutili v Ministre de l'intérieur*, ECLI:EU:C:1975:137.

169 European Social Charter signed and opened for signature on 18 October 1961, entered into force on 26 February 1965. By 2020 ratified by 27 states.

170 later Article 6(2) TEU.

171 OJ C 340, 10 November 1997, Article 13.

Despite the fact that the Charter became *de lege lata* the major pillar of human rights protection in the EU, its entry into force did not eliminate the rights constituting general principles of EU law. According to Article 6(3) TEU, fundamental rights guaranteed by the ECHR and resulting from the constitutional traditions common to the Member States constitute general principles of EU law.[172] The closed catalogue of the Charter rights is supplemented by fundamental rights resulting from general principles. These may be extended at any time and complemented by the Court of Justice.[173] As a result, fundamental rights as general principles of EU law cannot be underestimated as they constitute the heritage of the Court of Justice shaped before the Charter became effective. They affect the process of law interpretation and are a starting point for a law-making process and, as a result, ensure uniform law interpretation. They continue to play an important role in the field of fundamental rights for two primary reasons, firstly owing to thowing to the their broad subjective scope. What is more, proper understanding of fundamental rights in the EU requires one to follow and analyse the judgments of the Court of Justice as they give meaning and develop the general formulations of the Charter.[174]

Article 6(3) TEU clearly indicates that the Charter did not replace the provisions of the ECHR.[175] The ECHR has remained a major source for the general principles of EU law in the field of human and fundamental rights protection as principles shared by all the Member States which ratified the ECHR.[176] Since the beginning of adjudicating in the area of human rights, the Court of Justice has treated the ECHR as well as the jurisprudence of the ECtHR and the EU Member States constitutional traditions as arguments supporting the process of building fundamental rights as general principles of law. The ECHR which sets out the general norms in the area of human rights violation in Europe[177] helped the Court of Justice to shape an autonomous system of human rights protection. The Court availed itself of ready normative solutions and Strasbourg jurisprudence standards, and at the same time, did not deprive itself of the right to make different interpretations adequate to the

172 OJ 2016 C 202, 7 June 2016.

173 Andrzej Wróbel (ed.), *Karta Praw Podstawowych Unii Europejskiej. Komentarz*, Warszawa: C.H.Beck, 2013, 6.

174 Bartosz Liżewski, "Wykładnia Poszczególnych Rodzajów i Gałęzi Prawa UE", in: Leszek Leszczyński (ed.), *System Prawa Unii Europejskiej. Tom 3. Wykładnia prawa*. C.H. Beck, 2019, 275.

175 Filip Jasiński, *Karta Praw Podstawowych Unii Europejskiej*, Dom Wydawniczy ABC, 2003.

176 Ivo Pospíšil, "The Protection of National Minorities and the Concept of Minority in the EU Law", *Referat Prezentiran Na* 3, 2006, 21–3.

177 Ewa Łętowska, "Multicentryczność Współczesnego Systemu Prawa i Jej Konsekwencje", *Państwo i Prawo*, Vol. 4, 2005, 6–7.

specifics and nature of the EU.[178] The judgments of the ECtHR were treated by the Court of Justice as a persuasive authority strengthening its reasoning, in particular in deficiencies of its own instruments protecting human rights.[179] Moreover, the ECHR and the jurisprudence of the ECtHR are considered the substantial source of general principles of law in particular in the areas where the EU had no powers granted in the Treaties.[180]

The other major sources of fundamental rights are constitutional traditions common to the Member States. They often reflect the provisions of international treaties for the protection of human rights.[181] Apart from the ECHR, the key international law human right instruments including language-related guarantees incorporated into the national legal orders of the majority of Member States entail the ECMRL[182] and the FCNM,[183] and the United Nations ICCPR,[184] the ICESCR,[185] and the CRC.[186] De Witte (2019) draws attention to the distinctiveness of the EU's approach to the protection of rights which can play a part in ensuring the effective enjoyment of human right in the world.[187]

4.3.3 Language rights entrenched in the Charter

The Charter became the first formal EU instrument which systematised and consolidated the human rights sphere in the EU. The Charter did not grant any rights which would alter the extent of powers granted under the Treaties, nor did it provide a legal basis to adopt EU legislation or strike down any national legislation. It codified some of the fundamental rights already acknowledged as general principles of EU law. Formally, the rights, freedoms and principles set out in the Charter are recognised in Article 6(1) TEU, which also provides that the Charter does not extend in any way the competences of the Union defined in the Treaties. The Charter created a normative exhaustive catalogue of fundamental rights which became a formal source of rights thereby affecting the judicial decision-making

---

178 Liżewski, 276.
179 Liżewski, 276.
180 Cezary Mik, "The Charter of Fundamental Rights: Determinants of Protective Standards", in: Jan Barcz (ed.) *Fundamental Rights Protection in the European Union*, C.H. Beck, 2009, 73–4.
181 Judgment of the Court in the case C 4/73, para. 13.
182 Vide supra 39.
183 Vide supra 10.
184 Vide supra 13.
185 Vide supra 37.
186 Vide supra 14.
187 Bruno De Witte, "The Relative Autonomy of the European Union's Fundamental Rights Regime", *Nordic Journal of International Law*, Vol. 88, No. 1, 2019, 65.

process.[188] As a result, it became the reference text for the assessment of fundamental rights by the Court of Justice and national courts[189] as well as the basis for interpretation by advocates general.[190]

The Charter reflected the common standards respecting the national constitutional laws of EU Member States often drawn from relevant international law instruments, in particular from the ECHR.[191] The impact of the ECHR on the Charter is obvious, as the rights divided in the Charter under six chapters including dignity, freedoms, equality, solidarity, citizen's rights, and justice,[192] include, firstly, the rights which correspond to those guaranteed by the ECHR and secondly, the rights which depend on the Union or Member State legislation. In the latter case, their implementation must be performed in accordance with national laws. Despite being inspired by the ECHR, the Charter mirrored changes in society, social progress as well as the scientific, technological, political, and social development of the Union.[193]

The Charter has a limited scope of application as its provisions are addressed to the institutions and bodies of the Union with due regard for the principle of subsidiarity and to the Member States only when they implement Union law. It provides a basis to review the acts of Union institutions and bodies when they exercise powers conferred under the Treaties.[194] The above entities are bound by three categories of privileges – rights, freedoms, and principles. They must respect the rights, observe the principles, and promote their application within the limits of their powers. The Charter rights are imperative and unconditional. The principles need to be contained in directives to be transposed at a national level. They do not entitle the Union institutions to implement them in the Member States, nor oblige any Member State to recognise them otherwise than under its national legal order. They may be considered as rights, freedoms or principles only within the scope in which they are determined as such in a national legal order or the spheres of competence provided for by the Union law.[195]

---

188 Liżewski, 282.

189 Anna Zawidzka-Łojek, "Źródła prawa antydyskryminacyjnego", in: Anna Zawidzka-Łojek and Aleksandra Szczerba-Zawada (eds.), *Prawo antydyskryminacyjne Unii Europejskiej*, EuroPrawo, Warszawa, 2015, 47.

190 Joint communication from Presidents Costa and Skouris on the meeting of delegations from the European Court of Human Rights (ECHR) and the Court of Justice of the European Union (CJEU) as of 17 January 2011.

191 Steve Peers [et al.] (eds.), *The EU Charter of Fundamental Rights: A Commentary*, Hart Publishing, 2014, 3.

192 OJ C 202, 7 June 2016, Article 51(1).

193 Preamble to the Charter.

194 Peers [et al.] (eds.), 593.

195 Adam Bodnar, "The Charter of Fundamental Rights: Differentiated Legal Character of Charter's Provisions, Their Consequences for Individuals, Courts and

The Charter includes a range of rights, freedoms and principles which have clear linguistic dimensions. First and foremost, these include non-discrimination on the grounds of language and nationality (Article 21) and respect for linguistic diversity (Article 22). The Charter also includes a number of rights and freedoms which in certain circumstances may entail linguistic aspects. Such rights can be directly invoked before national courts and, on the basis of them, effective legal norms can be created.[196] The list includes respect for private and family life (Article 7), freedom of expression and information (Article 11), the right to education (Article 14), the right to good administration (Article 41(4)), the right of access to documents (Article 42), the right to address the Ombudsman (Article 43), the right to petition (Article 44), freedom of movement and residence (Article 45), the right to a fair trial (Article 47), and the right to defence (Article 48). Moreover, it should be noted that the background to all the above rights is respect for human dignity, which not without reason, is set out in Article 1 of the Charter. This implies that none of the rights laid down in the Charter may be used to harm dignity of another person, and that, dignity is part of the substance of the rights laid down there.[197] Hence, respect for the person's dignity comprises respect for a person's language and respect for the person's identity.[198]

4.4 Language rights provided in the Charter of Fundamental Rights of the European Union

4.4.1 Non-discrimination on the grounds of language and nationality

Before the entry into force of the Lisbon Treaty, the ban on discrimination was treated by the Court of Justice as a general principle of the Union law. When the Treaty became effective, non-discrimination became the fundamental right enshrined in Article 21 of the Charter.[199] Article 21 fell into a broader pattern of the Union's ban on discrimination, in particular non-discrimination constituting the EU's core value (Article 2 TEU), combating of discrimination as the Union's core objective (Article 3(3) TEU) as well as prohibiting discrimination on the grounds of nationality (Article 18 TFEU). Article 21 obliges the Union institutions and bodies

Legislator", in: Jan Barcz (ed.) *Fundamental Rights Protection in the European Union*, Warszawa: C.H. Beck 2009, 148, 157.

196 Bodnar, "The Charter of Fundamental Rights: Differentiated Legal Character of Charter's Provisions, Their Consequences for Individuals, Courts and Legislator", 157.

197 Wróbel (ed.), *Karta Praw Podstawowych Unii Europejskiej. Komentarz,* 2019, 21.

198 Mancini and De Witte, 247.

199 Wróbel (ed.), *Karta Praw Podstawowych Unii Europejskiej: Komentarz,* 2019, 685.

as well as the Member States to exercise non-discrimination in compliance with the guarantees provided by the Treaty while implementing the EU law.[200]

Article 21 has two limbs, discrimination based on the status grounds and on nationality, and in both cases it includes direct and indirect discrimination.[201] The fact that discrimination on the grounds of nationality is treated separately signals its distinctive contours in the EU. However, as sustained by Advocate General Kokott in his opinion to *Italy v Commission,* the prohibition of discrimination on the grounds of language set out in Article 21(1) of the Charter is an expression of the general prohibition on the grounds of nationality.[202] Based on such understanding, both types of discrimination are closely related, as discriminatory treatment based on language somewhat demonstrates discrimination on the grounds of nationality.

Firstly, Article 21(1) reads that "any discrimination based on any ground such as sex, race, colour, ethnic and social origin, genetic features, language, religion, or belief, political or any other opinion, membership of a national minority, birth, disability, age, or sexual orientation shall be prohibited".[203] Article 21(1) is related to a significant body of EU equality and anti-discrimination legislation, mainly contained in directives, required to be transposed at the national level.[204] As noted by Wróbel (2019), the 'post-Lisbon" case-law of the Court of Justice has evolved in terms of the legal qualification of Article 21 from the EU's principle into the subjective right. A landmark judgment of the Court of Justice in respect of the legal nature of Article 21(1) was issued in the case of *Egenberger*[205] (2018), where the Court stated that "prohibition, which is laid down in Article 21(1) of the Charter, is sufficient in itself to confer on individuals a right which they may rely on as such in disputes between them in a field covered by EU law".[206] As a result of the *Egenberger* judgment, Article 21(1) gained imperative nature and individuals were

200 Wróbel (ed.), *Karta Praw Podstawowych Unii Europejskiej. Komentarz.* 2013, 750–1.

201 Justyna Maliszewska-Nienartowicz (ed.), *Prawo antydyskryminacyjne. System Prawa Unii Europejskiej. Tom 6,* CH Beck, 2020, 15.

202 Opinion of Advocate General Kokott in the case 566/10 P *Italian Republic v European Commission* delivered on 21 June 2012, ECLI:EU:C:2012:368, para. 77.

203 OJ 2016 C 202, 7 June 2016.

204 Directive 2000/43/EC the Race Equality Directive; Directive 2000/78/EC Framework Equal Treatment Directive; Directive 2004/113/EC Gender Equality in Goods and Services Directive; Directive 2006/54 Gender Equality in Employment Directive; Directive 79/7/EEC on Gender Equality in Social Security; Directive 2010/41/EU on Gender Equality in Self-Employment.

205 Judgment of the Court of 17 April 2018 in the case C-414/16 *Vera Egenberger v Evangelisches Werk für Diakonie und Entwicklung e.V,* ECLI:EU:C:2018:257.

206 Judgment of the Court in the case C-414/16, para. 76.

granted enforceable subjective rights. The Court's position on the legal status of Article 21(1) was sustained in the *Cresco*[207](2019) judgment.

As a result of the jurisprudence of the Court of Justice, an individual may directly invoke Article 21(1) of the Charter in matters concerning discrimination on the grounds of language, as one of the status grounds, against the Union institutions and the Member State or its authorities (vertical direct effect). The horizontal direct effect of the Article was also recognised by the Court of Justice in a number of cases.[208] The Court held that Article 21(1) may constitute an independent source of rights to an individual and that the right may be adduced directly in a dispute against a private entity in one of the areas subject to the EU law.[209]

The multiplication of prohibited grounds listed in Article 21(1) triggered the need to consider the phenomenon of intersectional discrimination,[210] which stands for discrimination against an individual on more than one grounds at the same time,[211] for instance language and sex, language and race, or language and ethnic origin. As noted by Domańska (2019), such intersection of status grounds defines the identity of individuals which results from the synergy of the features affecting the way how they are identified in society, by making their position more or less privileged (sensitive). Domańska emphasises that intersectional discrimination may constitute the basis for establishing identity theory, which should aim to protect against such discrimination.[212] The phenomenon of intersectional discrimination may be considered when the discrimination on the grounds of language and membership of a national minority happen at the same time. Although the ban on discrimination against such a membership cannot be understood as obliging the Union or the Member States to take any positive measures, nor should it constitute the basis for claiming collective rights of a minority, the membership in a particular national minority may strengthen the protection of individuals belonging to such a minority who claim that their unequal treatment may be the result of applying against them the criterion of language, religion, race, or colour.[213]

---

207 Judgment of the Court of 22 January 2019 in the case C-193/17 *Cresco Investigation GmbH v Markus Achatzi*, ECLI:EU:C:2019:43.

208 C-193/17, para. 76–77, C-414/16, para.76, C-68/17, para. 69, C-176/12, para. 47.

209 Wróbel (ed.), *Karta Praw Podstawowych Unii Europejskiej: Komentarz*, 2019, 689–90.

210 The paradigm for intersectional discrimination are Afro-American feminists who suffered from discrimination which was not a simple sum of experience of every woman (sex) and every Afro-American (race and ethnic origin). Experiences of an Afro-American woman were not equivalent to those of Afro-American man.

211 Monika Domańska, *Zakaz dyskryminacji ze względu na więcej niż jedno zabronione kryterium,* Wolters Kluwer, 2019, 136–7.

212 Domańska, 149–53.

213 Wróbel (ed.) *Karta Praw Podstawowych Unii Europejskiej: Komentarz*, 2019, 726.

The second limb of the ban on discrimination is entrenched in Article 21(2) which stipulates that "any discrimination based on nationality shall be prohibited". It clearly draws on the wording of Article 18(1) TFEU. Article 21(2) may be applied independently, exclusively in situations subject to the EU law where the Treaty does not include any specific rules on non-discrimination on the grounds of nationality. It would not apply with reference to the free flow of workers as their rights are separately regulated in Article 45 TFEU.[214] The addressees of obligations arising out of Article 21(2) are the Union and the Member States implementing the EU law. As Article 21(2) applies only within the limits of the Treaty, the limitations to the right attached to Article 18 TFEU would also apply to the Charter. Therefore, the right set out in Article 21(2) is not absolute and may be limited when it is objectively justified and the measures applied are compliant with the principle of proportionality. No contradiction or incompatibility between Article 21(2) of the Charter and Article 18(1) TFEU arises as the provisions have different purpose and scope of beneficiaries. Firstly, Article 18 TFEU confers powers on the Union to adopt legislative acts, including harmonisation of the Member States' laws, so as to combat certain forms of discrimination listed in the Treaty, Article 21(2) of the Charter does not provide for any power to enact anti-discrimination law. Secondly, the beneficiaries of Article 21(2) are not only the citizens of the EU Member States, but also organizational units without legal capacity as well as third-country nationals whose rights are covered by Union law.[215]

Both limbs of Article 21 raise an important question of what added value the Charter brings to the existing law in terms of language rights. Article 21(1) of the Charter is viewed by the Court as having little added value in relation to Member States' laws and practices in the area of non-discrimination on the grounds of language. Similarly, Article 21(2) adds little to what is already a primary Treaty right set out in Article 18 TFEU.[216] This state of facts is somewhat confirmed in the Court of Justice jurisprudence. In no case involving the Union in the vast spectrum of relevant Treaty provisions and secondary legislation on free movement and citizenship related to non-discrimination on the grounds of nationality, the Court invoked Article 21(2) of the Charter.[217]

214 Wróbel (ed.), *Karta Praw Podstawowych Unii Europejskiej: Komentarz*, 2019, 717.

215 In fact the following situations are possible: 1) they are family members of the Union citizen, 2) they are citizens of the country which entered into an international association agreement with the Union, 3) they are citizens of the country belonging to the European Economic Area, 4) they are beneficiaries of Directive 2003/86/EC on the right of family unification, 5) they are beneficiaries of Directive 2004/38/EC on the right of movement and residence.

216 Peers [et al.] (eds.), 598.

217 Peers [et al.] (eds.), 599.

4.4.2 Respect for linguistic diversity

Respect for cultural, religious and linguistic diversity constituted the general principle of EU law in the period from the Treaty establishing the European Community to the LT. The Charter lifted this respect to the fundamental status and made it a principle, but not a fundamental right *sensu stricto* which would result in an individual subjective right for the use of language.[218] The principle of respect for cultural, religious and linguistic diversity enshrined in Article 22 of the Charter aims to reflect the diversity of its Member States.[219] Therefore, the Union's respect concerns only the diversity occurring at the supranational level, and only such diversity affects the scope of the Union's duties and obligations. This implies that the EU must not interfere into the internal diversity of individual Member States, as it remains their sole competence. Such understanding is compliant with Article 3(3) TEU which expressly states that the Union "shall respect its rich cultural and linguistic diversity".[220] Such a formulation obliges the Union to respect linguistic diversity while pursuing the process of European integration. Arguably, the same provision obliges the Union to take actions supporting such diversity.[221] Nevertheless, the EU institutions are required to observe the principle expected to promote its application in their respective areas of authority. At the same time, the principle of respect for linguistic diversity does not oblige the Union to treat all the languages occurring on the territories of its Member States equally. The major reason is that the languages have different constitutional status within the domestic legal orders, so an obligation to treat them equally could give rise to a claim for acknowledging an official status of regional languages. This, in turn, would challenge the competences of the Member States in the area of 'internal' linguistic diversity which the Union should respect.[222] Diversity must occur at the Union level in order to fall within the scope of the Charter, which justifies the fact that the single addressee of an obligation established by Article 22 of the Charter is the Union. The Member States are not bound to respect their cultural, religious and linguistic diversity on the grounds of this provision.[223]

The principle of respect for cultural, religious, and linguistic diversity cannot be classified as a norm of competence and, as a result, the guarantee of linguistic diversity enshrined in the Charter cannot be directly claimed in court, as no

---

218 Nikos Vogiatzis, "The Linguistic Policy of the EU Institutions and Political Participation Post-Lisbon", *European Law Review*, No. 2, 2016, 188.

219 Xabier Arzoz, "The protection of linguistic diversity through Article 22 of the Charter of Fundamental Rights", in: Xabier Arzoz (ed.), *Respecting Linguistic Diversity in the European Union*, Amsterdam, 2008, 145–74.

220 Wróbel (ed.), *Karta Praw Podstawowych Unii Europejskiej: Komentarz*, 2019, 734.

221 Wróbel (ed.), *Karta Praw Podstawowych Unii Europejskiej: Komentarz*, 2019, 1095.

222 Wróbel (ed.), *Karta Praw Podstawowych Unii Europejskiej: Komentarz*, 2019, 732–3.

223 Wróbel (ed.), *Karta Praw Podstawowych Unii Europejskiej: Komentarz*, 2019, 735.

legislative, regulatory, or administrative measures are established which could be deemed to be the basis for the establishment of its scope.[224] Moreover, Article 22 does not grant any specific grounds for the protection of minority languages. Hence, it cannot be treated as a basis for constructing the collective rights of a community.[225] Although in *Spain v European Parliament*[226] the Court of Justice refers to Article 22 of the Charter and notes that the language to be used in exchanges with the institutions, such as the European Parliament, is fundamental in nature, at the same time, it stresses that an obligation to respect linguistic diversity cannot imply that "there is a general principle of law entitling each person to have everything likely to affect his or her interests drafted in his or her language in all circumstances, and that the institutions are required, without any derogation being permissible, to use all the official languages in all situations".[227]

The EU's respect for cultural and linguistic diversity expressed in the Charter seems not to refer to the issue of minority protection which presupposes diversity inside the Member States. However, the Union's respect for linguistic diversity contains an element of respect for identity, which may refer not only for national identity but also the identity of minorities.[228] Hence, some researchers[229] maintain that Article 22 is meant to target minorities' concerns about the protection of their identities at the Union level. Such a view is supported with the EC's scrutiny of legislative proposals to ensure that such proposals are not in breach with the Union's duty to respect cultural, religious and linguistic diversity.[230] De Witte (2008) explicitly claims Article 22 constitutes a minority protection clause as it addresses the most basic protection needs of minorities, including culture, religion and language, which are common international minority rights standards, enshrined in particular in Article 27 ICCPR.[231] The discussion on the EU's respect for linguistic diversity shows that this is a sphere of action that still has to materialise itself with

224 Urrutia and Lasagabaster, "Language Rights as a General Principle of Community Law", 2005.
225 Wróbel (ed.), *Karta Praw Podstawowych Unii Europejskiej: Komentarz*, 2019, 725.
226 Judgment of the Court of 26 March 2019 in the case C-377/16 *Kingdom of Spain v European Parliament*, ECLI:EU:C:2019:249.
227 Judgment of the Court of 26 March 2019 in the case C-377/16, para. 36–7. To that effect also judgments: C-361/01 P *Kik v OHIM*, para. 82; C-566/10 P *Italy v Commission*, C-566/10 P, para. 88; and C-643/15 and C-647/15 *Slovakia and Hungary v Council*, para. 203.
228 Wróbel (ed.), *Karta Praw Podstawowych Unii Europejskiej: Komentarz*, 2019, 18.
229 De Witte, 2004, 115; Henrard, 2011, 83.
230 Henrard, 83.
231 Bruno De Witte, "The protection of linguistic diversity through provisions of the EU Charter other than Article 22", in: Xavier Arzoz (ed.) *Respecting Linguistic Diversity in the European Union*, Amsterdam, 2008, 163–4.

specific measures that guarantee the development of linguistic diversity.[232] Certainly, the inclusion of an explicit reference to the principle in the Charter raises awareness of linguistic diversity and fosters political climate to its preservation.[233]

4.4.3 Right to education

At the beginning of the European integration, education was perceived to be a national value and competence. For this reason, the powers were conferred on the Community to carry out education policy. The evolution of the EU legal order resulted in linking the right of equal access to education with the free movement of Union citizens,[234] limited by residence restrictions and by the secondary legislation, in particular Directive 2004/38/EC.[235] Article 14 of the Charter expressly providing every individual with the right to education reaffirms the fundamental nature of the right guaranteed in the constitutional constitutions of the Member States and in Article 2 of the Protocol to the ECHR.[236] However, given the fact that the competence to provide education remains the domain of the Member States, Article 14 became relevant mainly in litigation concerning freedom of movement and equal treatment, most probably in combination with Article 45 of the Charter. As a result, the substantive scope of the EU right to education included:

1) the right to access education and vocational training, including the right to study, train, and research in another EU Member State under the same conditions as the nationals of the host State,
2) the right of residence in that state for the length of the education, and
3) ancillary social rights, such as social security cover and social benefits, maintenance aid, or grants.[237]

The judgments of the Court of Justice in the 'post-Lisbon' cases show that protection of the right to education is afforded in connection with the freedom to move and reside. Hence, it is the state that must establish an education system, make it accessible, and ensure the enforceability of the right to education. Therefore, a conclusion may be drawn that Article 14 constitutes an additional legal

232 Urrutia and Lasagabaster, "Language Rights as a General Principle of Community Law", 2003–4.

233 De Witte, "The protection of linguistic diversity through provisions of the EU Charter other than Article 22", 165.

234 As discussed in chapter 3, section 3.3.2.1.

235 As discussed in chapter 3, section 3.3.1.2.

236 Explanations relating to the Charter of Fundamental Rights, 2007 c 303/02, https://eur-lex.europa.eu/LexUriServ/LexUriServdo?uri=OJ:C:2007:303:0017:0035:en:PDF [retrieved on 15 April 2020].

237 Peers [et al.] (eds.), 419.

benchmark in the area of education but seems to add no substance to the right itself.[238] This exposes the importance of the status of the right to education, under international law instruments binding upon the Union Member States. Any solutions to the problematic aspects of the right to education in a minority language must be sought in the general principles of EU law, in particular the ECHR, the FCNM, the ECRML, the ICCPR, and the CRC.

4.4.4 Citizen's rights enshrined in the Charter

Title V of the Charter entitled 'Citizen's Rights' includes a catalogue of rights which correspond to those enshrined under the Treaty, and they should be applied under the conditions and within the limits defined in the Treaties. The fact that the citizen's rights have been incorporated into the Charter raises their importance in the light of the law. Hence, in the case of any collision of those rights with other provisions, their special status may support their priority. Although *prima facie* identical, the guarantees of the Treaty and the Charter differ in terms of their *rationae personae*. Whereas the Treaty in principle refers to the Union citizen as a beneficiary, the Charter does not limit its *rationae personae*, exclusive of the right to vote and stand as a candidate at elections to the European Parliament (Article 39) and at municipal elections (Article 40) and the freedom of movement and of residence (Article 45), provided that the latter may be extended onto the third-country nationals who legally stay on the territory of a Member State.[239] Whereever the linguistic aspects of particular Union citizen's rights could be distinguished in the Treaty, the same might be done in the context of the Charter. Hence, the rights with language-related aspects include right of access to documents (Article 42), the right to address European Ombudsman (Article 43), the right to petition the European Parliament (Article 44), freedom of movement and of residence (Article 45), the right for diplomatic and consular protection (Article 46).

Moreover, the Charter specifies the right to good administration (Article 41), which is considered to be a human right of third generation. 'Good administration' implies the right to fair procedure *vis-à-vis* the Union institutions. It aims to guarantee quick, effective and just operation of the EU administration. The concept was coined in Article 41 of the Charter, and it is based on the existence of the Union as subject to the rule of law and good administration. The right was acknowledged by the case-law of the Court of Justice as a general principle of EU law.[240] The right to good administration constitutes a key element of relations between the Union institutions and individuals, who are assured of particular substantive and

---

238 Peers [et al.] (eds.), 420–1.

239 Wróbel (ed.), *Karta Praw Podstawowych Unii Europejskiej: Komentarz*, 2013, 255.

240 To that effect: C-255/60, T-167/94, T-231/97. Following: Explanations relating to the Charter of Fundamental Rights, https://fra.europa.eu/en/eu-charter/article/41-right-good-administration [retrieved on 20 October 2020].

procedural entitlements. Procedural entitlements guarantee impartial and honest proceedings, and substantive entitlements grant an individual the right to demand effective and appropriate administration.[241]

One of the key aspects of the right to good administration is the citizen's right to address in writing the Union institutions or bodies in one of the treaty languages and the right to receive an answer in the same language. Article 41(4) of the Charter states that "[e]very person may write to the institutions of the Union in one of the languages of the Treaties and must have an answer in the same language".[242] The wording draws on:

1) Article 20(2)(d) TFEU and Article 24(4) TFEU, and
2) Article 55 TEU, including a list of treaty languages.

The right is based on the Treaty and is exercised on general principles specified in Article 52(2) of the Charter. [243] Article 41 of the Charter grants the right to good administration to every person, as opposed to Article 20(2)(d) and Article 24 TFEU which limit the scope of the right to the Unions citizen. The catalogue of institutions bound by the right to good administration entails those listed in Article 6 TEU.[244] The fundamental nature of the right to good administration strengthens the democratic entitlement to communicate with the EU in one's own language enshrined in the Treaty which renders it very hard to justify the restrictive manner in which it is applied.[245]

4.4.5 Right to a fair trial and the right of defence

4.4.5.1 The right to a translator/interpreter in criminal proceedings

The right to a fair trial is enshrined in Article 47 of the Charter. It has the status of a principle which needs implementing legislation in order to be effective. The right to a fair trial is closely tied to the right of defence (Article 48 of the Charter) when considering language rights in criminal proceedings. In fact, the right of defence is an essential element of the right to a fair trial, as it guarantees the right to an

241 Izabela Skomerska-Muchowska and Anna Wyrozumska, *Obywatel Unii, Vol.* 6, No. 1, Instytut Wydawniczy EuroPrawo, 2010, 18–9.

242 OJ 2016 C 202, 7 June 2016.

243 Skomerska-Muchowska and Wyrozumska, 121.

244 The European Parliament, European Council, Council of the European Union, Commission, Court of Justice of the European Union, European Central Bank, Court of Auditors, Union advisory bodies i.e. the European Economic and Social Committee, Committee of the Regions and the European Ombudsman.

245 Erik Hertog, *Directive 2010/64/EU of the European Parliament and of the Council on the Right to Interpretation and Translation in Criminal Proceedings: Transposition Strategies with Regard to Interpretation and Translation*, MonTI, 2015, 78.

effective remedy. The significant feature of the right to a fair trial is its scope which covers everyone suffering from a violation of the rights and freedoms guaranteed under EU law. The various components of Article 47 cover the right to effective judicial protection and remedies both before the Court of Justice and Member State courts.

The linguistic aspects of the right to a fair trial and the right of defence are implemented through Directive 2010/64/EU[246] compliant with Article 82(2)(b) TFEU.[247] The Directive helps implement the minimum EU-wide rules on the right to interpretation and translation in criminal proceedings and in proceedings for the execution of the European Arrest Warrant. The Directive was an essential step in the direction of guaranteeing that persons requiring linguistic assistance would be assured of fair treatment when confronted with measures depriving them of their liberty, charging them with crimes, or making judgments against them. The adoption of the Directive alerted the ministries of justice in the Member States to the issues involved in legal interpreting and translation.[248]

First and foremost, the Directive obliges the Member States to ensure that suspected and accused persons who do not speak or understand the language of the criminal proceedings are provided legal assistance without delay. Such assistance includes interpreting before investigative and judicial authorities, such as during police questioning, all court hearings and any necessary interim hearings, as well as interpretation of communications between suspected and accused persons and their legal counsels (Article 2). Next, essential documents of the case, such as a decision depriving a person of his or her liberty, any charge or indictment, any judgment, a European Arrest Warrant, or any other documents qualified as essential must be translated in order to ensure that the right of defence and fairness of the proceedings are assured (Article 3). Article 5 of the Directive sets out that interpretation and translation provided to a suspected or arrested person must be of a quality sufficient to safeguard the fairness of the proceedings. The

---

246 Directive 2010/64/EU of the European Parliament and of the Council of 20 October 2010 on the right to interpretation and translation in criminal proceedings. OJ L280/1, 26 October 2010.

247 "To the extent necessary to facilitate mutual recognition of judgments and judicial decisions and police and judicial cooperation in criminal matters having a cross-border dimension, the European Parliament and the Council may, by means of directives adopted in accordance with the ordinary legislative procedure, establish minimum rules. Such rules shall take into account the differences between the legal traditions and systems of the Member States. They shall concern: (...) (b) the rights of individuals in criminal procedure; (...)".

248 Liese Katschinka, *The Impact of Directive 2010/64/EU on the Right to Interpretation and Translation in Criminal Proceedings,* 2014, https://www.openstarts.units.it/bitstream/10077/ 9841/1/9_Katschinka.pdf [retrieved on 17 April 2020].

translation/interpretation should provide a suspected or accused person with sufficient knowledge to exercise his or her right of defence. The provision of inadequate legal interpreting and translation in criminal proceedings leads to an infringement of the fundamental right to an effective remedy and undermines the EU fundamental rights.[249]

The Court of Justice has analysed the right to interpretation and translation in criminal proceedings in a number of cases. In *Gavril Covaci*,[250] (2015) it examined the request for a preliminary ruling filed by *Amtsgericht Laufen* (district court Germany) in the context of criminal proceedings against Mr Covaci for road traffic offences committed by him. Mr Covaci was a Romanian citizen who was driving in Germany a vehicle with no valid mandatory motor vehicle civil liability insurance. Later, he also submitted to the German authorities a forged green card.[251] One major question asked by the referring court was whether Articles 1 and 3 of Directive 2010/64 precluded national legislation according to which an individual against whom a penalty order was issued was not allowed to lodge an objection in a language other than the language of the proceedings (German).[252] The Court of Justice ruled that the Directive did not preclude national legislation from imposing on individuals against whom a penalty order was issued certain language requirements. However, the Court noted that the requirement of lodging an objection against the penalty order in a language of the main proceedings was admitted by the Court of Justice on condition that in the light of Article 3(3) of the Directive such an objection was not an essential document for the purposes of the proceedings.[253] If any document was considered essential, it would have to be translated into the language of the concerned party.

In *Franck Sleutjes*[254] (2017), the Court of Justice had to decide whether an order imposing sanctions issued in a simplified unilateral procedure under national law constituted an 'essential document' with the meaning of Directive 2010/64/EU. The Court ruled that under Article 3(1) such an order constituted an essential document and must be translated for the purposes of enabling the suspected and accused to exercise their right of defence and thus safeguarding the fairness of the proceedings.[255]

---

249 Hertog, 78.

250 The judgment of the Court of 15 October 2015 in the case C-216/14 *Gavril Covaci*, ECLI:EU:C:2015:686.

251 Judgment of the Court in the case C-216/14, para. 16.

252 Judgment of the Court in the case C-216/14, para. 25.

253 Judgment of the Court in the case C-216/14, para. 51.

254 Judgment of the Court of 12 October 2017 in the case C-278/16 *Frank Sleutjes v Staatsanwaltschaft Aachen*, ECLI:EU:C:2017:757.

255 Judgment of the Court in the case C-278/16, para. 34.

The language rights resulting from the right to a fair trial are also implemented through Directive 2012/29/EU.[256] The Directive obliges the Member States to guarantee crime victims necessary linguistic assistance if requested in the case when a victim wants to make a complaint with regard to a criminal offence or does not understand the language of the competent authority. The victims are entitled to receive the free of charge translation of the written acknowledgement of their complaint[257] and must be provided with interpretation while being interviewed or questioned before investigative and judicial authorities.[258]

4.5 Impact of the EU accession to the ECHR on human rights protection in the EU

4.5.1 EU's obligation to accede to the ECHR

Today, the European Convention for the Protection of Human Rights and Fundamental Freedoms constitutes one of the pillars for fundamental rights protection in the EU. The ECHR is still a major source for the general principles of law in the Union, in particular in the areas not covered by the Charter or falling outside the Union's powers.[259] The reason for such a state of affairs is that the ECHR exerted strong impact on the development of the EU's own human rights standards and their entrenchment in the Charter.[260] Certainly, the Charter did not replace the provisions of the ECHR, despite being deemed to do so by modifying and adjusting the ECHR provisions to the UE needs,[261] but took a lot from the ECHR solutions.[262]

Despite a close relationship between the EU and the ECHR, there still exist two parallel supranational and mutually supporting systems of human rights protection in Europe, i.e. the system established by the European Union through the Charter and the system created by the Council of Europe through the ECHR. The linkage between them is provided mainly by the states which are members of the first and parties to the second system. At the same time, the involvement of the same states in both systems generates possible tensions which may be manifested

256 Directive 2012/29/EU of the European Parliament and of the Council of 25 October 2012 establishing minimum standards on the rights, support and protection of victims of crime, and replacing Council Framework Decision 2001/220/JHA.OJ L 315, 14 November 2012.

257 OJ L 315, 14 November 2012.

258 OJ L 315, 14 November 2012.

259 Pospíšil, 21–3.

260 Christina Eckes, "EU Accession to the ECHR: Between Autonomy and Adaptation", *The Modern Law Review, Vol.* 76, No. 2, 2013, 257.

261 Jasiński, 2003.

262 Szczerba-Zawada, "Ochrona praw człowieka w Unii Europejskiej", 113.

by conflicts in jurisprudence of the ECtHR and the Court of Justice. A structural conflict may result in a situation where the Union law could appear to be in conflict with the ECHR and could put its Members States into a dilemma as to which international obligations should be given priority.[263] The dilemma was resolved in the *Bosphorus Airways* judgement (2005),[264] where the ECtHR ruled that owing to the fact that the Union law had a nature equivalent to the protection resulting from the ECHR, the ECtHR would not interfere unless the Union protection was deemed to be insufficient.[265] Still, the status quo is that the co-existence of two systems is difficult in legal terms.

The entry into force of the Lisbon Treaty created the legal basis and an obligation for the Union to accede to the ECHR. Article 6(2) TEU states that "the Union shall accede to the European Convention for the Protection of Human Rights and Fundamental Freedoms".[266] The procedure of the Union's accession to the ECHR was specified in Article 218 TFEU[267] and the detailed legal framework in Protocol No. 8 to Article 6(2).[268] On the side of the Convention, the legal grounds for the EU accession were created by way of amendments to Article 59(2) ECHR introduced by Protocol No. 14[269] which entered into force on 1 June 2010, having been ratified by all parties to the Convention.[270] The Protocol amended Article 59 of the ECHR

263 Zdzisław Kędzia, "Relationship between the European Convention on Human Rights and the Chapter of Fundamental Rights after the European Union's Accession to the Convention", in: Jan Barcz (ed.) *Fundamental Rights Protection in the European Union*, 2009, 224–5.

264 Judgment of the ECtHR of 30 June 2005 in the case *Bosphorus Hava Yollari Turizm v Ireland* (application No. 45036/98).

265 Leszek Garlicki, "Przystąpienie UE do Europejskiej Konwencji Praw Człowieka – przygotowania i problemy", *Europejski Przegląd Sądowy*, No. 1, 2011, 14.

266 OJ 2016 C 2020, 7 June 2016.

267 Jan Barcz, "Umowy międzynarodowe Unii Europejskiej z państwami trzecimi lub organizacjami międzynarodowymi", in: Jan Barcz, (ed.), *Źródła prawa Unii Europejskiej*, Vol. 4, No. 2, Warszawa: Instytut Wydawniczy EuroPrawo, 2010, 93–4.

268 Protocol No. 8 relating to Article 6(2) of the Treaty on European Union on the Accession of the Union to the European Convention of Human Rights and Fundamental Freedoms.

269 Protocol No. 14 to the Convention for the Protection of Human Rights and Fundamental Freedoms amending the control system of the Convention, Strasbourg 13 May 2004.

270 Garlicki, 14–5: *Protocol No. 8* does not specify the type of agreement. Under maximalistic interpretation the agreement should be an instrument of a treaty between the Union and international organisation within the meaning of Article 218 TFEU, which implies unanimous decision of the EU Council, approval of the European Parliament and approval of all the EU Member States acquired in line with their procedural requirements. The Strasbourg stage would include a formal

by adding paragraph 2 which expresses permission for the European Union's accession to the Convention. This accession is accompanied by a range of constraints specifying the scope of the EU accession.[271] Firstly, the constraints comprise the warrant, set forth in Article 6(2) TEU and specified in Article 2 of Protocol No. 8 to Article 6(2), that EU "accession shall not affect the Union's competences as defined in the Treaties".[272] This warrant implies that the Union shall comply with the principle of conferred powers and that the accession to the ECHR shall not affect the competences of the EU institutions. Secondly, Protocol No. 8 includes a covenant on the necessity of the retaining by the EU of specific features of an organization, including EU participation in the statutory bodies of the Council of Europe (the Parliamentary Assembly and the Committee of Ministers) when they act under the ECHR, and retaining the autonomy of the Union law. Thirdly, the EU accession to the Convention shall not affect an obligation of the Member States not to submit a dispute concerning the interpretation and application of the Treaties to any method of settlement other than those provided for in the Treaties (Article 3 of Protocol No. 8 referring to Article 344 TFEU).[273]

To date, the EU has not acceded to the ECHR. The draft accession agreement raised numerous reservations expressed by the Court of Justice in its opinion of 18 December 2014.[274] The Court found the draft agreement not to be compliant with EU law and indicated that the draft failed to include any provisions coordinating the relationship between the EU Charter and the ECHR. According to the Court of Justice, it did not take into account the specific characteristics and autonomy of EU law and the procedure of preliminary ruling (under Article 267 TFEU).[275] Following the Court' opinion, the negotiations were suspended for five years. By a

conclusion of the agreement between the EU and state parties of the ECHR and would require ratification of the agreement by all 47 parties to the Convention. Under minimalistic interpretation the EU would be obligated to notify the CoE of its readiness to accede and conditions of this accession, as is the case with new Member States acceding to the ECHR. According to this solution, the decision would be taken at the level of the Council of Europe and detailed issues would be regulated at the non-contractual basis e.g. in the Regulations of the ECtHR. Such procedure would accelerate the entire accession process and would not require any actions by state parties to the ECHR.

271 Anastazja Gajda, "Przystąpienie Unii Europejskiej Do Europejskiej Konwencji o ochronie praw człowieka i podstawowych wolności", *Kwartalnik Kolegium Ekonomiczno-Społecznego „Studia i Prace"* No. 1/2013, 16.

272 OJ C 202, 7 June 2016.

273 Skomerska-Muchowska and Wyrozumska, 237–8.

274 Opinion 2/13 of the Court of Justice (Full Court) on EU accession to the ECHR given on 18 December 2014.

275 Kędzia, 224–5.

letter of 31 October 2019, the EU informed the Secretary General of the Council of Europe of its readiness to resume the negotiations, which were again incorporated into the agenda of both organizations.[276]

The interrupted negotiation process exposed sensitive areas of human rights protection in the context of the EU accession to the ECHR. These areas are closely interlinked with the concept of national identity, ultimately being the matter of sovereign states. The standards of human rights in such areas, and the relationship between the Court of Justice, the ECtHR and national courts, have been brought to the severest test, which so far has been failed. The matter constitutes the background for further negotiations as well as the EU's discussion on how much 'united in diversity' the Union should be.[277]

4.5.2 Language rights upon the Union's accession to the ECHR

The EU accession to the ECHR is seen as a major step in the development of human rights in Europe, mainly owing to the EU's wish to recognise the guarantees of human rights established by the Strasbourg system. Both the EU and the CoE believe that the EU accession to the ECHR will further strengthen the protection of human rights in Europe by submitting the EU to independent external control in respect of rights enshrined in the Convention.[278] The ECHR is considered to be a minimum standard vis-à-vis the Charter, and the Articles of the Charter are intended to be interpreted like corresponding ECHR Articles. The influence of the ECHR on the EU law will also be manifested through the influence of the ECtHR jurisprudence on the EU legal order. Upon the EU accession, the Court of Justice will be bound by the case-law of the ECtHR.[279] This does not change the fact that the Court of Justice will retain its judicial autonomy, but the interpretations of the ECHR provisions by the ECtHR will become directly enforceable against the EU institutions and its EU Member States when acting within the scope of EU law. This means that the Member States will be subject to additional constraints when acting under the ECHR system.[280]

---

276 EU accession to the ECHR, https://www.coe.int/en/web/human-rights-intergovernmental-cooperation/accession-of-the-european-union-to-the-european-convention-on-human-rights [retrieved on 27 April 2020].

277 Eckes, 285.

278 Jan Barcz, *Traktat z Lizbony: Wybrane Aspekty Prawne Działań Implementacyjnych*, LexisNexis, 2012, 329–76.

279 Judgment of the Court (Third Chamber) of 5 October 2010 in the case C-400/10 PPU *J. McB. v L. E.*, ECLI:EU:C:2010:582.

280 Eckes, 255, 258.

The merger of the two systems is considered to contribute to the consolidation of the rights in the sphere of language use, in particular in respect to procedural language rights.[281] Individuals will be able to invoke the provisions of the ECHR and the relevant case-law of the ECtHR in order to claim for or defend their language rights against the Union and before national courts. The accession to the ECHR will most probably trigger the EU accession to the other conventions and agreements which are strictly linked to the ECHR system, in particular the FCNM. However, it remains a matter of discussion whether the accession will positively affect the language rights of persons belonging to minorities on the territory of the EU. The reason is that the ECtHR is rather resistant in matters concerning minority language rights protection mainly due to the fact that it leaves a wide margin of appreciation for the states to decide about language related matters and considers some claims for the rights to be unfounded, for instance in the fields of legal proceedings[282] or education.[283]

Upon the Union's accession, the ECHR is likely take the space which is left outside the application of the Charter. Article 51 of the Charter draws a clear boundary between the scope of the Charter, national constitutional orders and international instruments. This will allow the ECHR to be applied within the EU legal order without creating collisions. Whereas the Charter limits its application to the EU institutions and bodies and Member States implementing the EU law, the ECHR is general in nature and the ECtHR exercises universal jurisdiction. As a result, an individual will be allowed to submit complaints directly to the ECtHR and adduce the right to liberty and security (Article 5(2)), the right to a fair trial (Article 6(3)(e), and prohibition of discrimination (Article 14) of the ECHR in order to defend his or her language rights.[284]

4.6 Conclusions

- The three major aims of protecting language rights – the preservation of peace and security, promotion of fair treatment of individuals, and preservation of linguistic diversity – demonstrated different aspects of the rights and gave rise to the debate on their scope and nature.
- The above aims manifest both the individual and collective nature of language rights. Although the debate is still in progress in the matter, the prevailing view is that language rights are in principle individual. The collective conception is

281 *Brozicek v Italy (1989), Delcourt v Belgium (1970), Kamasinski v Austria (1989), Öztürk v Germany (1984), Shamayev and 12 Others v Georgia and Russia (2005).*

282 *Isop v Austria* (application No. 808/60)

283 *Belgian Linguistic Case v Belgium* (applications No. 1474/62; 1677/62; 1691/62; 1769/63; 1994/63; 2126/64.

284 As discussed in 4.2.5 of this chapter.

justified when the right holder is an individual member of a group (minority) but not the group as a whole. Such understanding is supported by the narrow interpretation of Article 27 ICCPR.

- The classification of individual language rights into human rights is not straightforward for all the academic scholars in the field.
  - The distinction by Kloss and Mälksoo between 'tolerance-oriented language rights' as the language rights in the private sphere and 'promotion-oriented language rights' as the rights in the public sphere reflects the nature of the rights. The former are considered to be inalienable and should be unconditionally guaranteed under international law instruments. The latter are not comprehensively protected, as they depend on the implementation at the state level.
  - The human rights-based approach to language rights represented by. Skutnabb-Kangas and Philipson exposes educational aspects of 'linguistic human rights' which may be either necessary and, therefore, inalienable or enrichment-oriented, therefore deemed to be a privilege.
  - Arzoz presented the view that no general equation between language rights and human rights should be made as the fundamental nature of the rights depends on the state constitutional laws.
- The classifications of language rights allow one to distinguish the nature of rights based on their use in the private and public sphere. The private use of language appears to be a fundamental and unconditional right, which is based on state non-interference. The public use of language may be fundamental when relating to the rights guaranteeing linguistic fairness in the course of judicial proceedings. Such rights do not have fundamental status when they refer to the public use of minority languages which depends on the quantity condition (sufficient number of minority members).
- The concepts of negative and positive language rights have also been distinguished in order to indicate the rights which could be effectively enjoyed without state intervention and positive rights which require the active participation of the state in order to be exercised.
- The Union's system for the protection of fundamental rights in the EU is based on three pillars: the Charter of Fundamental Rights, the European Convention for the Protection of Human Rights and Fundamental Freedoms, and the general principles of EU law enshrined in international law instruments ratified by the Member States. They remain complementary sources of fundamental rights.
- The debate on the fundamental nature of language rights guaranteed in the EU law exposes diverging views on the part of experts in the field:
  - language rights cannot fall within this category as there are not legal basis for that (Arzoz),
  - language rights in the EU are only the result of the organization's different levels of multilingualism and well developed language rules and, hence, they cannot be qualified as human rights (Schilling),

   - language rights constitute fundamental rights protected in the European law, including the EU and the Council of Europe instruments (Mancini and De Witte, Urrutia and Lasagabaster).
- The international human rights instruments, in particular the ECHR, the FCNM, and the ICCPR, widely ratified by the EU Member States, remain the source of language rights to persons belonging to minorities having the status of general principles of EU law.
- Language rights in the light of international law are mostly embedded in the universal human rights, such as freedom of expression, the right of non-discrimination on the grounds of language, including the right to education, and procedural linguistic rights.
   - The lack of direct references to language guarantees while exercising freedom of expression in major international law instruments (Article 10(1) ECHR, Article 19(2) ICCPR) results in a limited reach of freedom in respect of language rights protection. The freedom of expression affects only the private use of a minority language in the public sphere.
   - The right of non-discrimination on the grounds of language (Article 27 ICCPR and Article 14 ECHR) plays a crucial role in the protection of language rights under international law. On the basis of the case-law of the ECHR and the UNHRC, it may be observed that rights in the public realm are implemented only at a minimum level which prevents discrimination based on linguistic status, and merely until these speakers complete their transition into the linguistic mainstream of society and its dominant cultural practice.
   - The right to education in a minority language is deeply entrenched in the right of non-discrimination. Although the formative *Belgian Linguistic Case* demonstrated a limited impact of non-discrimination on the language of instruction, the recent cases, in particular *Cyprus v Turkey*, show that the right of non-discrimination on the grounds of language affects the right to education in a minority language and may influence the language of instruction.
   - Procedural linguistic human rights include language rights resulting from procedural human rights such as the right to liberty and security (Article 9 ICCPR and Article 5 ECHR) and the right to a fair trial (Article 14 ICCPR and Article 6 ECHR). Their linguistic aspects focus on assuring free-of-charge interpretation and translation assistance so that a person detained or charged, who does not speak the language of the main proceedings, could effectively defend himself or herself. The practical implementation of language assistance turns out to be problematic in particular in terms of the extent of the free-of-charge translation and interpretation (*Leudicke, Belkacem and Koc v Germany, Kamasinki v Austria*).
- The analysis of the relevant provisions on the language rights and the case-law of the UNHRC and the ECtHR leads to the conclusion that in the public sphere only a thin layer of language rights focused on fairness and the needs of the individual is guaranteed. It seems that demands which promote the most minimal redistribution of resources are promoted. It is manifested through the

right to an interpreter in criminal proceedings only for those defendants who are completely unfamiliar with the court language, but not those who know the language insufficiently. At the same time, in the private sphere, the UNHRC and the ECtHR support a thick layer of cultural and linguistic preservation and complete freedom to defend and to develop minorities' distinct linguistic identity and cultural practices.

- The Charter of Fundamental Rights exposes a few rights and principles which have linguistic aspects.
  - The right of non-discrimination under the Charter has two limbs related to language matters. The non-discrimination on the grounds of language (Article 21(1)) is a subjective right which may be relied on by an individual in disputes with the EU institutions, the Member States (vertical direct effect) as well as against private entities (horizontal direct effect) covered by the EU law (*Egenberger, Cresco*). The non-discrimination on the grounds of nationality (Article 21(2)) draws on the primary law right included in Article 18 TFEU and is considered to add little value to the right already existing in the Treaty.
  - Respect for linguistic diversity is a Charter principle which does not generate any subjective rights for individuals. The principle must be observed at the EU level by the Union institutions. The Union's respect for diversity at the supranational level is also an expression of respect for the Member States' national identities, including respect for identity of minorities.
  - The right to education (Article 14) is deemed to be afforded in connection with the freedom to move and reside. The Charter seems to add no substance to the right, but reaffirms the right of equal access to education by non-nationals of a host State under the same conditions as the citizens of the state.
  - The civic rights enshrined in the Charter reflect the Treaty rights granted to the Union citizen. The fundamental status of the same rights stresses their importance, but adds little in terms of the enforcement of the right. The legal basis remains Articles 20–24 TEFU, including the language-related rights. The Charter rights have an additional value for the third-country nationals.
  - The right to a fair trial and the right of defence are the Charter principles implemented in particular by means of Directive 2010/64/EC. The Directive guarantees suspected and accused persons who do not speak or understand the language of the criminal proceedings, language assistance, including interpreting and translation. The lack of such support or inadequate support leads to the infringement of fundamental rights to an effective remedy.
- The EU accession to the ECHR is considered to be a step towards strengthening the language rights of individuals mainly owing to the consolidation of human fundamental rights existing in the systems of the Council of Europe and the Union. However, owing to the ECtHR resistance to granting language rights to minority members, it remains a matter of discussion whether the language rights of persons belonging to national minorities will actually be strengthened.

Final conclusions

1. The primary objective of this dissertation was to prove that the language rights of the Union citizen are an important element of the European Union's respect for the national identities of its Member States guaranteed in the Treaties. With the aim of verifying the thesis, four research hypotheses were formulated. According to them, firstly, language rights are an integral part of the European Union language policy, secondly, the European Union maintains linguistic regime which constitutes the grounds for language rights, thirdly, Union citizenship strengthens the legal basis for the protection of language rights of Member States' citizens and finally, the European Union respects selected language rights as fundamental rights. The justification of the above hypotheses required the examination of the following research problems: analysis of the legal aspects of European Union's language policy, examination of the language rights resulting from the EU multilingual law, exploration of the rights of Member States' citizens related to language use in communication with the EU institutions, analysis of language rights resulting from the rights expressly granted to the Union citizen in the Lisbon Treaty, investigation into those universal human rights having linguistic aspects constituting general principles of EU law enshrined in international law instruments, and scrutiny of language rights resulting from the protection of fundamental rights laid down in the Charter of Fundamental Rights of the European Union.

2. The examination of the formulated research problems has led me to the following conclusions:

2.1 The analysis of the European Union's language policy demonstrates that the legal aspects of the policy are first and foremost reflected in the Union's linguistic regime which regulates the status of languages. Through its regime, the Union respects one official language of every Member State as listed in Regulation No. 1/58.[1] All the EU official languages enjoy equal status in the light of the law. The linguistic equality of the Member States constitutes the basis for the rights rooted in the EU language policy, in particular in the Union multilingual law (legal multilingualism) and in the linguistic regimes of the Union's institutions (institutional multilingualism). In this sense, the EU language policy is distinct when compared to the language policies of the United Nations (UN) and the Council of Europe (CoE). The EU is the only international organization whose language policy is a source of enforceable language rights for the citizens of its Member States. As a result, the current shape of the EU linguistic regime does not admit the introduction of a single EU official language. The reduction in a number of the organization's official languages would be in contrast with the Union's respect for the linguistic

1 OJ 17, 1 July 2013.

diversity of its Member States. Such a reduction would also mean that the citizens of the Union would not be able to exercise their language rights to access directly effective EU law or to contact the Union institutions in their own languages.

2.2 The main conclusion that can be drawn from the examination of language rights resulting from the EU multilingual law is that the direct effect of the EU law and its supremacy over national laws of Member States impose on the EU an obligation to provide Member States' citizens with access to EU law in their languages. The linguistic equality of all the EU official languages guarantees the Union citizen the right to be unilingual, i.e. the right to rely solely on one authentic language version of the EU legislation to acquaint himself or herself with the content of law. The right is guaranteed by a number of principles: firstly, the principle of legal multilingualism (*Skoma-Lux*[2]), secondly, the principle of equal authenticity (*Stauder,*[3] *CILFIT*[4]) and thirdly, the principle of uniform law interpretation and application (*CILFIT, EMU Tabac*[5]). The above principles aim to guarantee legal certainty for the addressee of the law (Union citizen). Despite assertions of the lack of exact equivalence between language versions, whatever the effort of the legislator or the Court of Justice, the citizen's right to be unilingual seems to remain unaffected (*UAB Profisa,*[6] *Research*[7]). Neither the principles guaranteeing legal certainty nor judgments issued by the Court of Justice require the Union citizen to read EU law in more than one official language.

2.3 The investigation into the rights of Member States' citizens related to language use in communication with the EU institutions provides evidence for a short list of citizen's rights to contact the Union institutions in any of the EU official languages (external linguistic regime). In principle, the Union citizen is entitled to use any official language while contacting the EU institutions listed in Article 13 TEU and the EU bodies which comply with the language rules governed by Regulation

---

2 Judgment of the Court of 11 December 2007 in the case C-161/06 *Skoma-Lux sro v Celní ředitelství Olomouc,*. ECLI:EU:C:2007:773.

3 Judgment of the Court of 12 November 1969 in the case C 29-69 *Erich Stauder v City of Ulm – Sozialamt,* ECLI:EU:C:1969:57.

4 Judgment of the Court of 6 November 1982 in the case C 283/81 *Srl CILFIT and Lanificio di Gavardo SpA v Ministry of Health,* ECLI:EU:C:1982:335.

5 Judgment of the Court of 2 April 1998 in the case C 296/95 *The Queen v Commissioners of Customs and Excise, ex parte EMU Tabac SARL, The Man in Black Ltd, John Cunningham,* ECLI:EU:C:1998:152.

6 Judgment of the Court of 19 April 2007 in the case C-63/06 *UAB Profisa v Muitinės departamentas prie Lietuvos Respublikos finansų ministerijos,* ECLI:EU:C:2007:233.

7 Judgment of the General Court of 21 May 2014 T-61/13 *Research and Production Company 'Melt Water' UAB v Office for Harmonisation in the Internal Market (Trade Marks and Designs) (OHIM),* ECLI:EU:T:2014:265.

No. 1/58. In turn, these are obliged to respond in the same language (Articles 2 and 3 of Regulation No. 1/58).

The right of the Union citizen to use any EU official language is also maintained when applying to the Court of Justice, whose linguistic regime is specifically governed by its Rules of Procedure.[8] The language chosen does not have to be the native language of the applicant. If the case is brought by more than one applicant, the applicants must choose a common language or file separate applications. Once the language of the case is specified, the further right to rely on specific language version of the judgment concerns only the selected languages, including the language of the case. This is justified by the fact that the Court's judgments are authentic only in the language of the case or where applicable in another authorised language.

The study reveals that the right to use any Union official language in contacts with the EU administration is not absolute. It is not guaranteed in respect of the EU bodies and agencies whose linguistic regime is not governed by Regulation No. 1/58 (*Kik*[9]). The limitations of such administrative language rights are considered to be in compliance with the EU law when applied in a non-discriminatory manner and being substantiated by the argument that it is not a general principle of Community law that every citizen has the right to "have a version of anything that might affect his interests drawn up in his language in all circumstances".[10]

The language rights of the citizens of the Union are also exercised within the internal linguistic regimes of the EU institutions. The right of an elected European Parliament representative to express himself or herself and to work in his or her own language constitutes the most striking example. The right constitutes an inalienable part of democratic legitimacy allowing a deputy to carry out his or her mandate. Elsewhere, the internal language arrangements of the EU institutions remain largely unregulated. Practical solutions expose the imbalance in the treatment of various languages, in particular in favour of English. As a result, the restricted internal linguistic regimes of the institutions prevent the users of languages not used by the institutions in a 'working mode' from the democratic right of access to information about the EU in one of the EU official languages. The major affected areas or channels of communication include publications made available on the internet websites of some EU institutions, public consultations, recruitment procedures for the EU staff, and invitations to tenders.

The research shows that the Union institutions bear no consequences for failure to publish documents of non-binding force or information in all the official

8 Articles 36–38 of the Rules of Procedure of the Court of Justice of the European Union.

9 Judgment of the Court of 9 September 2003 in the case C-361/01 P *Christina Kik v Office for Harmonisation in the Internal Market (Trade Marks and Designs) (OHIM)*, ECLI:EU:C:2003:434.

10 Judgment of the Court in the case C-361/01, para 82.

languages. In such as case, the Union citizen has no solid legal grounds, except for relying on the Union's policy of openness and transparency supported with the right to good administration (Article 41 of the Charter), to sue the EU institutions. The limitation of languages in the process of public consultations and invitations to tenders is considered to be unequal treatment which may be justified when proportionate and based on reasonable and objective justification. Moreover, the restricted number of languages in the calls for proposal or invitations to tenders may be justified by cost considerations when the legislator has made a decision to that effect.[11] The issue of citizen's language rights may also arise in the recruitment procedure for EU staff. The general rule is that the job announcements should be published in all the EU official languages.[12] Hence, any limitation of languages should not favour the candidates using particular languages and adversely affect the other candidates. Different treatment of languages in the recruitment procedures may amount to a claim for discrimination if a particular institution fails to provide candidates with the grounds for the difference in treatment by way of clear, objective, and foreseeable criteria.[13] This does not mean that linguistic requirements towards candidates are not founded. The knowledge of a specific language is considered to be compatible with EU law if objectively justified by the interests of the service, with the reservation that the required level of language command is proportionate to the genuine needs of the service. As in principle, thorough knowledge of one EU official language and a satisfactory knowledge of another one is expected from the candidates, the institutions must be able to justify the choice of languages in terms of their usefulness for the performance of the duties.[14]

2.4 The examination of the rights expressly granted to the Union citizen in the Lisbon Treaty proves that this is an area which generates a number of rights in the field of language use. It is so because the day-to-day life of the Union citizen who enjoys the right to move and reside freely results in a multitude of situations concerning the use of one's own language. The jurisprudence of the Court of Justice evidences that the rights granted to the Union citizen in Article 20(2) TFEU and developed in Articles 21–24 include linguistic aspects. One of the principal aims of such rights, including social, personal and political sphere, is to guarantee to

11 European Ombudsman's decision 259/2005, para. 11.

12 Judgment of the Court of 26 March 2019 in the case C-621/16 P *European Commission v Italy*, ECLI:EU:C:2019:251.

13 T-185/05 *Italy v Commission*, C-566/10 P *Italy v Commission*, C-377/16 *Kingdom of Spain v European Parliament*, C-621/16 P *European Commission v Italy*.

14 Judgment of the Court of 26 March 2019 in the case C-377/16 *Kingdom of Spain v European Parliament*, ECLI:EU:C:2019:249.

moving citizens of the Union the same legal position as the nationals residing in their homeland (*Bickel and Franz*[15]).

The citizen's right to move and reside freely is subject to two major limitations (*Baumbast*[16]), which affect the linguistic aspects of the right. Firstly, the right may be restricted if it constitutes an unreasonable burden on the social security system of the host State (Article 7 of Directive 2004/38/EC). Despite the fundamental status of the citizenship of the Union, this limitation exposes the difference in treatment between economically active and inactive citizens. Accordingly, the latter do not enjoy all the rights granted under Article 21 TFEU, under the conditions of self-sufficiency specified in Directive 2004/38. Secondly, the right is subject to the Member State's public policy, public security or public health (Article 27 of the Directive). Accordingly, a Member State may reserve some areas of public operations for its nationals only. Still, the exclusion of some specific areas earmarked for the nationals of the host State does not change the fact that the Union citizen exercising the right to move and reside freely has been brought to a position very close to that enjoyed by the nationals of the host State.

The Union citizen's right to move and reside freely read in conjunction with the principle of non-discrimination on the grounds of nationality constitute the basis for a number of language rights. The first one is the right of equal access to education which potentially entails language-related dimension. However, the analysis shows that it appears not to guarantee the right to education in the individual's own language. The case-law of the Court of Justice[17] clearly shows that the right concerns mostly the non-discriminatory treatment of Member State citizens in terms of financial aspects and quotas and does not refer to education in a particular language.

Secondly, the analysis proves that the moving Union citizen is guaranteed the right to use his or her own language before Member State courts on no less favourable conditions than the nationals of the host State. The right applies both to criminal proceedings (*Bickel and Franz*) and civil proceedings (*Rüffer*[18]).

15 Judgment of the Court of 24 November 1998 in the case C-274/96 *Criminal proceedings against Horst Otto Bickel and Urlich Franz*, ECLI:EU:C:1998:563.

16 Judgment of the Court of 17 September 2002 in the case C-413/99 *Baumbast and R v Secretary of State for the Home Department*, ECLI:EU:C:2002:493.

17 Judgment of the Court of 1 July 2004 in the case C-65/03 *Commission v Belgium*, ECLI:EU:C:2004:402; judgment of the Court of 7 July 2005 in the case C-147/03 *Commission v Austria*, ECLI:EU:C:2005:427; judgment of the Court of 13 April 2010 in the case C-73/08 *Nicolas Bressol and Others and Céline Chaverot and Others v Gouvernement de la Communautéfrançaise*, ECLI:EU:C:2010:181.

18 Judgment of the Court of 27 March 2014 in the case C-322/13 *lrike Elfriede Grauel Rüffer v Katerina Pokorná*. ECLI:EU:C:2014:189.

Thirdly, the right to move and reside freely together with the principle of non-discrimination on the grounds of nationality creates a higher standard of protection for the citizen's right to choose his or her name and surname. This higher standard results from the case-law of the Court of Justice, according to which the right must be guaranteed when: 1) a distorted pronunciation of a (sur)name causes inconvenience in pursuing one's occupation by exposing one to a risk of losing clients (*Konstantinidis*[19]), and 2) using different (sur)names in the Member State of nationality in the Member State of birth and residence is liable to hamper the exercise of the right to move and reside freely. The Court of Justice specified clear conditions when a national court may deem a change in one's name and surname to be in breach of Union law. The Court gave the competent national courts a prerogative to carry out the 'serious inconvenience test'. The national court must determine if the refusal to amend the name gives rise to serious inconvenience at administrative, professional and private levels. If the answer is in the affirmative, the person concerned should be entitled to use a (sur)name according to the law and tradition of the Member State of nationality in order to avoid doubts about his or her identity (*Garcia Avello,*[20] *Leonhard Matthias,*[21] *Runevič-Vardyn and Wardyn*[22]).

At the same time, the analysis demonstrates that the right to choose one's name and surname may be limited by the principle of the EU's respect for national identities of its Member States (Article 4(2) TEU) expressed through the EU's respect for state constitutional values. The case of *Sayn-Wittgenstein*[23] evidences that the national law on the abolition of noble titles may justify precluding a person from holding a noble title considered to be part of a surname. Moreover, in the reasoning of the Court of Justice, the right to choose one's name and surname could be restricted by the national norms which aim to protect the state's national language constituting a fundamental element of the Member State's national identity

19 Judgement of the Court of 30 May 1993 in the case C-168/91 *Christos Konstantinidis v Stadt Altensteig – Standesamt and Landrastamt Calw- Ordnungsamt,* ECLI:EU:C:1993:115.

20 Judgment of the Court of 2 October 2003 in the case C-148/02 Carlos Garcia Avello v Belgian State. ECLI:EU:C:2003:539.

21 Judgment of the Court of 27 April 2006 in the case C-96/04 *Standesamt Stadt Niebüll.* ECLI:EU:C:2006:254.

22 Judgment of the Court of 12 May 2011 in the case C-391/09 *Malgožata Runevič-Vardyn and Łukasz Paweł Wardyn. Vilniaus miesto savivaldybės administracija and Others.* ECLI:EU:C:2011:291.

23 Judgment of the Court of 22 December 2012 in the case C-208/09 *Ilonka Sayn-Wittgenstein v Landeshauptmann von Wien,* ECLI:EU:C:2010:806.

(*Runevič-Vardyn and Wardyn*). The restriction is subject to the 'serious inconvenience test'.[24]

Union citizenship as a fundamental status of every Member State national guarantees a worker or a self-employed person the right to move and reside freely and to participate in the EU internal market on a non-discriminatory basis. The principle of non-discrimination on the grounds of nationality and the right to move and reside freely trigger language entitlements for economically active citizens. They are not absolute and may be limited by objectively justified requirements resulting from the Member State's national regulations. Such requirements should be perceived as exceptions rather than general rules and must be applied in a non-discriminatory and proportionate manner (*Groener*[25]). Language requirements are justified when they are necessary to practise some regulated professions[26] or if they determine someone's ability to work adequately according to the expectations of an employer. Therefore, the language skills of moving citizens participating in the internal market are subject to testing, if required. Invariably, the imposed language requirements should not go beyond what is necessary to attain professional objectives. If the required linguistic skills are not justified by actual needs, they might be considered discriminatory and disproportionate (*Haim*,[27] *Hocsman*,[28] *Angonese*[29]).

Next, the right to petition the EP, to apply to the European Ombudsman, and the right to address the EU institutions in one of the Treaty languages reinforces the language rights resulting from the EU legal system enshrined in Regulation No. 1/58 by lifting them to the status of primary law rights. The inclusion of the right into the catalogue of the Union citizen's rights strengthens the linguistic aspects of the Union's democratic communication mechanisms, such as the right to control the institutions and obtain information about the EU, and the EU makes a simple procedure of amending Regulation No. 1/58 impossible.

Finally, language rights granted to consumers reflect the EU's attempt to balance between ensuring smooth functioning of the internal market, on the one

24 *Vilnus City District Court allows for original spelling of Malgorzata*, http://cn.cfhr.eu/2019/11/20/vilnius-city-district-court-allows-for-original-spelling-of-malgorzata/ [retrieved on 22 July 2020].

25 Judgment of the Court of 28 November 1989 in the case C-379/87 *Anita Groener v Minister for Education and the City of Dublin Vocational Educational Committee*, ECLI:EU:C:1989:599.

26 Article 53 of Directive 2005/36/EC.

27 Judgment of the Court of 4 July 2000 in the case C-424/97 *Salomone Haim v Kassenzahnärztliche Vereinigung Nordrhein*, ECLI:EU:C:2000:357.

28 Opinion of Advocate General Jacobs delivered on 16 September 1999 in the case C-238/98.

29 Judgment of the Court of 6 June 2000 in the case C-281/98 *Angonese v Cassa di Risparimo di Bolzano SpA*, ECLI:EU:C:2000:296.

hand, and preserving linguistic diversity of EU Member States, on the other hand. In principle, consumers are entitled to be informed of the characteristics of the product placed on the relevant market in the required language (*Cassis de Dijon*[30]). This does not automatically mean the use of an official language of a given state (*Piageme I*[31] (1991) and *Piageme II*[32] (1995)). The consumer is entitled to receive necessary information by 'use of language easily understood' rather than to demand the use of a specific language. The results of the study evidence that the EU protects consumers' language rights only when Member States cannot guarantee adequate protection and the EU protection is justified by higher rank objectives, such as: 1) the protection of the consumer as a weaker party to a cross-border contract and in a cross-border dispute or 2) the protection of consumer's health and safety. In the first case, the protection is implemented by means of a range of directives which do not prejudice Member States from setting more stringent rules regarding the use of languages than those imposed by the Union if this is justified by consumer protection. The EU – acting within its powers – assists consumers to exercise their language entitlements in cross-border disputes by way of the European Consumer Centres' Network (ECC-Net). The ECCs founded in every Member State are also expected to provide consumers with linguistic support and translation assistance. Another overriding reason substantiating the Union's intervention into language matters occurs when consumer's health and safety are at stake. Under the EU law, one may distinguish language entitlements with respect to three categories of products. These are medical devices, toys and cosmetic products. The most stringent rights concern medical products – where the consumer has the right to obtain the entire package leaflet of the product in his or her official language or the language of the state where the product is marketed. In respect of toys, less stringent rules apply. The consumer is entitled to receive instructions and safety information in an intelligible language understood by him or her. As regards cosmetic products, the rules are most flexible, with the condition that the language of the information provided on the label should be understandable to the end user.

2.5 The investigation into the universal human rights constituting the general principles of EU law enshrined in international law instruments proves that language rights are protected under freedom of expression, the right of non-discrimination on the grounds of language, the right to education, the right to liberty and security, and the right to a fair trial. The analysis shows that language

30 Judgment of the Court of 20 February 1979 in the case C-120/78 *Rewe-Zentral AG vs Bundesmonopolverwaltung Für Branntwein*, ECLI:EU:C:1979:42.

31 Judgment of the Court of 18 June 1991 in the case C-369/89 *Piageme and others v BVBA Peeters,*, ECLI:EU:C:1991:256.

32 Judgment of the Court of 12 October 1995 in the case C-85/94 *Groupement des Producteurs, Importateurs et Agents Généraux d'Eaux Minérales Etrangères VZW (Piageme) and others v Peeters NV*, ECLI: EU: C:1995:312.

rights in this context are divided into those which concern the private use of language and public use of language. The former constitute fundamental unconditional rights which cannot be arbitrarily or unlawfully interfered with by the public authority. The latter concern the rights to use a language publicly, which is not always regarded as fundamental as it depends on how the state organises communication with minorities. The right to use a minority language in the public usually arises when a sufficient number of language speakers request a particular type of public service in their language (e.g. civil ceremonies). When the number of speakers is too low, and it is too onerous to use a minority language in a certain type of public service, the right to use a minority language in the public sphere is not considered to be violated.

The research results prove that freedom of expression is a universal human right which has a limited impact on language rights. The reason is that it concerns only private communication between persons using the same (minority) language in a majority language environment (*Ballantyne*[33]). Preventing someone from expressing himself or herself in a minority language in the public sphere is analysed by judicial bodies as discrimination based on language rather than violation against freedom of expression.

Next, the right of non-discrimination on the grounds of language constitutes the basis for a number of language rights awarded under international human rights instruments. The rights affect both minority-specific and non-minority-specific rights to language use. They include respect for private and family life, the right to personal identity, or the right to education. One of the frequently raised aspects of the right of non-discrimination on the grounds of language entails the right to education in a minority language. The right understood as a positive one – requiring the state to take actions – in the public sphere is not guaranteed unconditionally. The international law provides no straightforward legal grounds for the right to be educated in one's own language. Article 27 of the International Covenant on Civil and Political Rights (ICCPR) and Article 29 of the Convention on the Rights of the Child (CRC) fail to provide a general, unambiguous, and legally binding obligation for the right. Article 14 of the Framework Convention on National Minorities (FCNM) and Article 8 of European Convention on Regional and Minority Languages (ECRML) offer more specific basis for education in minority languages, but they limit the right to situations when a right is justified and reasonable or when a number of students in part of a territory is substantial or sufficient. To put it in other words, the right to education in a minority language is not absolute and depends on the number of speakers and feasibility considerations. Although

33 Communications of the UN Human Rights Committee, Nos. 359/1989 and 385/1989 in the case *Ballantyne, Davidson, McIntyre v Canada,* U.N. Doc. CCPR/C/47/D/359/1989 and 385/1989/Rev1 (1993).

the ECtHR case-law in this area (*Cyprus v Turkey*[34]) indicates that the language of education should not simply be left to the state's determination or discretion, in principle the freedom to decide about actual educational measures still remains within the competence of the state authorities. The evolution in adjudications may, however, breathe new life into the existing legal standards in this area in the years to come.

Another important group of language rights embedded in universal human rights is procedural linguistic human rights. They are derivatives of the other procedural human rights, such as the right to liberty and security and the right to a fair trial (Articles 5 and 6 ECHR and Articles 9 and 14 ICCPR). The right to free language assistance by a translator and an interpreter at different stages of criminal proceedings is a human right which prevents abuses of the state and puts an obligation on the state to provide actively for the realisation of the right (*Delcourt v Belgium*,[35] *Öztürk v Germany*[36]). The results of the study reveal that the arrested has the right to be provided with free-of-charge language support so that he or she can understand the charges (*Brozicek v Italy*[37]) and the hearing (*Luedicke, Belkacem and Koc v Germany*[38]). The linguistic support should be provided when requested and it should include translation of documentary material as well as interpretation of pre-trial hearing and main hearing unless it is evidenced that the request is not justified (*Kamasinski v Austria*[39]). The underlying reason for granting professional language support is that the accused must be able to effectively participate in proceedings and protect his or her interests. In a case when the accused declares to even roughly knows the language of the proceedings, the right might be rejected (*Cuscani v Italy*[40]).

2.6 The examination of the scope of fundamental rights enshrined in the Charter of Fundamental Rights of the European Union proves that it is the source of several language rights. The examination of the Charter reveals that the rights are vested

34 Judgment of the ECtHR of 10 May 2001 in the case *Cyprus v Turkey* (application No. 25781/94).

35 Judgment of the ECtHR of 17 January 1970 in the case *Delcourt v Belgium* (application No. 2689/65).

36 Judgment of the ECtHR of 21 February 1984 in the case *Öztürk v Germany* (application no 8544/79).

37 Judgment of the ECtHR of 19 December 1989 in the case *Brozicek v Italy* (application No. 10964/84).

38 Judgment of the ECtHR of 28 November 1978 in the case *Luedicke, Belkacem and Koc v Germany* (application No. 6210/73, 6877/75, 7132/75).

39 Judgment of the ECtHR of 9 December 1989 in the case *Kamasinski v Austria* (application No. 9783/82).

40 Judgment of the ECtHR of 24 September 2002 in the case *Cuscani v Italy* (application No. 32771/96).

in every individual, not only the Union citizen, are dispersed in a number of the Charter provisions and are of a varied nature.

Firstly, the right to non-discrimination based on language (Article 21(1)) is an enforceable subjective right in the light of the Court of Justice's case-law (*Egenberger*,[41] *Cresco*[42]), which has both horizontal and vertical direct effects. As a result, the right may be directly adduced before Member State courts by an individual with reference to disputes against the Union institutions and a Member State or its authorities as well as against a private entity in one of the areas subject to the EU law.

Secondly, the right to non-discrimination on the grounds of nationality (Article 21(2)) applies within the limits of the Treaty, and the limitations to the right attached to Article 18 TFEU also apply to the Charter. In practice, the right seems to have little added value to what is already a primary law right set out in Article 18 TFEU. The inclusion of the right in the Charter underlines its fundamental nature.

Thirdly, respect for linguistic diversity (Article 22) is a principle, not a subjective right, and therefore, it cannot be claimed directly by an individual before a Member State court. The reason is that the scope of respect concerns only diversity at a supranational level while pursuing European integration, and its sole addressee is the Union.

Next, Article 14 of the Charter does not constitute the grounds for the right to education in a minority language. The legal grounds must be sought in the general principles of EU law.

The citizen's rights enshrined in the Charter (Articles 39–46) must be applied under the conditions and limits defined in the Treaties, also in respect of language use. In fact, the inclusion of citizen's rights into the Charter raises their importance, without much affecting their actual application. The right which deserves special attention is the right to good administration (Article 41) which legally reinforces the right to communicate with the EU in all its official languages and, as a result, renders it very hard to justify the restrictive manner in which such communication is held.

Finally, the right to interpretation and translation in criminal proceedings arising from the right to a fair trial and right of defence (Articles 47 and 48) guarantees linguistic assistance for individuals not acquainted with the language of the proceedings. The right entails interpreting before investigative and judicial authorities, all court hearings and any necessary interim hearings, interpretation of

41 Judgment of the Court of 17 April 2018 in the case C-414/16 *Vera Egenberger v Evangelisches Werk für Diakonie und Entwicklung e.V*, ECLI:EU:C:2018:257.

42 Judgment of the Court of 22 January 2019 in the case C-193/17 *Cresco Investigation GmbH v Markus Achatzi*, ECLI:EU:C:2019:43.

communication between suspected and accused persons and their legal counsels, as well as translation of essential documents (*Gavril Covaci*,[43] *Franck Sleutjes*[44]).

3. The findings from the analysis of the above research problems support the research hypotheses made at the beginning of the study. Certainly, language rights are an integral part of the European Union language policy. The policy generates the administrative language entitlements of EU official language users and expresses the EU's respect for the Member States' linguistic diversity.

3.1 The EU maintains a linguistic regime which constitutes the grounds for language rights. They are entrenched at two levels: EU multilingual law and EU institutional multilingualism. The EU multilingual law guarantees the citizen's right to be unilingual, i.e. to base their knowledge about the EU law solely on one authentic language version. The latter guarantees a range of rights associated with the external communication of the EU institutions with the Union citizens and the rights affected by the internal regimes of particular institutions.

3.2 Citizenship of the Union strengthens the protection of language rights of Member States' citizens. The rights expressly granted to the Union citizens in Articles 20–24 TFEU include linguistic aspects. As the concept of Union citizenship is the fundamental status of Member States' nationals, it may be deemed to be the source of language rights.

3.3 Finally, the European Union respects selected language rights as fundamental rights. They result from two sources: the general principles of EU law and the Charter. The former are accorded to individuals under international human rights instruments, in particular in the ECHR, the ICCPR, the CRC, and the FCNM.

4.The above conclusions and findings support the main thesis of the dissertation according to which the language rights of the Union citizen are an important element of the Union's respect for the national identities of its Member States.

4.1 The EU's respect for the national identities of its Member States is expressed by granting equal status to the official languages of all Member States. The equality of state languages demonstrates the Union's intention to protect Member States' national languages and their users and, as a consequence, to grant specific language rights only to the users of such languages. Accordingly, Union citizens are allowed to use their national languages in a variety of situations on a non-discriminatory basis and their rights in this regard may be limited only in an objectively justified and proportionate manner.

4.2 The findings presented in the dissertation have clearly exposed several unresolved problems and tensions resulting from the Union's multilingualism which

43 Judgment of the Court of 15 October 2015 in the case C-216/14 *Gavril Covaci*, ECLI:EU:C:2015:686.

44 Judgment of the Court of 12 October 2017 in the case C-278/16 *Frank Sleutjes v Staatsanwaltschaft Aachen*, ECLI:EU:C:2017:757.

should be considered in further research and may be of some value for policy-makers and scholars.

Firstly, owing to the limited powers of the EU institutions in language matters, Member States play an important role in defining citizen's language rights and their limitations, in particular in the context of the Union internal market. For instance, in the area of the consumer's rights protection, the major role of assuring language rights lies with individual Member States.

Secondly, the issue of neglecting users of EU non-official languages is perceived by some scholars as problematic and questioning the legitimacy of the principle of respect for linguistic diversity remaining the symbol of the Union.

Thirdly, the infringement of the Union citizen's administrative language rights vis-à-vis EU institutions results in no legal consequences. As the only measure used by the European Ombudsman in such a case is publishing recommendations for the relevant EU institutions in respect of language use, in fact the citizen is left with no specific recovery measures.

Next, the lack of publication of the Court of Justice's judgments in all language versions may generate serious legal problems. When a language of the case is not a popular one, mostly the English language version is authorised and relied on. If the English version is mistranslated, its application results in inequality of law (*Associação Sindical dos Juízes Portugueses, European Commission v Republic of Poland*[45]).

Finally, it should be noted that language rights are evolving and their status may be affected once the EU accedes to the ECHR. Although the Strasbourg system is already present in the EU human rights system as general principles of law, the accession will result into the consolidation of the two systems in the field of human rights protection, also in the sphere of language rights. Moreover, the universal jurisdiction of the ECtHR will make it possible for individuals to submit claims to defend their language rights vis-à-vis EU institutions or Member State authorities or private entities directly to the Strasbourg Court. This will require from the EU to be prepared for such claims. Yet, as analysis proves, the accession may not guarantee better protection of language rights of national minorities.

4.3 The dissertation contributes to the existing academic knowledge by systematising the rights vested in the Union citizen in the area of language use. I hope it will constitute the groundwork for future research into the comparative analysis of language rights, mostly in the context of highly-resourced and less-resourced languages. I note, however, that owing to the extensiveness of the case-law of the Court of Justice in the field, the dissertation has only partially analysed the practical implementation of language rights. Nevertheless, I believe this has not affected the final conclusions drawn based on the analysed jurisprudence.

45 Judgment of the Court of 27 February 2018 in the case C-64/16 *Associação Sindical dos Juízes Portugueses v Tribunal de Contas*, ECLI:EU:C:2018:117.

4.4 Looking into the future, I believe that there is a need to conduct further research into language rights which should account for the development of relevant technologies and emerging human-machine era. They are very likely to influence language rights where a growing number of people speak *through* and *to* technology, also in the public sphere.

References

A. Books and monographs

Arzoz, Xabier (ed.), *Respecting Linguistic Diversity in the European Union*, Amsterdam: John Benjamins Publishing, 2008.

Athanassiou, Phoebus, *The Application of Multilingualism in the European Context, Legal Working Paper Series*, No. 2, European Central Bank, 2006.

Aust, Anthony, *Modern Treaty Law and Practice*, Cambridge University Press, 2013.

Baaij, Cornelis J.W., *Fifty Years of Multilingual Interpretation in the European Union*, The Oxford Handbook of Language and Law, 2012.

Baaij, Cornelis J.W., *Legal Integration and Linguistic Diversity. Rethinking Translation in EU Lawmaking*, Oxford Studies in Language and Law, 2018.

Barcz, Jan (ed.), *Prawo Unii Europejskiej. Zagadnienia systemowe. Prawo materialne i polityki*, Warszawa: Wydawnictwo Prawo i Praktyka Gospodarcza, 2006.

Barcz, Jan, *Przewodnik po Traktacie z Lizbony. Traktaty stanowiące UE. Stan obecny oraz teksty skonsolidowane w brzmieniu Traktatu z Lizbony*, Warszawa: LexisNexis, 2008.

Barcz, Jan (ed.), *Fundamental Rights Protection in the European Union*, Warszawa: Wydawnictwo C.H. Beck, 2009.

Barcz, Jan (ed.), *Polityki Unii Europejskiej: polityki społeczne, Vol.* XXVII, Warszawa: Instytut Wydawniczy EuroPrawo, 2010.

Barcz, Jan (ed.), *Źródła prawa Unii Europejskiej*, Vol. 4, No. 2, Warszawa: Instytut Wydawniczy EuroPrawo, 2010.

Barcz, Jan, *Traktat z Lizbony: Wybrane Aspekty Prawne Działań Implementacyjnych.* LexisNexis, 2012.

Carson, Lorna (ed.), *Multilingualism in Europe. A Case Study*, Brussels, 2003.

Cieśliński, Aleksander, *Konstrukcja Prawna Swobód Rynku Wewnętrznego Unii Europejskiej*, Prawnicza i Ekonomiczna Biblioteka Cyfrowa, 2013.

Checkel, Jeffrey T. and Peter J. Katzenstein (eds.), *European Identity*, Cambridge: Cambridge University Press, 2009.

Cooper, Robert L., *Language Planning and Social Change*, Cambridge University Press, 1989.

Coulmas, Florian, *A Language Policy for the European Community: Prospects and Quandaries*, Vol. 61, De Gruyter Mouton, 1991.

Creech, Richard L., *Law and Language in the European Union: the Paradox of a Babel "United in Diversity"*, Groningen: Europa Law Publishing, 2005.

Czapliński, Władysław and Cezary Mik, *Traktat o Unii Europejskiej. Komentarz*, Warszawa: ABC 2005.

Dagilytė, Eglė, *The Right to Education and Free Movement of Persons: Whose Right Is It and How Does the EU Protect It?*, https://www.academia.edu /1665538/the_Right_to_Education_and_Free_Movement_of_Persons_Whose_Right_is_it_and_how_does_the_EU_Protect_it [retrieved on 1 January 2018].

Davis, William D., and Stanley Dubinsky, *Language Conflict and Language Rights: Ethnolinguistic Perspectives on Human Conflict*, Cambridge University Press, 2018.

De Swaan, Abram, *Words of the World: The Global Language System*, Wiley, 2002.

De Varennes, Fernand, *Language, Minorities and Human Rights (International Studies in Human Rights)*, Brill Nijhoff, 1996.

De Varennes Fernand, *Discrimination and the Right to Education and language in main documents and conclusions from UN mechanisms*, Reference Document – Education and Language, 20 October 2014.

Derlén, Mattias, *Multilingual Interpretation of European Union Law*, Wolters Kluwer Law & Business, 2009.

Dinstein, Yorman and Mala Tabory (eds.), *The Protection of Minorities and Human Rights*, Dordrecht: Martinus Nijhoff, 1992.

Domańska, Monika, *Zakaz dyskryminacji ze względu na więcej niż jedno zabronione kryterium*, Wolters Kluwer, 2019.

Elias, Taslim Olawale, *The Modern Law of Treaties*, Oceana Publications, 1974.

Fall, Papa Luis and Yishan Zhang, *Multilingualism in the United Nations system organizations: Status of implementation*. JIU/REP/2011/4. Geneva: United Nations, 2011.

Frankowska, Maria, *Umowy międzynarodowe. Wprowadzenie do prawa traktatów*, Warsaw, 1972.

Frankowska, Maria, *Prawo Traktatów*, Warszawa: Szkoła Główna Handlowa, 1997.

Gazzola, Michele, *Research for CULT Committee – European Strategy for multilingualism: benefits and costs. Study*, http://www.michelegazzola.com /attachments/File/Papers/EP.pdf2016 [retrieved on 28 September 2020].

Groussot, Xavier, *General Principles of Community Law*, Europa Law Publishing, 2006.

Habermas, Jürgen, *The Inclusion of the Other: Studies in Political Theory*, Cambridge: Polity Press, 2005.

Haraszti, György, *Some Fundamental Problems of the Law of Treaties*, Akademia Kiadó, 1973.

Harmsen, Robert and Thomas M. Wilson (eds.), *Europeanization: Institution, Identities and Citizenship*, Amsterdam; Atlanta, GA: Rodopi (Yearbook of European Studies, 14), 2000.

Harvard Law School, *Draft Convention on the Law* of *Treaties prepared as part of the Harvard Research in International Law*, Research in International Law under the Auspices of the Harvard Law School, 1935.

Helios, Joanna and Wioletta Jedlecka, *Wykładnia Prawa Unii Europejskiej Ze Stanowiska Teorii Prawa*, E-Wydawnictwo. Prawnicza i Ekonomiczna Biblioteka Cyfrowa. Wydział Prawa, Administracji i Ekonomii Uniwersytetu Wrocławskiego, 2018.

Hertog, Erik, *Directive 2010/64/EU of the European Parliament and of the Council on the Right to Interpretation and Translation in Criminal Proceedings: Transposition Strategies with Regard to Interpretation and Translation*, MonTI, 2015.

Iben Jensen, Ulla, *Analytical Note for 2013. The Language Requirements under EU Law on Free Movement of Workers*, https://ec.europa.eu/social/keyDocuments jsp? type=0&policyArea=25&subCategory=475&country=0&year=0&advSearchKey=FMWthematic&mode=advancedSubmit&langId=en [retrieved on 10 May 2017].

Jasiński, Filip, *Karta Praw Podstawowych Unii Europejskiej*, Dom Wydawniczy ABC, 2003.

Kadelbach, Stefan, *Union Citizenship*, New York University, School of Law, 2003.

Kalisz, Anna, *Wykładnia i stosowanie prawa wspólnotowego*, Wolters Kluwer, 2007.

Katschinka, Liese, *The Impact of Directive 2010/64/EU on the Right to Interpretation and Translation in Criminal Proceedings*, 2014, https://www.openstarts.units. it/bitstream/10077/9841/1/9_Katschinka.pdf [retrieved on 17 April 2020].

Kitzinger, Arianna, *The Theory and Practice of Multilingualism in the European Union*, Saarbrücken: VDM Verlag Dr. Müller, 2009.

Kjær, Anne Lise and Silvia Adamo (eds.), *Linguistic Diversity and European Democracy*, Ashgate Publishing, 2013.

Kontra, Miklós, Robert Phillipson, Tove Skutnabb-Kangas and Tibor Várady (eds.), *Language: A right and a resource: Approaching linguistic human rights*, Budapest: Central European University Press, 1999.

Kornobis-Romanowska, Dagmara, *Pewność prawa w Unii Europejskiej: pomiędzy autonomią jednostki a skutecznością prawa UE*, C.H. Beck, 2018.

Koskinen, Kaisa, *Beyond ambivalence: Postmodernity and the ethics of translation*, Tampere University Press, 2000.

Kraus, Peter A., *A Union of Diversity. Language, Identity and Polity-Building in Europe*, Cambridge University Press: Cambridge, 2008.

Kuzborska, Elżbieta (ed.), *Integration and Exclusion. Linguistic rights of national minorities in Europe*, Vilnus, 2015.

Kuzborska, Elżbieta, *European Practices in Multilingual Legal Education,* Cluj-Napoka, Romania, 2017.

Labrie, Normand, *La construction linguistique de la Communauté européenne,* Honoré Champion, Vol. 1, 1993.

Lankosz, Kazimierz, (ed.), *Traktat o Unii Europejskiej. Komentarze Becka,* C.H. Beck: Warszawa, 2003.

Lenaerts, Koen, Dirk Arts, and Ignace Maselis, *Procedural law of the European Union,* Sweet and Maxwell, 2006.

Leszczyński, Leszek (ed.), *System Prawa Unii Europejskiej. Tom 3. Wykładnia prawa,* C.H. Beck, 2019.

Lubaś, Władysław, *Polityka językowa,* Opole: University of Opole, 2009.

Łuczak, Jacek, *Polityka językowa Unii Europejskiej,* Warszawa: Oficyna Wydawnicza ASPRA-JR, 2010.

MacCormick, Neil and Robert S. Summers, *Interpreting Statutes,* 1991.

Maliszewska-Nienartowicz, Justyna (ed.), *Prawo antydyskryminacyjne. System Prawa Unii Europejskiej. Tom 6,* C.H. Beck, 2020.

Marácz, László and Mireille Rosello (eds.), *Multilingual Europe, Multilingual Europeans,* Brill, 2012.

Martyniuk, Waldemar and José Noijons, *Executive summary of results of a survey on the use of the CEFR at national level in the Council of Europe Member States,* 2007, https://rm.coe.int/168069b7ad [retrieved on 10 January 2020].

May, Stephen, *Language and Minority Rights: Ethnicity, Nationalism and the Politics of Language,* Routledge, 2013.

Mensah, Barbara, *European Human Rights Case Summaries,* Routledge-Cavendish, 2002.

Mollin, Sandra, *Euro-English: Assessing Variety Status,* Vol. 33, Gunter Narr Verlag, 2006.

Montanari, Simona and Suzanne Quay (eds.), *Multidisciplinary Perspectives on Multilingualism,* De Gruyter Mouton, 2019.

Nahlik, Stanisław Edward, *Kodeks Prawa Traktatów,* Państwowe Wydawnictwo Naukowe, 1976.

Nettle, Daniel, *Linguistic Diversity,* Oxford University Press, 1999.

Nikadem-Malinowska, Ewa, *Język–prawo–społeczeństwo,* Opole: University of Opole, 2004

Nowak-Far, Artur, *Prawo Unii Europejskiej. Języki, struktury, działanie w praktyce,* C.H. Beck, 2020.

Paluszek, Karolina, *Komparatystyka językowa jako narzędzie interpretacyjne Trybunału Sprawiedliwości Unii Europejskiej,* Difin, 2019.

Pariente, Audrey (ed.), *Translation at the European Commission – a history*, Office for Official Publications of the European Communities, 2010, 57.

Paunio, Elina, *Legal Certainty in Multilingual EU Law: Language, Discourse and Reasoning at the European Court of Justice*, Routledge, 2013.

Peers, Steve [et al.] (eds.), *The EU Charter of Fundamental Rights: A Commentary*, Hart Publishing, 2014.

Phillipson, Robert, *English-Only Europe?: Challenging Language Policy*, London and New York: Routledge, 2003.

Phillipson, Robert, *Linguistic Imperialism Continued*, London and New York: Routledge, 2003.

Pisarek, Walery, *Wstęp do nauki o komunikowaniu*, Wydawnictwa Akademickie i Profesjonalne, 2008.

Pool, Jonathan, *Optimal Language Regimes for the European Union*, Berlin/New York: Walter de Gruyter, 1996.

Pozzo, Barbara and Valentina Jacometti (eds.), *Multilingualism and the Harmonisation of European Law*, Kluwer Law International, 2006.

Prutsch, Markus, *Research for CULT Committee: European Identity*. Study of the European Parliament's Committee on Culture and Education, 2017.

Pudzianowska, Dorota, *Obywatelstwo w Procesie Zmian*, Wolters Kluwer, 2013.

Raitio, Juha, *The Principle of Legal Certainty in EC Law*, Kluwer Academic Publishers, 2003.

Reuter, Paul, *Introduction to the Law of Treaties*, Pinter Publishers, 1989.

Ricento, Thomas (ed.), *An Introduction to Language Policy. Theory and Method*, Blackwell Publishing, 2006.

Robertson, Colin D., *Multilingual Law: A Framework for Analysis and Understanding*, Routledge, 2016.

Root, Amanda, *Market Citizenship: Experiments in Democracy and Globalization*, Sage, 2007.

Rosenne, Shabtai, *Developments in the Law of Treaties*, 1945–1986, Cambridge: Cambridge University Press, 1989.

Šarčević, Susan, *New Approach to Legal Translation*, Kluwer Law International, 1997.

Šarčević, Susan (ed.), *Language and Culture in EU Law: Multidisciplinary Perspectives*. Routledge, 2017.

Seubert, Sandra, Oliver Eberl and Frans van Waarden, *Reconsidering EU Citizenship: Contradictions and Constraints*, Edward Elgar Publishing, 2018.

Sinclair, Ian McTaggart and Ian Robertson Sinclair, *The Vienna Convention on the Law of Treaties*, Manchester University Press, 1984.

Skomerska-Muchowska, Izabela and Anna Wyrozumska, *Obywatel Unii, Vol.* 6, No. 1, Instytut Wydawniczy EuroPrawo, 2010.

Skutnabb-Kangas, Tove and Robert Phillipson (eds.), *Linguistic Human Rights. Overcoming Linguistic Discrimination*, Berlin/New York: Mouton De Gruyter, 1995.

Szczerbiak, Aleks and Paul Taggart (eds.), *Opposing Europe? The Comparative Party Politics of Euroscepticism*, Oxford; New York, NY: Oxford University Press, 2008.

Szpotowicz, Magdalena, *Polityka Językowa w Europie: Raport Analityczny*, Instytut Badań Edukacyjnych, 2013.

Tabory, Mala, *Multilingualism in International Law and Institutions*, Brill Archive, 1980.

Thornberry, Patrick, *International Law and the Rights of Minorities*, Oxford University Press, 1992.

Tridimas, Takis, *The General Principles of EU Law*, Oxford European Union Law Library, 2007.

Tryfonidou, Alina, *Reconceptualising the EU's Market Freedoms as Union Citizenship Rights. Towards a Citizenship Right to Pursue an Economic Activity in a Cross-Border Context?*, 2011, https://eustudies.org/assets/files/papers/Tryfonidou% 20-%20EUSA% 20Paper%202011.pdf [retrieved on 21 July 2020].

Tryfonidou, Alina, *Impact of Union Citizenship on the EU's Market Freedoms.* Hart Publishing, 2018.

Van Dongera, Rixt, Cor Van Der Meer and Richt Sterk, *Research for CULT Committee – Minority Languages and education: best practices and pitfalls. Study*, https://www.europarl.europa.eu/RegData/etudes/STUD/2017/585915/IPOL_STU(2017) 585915_EN.pdf [retrieved on 19 October 2020].

Urrutia, Iñigo and Iñaki Lasagabaster, *Language Rights and Community Law*, European Integration Online Papers, Vol. 14, 2008.

Van der Jeught, Stefaan, *EU Language Law*, Groninger: Europa Law Publishing, 2015.

Williams, Glyn and Gruffudd Williams, *Language, Hegemony and the European Union: Re-Examining 'Unity in Diversity'*, Springer, 2016.

Wright, Sue, *Community and Communication: the Role of Language in Nation State Building and European Integration*, Clevedon: Multilingual Matters Ltd, 2000.

Wright, Sue, *Language Policy and Language Planning. From Nationalism to Globalisation*, Palgrave Macmillan, 2016.

Wróbel, Andrzej (ed.), *Stosowanie prawa Unii Europejskiej przez sądy*, Vol. 1, No. 2, Warszawa, 2010.

Wróbel, Andrzej (ed.), *Karta Praw Podstawowych Unii Europejskiej. Komentarz*, No. 1, Warszawa: C.H. Beck, 2013.

Wróbel, Andrzej (ed.), *Karta Praw Podstawowych Unii Europejskiej. Komentarz*, No. 2, Warszawa: C.H. Beck, 2019.

Wróbel, Andrzej, Dawid Miąsik and Nina Półtorak (eds.), *Traktat o funkcjonowaniu Unii Europejskiej. Komentarz*, Vol. 1, Warszawa, 2012.

Wróbel, Andrzej, Krystyna Kowalik-Bańczyk and Monika Szwarc-Kuczer (eds.), *Traktat o funkcjonowaniu Unii Europejskiej*, Vol. 2, Warszawa, 2012.

Wróbel, Andrzej, Justyna Łacny and Dagmara Kornobis-Romanowska (eds.), *Traktat ustanawiający Wspólnotę Europejską. Komentarz*, Vol. 3, Warszawa, 2009.

Wronkowska, Sławomira (ed.) *Polska kultura prawna a proces integracji europejskiej*, Zakamycze Kantor Wydawniczy, 2005.

Wyrozumska, Anna, *Umowy międzynarodowe: teoria i praktyka*, Wydawnictwo Prawo i Praktyka Gospodarcza, 2006.

Zawidzka-Łojek, Anna and Aleksandra Szczerba-Zawada (eds.), *Prawo antydyskryminacyjne Unii Europejskiej*, EuroPrawo, Warszawa 2015.

Zawidzka-Łojek, Anna and Adam Łazowski (eds.), *Podręcznik Prawa Unii Europejskiej. Instytucje i porządek prawny. Prawo materialne*, Instytut Wydawniczy EuroPrawo, 2017.

Żuk, Mateusz, *Relacja między obywatelem Unii Europejskiej a swobodami rynku wewnętrznego*, Warszawa: Wydawnictwo C.H. Beck, 2013.

B. Research papers and chapters in collective works

Albi, Anneli, "Europe Articles in the Constitutions of Central and Eastern European Countries", *Common Market Law Review*, Vol. 42, No. 2, 2005, 399–423.

Ammon, Ulrich, "Language conflicts in the European Union", *International Journal of Applied Linguistics*, Vol. 16, No. 3, 2006.

Arzoz, Xabier, "The protection of linguistic diversity through Article 22 of the Charter of Fundamental Rights", in: Xabier Arzoz (ed.), *Respecting Linguistic Diversity in the European Union*, Amsterdam, 2008, 145–74.

Arzoz, Xabier, "The Nature of Language Rights", *JEMIE* 6, 2007.

Baaij, Cornelis J.W., "The EU policy on institutional multilingualism: between principles and practicality", *International Journal of Language and Law*, Vol. 1, 2012.

Bandov, Goran, "Language Policy of the European Union–Realization of the Multilingual Policy of the EU", *Međunarodne studije*, Vol., 65–84.

Barcz, Jan, "Umowy międzynarodowe Unii Europejskiej z państwami trzecimi lub organizacjami międzynarodowymi", in: Jan Barcz, (ed.), *Źródła prawa Unii Europejskiej*, Vol. 4, No. 2, Warszawa: Instytut Wydawniczy EuroPrawo 2010.

Barcz, Jan, "Polityki społeczne w systematyce Traktatów stanowiących Unię Europejską," in: Jan Barcz (ed.), *Polityki Unii Europejskiej: polityki społeczne.* Vol. XXVII, Warszawa: Instytut Wydawniczy EuroPrawo, 2010.

Bochmann, Klaus, Gy Szépe and A. Derényi, "A nyelvpolitika elmélete, módszerei és elemzése", in: Szépe György and Derényi András (eds.), *Nyelv, hatalom, egyenl Hoség. Budapest: Corvina*, 1999.

Bodnar, Adam, "Obywatelstwo UE a Ochrona Praw Podstawowych", *Obywatelstwo Unii Europejskiej. Zeszyty OIDE*, Wydawnictwo Sejmowe, 2008, 50–99.

Bodnar, Adam, "The Charter of Fundamental Rights: Differentiated Legal Character of Charter's Provisions, Their Consequences for Individuals, Courts and Legislator", in: Jan Barcz (ed.) *Fundamental Rights Protection in the European Union*, Warszawa: C.H. Beck, 2009.

Brannan, James, "Identifying written translation in criminal proceedings as a separate rights: scope and supervision under European law," *The Journal of Specialised Translation,* https://jostrans.org/issue27/art_brannan.php [retrieved on 20 October 2020].

Budzyńska, Izabela and Bartosz Pawłowski, "Polityka Jawności i Przejrzystości Unii Europejskiej Ze Szczególnym Uwzględnieniem Dostępu Do Dokumentów Publicznych", *Informacja BSE*, No. 731, Warszawa: KS Biuro Studiów i Ekspertyz, 2000.

Carl, Noah, James Dennison and Geoffrey Evans, "European but Not European Enough: An Explanation for Brexit", *European Union Politics*, Vol. 20, No. 2, 2019, 282–304.

Castiglione, Dario, "Political identity in a community of strangers", in: Jeffrey T. Checkel and Peter J. Katzenstein (eds.), *European Identity*, Cambridge: Cambridge University Press, 2009, 29–51.

Crook, John R., "The International Court of Justice and Human Rights", *Northwestern University Journal of International Human Rights,* Vol. 1, 2003.

Christiansen, Pia Vanting, "Language Policy in the European Union: European/English/Elite/Equal/Esperanto Union?", *Language Problems and Language Planning*, Vol. 30, No. 1, 2006, 21–44.

Cohen, Mathilde, "On the linguistic design of multinational courts", *International Journal of Constitutional Law*, Vol. 14, 2016, 498–51.

Crystal, David, "The Future of New Euro-Englishes", *World Englishes*, Vol. 36, No. 3, 2017, 330–35.

Currall, Julian, "Official languages inside and outside the institutions: An analysis of recent cases", *Georgia Journal of International & Comparative Law, Vol.* 39, 2010.

Derlén, Mattias, "In defence of (limited) multilingualism", in: Kjær Anne Lise and Silvia Adamo (eds.), *Linguistic Diversity and European Democracy*, Ashgate Publishing, 2011.

Darquennes, Jeroen and Peter Nelde, "German as a Lingua Franca", *Annual Review of Applied Linguistics*, Vol. 26, 2006, 61–77.

De Bazelaire De Ruppierre, Marta and Katarzyna Frączak, "Ochrona Konsularna Niereprezentowanych Obywateli Unii Europejskiej w Państwach Trzecich (Art. 23 TFUE)", *Przegląd Legislacyjny*, 2016, 25–48.

De Varennes, Fernand, "The Existing Rights of Minorities in International Law", in: Mikl¢s Kontra [et al.] (eds.), *Language: A Right and a Resource*, Central European University Press, 1999, 117–46.

De Varennes, Fernand, "Language Rights as an Integral Part of Human Rights", *International Journal on Multicultural Societies*, Vol. 3, No. 1, 2001, 15–25.

De Varennes, Fernand and Elżbieta Kuzborska, "Human Rights and a Person's Name: Legal Trends and Challenges," *Human Rights Quarterly*, Vol. 37, No. 4, 2015, 977–1023.

De Varennes, Fernand and Elżbieta Kuzborska, "International Law and Language Minority Education", *Language Policy and Political Issues in Education*, 2016, 1–12.

De Varennes, Fernand and Elżbieta Kuzborska, "Continued Relevance of an 'Oslo' Language Policy in a Changing World", in: Iryna Ulasiuk, Laurenţiu Hadîrcă, and William Romans (eds.), *Language Policy and Conflict Prevention,* 2018, Brill Nijhoff, 123–134.

De Witte, Bruno, "Language Law of the European Union: Protecting or Eroding Linguistic Diversity?" in: Richard Craufurd Smith (ed.) *Culture and European Union Law*, Oxford University Press, 2004.

De Witte, Bruno, "The protection of linguistic diversity through provisions of the EU Charter other than Article 22", in: Xavier Arzoz (ed.) *Respecting Linguistic Diversity in the European Union*, Amsterdam, 2008, 145–73.

De Witte, Bruno, "The Relative Autonomy of the European Union's Fundamental Rights Regime", *Nordic Journal of International Law*, Vol. 88, No. 1, 2019, 65–85.

Doczekalska, Agnieszka, "Interpretacja wielojęzycznego prawa Unii Europejskiej", *Europejski Przegląd Sądowy*, 5/2006, 14–21.

Doczekalska, Agnieszka, "Drafting and interpretation of EU law – paradoxes of legal multilingualism", in: Gunther Grewendorf and Monika Rathert, *Formal Linguistics and Law*, Berlin: Mouton De Gruyter, 2009, 339–70.

Doczekalska, Agnieszka, "Drafting or Translation – Production of Multilingual Legal Text", in: Frances Olsen, Alexander Lorz and Dieter Stein (eds.), *Translation Issues in Language and Law*, London, New York, Palgrave Macmillan Ltd, 2009, 116–35.

Doczekalska, Agnieszka, "Legal Multilingualism as a Right to Remain Unilingual – Fiction or Reality?", *Comparative Legilinguistics*, Vol. 20, 2014, 7–18.

Doczekalska, Agnieszka, "Zasada Pewności Prawa w Wykładni Wielojęzycznego Prawa Unii Europejskiej", *Europejski Przegląd Sądowy*, 5/2019, 12–18.

Dobbs, Mary, "The Shifting Battleground of Article 4(2) TEU: Evolving National Identities and the Corresponding Need for EU Management?", *European Journal of Current Legal Issues*, Vol. 21, No. 2, 2015.

Dunbar, Robert, "Minority Language Rights in International Law", *International & Comparative Law Quarterly*, Vol. 50, No. 1, 2001, 90–120.

Eckes, Christina, "EU Accession to the ECHR: Between Autonomy and Adaptation", *The Modern Law Review, Vol.* 76, No. 2, 2013.

Felici, Annarita, "Translating EU Law: Legal Issues and Multiple Dynamics", *Perspectives: Studies in Translatology, Vol.* 18, No. 2, 2010, 95–108.

Forrest, Alan, "The Politics of Language in the European Union", *European Review*, Vol. 6, No. 3, 1998, 299–319.

Foucher, Pierre, "Le Droit et La Langue Française Au Canada: Évolution et Perspectives", *Francophonies d'Amérique*, No. 26, 2008.

Frankowska, Maria, "The Vienna Convention on the Law of Treaties Before United States Courts", *Virgina Journal of International Law*, Vol. 28, 1987.

Frost, Amanda, "Restoring Faith in Government: Transparency Reform in the United States and the European Union", *European Public Law*, Vol. 9, No. 1, 2003, 87–104.

Fryźlewicz, Marcin, "Znaczenie komparatystyki językowej w wykładni sądów luksemburskich", in: Cezary Mik (ed.), *Wykładnia prawa Unii Europejskiej*, 2008, TNOiK.

Gajda, Anastazja, "Wielojęzyczność Unii Europejskiej", *Socjolingwistyka*, No. 27, 2013, 7–29.

Gajda, Anastazja, "Przystąpienie Unii Europejskiej do Europejskiej Konwencji o ochronie praw człowieka i podstawowych wolności", *Kwartalnik Kolegium Ekonomiczno-Społecznego „Studia i Prace"*, No. 1/2013, Warszawa, 11–35.

Gajda, Stanisław, "Program polskiej polityki językowej (rozważania wstępne)", in: Jan Mazur (ed.) *Polska polityka językowa na przełomie tysiącleci*, Wydawnictwo Uniwersytetu Marii Curie-Skłodowskiej, 1999,

Garlicki, Leszek, "Przystąpienie UE do Europejskiej Konwencji Praw Człowieka – przygotowania i problemy", *Europejski Przegląd Sądowy*, No. 1, 2011.

Gazzola, Michele, "Managing Multilingualism in the European Union: Language Policy Evaluation for the European Parliament", *Language Policy*, Vol. 5, No. 4, 2006.

Gazzola, Michele, "Multilingual Communication for Whom? Language Policy and Fairness in the European Union", *European Union Politics*, Vol. 17, No. 4, 2016, 546–69.

Goldner Lang, Iris, "Languages as a Barrier to Free Movement of Persons in the European Union", *Curriculum, Multilingualism and the Law*, Nakladni zavod Globus, 2009.

Grin, François, "The Economics of English in Europe," in: Thomas Ricento (ed.) *Language Policy and Political Economy: English in a Global Context,* Oxford Scholarship Online, 2015.

Green, Leslie, "Freedom of Expression and Choice of Language", *Law & Policy,* Vol. 13, No. 3, 1991, 215–29.

Grucza, Franciszek, "Język (narodowy) – tożsamość (narodowa) – integracja (europejska)", in: Elżbieta Jeleń [et al.] (ed.), *Zmiany i Rozwój Języka Oraz Tożsamości Narodowej–Trendy w Procesie Integracji Europejskiej,* Kraków, 2002, 25–49.

Grzeszczak, Robert, "Dwie Narracje o Obywatelstwie Unijnym – Obywatel Rynku i Obywatel Unii Europejskiej", in: Andrzej Bator (et al.), *Współczesne Koncepcje Ochrony Wolności i Praw Podstawowych,* Prawnicza i Ekonomiczna Biblioteka Cyfrowa, 2013.

Gubrynowicz, Aleksander, "Obywatelstwo Unii Europejskiej – Stan Obecny i Perspektywy", *Obywatelstwo Unii Europejskiej. Zeszyty OIDE,* Wydawnictwo Sejmowe, 2008, 5–48.

Henrard, Kristin, "An EU Perspective on New versus Traditional Minorities: On Semi-Inclusive Socio-Economic Integration and Expanding Visions of European Culture and Identity", *Columbia Journal of European Law,* Vol. 17, 2010.

Hilpold, Peter, "Union Citizenship and Language Rights", in: Xabier Arzoz (ed.) *Respecting Linguistic Diversity in the European Union,* Amsterdam: John Benjamins Publishing, 2008, 107–122.

Jedlecka, Wioletta, "Reguły językowe wykładni prawa UE", in: Leszek Leszczyński (ed.), *System Prawa Unii Europejskiej. Tom 3. Wykładnia prawa,* C.H.Beck, 2019, 137–52.

Juaristi, Patxi, Timothy Reagan and Humphrey Tonkin, "Linguistic diversity in the European Union: An Overview", in: Xabier Arzoz (ed.), *Respecting Linguistic Diversity in the European Union,* Amsterdam: John Benjamins Publishing, 2008.

Kaplan, Robert B. and Richard B. Baldauf, "Language Planning from Practice to Theory", *Multilingual Matters,* Vol. 108, 1997.

Kaya, Cemil, "The Role of the European Court of Justice in the Process of European Integration," *Annales de la Faculté de Droit d'Istanbul,* 2010, 215–29.

Kemp, Charlotte, "Defining Multilingualism", *The Exploration of Multilingualism,* Amsterdam: John Benjamins Publishing, 2009, 11–26.

Kędzia, Zdzisław, "Relationship between the European Convention on Human Rights and the Chapter of Fundamental Rights after the European Union's Accession to the Convention", in: Jan Barcz (ed.) *Fundamental Rights Protection in the European Union,* Warszawa: Wydawnictwo C.H. Beck, 2009, 224–46.

Kjaer, Anne Lise, "Recontextualization of concepts in European legal discourse", in: Edda Weigand (ed.), *Dialogue and Rhetoric,* 2008.

Kjær, Anne Lise and Silvia Adamo, "Linguistic Diversity and European Democracy: Introduction and Overview", in: Kjær Anne Lise and Silvia Adamo (eds.), *Linguistic Diversity and European Democracy,* Ashgate Publishing, 2011.

Kloss, Heinz, "Language Rights of Immigrant Groups", *International Migration Review,* Vol. 5, No. 2, 1971.

Komorowska, Hanna, "Polska polityka językowa na tle innych krajów Unii Europejskiej", in: Hanna Komorowska (ed.) *Nauczanie Języków Obcych – Polska a Europa,* Warszawa: Academica, 2007, 13–55.

Kowalczyk-Bańczyk, Krystyna, "Komentarz do artykułu 24 TFUE", in: Andrzej Wróbel, Dawid Miąsik and Nina Półtorak (eds.), *Traktat o funkcjonowaniu Unii Europejskiej, Komentarz,* Vol. 1, Warszawa, 2012.

Kraus, Peter A., "A one-dimensional diversity? European integration and the challenge of language policy", in: Xabier Arzoz, (ed.) *Respecting Linguistic Diversity in the European Union,* Amsterdam: John Benjamins Publishing, 2008.

Kraus, Peter A., "Neither United nor Diverse? The Language Issue and Political Legitimation in the European Union", in: Anne Lise Kjær and Silvia Adamo (eds.), *Linguistic Diversity and European Democracy,* Ashgate Publishing, 2013, 17–34.

Kugelmann, Dieter, "Minderheitenschutz Als Menschenrechtsschutz", *Archiv Des Völkerrechts,* Vol. 39, No. 3, 2001.

Kuzborska, Elżbieta, "Prawa językowe mniejszości narodowych na Litwie," *Państwo i Prawo,* 7/2012.

Kuzborska, Elżbieta and Łukasz Wardyn, "Ochrona mniejszości polskiej na Litwie oraz mniejszości litewskiej w Polsce w świetle realizacji konwencji ramowej o ochronie mniejszości narodowych oraz innych zobowiązań międzynarodowych", *Przegląd Sejmowy,* 6/2014, 2018–233.

Kuzborska, Elżbieta, "The Protection of Language Rights of Minorities in Lithuania", in: Elżbieta Kuzborska (ed.), *Integration and Exclusion. Linguistic rights of national minorities in Europe,* Vilnius 2015, 133–46.

Láncos, Petra Lea, "Linguistic Diversity Meets the Free Movement of Workers: The Las Case", *Hungarian Yearbook of International Law & European Law,* 2015.

Lang, Iris Goldner, "Languages as a Barrier to Free Movement of Persons in the European Union", *Curriculum, Multilingualism and the Law,* Nakladni zavod Globus, 2009.

Legrand, Pierre, "The Impossibility of 'Legal Transplants'", *Maastricht Journal of European and Comparative Law,* Vol. 4, 1997.

Lenaerts, Gilberte, "A failure to comply with the EU language policy: A study of the Council archives", *Multilingua,* Vol. 20, No. 3, 2001.

Liżewski, Bartosz, "Wykładnia Poszczególnych Rodzajów i Gałęzi Prawa UE", in: Leszek Leszczyński (ed.), *System Prawa Unii Europejskiej. Tom 3. Wykładnia prawa.* C.H. Beck, 2019.

Łazowski, Adam, "Obywatelstwo Unii Europejskiej – Uwagi Teoretyczne i Praktyczne w Dziesięć Lat Po Wejściu w Życie Traktatu z Maastricht", in: Eugeniusz Piontek and Anna Zawidzka (eds.), *Szkice z Prawa Unii Europejskiej*, Kraków, 2003.

Łętowska, Ewa, "Multicentryczność Współczesnego Systemu Prawa i Jej Konsekwencje", *Państwo i Prawo*, Vol. 4, 2005.

Luttermann, Claus and Karin Lutterman, "Ein Sprachenrecht für die Europäische Union", *Juristenzeitung*, Vol. 20, 1002–10.

Mälksoo, Lauri, "Language Rights in International Law: Why the Phoenix is Still in the Ashes", *Florida Journal of International Law*, Vol. 12, 1998.

Mancini, Susanna and Bruno De Witte, "Language Rights as Cultural Rights: A European Perspective", *International Studies in Human Rights*, Vol. 95, 2008.

Marcinkowska, Izabela, "Poszanowanie różnorodności językowej w Unii Europejskiej", *Europejski Przegląd Sądowy*, 1/2020.

Marshall, Thomas H., "Citizenship and Social Class", in: Jeff Manza and Michael Sauder (eds.), *Inequality and Society*, New York, 2009.

Maslowski, Solange, "The Expulsion of European Union Citizens from the Host Member State: Legal Grounds and Practice", *Central and Eastern European Migration Review*, Vol. 4, No. 2, 2015, 61–85.

May, Stephen, "Language Rights: The "Cinderella" Human Right", *Journal of Human Rights*, Vol. 10, No. 3, 2011, 265–89.

May, Stephen "Language, Imperialism, and the Modern Nation-State System", in: Nelson Flores, Ofelia Garcia and Massimiliano Spotti (eds.), *The Oxford Handbook of Language and Society*, Oxford Handbooks Online, 2016.

McCluskey, Brian, "Respecting multilingualism in the enlargement of the European Union – the organisational challenge," *Termonologie et traduction*, 2/2001.

Michałowska-Gorywoda, Krystyna, "Służby lingwistyczne Unii Europejskiej", *Studia Europejskie*, No. 3, 2001.

Mickonytė, Aistė, "The Right to a Name Versus National Identity in the Context of EU Law: The Case of Lithuania", *Review of Central and East European Law*, Vol. 42, No. 4, 2017, 325–63.

Mik, Cezary, "The Charter of Fundamental Rights: Determinants of Protective Standards", in: Jan Barcz (ed.) *Fundamental Rights Protection in the European Union*, C.H. Beck, 2009.

Modiano, Marko, "English in a Post-Brexit European Union", *World Englishes*, Vol. 36, No. 3, 2017, 313–27.

Nowak-Far, Artur, "Jednolitość prawa unijnego a jego wielojęzyczność", in: Cezary Mik (ed.), *Konferencja. Unia Europejska: zjednoczenie w różnorodności, Warszawa, 14–15 grudnia 2010*, 2012, 74–92.

Nowak-Far, Artur, "Co wielojęzyczność tekstów prawnych Unii Europejskiej mówi o naturze prawa?" in: Maciej Kłodawski, Alicja Witorska and Mariusz Lachowski (eds.), *Legislacja czasu przemian, przemiany w legislacji. Księga jubileuszowa na XX-lecie Polskiego Towarzystwa Legislacji,* Wydawnictwo Sejmowe, 2016, 283–307.

Ogonowska, Anna, "Dostęp Do Dokumentów Unii Europejskiej", *Źródła Informacji o Unii Europejskiej. Zarys Problematyki.* Wydawnictwo Sejmowe, Warszawa, 2006.

Ogonowska, Anna, "Dostęp Do Dokumentów Rady Unii Europejskiej", *Unia Europejska Istota Szanse Wyzwania,* CeDeWu, 2018, 85–106.

Paluszek, Karolina, "The equal authenticity of official language versions of European legislation in light of their consideration by the Court of Justice of the European Union", *Comparative Legilinguistics,* 18/2014.

Paluszek, Karolina, "Institutional Multilingualism in the European Union – Policy, Rules and Practice", *Comparative Legilinguistics, Vol.* 24, 2015, 119–42.

Patten, Alan and Will Kymlicka, "Introduction: Language Rights and Political Theory: Context, Issues, and Approaches", in: Allan Patten and Will Kymlicka (eds.), *Language Rights and Political Theory,* Oxford University Press, 2003.

Paunio, Elina and Susan Lindroos-Hovinheimo, "Taking Language Seriously: An Analysis of Linguistic Reasoning and Its Implications in EU Law", *European Law Journal,* Vol. 16, No. 4, 2010.

Pawłowski, Adam, "Problemy polityki językowej w Unii Europejskiej", *Sociolingwistyka,* Vol. 20, 7–17.

Pawłowski, Adam, "Zadania polskiej polityki językowej w Unii Europejskiej", in: Jacek Warchala and Danuta Krzyżyk (eds.), *Polska Polityka Językowa w Unii Europejskiej,* 2008, 113–47.

Paz, Moria, "The Failed Promise of Language Rights: A Critique of the International Language Rights Regime", *Harvard International law Journal,* Vol. 54, No.1, 2013.

Paz, Moria, "The Tower of Babel: Human Rights and the Paradox of Language", *European Journal of International Law,* 25/2, 2014.

Phillipson, Robert, "The EU and Languages: Diversity in What Unity?", in: Anne Lise Kjær and Silvia Adamo (eds.), *Linguistic Diversity and European Democracy,* Ashgate Publishing, 2013, 57–74.

Płachta, Agnieszka, "Zasada Ochrony Praw Podstawowych", in: Andrzej Wróbel (ed.), *Stosowanie Prawa Unii Europejskiej Przez Sądy,* Kraków, 2005.

Pospíšil, Ivo, "The Protection of National Minorities and the Concept of Minority in the EU Law", *Referat Prezentiran Na,* Vol. 3, 2006.

Pozzo, Barbara, "Multilingualism as a 'value' in the European Union", *The Multilanguage Complexity of European Law: Methodologies in Comparison,* European Press Academic Publishing, 2007, 133–44.

Ricento, Thomas, "Historical and theoretical perspective in language policy and planning", *Journal of Sociolinguistics*, Vol. 5, 2000, 196–213.

Ristikivi, Merike, "Latin: The Common Legal Language of Europe", *Juridica International Journal*, Vol. 10, 2005.

Salverda, Reinier, "Language diversity and international communication", English Today, 18/(03), 2002, 3–11.

Šarčević, Susan, "Multilingual Lawmaking and Legal (Un)Certainty in the European Union", *International Journal of Law, Language & Discourse*, Vol. 3, No. 1, 2013, 1–29.

Sayers, Dave and Petra Lea Láncos, "(Re) defining linguistic diversity: What is being protected in European language policy?", *SKY Journal of Linguistics*, Vol. 30, 2017, 35–73.

Schilling, Theodor, "Language Rights in the European Union", *German Law Journal*, Vol. 9, 2008.

Schilling, Theodor, "Beyond Multilingualism: On Different Approaches to the Handling of Diverging Language Versions of a Community Law", *European Law Journal*, Vol. 16, No. 1, 2010.

Schilling, Theodor, "Multilingualism and Multijuralism: Assets of EU Legislation and Adjudication", *German Law Journal*, Vol. 12, No. 7, 2011.

Schmidt, Susanne K. and Michael Blauberger, "Free movement and equal treatment in an unequal Union", *Journal of European Public Policy*, Vol. 25, 2018, 1391–402.

Schnettger, Anita, "Article 4(2) TEU as a Vehicle for National Constitutional Identity in a Shared European Legal System", in: Christian Calliess and Gerhard van der Schyff (eds.), *Constitutional Identity in a Europe of Multilevel Constitutionalism*, Cambridge University Press, 2019, 9–38.

Seymour, Edward, "A common EU legal language?" *Perspectives: studies in translatology*, Vol. 10,1/2020.

Skorupa-Wulczyńska, Aneta, "Polityka Językowa w Unii Europejskiej i Organizacji Narodów Zjednoczonych", *Sprawy Międzynarodowe*, No. 1, 2014, 119–35.

Skorupa-Wulczyńska, Aneta, "Erasmus+ as the EU answer to the educational challenges faced by Europe", in: Istvan Tarrósy and Susan Milford (eds.), *Recent Political Changes and their Implications in the Danube Region*, Pecs, Hungary, 2016, 43–60.

Skutnabb-Kangas, Tove and Robert Phillipson, "Wanted! Linguistic Human Rights", *ROLIG-papir*, No. 44, 1989.

Skutnabb-Kangas, Tove and Robert Philipson, "Linguistic Human Rights, Past and Present", in: Tove Skutnabb-Kangas and Robert Philipson (eds.), *Language Rights*, Routledge, 2017.

Solan, Lawrance M., "Interpretation of Multilingual Statues by the European Court of Justice", *Brooklyn Journal of International Law*, Vol. 42(2), 2009.

Stępkowska, Urszula, "Edukacja, kształcenie zawodowe, młodzież i sport", in: Jan Barcz (ed.), *Polityki Unii Europejskiej: Polityki Społeczne Aspekty Prawne*, Vol. XXVII, 2010, 58–63.

Suwara, Ewa, "Wyzwania Prawno-Proceduralne Dla Unii Europejskiej Związane z BREXIT-Em", *Europejski Przegląd Sądowy*, 9/2016, 11–17.

Szczerba-Zawada, Aleksandra, "Ochrona praw człowieka w Unii Europejskiej", in: Ewa Latoszek [et al.] (eds.), *Unia Europejska. Istota, Szanse, Wyzwania*, CeDeWu, 2018.

Szul, Roman, "The Linguistic Situation in Europe: Between Regionalism and European Integration", *The Polish Foreign Affairs Digest*, No. 1 (10) 2004, 127–67.

Szul, Roman, "Tożsamość europejska a kwestia językowa w Unii Europejskie", *Studia Regionalne i Lokalne*, **No.** 4, 2007, 66–75.

Szuniewicz, Marta, "Interpretacja prawa wspólnotowego - metody i moc wiążąca wykładni ETS", *Studia Prawnicze*, No. 1, 2006.

Tabory, Mala, "Language Rights as Human Rights", *Israel Yearbook on Human Rights*, Vol. 10, 1980.

Toggenburg, Gabriel N., "Who is Managing Ethnic and Cultural Diversity in the European Condominium? The Moments of Entry, Integration and Preservation", *Journal of Common Market Studies, Vol.* 43 (4), 2005.

Christian Tomuschat, "Protection of Minorities under Article 27 CCPR", in: Rudolf Bernhardt [et al.] (eds.), *Völkerrecht als Rechtsordnung, Internationale Gerichtsbarkeit, Menschenrechte*, Spinger, 1983.

Toscano Méndez, Manuel, "Language Rights as Collective Rights: Some Conceptual Considerations on Language Rights", *Res Publica: Revista de Filosofía Política*, Vol. 27, 2012, 109–118.

Urrutia, Iñigo and Iñaki Lasagabaster, "Language Rights as a General Principle of Community Law", *German Law Journal*, Vol. 8, No. 5, 2007, 479–500.

Urrutia, Iñigo and Iñaki Lasagabaster, "Language Rights and Community Law," *European Integration online Papers*, Vol. 14, 2008.

Van der Vlis, Evert-Jan, "The right to interpretation and translation in criminal proceedings", *The Journal of Specialised Translation*, No. 14, 2010.

Van Eijken, Hanneke, "Case Note on C-391/09, Malgožata Runevič-Vardyn and Łukasz Paweł Wardyn v Vilniaus Miesto Savivaldybės Administracija and Others", *Common Market Law Review*, 2012, 809–26.

Van Parijs, Philippe, "Linguistic diversity as curse and as by-product", in: Xabier Arzoz (ed.), *Respecting Linguistic Diversity in the European Union*, Amsterdam: John Benjamins Publishing, 2008.

Vogiatzis, Nikos, "The Linguistic Policy of the EU Institutions and Political Participation Post-Lisbon", *European Law Review*, No. 2, 2016.

Von Bogdandy, Armind and Stephan Schill, "Overcoming Absolute Primacy: Respect for National Identity under the Lisbon Treaty", *Common Market Law Review*, Vol. 48, 2011.

Wardyn, Łukasz, "The Observance of national minorities from the perspective of the European Union: selected aspects", in: Elżbieta Kuzborska (ed.), *Integration and Exclusion. Linguistic rights of national minorities in Europe*, Vilnus, 2015, 223–48.

Wardyn, Łukasz and Jan Fiala, "The 2009 Amendment of the Slovakian State Language Law and Its Impact on Minority Rights", *XXIX Polish Yearbook of International Law*, 2009.

Waszczuk, Katarzyna, "Znaczenie przekładu aktów prawnych Unii Europejskiej dla polskiego kontekstu kulturowego i dyskursu społeczno-politycznego", *Rocznik Przekładoznawczy*, 2008.

White, Johnathan, "A common European identity is an illusion", in: Hubert Zimmermann and Andreas Dür (eds.) *Key Controversies in European Integration*. Palgrave Macmillan, 2012, 103–11.

Wojciechowski, Maciej, "Wybrane aspekty problematyki pewności prawa", *Gdańskie Studia Prawnicze*, Vol. 24, 2010.

Wright, Sue, "Language and Power: Background to the Debate on Linguistic Rights", *International Journal on Multicultural Societies* Vol. 3, No. 1, 2001, 44–54.

Wright, Sue, "The Elephant in the Room: Language Issues in the European Union", *European Journal of Language Policy*, Vol. 1, No. 2, 2009, 93–119.

Wright, Sue, "Democracy, Communities of Communication and the European Union", in: Anne Lise Kjær and Silvia Adamo (eds.), *Linguistic Diversity and European Democracy*, Ashgate Publishing, 2013.

Wyrozumska, Anna, "Jednostka w Unii Europejskiej", in: Jan Barcz (ed.) *Prawo Unii Europejskiej. Zagadnienia Systemowe, Prawo materialne i polityki*, Warszawa: Wydawnictwo Prawo i Praktyka Gospodarcza, 2006.

Zawidzka-Łojek, Anna, "Źródła prawa antydyskryminacyjnego", in: Anna Zawidzka-Łojek and Aleksandra Szczerba-Zawada (eds.), *Prawo antydyskryminacyjne Unii Europejskiej*, EuroPrawo, Warszawa, 2015, 41–64.

Zienkiewicz, Adam and Michał Lasota, "Wielojęzyczność a Interpretacja Europejskiego Prawa Wspólnotowego", *Studia Prawnoustrojowe*, Vol. 9, 2009.

Zirk-Sadowski, Marek, "Wykładnia i rozumienie prawa w Polsce po akcesji do UE", in: Sławomira Wronkowska (ed.), *Polska kultura prawna a proces integracji europejskiej*, Kraków: Zakamycze, 2005.

Zygierewicz, Anna, "Wielojęzyczność Unii Europejskiej", *Analizy Biura Analiz Sejmowych*, No. 3 (28), 2010.

C) Internet websites

https://www.ab.gov.tr/
https://www.academia.edu
http://bookshop.europa.eu
http://www.cedefop.europa.eu
https://www.citizensinformation.ie/
https://www.coe.int
https://www.consilium.europa.eu
https://cordis.europa.eu/
https://curia.europa.eu
https://www.cvce.eu
https://digitallibrary.un.org/
https://eacea.ec.europa.eu
https://ec.europa.eu
https://www.eshre.eu
https://eur-lex.europa.eu
https://europa.eu/
https://europa.eu/epso
http://www.europarl.europa.eu
https://www.echr.coe.int
https://www.ecml.at
https://edps.europa.eu
https://en.efhr.eu
https://en.iyil2019.org
http://www.europarl.europa.eu
https://eustudies.org/
https://fra.europa.eu
https://idfi.ge
https://konsument.gov.pl/
http://www.linguapax.org
https://www.lrkt.lt/en
https://www.minderheitensekretariat.de
http://www.minority-safepack.eu
https://www.mjmf.org
http://oide.sejm.gov.pl

https://www.ombudsman.europa.eu
https://www.politico.eu
https://www.prawo.pl
https://publications.europa.eu
https://pure.uva.nl
https://www.ris.bka.gv.at
https://www.rp.pl/
https://secure.edps.europa.eu/
https://slator.com
https://www.un.org
http://www.unesco.org
http://wfdeaf.org

D. European Union documents

D.1. Primary law

Accession Treaty of Austria, Finland, and Sweden. Official Journal C 241, 29 August 1994.

Accession Treaty of Denmark, Ireland and the United Kingdom. Official Journal L 73, 27 March 1972.

Charter of Fundamental Rights of the European Union. Official Journal 2016 C 202/2, 7 June 2016.

Protocol No. 8 relating to Article 6(2) of the Treaty on European Union on the Accession of the Union to the European Convention of Human Rights and Fundamental Freedoms.

Treaty establishing the European Economic Community, Rome, 25 March 1957.

Treaty establishing the European Atomic Energy Community (EURATOM). Official Journal C 326, 26 October 2012.

Treaty of Amsterdam amending the Treaty on European Union, the Treaties establishing the European Communities and certain related acts. Official Journal C 340, 10 November 1997.

Treaty on European Union. Official Journal C 191, 29 July 1992.

Treaty on European Union and the Treaty on the Functioning of the European Union. Official Journal C 2020/1, 7 June 2016.

D.2. Secondary law

D.2.1. Regulations

Commission Implementing Regulation (EU) 2015/983 of 24 June 2015 on the procedure for issuance of the European Professional Card and the application of the alert mechanism pursuant to Directive 2005/36/EC of the European Parliament and of the Council. Official Journal L 159/27, 25 June 2015.

Council Regulation (EC) No. 40/94 of 20 December 1993 on the Community trade mark. Official Journal L 011, 14 January 1994.

Council Regulation (EC) No. 2062/94 of 18 July 1994 establishing a European Agency for Safety and Health at Work. Official Journal L 216, 20 August 1994.

Council Regulation (EC) No. 930/2004 of 1 May 2004 on temporary derogation measures relating to the drafting in Maltese of the acts of the institutions of the European Union. Official Journal L 169, 1 May 2004.

Council Regulation (EC) No. 1738/2006 of 23 November 2006 amending Regulation (EC) No. 930/2004 on temporary derogation measures relating to the drafting in Maltese of the acts of the institutions of the European Union. Official Journal L 329, 25 November 2006.

Council Regulation (EU) No. 1257/2010 of 20 December 2010 extending the temporary derogation measures from Regulation No. 1 of 15 April 1958 determining the languages to be used by the European Economic Community and Regulation No. 1 of 15 April 1958 determining the languages to be used by the European Atomic Energy Community introduced by Regulation (EC) No. 920/2005, Official Journal J L 343, 29 December 2010.

Council Regulation (EU, Euratom) No. 2015/2264 of 3 December 2015 extending and phasing out the temporary derogation measures from Regulation No 1 of 15 April 1958 determining the languages to be used by the European Economic Community and Regulation No. 1 of 15 April 1958 determining the languages to be used by the European Atomic Energy Community introduced by Regulation (EC) No. 920/2005. Official Journal L 322, 8 December 2015.

Regulation (EEC) No. 1612/68 of the Council of 15 October 1968 on freedom of movement for workers within the Community. Official Journal J L 257, 30 April 2004. In force until 15 June 2011.

Regulation (EEC) No. 1408/71 of the Council of 14 June 1971 on the application of social security schemes to employed persons and their families moving within the Community. Official Journal L 149, 1 May 2010.

Regulation (EEC) No. 337/75 of the Council of 10 February 1975 establishing a European Centre for the Development of Vocational Training. Official Journal L 39, 13 February 1975.

Regulation (EC) No. 1049/2001 of the European Parliament and of the Council of 30 May 2001 regarding public access to European Parliament, Council and Commission documents. Official Journal L 145, 31 May 2001.

Regulation (EC) No. 460/2004 of the European Parliament and of the Council of 10 March 2004 establishing the European Network and Information Security Agency. Official Journal L 077, 13 March 2004.

Regulation (EC) No. 881/2004 of the European Parliament and of the Council of 29 April 2004 establishing a European railway agency. Official Journal L 220, 21 June 2004.

Regulation (EC) No. 764/2008 of the European Parliament and of the Council of 9 July 2008 laying down procedures relating to the application of certain national technical rules to products lawfully marketed in another Member State and repealing Decision No. 3052/95/EC. Official Journal L 218, 13 August 2008.

Regulation (EC) No. 1223/2009 of the European Parliament and of the Council of 30 November 2009 on cosmetic products. Official Journal L 342, 22 December 2009.

Regulation (EU) No. 211/2011 of the European Parliament and of the Council of 16 February 2011 on the citizens' initiative. Official Journal L 65, 11 March 2011.

Regulation (EU) No. 492/2011 of the European Parliament and of the Council of 5 April 2011 on freedom of movement for workers within the Union Text with EEA relevance. Official Journal L141/1, 27 May 2011.

Regulation No. 1 determining the languages to be used by the European Economic Community. Official Journal 17, 1 July 2013.

Regulation (EU) No. 2016/794 of the European Parliament and of the Council of 11 May 2016 on the European Union Agency for Law Enforcement Cooperation (Europol) and replacing and repealing Council Decisions 2009/371/JHA, 2009/934/JHA, 2009/935/JHA, 2009/936/JHA and 2009/968/JHA. Official Journal L 135, 24 May 2016.

Regulation (EU) No. 2017/745 of the European Parliament and of the Council of 5 April 2017 on medical devices, amending Directive 2001/83/EC, Regulation (EC) No. 178/2002 and Regulation (EC) No. 1223/2009 and repealing Council Directives 90/385/EEC and 93/42/EEC. Official Journal L 117, 5 May 2017.

Regulation (EU) No. 2018/1727 of the European Parliament and of the Council of 14 November 2018 on the European Union Agency for Criminal Justice Cooperation (Eurojust), and replacing and repealing Council Decision 2002/187/JHA. Official Journal L 295, 21 November 2018.

Regulation (EU) No. 2019/788 of the European Parliament and of the Council of 17 April 2019 on the European citizens' initiative. Official Journal L 130, 17 May 2019.

Regulation No. 31 (EEC), No. 11 (EAEC), laying down the Staff Regulations of Officials and the Conditions of Employment of Other Servants of the European

Economic Community and the European Atomic Energy Community, Official Journal P 045, 1 January 2020.

D.2.2. Directives

Council Directive 79/7/EEC of 19 December 1978 on the progressive implementation of the principle of equal treatment for men and women in matters of social security. Official Journal L 6, 10 January 1979.

Council Directive 85/577/EEC of 20 December 1985 to protect the consumer in respect of contracts negotiated away from business premises. Official Journal L 372, 31 December 1985.

Council Directive 90/364/EEC of 28 June 1990 on the right of residence. Official Journal L 180, 13 July 1990. In force until 29 April 2006.

Council Directive 2000/43/EC of 29 June 2000 implementing the principle of equal treatment between persons irrespective of racial or ethnic origin. Official Journal L 180, 19 July 2000.

Council Directive 2000/78/EC of 27 November 2000 establishing a general framework for equal treatment in employment and occupation. Official Journal L 303, 2 December 2000.

Council Directive 2003/109/EC of 25 November 2003 concerning the status of third-country nationals who are long-term residents. Official Journal L 16, 20 May 2011.

Council Directive 2004/113/EC of 13 December 2004 implementing the principle of equal treatment between men and women in the access to and supply of goods and services. Official Journal L 153M, 7 June 2006.

Council Directive (EU) 2015/637 of 20 April 2015 on the coordination and cooperation measures to facilitate consular protection for unrepresented citizens of the Union in third countries and repealing Decision 95/553/EC. Official Journal L 106, 24 April 2015.

Directive 97/7/EC of the European Parliament and of the Council of 20 May 1997 on the protection of consumers in respect of distance contracts. Official Journal L 144, 4 June 1997.

Directive 98/79/EC of the European Parliament and of the Council of 27 October 1998 on in vitro diagnostic medical devices. Official Journal L 331, 7 December 1998.

Directive 1999/44/EC of the European Parliament and of the Council of 25 May 1999 on certain aspects of the sale of consumer goods and associated guarantees. Official Journal L 171, 7 July 1999.

Directive 2000/31/EC of the European Parliament and of the Council of 8 June 2000 on certain legal aspects of information society services, in particular electronic commerce, in the Internal Market. Official Journal L 178, 17 July 2000.

Directive 2001/83/EC of the European Parliament and of the Council of 6 November 2001 on the Community code relating to medicinal products for human use. Official Journal L 311, 28 November 2001.

Directive 2001/95/EC of the European Parliament and of the Council of 3 December 2001 on general product safety. Official Journal L 11, 15 January 2002.

Directive 2004/38/EC of the European Parliament and of the Council of 29 April 2004 on the right of citizens of the Union and their family members to move and reside freely within the territory of the Member States amending Regulation (EEC) No 1612/68 and repealing Directives 64/221/EEC,68/360/EEC, 72/194/EEC, 73/148/EEC, 75/34/EEC, 75/35/EEC, 90/364/EEC, 90/365/EEC and 93/96/EEC. Official Journal L 158/77, 30 April 2004.

Directive 2005/29/EC of the European Parliament and of the Council of 11 May 2005 concerning unfair business-to-consumer commercial practices in the internal market and amending Council Directive 84/450/EEC, Directives 97/7/EC, 98/27/EC and 2002/65/EC of the European Parliament and of the Council and Regulation (EC) No. 2006/2004 of the European Parliament and of the Council ('Unfair Commercial Practices Directive'). Official Journal L 149, 11 June 2005.

Directive 2005/36/EC of the European Parliament and of the Council of 7 September 2005 on the recognition of professional qualifications. Official Journal L 255, 30 September 2005.

Directive 2006/54/EC of the European Parliament and of the Council of 5 July 2006 on the implementation of the principle of equal opportunities and equal treatment of men and women in matters of employment and occupation (recast). Official Journal L 204, 26 July 2006.

Directive 2006/123/EC of the European Parliament and of the Council of 12 December 2006 on services in the internal market. Official Journal L 376, 27 December 2006.

Directive 2008/122/EC of the European Parliament and of the Council of 14 January 2009 on the protection of consumers in respect of certain aspects of timeshare, long-term holiday product, resale and exchange contracts. Official Journal L 33, 3 February 2009.

Directive 2009/48/EC of the European Parliament and of the Council of 18 June 2009 on the safety of toys. Official Journal L 170, 30 June 2009.

Directive 2010/41/EU of the European Parliament and of the Council of 7 July 2010 on the application of the principle of equal treatment between men and women engaged in an activity in a self-employed capacity and repealing Council Directive 86/613/EEC. Official Journal L 180, 15 July 2010.

Directive 2010/64/EU of the European Parliament and of the Council of 20 October 2010 on the right to interpretation and translation in criminal proceedings. Official Journal L 280, 26 October 2010.

Directive 2011/83/EU of the European Parliament and of the Council of 25 October 2011 on consumer rights, amending Council Directive 93/13/EEC and Directive 1999/44/EC of the European Parliament and of the Council and repealing Council Directive 85/577/EEC and Directive 97/7/EC of the European Parliament and of the Council. Official Journal L 304, 22 November 2011.

Directive 2012/29/EU of the European Parliament and of the Council of 25 October 2012 establishing minimum standards on the rights, support and protection of victims of crime, and replacing Council Framework Decision 2001/220/JHA. Official Journal L 315, 14 November 2012.

Directive 2013/55/EU of the European Parliament and of the Council of 20 November 2013 amending Directive 2005/36/EC on the recognition of professional qualifications and Regulation (EU) No. 1024/2012 on administrative cooperation through the Internal Market Information System ('the IMI Regulation'). Official Journal L 354, 28 December 2013.

D.2.3. Decisions

Decision No. 1934/2000/EC of the European Parliament and of the Council of 17 July 2000 on the European Year of Languages 2001. Official Journal L 232/1, 17 July 2000.

D.3. Case law

D.3.1. The Court of Justice of the European Union

Judgment of the Court of 5 February 1963 in the case 26/62NV Algemene Transport- en Expeditie Onderneming van Gend en Loos v Nederlandseadministratie der belastingen, ECLI:EU:C:1963:1.

Judgment of the Court of 6 June 2000 in the case C-281/98 Angonese v Cassa di Risparimo di Bolzano SpA, ECLI:EU:C:2000:296.

Judgment of the Court of 28 November 1989 in the case C-379/87 Anita Groener v Minister for Education and the City of Dublin Vocational Educational Committee, ECLI:EU:C:1989:599.

Judgment of the Court of 16 April 2013 in the case C-202/11 Anton Las v PSA Antwerp N, ECLI:EU:C:2013:23.

Judgment of the Court of 27 February 2018 in the case C-64/16 Associação Sindical dos Juízes Portugueses v Tribunal de Contas, ECLI:EU:C:2018:117.

Judgment of the Court of 14 July 1972 in the case 57-69 Azienda Colori Nazionali – ACNA S.p.A. v Commission of the European Communities, ECLI:EU:C:1972:78.

Judgment of the Court of 17 September 2002 in the case C-413/99 Baumbast and R v Secretary of State for the Home Department, ECLI:EU:C:2002:493.

Judgment of the Court of 29 October 1975 in the case 22-75 Berthold Küster v European Parliament, ECLI:EU:C:1975:140.

Judgment of the Court of 2 October 2003 in the case C-148/02 Carlos Garcia Avello v Belgian State, ECLI:EU:C:2003:539.

Judgment of the Court of 9 September 2003 in the case C-361/01 P Christina Kik v Office for Harmonisation in the Internal Market (Trade Marks and Designs) (OHIM), ECLI:EU:C:2003:434.

Judgment of the Court of 30 May 1993 in the case C-168/91 Christos Konstantinidis v Stadt Altensteig – Standesamt and Landratsamt Calw- Ordnungsamt, ECLI:EU:C:1993:115.

Judgment of the Court of 3 June 1999 in the case C-33/97 Colim NV v Bigg's Continent Noord NV, ECLI:EU:C:1999:274.

Judgment of the Court of 7 July 2005 in the case C-147/03 Commission v Austria, ECLI:EU:C:2005:427.

Judgment of the Court of 1 July 2004 in the case C-65/03 Commission v Kingdom of Belgium, ECLI:EU:C:2004:402.

Judgment of the Court of 23 March 2006 in the case C-147/03 Commission v Kingdom of Belgium, ECLI:EU:C:2006:192.

Judgment of the Court of 22 January 2019 in the case C-193/17 Cresco Investigation GmbH v Markus Achatzi, ECLI:EU:C:2019:43.

Judgment of the Court of 24 November 1998 in the case C-274/96 Criminal proceedings against Horst Otto Bickel and Urlich Franz, ECLI:EU:C:1998:563.

Judgment of the Court of 11 July 1985 in the case C 37/84 Criminal proceedings against Robert Heinrich Maria Mutsch, ECLI:EU:C:1985:335.

Judgment of the Court of 18 January 1984 in the case C 327/82 Ekro BV Vee- en Vleeshandel v Produktschap voor Vee en Vlees, ECLI:EU:C:1984:11.

Judgment of the Court of 12 November 1969 in the case C 29-69 Erich Stauder v City of Ulm – Sozialamt, ECLI:EU:C:1969:57.

Judgment of the Court of 26 March 2019 in the case C-621/16 P European Commission v Italian Republic, ECLI:EU:C:2019:251.

Judgment of the Court of 24 June 2019 in the case C-619/18 European Commission v Republic of Poland, ECLI:EU:C:2019:531.

Judgment of the Court of 12 October 2017 in the case C-278/16 Frank Sleutjes v Staatsanwaltschaft Aachen, ECLI:EU:C:2017:757.

Judgment of the Court of 8 April 1976 in the case C-43/75 Gabrielle Defrenne v Société anonyme belge de navigation aérienne Sabena, ECLI:EU:C:1976:56.

The judgment of the Court of 15 October 2015 in the case C-216/14 Gavril Covaci, ECLI:EU:C:2015:686.

Judgment of the Court of 29 April 2004 in joined cases C-482/01 Georgios Orfanopoulos and Others and C-493/01 Raffaele Oliveri v Land Baden-Württemberg, ECLI:EU:C:2004:262.

Judgment of the Court of 8 March 2011 in the case C-34/09 Gerardo Ruiz Zambrano v Office national de l'emploi (ONEm), ECLI:EU:C:2011:124.

Judgment of the Court of 1 April 2008 in the case C-212/06 Government of the French Community and Walloon Government v Flemish Government, ECLI:EU:C:2008:178.

Judgment of the Court of 12 October 1995 in the case C-85/94 Groupement des Producteurs, Importateurs et Agents Généraux d'Eaux Minérales Etrangères VZW (Piageme) and others v Peeters NV, ECLI: EU: C: 1995: 312.

Judgment of the Court 14 October 2008 in the case C-353/06 Grunkin-Paul v Standesamt Niebüll, ECLI:EU:C:2008:559.

Judgment of the Court of 17 November 2011 in the case C-430/10 Hristo Gaydarov v Direktor na Glavna direktsia 'Ohranitelna politsia' pri Ministerstvo na vatreshnite raboti, ECLI:EU:C:2011:749.

Judgment of the Court of 14 September 2000 in the case C-238/98 Hugo Fernando Hocsman v Ministre de l'Emploi et de la Solidarité, ECLI:EU:C:2000:440.

Judgment of the Court of 2 February 1989 in the case 186/87 Ian William Cowan v Trésor public. Reference for a preliminary ruling: Tribunal de grande instance de Paris – France, ECLI:EU:C:1989:47.

Judgment of the Court of 22 December 2012 in the case C-208/09 Ilonka Sayn-Wittgenstein v Landeshauptmann von Wien, ECLI:EU:C:2010:806.

Judgment of the Court of 27 March 2014 in the case C-322/13 lrike Elfriede Grauel Rüffer v Katerina Pokorná, ECLI:EU:C:2014:189.

Judgment of the Court of 17 December 1970 in the case C 11/70 Internationale Handelsgesellschaft mbH v Einfuhr- und Vorratsstelle für Getreide und Futtermittel, ECLI:EU:C:1970:114.

Judgment of the Court of 27 November 2012 in the case C-566/10 P Italian Republic v European Commission, ECLI:EU:C:2012:752.

Judgment of the Court of 5 October 2010 in the case C-400/10 PPU J. McB. v L. E., ECLI:EU:C:2010:582.

Judgment of the Court of 14 May 1974 in the case C 4/73 J. Nold, Kohlen- und Baustoffgroßhandlung v Ruhrkohle Aktiengesellschaft, ECLI:EU:C:1974:151.

Judgment of the Court of 2 May 2018 in joined cases of C-331/16 and C-366/16 K. v Staatssecretaris van Veiligheid en Justitie (C-331/16), H.F v Belgische Staat (C-366/16).

Judgment of the Court of 15 March 2005 in the case C-160/03 Kingdom of Spain v Eurojust, ECLI:EU:C:2005:168.

Judgment of the Court of 26 March 2019 in the case C-377/16 Kingdom of Spain v European Parliament, ECLI:EU:C:2019:249.

Judgment of the Court of 26 May 2005 in the case C-498/03 Kingscrest Associates Ltd and Montecello Ltd v Commissioners of Customs & Excise, ECLI:EU:C:2005:322.

Judgment of the Court of 6 April 1962 in the case 13-61 Kledingverkoopbedrijf de Geus en Uitdenbogerd v Robert Bosch GmbH and Maatschappij tot voortzetting van de zaken der Firma Willem van Rijn, ECLI:EU:C:1962:11.

Judgment of the Court of 19 October 2004 in the case C-200/02 Kunqian Catherine Zhu and Man Lavette Chen v Secretary of State for the Home Department, ECLI:EU:C:2004:639.

Judgment of the Court 12 May 1998 in the case C-85/96 María Martínez Sala v Freistaat Bayern, ECLI:EU:C:1998:217.

Judgment of the Court of 12 May 2011 in the case C-391/09 Malgožata Runevič-Vardyn and Łukasz Paweł Wardyn v Vilniaus miesto savivaldybės administracija and Others, ECLI:EU:C:2011:291.

Judgment of the Court of 9 August 1994 in the case C-51/93 Meyhui NV v Schott Zwiesel Glaswerke AG, ECLI:EU:C:1994:312.

Judgment of the Court of 7 February 1979 in the case C-11/76 Netherlands v Commission, ECLI:EU:C:1979:28.

Judgment of the Court of 13 April 2010 in the case C-73/08 Nicolas Bressol and Others and Céline Chaverot and Others v Gouvernement de la Communautéfrançaise, ECLI:EU:C:2010:181.

Judgment of the Court of 18 June 1991 in the case C-369/89 Piageme and others v BVBA Peeters, ECLI:EU:C:1991:256.

Judgment of the Court of 23 November 1999 in the case C-149/96 Portuguese Republic v Council of the European Union, ECLI:EU:C:1999:574.

Judgment of the Court of 11 July 1974 in the case 8/74 Procureur du Roi v Benoit and Gustave Dassonville, ECLI:EU:C:1974:82.

Judgment of the Court of 20 February 1979 in the case C-120/78 Rewe-Zentral AG vs Bundesmonopolverwaltung Für Branntwein, ECLI:EU:C:1979:42.

Judgment of the Court of 7 December 1995 in the case C-449/93 Rockfon A/S v Specialarbejderforbundet and Danmark, ECLI:EU:C:1995:420.

Judgment of the Court of 28 October 1975 in the case 36/75 Roland Rutili v Ministre de l'intérieur, 28 October 1975, ECLI:EU:C:1975:137.

Judgment of the Court of 20 September 2001in the case C-184/99 Rudy Grzelczyk v Centre public d'aidesocialed' Ottignies-Louvain-la-Neuve, ECLI:EU:C:2001:458.

Judgment of the Court of 4 July 2000 in the case C-424/97 Salomone Haim v Kassenzahnärztliche Vereinigung Nordrhein, ECLI:EU:C:2000:357.

Judgment of the Court of 11 December 2007 in the case C-161/06 Skoma-Lux sro v Celní ředitelství Olomouc, ECLI:EU:C:2007:773.

Judgment of the Court of 22 March 1961 in the joined cases 42 and 49/59 Société nouvelle des usines de Pontlieue – Aciéries du Temple (S.N.U.P.A.T.) v High Authority of the European Coal and Steel Community, ECLI:EU:C:1961:5.

Judgment of the Court of 6 October 1982 in the case 283/81 Srl CILFIT and Lanificio di Gavardo SpA v Ministry of Health, ECLI:EU:C:1982:335.

Judgment of the Court of 27 April 2006 in the case C-96/04 Standesamt Stadt Niebüll, ECLI:EU:C:2006:254.

Judgment of the Court of 2 April 1998 in the case C 296/95 The Queen v Commissioners of Customs and Excise, ex parte EMU Tabac SARL, The Man in Black Ltd, John Cunningham, ECLI:EU:C:1998:152.

Judgment of the Court of 19 April 2007 in the case C-63/06 UAB Profisa v Muitinės departamentas prie Lietuvos Respublikos finansų ministerijos, ECLI:EU:C:2007:233.

Judgment of the Court of 17 April 2018 in the case C-414/16 Vera Egenberger v Evangelisches Werk für Diakonie und Entwicklung e.V, ECLI:EU:C:2018:257.

Opinion 2/13 of the Court of Justice (Full Court) on EU accession to the ECHR given on 18 December 2014.

D.3.2. General Court (formerly the Court of First Instance) and Civil Service Tribunal

Judgment of the Court of First Instance of 19 June 1975 in the case 79-74 ***Berthold Küster v European Parliament,*** ECLI:EU:C:1975:85.

Judgment of the Court of First Instance of 12 July 2001 in the case T-120/99 ***Christina Kik v Office for Harmonisation in the Internal Market (OHIM),*** ECLI:EU:T:2001:189.

Judgment of the Court of First Instance of 20 November 2008 in the case T-185/05 ***Italian Republic v Commission,*** ECLI:EU:T:2008:519.

Judgment of the General Court of the European Union of 13 September 2010 in joint cases T-166/07 and T-285/07 ***Italian Republic v European Commission***, ECLI:EU:T:2010:393.

Judgment of the Court of First Instance of 15 September 2016 in joint cases T-353/14 and T-17/15 ***Italian Republic v European Commission***, ECLI:EU:T:2016:495.

Judgment of the General Court (Fourth Chamber) of 5 October 2005 in the case T-203/03 ***Lars Bo Rasmussen v European Commission***, ECLI:EU:T:2005:346.

Judgment of the General Court (Fourth Chamber) of 17 May 2006 in the case T-95/04 ***Luciano Lavagnoli v European Commission***, ECLI:EU:T:2006:131.

Judgment of the Civil Service Tribunal of 29 June 2011 in the case F-7/0 ***Marie-Thérèse Angioi v Commission,*** unreported.

Judgment of the Court of First Instance of 14 July 1994 in the case T-77/92 ***Parker Pen Ltd v Commission of the European Communities***, ECLI:EU:T:1994:85.

Judgment of the General Court of 21 May 2014 in the case T-61/13 ***Research and Production Company "Melt Water" UAB v OHIM***, ECLI:EU:T:2014:265.

D.3.3. Opinions of Advocates General

Opinion of Advocate General Jacobs in the case C-338/95 delivered on 10 July 1997, ECLI:EU:C:1997:352.

Opinion of Advocate General Mischo in the case C-424/97 delivered on 19 May 1999, ECLI:EU:C:1999:253.

Opinion of Advocate General Jacobs in the case C-238/98 delivered on 16 September 1999, ECLI:EU:C:1999:426.

Opinion of Advocate General Stix-Hackl in the case C-247/02 delivered on 1 July 2004, ECLI:EU:C:2004:399.

Opinion of Advocate General Maduro in the case C-160/03 delivered on 16 December 2004, ECLI:EU:C:2004:817.

Opinion of Advocate General Stix-Hackl in the case C-495/03 delivered on 12 April 2005, ECLI:EU:C:2005:215.

Opinion of Advocate General Ruiz-Jarabo Colomer in the case C-408/03 delivered on 25 October 2005, ECLI:EU:C:2005:638.

Opinion of Advocate General Francis Jacobs in the case C-96/04 delivered on 30 June 2005, ECLI:EU:C:2005:419.

Opinion of Advocate General Kokott in the case 566/10 P delivered on 21 June 2012, ECLI:EU:C:2012:368.

Opinion by Advocate General Sharpston in the case C-377/16 delivered on 25 July 2018, ECLI:EU:C:2018:610.

Opinion of Advocate General Tanchev in the case C-619/18 delivered on 11 April 2019, ECLI:EU:C:2019:325.

D.4. Decisions of the European Ombudsman

European Ombudsman's decision of 17 November 1999 on complaint 281/99/VK against the European Commission.

European Ombudsman's decision of 23 March 2007 on complaint 259/2005 (PB)GG against the European Commission.

European Ombudsman's decision of 24 April 2007 on complaint 2580/2006/TN against the Council of the European Union.

European Ombudsman's decision of 22 November 2007 on complaint 3191/2006/(SAB)MHZ against the European Commission.

European Ombudsman's decision of 30 April 2008 on compliant 259/2005(PB) GG against the European Commission.

European Ombudsman's decision of 4 October 2012 on complaint 640/2006 against the European Commission.

European Ombudsman's decision of 4 October 2012 on complaint 640/2011/AN against the European Commission.

D.5. Other European Union documents

Administrative Arrangement between the European Commission and the Kingdom of Spain. Official Journal C 73/14, 25 March 2006.

Administrative Arrangement between the Government of the United Kingdom of Great Britain and Northern Ireland and the Council of the European Union. Official Journal C 194/04, 31 July 2008.

Administrative Arrangement between the Kingdom of Spain and the Council of the European Union. Official Journal C 40/02, 17 February 2006.

Agreement between the European Union and the government of the United States of America on the security of classified information. Official Journal L115, May 2007.

Agreement between the Government of the United States of America and the Commission of the European Communities regarding the application of their competition laws. Official Journal L 95, 27 April 1995.

Annual Report of the European Ombudsman 2011, published on 13 February 2012.

Bologna Declaration of 19 June 1999. Joint Declaration of the European Ministers of Education. *The European Higher Education Area.*

Bulletin of the European Communities, 1975 (8) II.

Code of Conduct on Multilingualism adopted by the Bureau of the European Parliament of 1 July 2019.

Commission Communication of 1 August 2005 – The European Indicator of Language Competence COM(2005) 356 final. Not published in the Official Journal.

Commission Regulation (EEC) No. 2454/93 of 2 July 1993 laying down provisions for the implementation of Council Regulation (EEC) No. 2913/92 establishing the Community Customs Code. Official Journal L 253, 11 October 1993.

Communication from the Commission to the Council and the European Parliament concerning language use in the information of consumers in the Community. COM(93) 456 final, 10 November 1993.

Communication from the Commission on making a European area of lifelong learning a reality. COM(2001) 678. 21 November 2001. Not published in the Official Journal.

Communication from the Commission to the Council, the European Parliament, the European Economic and Social Committee and the Committee of the Regions: Promoting Language Learning and Linguistic Diversity. An Action Plan 2004–2006. COM(2003) 449. 24 July 2003. Not published in the Official Journal.

Communication from the Commission to the Council, the European Parliament, the European Economic and Social Committee and the Committee of the Regions – A New Framework Strategy for Multilingualism. COM(2005) 596. 22 November 2005. Not published in the Official Journal.

Communication to the Spring European Council – Working together for growth and jobs. A new start for the Lisbon Strategy – Communication from President Barroso in agreement with Vice-President Verheugen. COM(2005) 24. 2 February 2005. Not published in the Official Journal.

Communication from the Commission to the European Parliament, the Council, the European Economic and Social Committee and the Committee of the Regions Multilingualism: an asset for Europe and a shared commitment COM(2008) 566. 18 September 2008.

Communication from the Commission to the European Parliament and the Council on guidance for better transposition and application of Directive 2004/38/EC on the right of citizens of the Union and their family members to move and reside freely within the territory of the Member States COM(2009) 313, 2 July 2019.

Communication from the Commission to the European Parliament, the European Council, the Council, the European Economic and Social Committee and the Committee of the Regions A Modern Budget for a Union that Protects, Empowers and Defends The Multiannual Financial Framework for 2021–2027 COM(2018) 321.

Council conclusion of 13 June 2005 on the official use of additional languages within the Council and possibly other Institutions and bodies of the European Union. Official Journal C 148/01, 18 June 2005.

Council conclusions on the European Indicator of Language Competence. Official Journal C172/01, 25 July 2006.

Council conclusions of 12 May 2009 on a strategic framework for European cooperation in education and training ('ET 2020'). 28 May 2009. Official Journal 2009/C 119/02.

Council Resolution of 27 June 2002 on lifelong learning. Official Journal C 163, 9 July 2002.

Council Resolution on a European strategy for multilingualism. 2905th Education, Youth and Culture Council meeting, Brussels. 21 November 2008.

Declaration of the European Ministers of Vocational Education and Training and the European Commission, 29–30 November 2002 on enhanced European cooperation in vocational education and training (Copenhagen Declaration).

Declaration on European Identity, Copenhagen. 14 December 1973, Bulletin of the European Communities. December 1973, No. 12.

Declaration on nationality of a Member State. Official Journal C 191, 29 July 1992.

Detailed work programme on the follow-up of the objectives of education and training systems in Europe. Official Journal C 142/01, 14 June 2002.

Directorate-General for Education and Culture EC, *A Rewarding Challenge. How the Multiplicity of Languages could strengthen Europe: Proposals from the Group of Intellectuals for Intercultural Dialogue set up at the initiative of the European Commission*, Office for Official Publications of the European Union, 2008.

Directorate-General for Education, Youth, Sport and Culture, *Euromosaic III. Presence of Regional and Minority Language Groups in the New Member States,* Office for Official Publications of the European Union, 2006, 2009 and 2012.

Directorate-General for Translation EC, *Study on translation and multilingualism. Language and Translation in International Law and EU Law*, Office for Official Publications of the European Union, 2012.

'Education & Training 2010', The Success of the Lisbon Strategy Hinges on Urgent Reforms – Joint Interim Report of the Council and the Commission on the Implementation. Official Journal C 104/1, 30 April 2004.

Eurobarometer 85. Spring 2016. Report. European citizenship. Fieldwork May 2016.

European Indicator of Language Competence COM(2005) 356. 1 August 2005. Not published in the Official Journal.

European Union Agency for Fundamental Rights, *Making EU Citizens' Rights a Reality: National Courts Enforcing Freedom of Movement and Related Rights,* 2018.

European Parliament resolution of 14 January 2003 on the role of regional and local authorities in European integration (2002/2141(INI)). Official Journal C 38E/167, 12 February 2003.

European Parliament resolution of 15 November 2006 on a new framework strategy for multilingualism (2006/2083(INI)). Official Journal C 314 E/207, 21 December 2006.

European Parliament resolution of 4 September 2003 with recommendations to the Commission on European regional and lesser-used languages — the languages of minorities in the EU — in the context of enlargement and cultural diversity. Official Journal C 76 E/374, 25 March 2004.

European Parliament Resolution on Multilingualism: an asset for Europe and a shared commitment (2008/2225 (INI)). 24 March 2009.

Explanations relating to the Charter of Fundamental Rights, https://fra.europa.eu/en/eu-charter/article/41-right-good-administration [retrieved on 20 October 2020].

Final Report Summary of the research project – Languages in a network of European excellence (LINEE), 3 November 2011, https://cordis. europa.eu/project/id/28388/ reporting [retrieved on 8 October 2020].

Flash Eurobarometer Series 186: Business attitudes towards cross-border sales and consumer protection, 2006.

Flash Eurobarometer Series 321: B2C on the European contract law, 2011.

Flash Eurobarometer 397: Consumer attitudes towards cross-border trade and consumer protection, 2015.

Lisbon European Council 23 and 24 March 2000 Presidency Conclusions.

Opinion of the Committee of the Regions on Multilingualism. 18–19 June 2008. 75th Plenary Session of the Committee of the Regions. Official Journal C 257/06, 9 October 2008.

Opinion of the Committee of the Regions on the Communication from the Commission to the Council, the European Parliament, the European Economic and Social Committee and the Committee of the Regions on A New Framework Strategy for Multilingualism. Official Journal 2006/C 229/05, 22 September 2006.

Opinion of the Economic and Social Committee on 'Multilingualism'. Official Journal 2009/C 77/25, 31 March 2009.

Opinion of the European Economic and Social Committee on the Communication from the Commission to the Council, the European Parliament, the European Economic and Social Committee and the Committee of the Regions – A new framework strategy for multilingualism. Official Journal C 324/68, 30 December 2006.

Presidency Conclusions. Barcelona European Council. 15 and 16 March 2002, http://ec.europa.eu/invest-in-esearch/pdf/download_en/barcelona_european_council.pdf [retrieved on 14 March 2019].

Proposals from the Group of Intellectuals for Intercultural Dialogue set up at the initiative of the European Commission, *A Rewarding Challenge: how the multiplicity of languages could strengthen Europe*, https://ec.europa.eu/ education/sites/education /files/rewarding-challenge-report_en.pdf [23 July 2018].

Protocol No. 3 on the Statute of the Court of Justice of the European Union. Official Journal C 83/210, 30 March 2010.

Recommendation of the European Parliament and the Council on of 18 December 2006 on key competences for lifelong learning. Official Journal L 394/10, 30 December 2006.

Reference for a preliminary ruling from the Amtsgericht Flenburg (Germany) filed on 28 August 2006, C 281.

Report from the Commission on the Application in 2018 of Regulation (EC) No. 1049/2001 Regarding Public Access to European Parliament, Council and Commission Documents COM(2019) 356 Final, 29 July 2019.

Report of the European Parliament with the recommendations of the Commission on European regional and lesser-used in the context of enlargement and cultural diversity Session document (A5-0271/2003). 14 July 2003.

Report on the implementation of the Action Plan "Promoting language learning and linguistic diversity". SEC (2007) 1222. COM (2007) 554. Working Paper. Not published in the Official Journal.

Resolution of the European Parliament on the use of the official languages in the institutions of the European Union. Official Journal C 043, 20 February 1995.

Resolution of the European Parliament of 14 June 2012 on public consultations and their availability in all EU languages. Official Journal C 332 E/68, 15 November 2013.

Resolution on the use of the official languages in the institutions of the European Union. Official Journal C 043, 20 February 1995.

Rules of Procedure of the Committee of the Regions of 31 January 2014. Official Journal L 65/41 5 March 2014.

Rules of Procedure of the Council of the European Union. Official Journal L 325, 11 December 2009.

Rules of Procedure of the Court of Justice. Official Journal L 265/1, 29 September 2012.

Rules of Procedure of the European Central Bank. Official Journal L 338, 15 December 1998.

Rules of Procedure of the European Commission. Official Journal L 308, 8 December 2000.

Rules of Procedure of the European Council. Official Journal L 315, 2 December 2009.

Rules of Procedure of the European Economic and Social Committee. Official Journal L 324/52, 9 December 2010.

Rules of Procedure of the European Parliament 2019–2024, 9th parliamentary term.

Seminars on Equality of Legislation. How to interpret legislation which is equally authentic in twenty languages. Lecture by Advocate General Franics Jacobs. Brussels, 20 October 2003. Published on 26 November 2003.

Special Eurobarometer No. 386. Europeans and Languages. Report. Fieldwork: February-March 2012. Published in June 2012.

Standard Eurobarometer 91. Spring 2019. Public opinion in the European Union. Published in June 2019.

Statute of the Court of Justice of the European Economic Community, published by the Publishing Services of the European Communities, 8012/5/XII/1962/5.

E. Documents of the Council of Europe

E.1. Conventions

European Cultural Convention opened for signature on 19 December 1954, entered into force on 5 May 1955. By 2020 ratified by 50 states.

European Convention for the Protection of Human Rights and Fundamental Freedoms signed on 4 November 1950, entered into force on 3 September 1953. By 2020 ratified by 47 states.

European Charter for Regional or Minority Languages opened for signature on 5 November 1992, entered into force on 1 March 1998. By 2020 ratified by 25 states.

European Social Charter signed and opened for signature on 18 October 1961, entered into force on 26 February 1965. By 2020 ratified by 27 states.

Framework Convention for the Protection of National Minorities opened for signature on 1 February 1995, entered into force on 1 February 1998. By 2020 ratified by 39 states.

Protocol No. 14 to the Convention for the Protection of Human Rights and Fundamental Freedoms amending the control system of the Convention, Strasbourg 13 May 2004.

Statute of the Council of Europe opened for signature on 5 May 1949, entered into force on 3 August 1949. By 2020 ratified by 47 states.

E.2. Other documents of the Council of Europe

Common European Framework of Reference for Languages: Learning, Teaching, Assessment (CEFR), Language Policy Unit, Strasbourg, https://rm.coe.int/16802fc1bf [retrieved on 1 September 2020].

Explanatory Memorandum on the official languages of the Council of Europe, Committee on Political Affairs and Democracy, doc. 1039, 14 September 1959.

Explanatory Report to the European Charter for Regional and Minority Languages, Strasbourg, 5 November 1992, https://rm.coe.int/16800cb5e5 [retrieved on 19 October 2020].

Explanatory Report to the Framework Convention for the Protection of National Minorities, Strasbourg, H (95)10, 10–27, https://rm.coe.int/ 16800c10cf, [retrieved on 19 October 2020].

Rules of the European Court of Human Rights of 1 January 2020, Strasbourg.

E.3. Case law of the European Court of Human Rights

Judgment of the ECtHR of 23 July 1968 in the case ***Belgian Linguistic Case v Belgium*** (applications No. 1474/62; 1677/62; 1691/62; 1769/63; 1994/63; 2126/64).

Judgment of the ECtHR of 30 June 2005 in the case ***Bosphorus Hava Yollari Turizm v Ireland*** (application No. 45036/98).

Judgment of the ECtHR of 19 December 1989 in the case ***Brozicek v Italy*** (application No. 10964/84).

Judgment of the ECtHR of 22 February 1994 in the case ***Burghartz v Switzerland***, 18 E.H.R.R.101.

Judgment of the ECtHR of 24 September 2002 in the case ***Cuscani v Italy*** (application No. 32771/96).

Judgment of the ECtHR of 10 May 2001 in the case ***Cyprus v Turkey*** (application No. 25781/94).

Judgment of the ECtHR of 17 January 1970 in the case ***Delcourt v Belgium*** (application No. 2689/65).

Judgment of the ECtHR of 8 June 1976 in the case ***Isop v Austria*** (application No. 808/60).

Judgment of the ECtHR of 9 December 1989 in the case ***Kamasinski v Austria*** (application No. 9783/82).

Judgment of the ECtHR of 14 January 2003 in the case ***Lagerblom v Sweden*** (application No. 26891/95).

Judgment of the ECtHR of 28 November 1978 in the case ***Luedicke, Belkacem and Koc v Germany*** (application No. 6210/73, 6877/75, 7132/75).

Judgment of the ECtHR of 10 March 1980 in the case ***Luedicke, Belkacem and Koc v Germany*** (Article 50) (application No. 6210/73, 6877/75, 7132/75).

Judgment of the ECtHR of 7 December 2004 in the case ***Mentzen v Latvia*** (application No. 71074/01).

Judgment of the ECtHR of 21 February 1984 in the case ***Öztürk v Germany*** (application no 8544/79).

Judgment of the ECtHR of 12 April 2005 in the case ***Shamayev and 12 Others v Georgia and Russia*** (application No. 36378/02).

F. Documents of the United Nations

F.1. UN Charter and other Conventions

Charter of the United Nations signed on 26 June 1945, entered into force on 24 October 1945.

Constitution of the United Nations Educational, Scientific and Cultural Organization signed on 16 November 1945, entered into force on 4 November 1946. By 2020 ratified by 193 states.

Convention on the Rights of the Child adopted by the UN General Assembly on 20 November 1989 by resolution No. 45/25, entered into force on 2 September 1990. By 2020 ratified by 196 states.

Declaration on the Rights of Persons Belonging to National or Ethnic, Religious and Linguistic Minorities adopted by the UN General Assembly on 18 December 1992 by resolution No. 47/135.

International Covenant on Civil and Political Rights adopted by the UN General Assembly on 16 December 1966 by resolution No. 2200 A, entered into force on 23 March 1976. By 2020 ratified by 173 states.

International Covenant on Economic, Social and Cultural Rights adopted by the UN General Assembly on 16 December 1966 by resolution No. 2200 A, entered into force on 3 January 1976. By 2020 ratified by 171 states.

International Convention on the Protection of the Rights of All Migrant Workers and Members of Their Families signed on 18 December 1990, into force since 1 July 2003. By 2020 ratified by 55 states.

UNSECO Convention against Discrimination in Education adopted on 14 December 1960, entered into force on 22 May 1962. By 2019 ratified by 104 states.

Universal Declaration of Human Rights adopted by the UN General Assembly on 10 December 1948 by resolution No. 217 A.

Vienna Convention on Consular Relations of 24 April 1963, Treaty Series, Vol. 596, in force since 19 March 1967. By 2020 ratified by 180 states.

Vienna Convention on the Law of Treaties of 23 May 1969, into force since 27 January 1980. *United Nations Treaty Series*, Vol. 1155. By 2018 ratified by 116 states.

F.2. Other documents of the United Nations

Commentary of the Working Group on minorities to the United nations Declaration on the Rights of Persons Belonging to National or Ethnic, Religious and Linguistic Minorities, E/CN.4/Sub.2/AC.5/2005/2, 4 April 2005.

Communication No. 453/1991 of the United Nations Human Rights Committee in the case *Coeriel and Aurik v Netherlands,* U.N. Doc. CCPR/C/52/D/453/1991 (1994).

Communications of the UN Human Rights Committee, Nos 359/1989 and 385/1989 in the case *Ballantyne, Davidson, McIntyre v Canada,* U.N. Doc. CCPR/C/47/ D/ 359/1989 and 385/1989/Rev1 (1993).

Declaration on the Responsibilities of the Present Generations Towards Future Generations, adopted on 12 November 1997 by the General Conference of UNESCO.

Declaration on the Rights of Persons Belonging to National and Ethnic or Religious Minorities adopted by the UN General Assembly on 18 December 1992 by resolution No. 47/135.

Multilingualism: Report of the Secretary-General. A/61/317, 6 September 2006.

Report of the Joint Inspection Unit on the implementation of multilingualism in the United Nations System: note by the Secretary-General, A/58/251, 10 June 2003.

Resolutions proclaimed by General Assembly on 2 November 1995 (A/RES/50/11), and adopted by the General Assembly on 24 May 2017 (A/RES/71/288), on 21 January 2000, (A/RES/54/64), on 24 May 2017 (A/71/L.68) and on 19 December 2017 (A/RES/72/161).

G. Other documents

Act of the Polish Parliament of 6 January 2005 on national and ethnic minorities and on national language. Journal of Laws 17, item, 141 as amended.

Act of the Polish Parliament of 25 June 2015 Consular Law. Journal of Laws 2015, item 1274.

Bond, Esther, *EU provides clarity on post-Brexit future for English language*, 2018, https://slator.com/demand-drivers/eu-provides-clarity-on-post-brexit-future-for-english-language/ [retrieved on 6 November 2019].

Brannan, James, *ECHR Case-Law on the Right to Language Assistance in Criminal Proceedings and the EU Response*, A Seminar Organised by the AIIC Committee for Court and Legal Interpreting at the European Court of Human Rights: Droits de l'Homme En Europe et Interprétation Juridique, Strasbourg, 2010.

Constitution of Ireland, http://www.irishstatutebook.ie/eli/cons/en/html#part2 [retrieved on 17 February 2020].

Constitution of Malta, https://www.constitution.org/cons/malta/chapt0.pdf [retrieved on 17 February 2020].

Convention for the strengthening of the Inter-American Tropical Tuna Commission established by the 1949 Convention between the United States of America and the Republic of Costa Rica. Official Journal L 224/24, 16 August 2006.

Decree No. IR-294 of the Minister for Justice of 22 July 2008 confirming the civil registration rules (Žin., 2008, No. 88–3541).

De La Baume, Maïa, *As Britain leaves, English on rise in EU- to French horror*, 5 October 2018, https://www.politico.eu/article/french-english-language-bre xit-europ ean-parliament-ecj-commission-eu-next-waterloo/ [retrieved on 6 November 2019],

European Convention for the Protection of Animals during International Transport. Official Journal L 241/22, 13 July 2004.

German Institute for Standardisation (DIN), *Studie des Verbraucherrates des DIN: Folgen fehlerhafter Anleitungen am Markt und Lösungsansätze zur Verbesserung technischer Anleitungen*, 2010.

Gontarski, Waldemar, *Karlsruhe blokuje Luksemburg i Brukselę – wyrok TSUE ws. Polski komentuje Waldemar Gontarski,* https://www.rp.pl/Rzecz-o-prawie /310019956-Karlsruhe-blokuje-Luksemburg-i-Bruksele---wyrok-TSUE-ws-Polski-komentuje-Waldemar-Gontarski.html [retrieved on 19 November 2019].

Joint communication from Presidents Costa and Skouris on the meeting of delegations from the European Court of Human Rights (ECHR) and the Court of Justice of the European Union (CJEU) as of 17 January 2011.

Judgment of the Austrian Constitutional Court Verfassungsgerichtshof (VfGH), B 557/03, 27 November 2003, https://www.ris.bka.gv.at/VfghEntscheidung.wxe? Abfrage=Vfgh&Dokumentnummer=JFT_09968873_03B00557_2_00&IncludeSelf=True [retrieved on 1 September 2020].

Judgment in the name of the Republic of Latvia on Compliance with Article 19 of the Language Law and the Cabinet of Ministers, 22 August 2000, Regulations No. 295 "Regulations on Spelling and Identification of Names and Surnames" with Article 86 and 116 of the Satversme (Constitution).

Judgment of the Constitutional Court of Latvia of 21 December 2001, No. 2001-04–0103, http://www.satv.tiesa.gov.lv/upload/2001-04-0103E.rtf [retrieved on 24 October 2019].

Olszański, Tadeusz A., *Ukraińcy nie gęsi...Ustawa o języku państwowym Ukrainy,* https://www.osw.waw.pl/pl/publikacje/komentarze-osw/2019-06-11/ukraincy-nie-gesi-ustawa-o-jezyku-panstwowym-ukrainy [retrieved on 28 October 2020].

Ruling on the compliance of the 31 January 1991 Supreme Council of the Republic of Lithuania Resolution "On Writing Names and Family Names in Passports of Citizens of the Republic of Lithuania" with the Constitution of the Republic of Lithuania. Judgment of the Constitutional Court of Lithuania of 21 October 1999, No. 14/98, https://www.lrkt.lt/en/court-acts/search/170/ta1147/summary [retrieved on 24 October 2019].

The Oslo Recommendations regarding the Linguistic Rights of National Minorities and Explanatory Note, OSCE, February 1998.

Trade, Development and Cooperation Agreement (TDCA) between the European Community and the Republic of South Africa. Official Journal L 311, 4 December 1999.

Treaty between the Republic of Poland and the Republic of Lithuania on Good Neighbourhood and Friendly Cooperation of 26 April 1994 (Journal of Laws of 1995, No. 15, item. 71).

Van der Jeught, Stefaan, *What You Need To Know About EU Language Law,* 2016, https://slator.com/features/what-you-need-to-know-about-eu-language-law/ [retrieved on1 October 2020].

Index of Names

Ius, Lex et Res Publica

Studies in Law, Philosophy and Political Cultures

Edited by
Anna Jaroń

Vol. 1 Anna Jaroń: Socio-Economic Constitutional Rights in Democratisation Processes. An Account of the Constitutional Dialogue Theory. 2012.

Vol. 2 Stanisław Filipowicz: Democracy – The Power of Illusion. 2013.

Vol. 3 Teresa Dukiet-Nagórska (ed.): The Postulates of Restorative Justice and the Continental Model of Criminal Law. As Illustrated by Polish Criminal Law 2014.

Vol. 4 Agnieszka Kupzok: Enforcement of Patents on Geographically Divisible Inventions. An Inquiry into the Standard of Substantive Patent Law Infringement in Cross-Border Constellations. 2015.

Vol. 5 Alicja Jagielska-Burduk / Wojciech Szafrański: Legal Issues in Cultural Heritage Management. A Polish Perspective. 2016.

Vol. 6 Maciej Mataczyński (ed.): The Takeover of Public Companies as a Mode of Exercising EU Treaty Freedoms. 2017.

Vol. 7 Maciej Barczewski (ed.): Value of Information. Intellectual Property, Privacy and Big Data. 2018.

Vol. 8 Pawel Smoleń, Marcin Burzec: Introduction to Polish Tax Law. 2018.

Vol. 9 Łukasz Pohl, Konrad Burdziak: Judicial Interpretation of the 1997 Criminal Code Provisions on Self-Defence. 2019.

Vol. 10 Adam Szot: Judicial Review of Administrative Discretion. The Influence of Court Decisions on Administrative Actions. 2019.

Vol. 11 Michał Peno / Konrad Burdziak (eds.): The Concept of Modern Law. Polish and Central European Tradition. 2019.

Vol. 12 Leszek Leszczyński / Bartosz Liżewski / Adam Szot (eds.): Potential of Precedent in the Statutory Legal Order. 2019.

Vol. 13 Łukasz Bolesta: In Search of a Model for the Legal Protection of a Whistleblower in the Workplace in Poland. A legal and comparative study. 2020.

Vol. 14 Paweł Chmielnicki / Adam Sulikowski (eds.): New Perspectives on Legislation. A Comparative Approach. 2020.

Vol. 15 Marcin Burzec / Beata Kucia-Guściora / Paweł Smoleń: Agricultural Activity in Poland: A Fiscal and Legal Study. 2020.

Vol. 16 Magdalena Półtorak / Ilona Topa (eds.): Women, Children and (Other) Vulnerable Groups. Standards of Protection and Challenges for International Law. 2021.

Vol. 17 Josef Albert Fox: Die polnische Verfassung vom 3. Mai 1791. Hintergründe der Entstehung und der Außerkraftsetzung. Stellung Polens im Zeitalter der Aufklärung. 2021.

Vol. 18 Barbara Janusz-Pohl (ed.): Juvenile Justice Systems: Poland-Brazil-Portugal. 2021.

Vol. 19 Leszek Leszczyński: General Reference Clauses in the Judicial Process. Context of Legislative Intentions Interpretative Discretion. 2021.

Vol. 20 Francisco J. Campos Zamora: Das Problem der Begründung richterlicher Entscheidungen. Eine Analyse auf der Grundlage der Theorie der juristischen Argumentation. 2021.

Ius, Lex et Res Publica
Studies in Law, Philosophy and Political Cultures

Edited by
Barbara Janusz-Pohl and Anna Jaroń

Vol. 21 Aneta Skorupa-Wulczyńska: Language Rights of the Citizen of the European Union. 2022.

www.peterlang.com

www.ingramcontent.com/pod-product-compliance
Ingram Content Group UK Ltd.
Pitfield, Milton Keynes, MK11 3LW, UK
UKHW020834290926
15470UKWH00004B/1338

9 783631 881583